Between Past and Future

Between Past and Future

The Revolutions of 1989
and Their Aftermath

Edited by

SORIN ANTOHI
and
VLADIMIR TISMANEANU

CEU PRESS

Central European University Press

Published by
Central European University Press

Október 6. utca 12
H–1051 Budapest
Hungary

400 West 59th Street
New York, NY 10019
USA

Distributed in the United Kingdom and Western Europe by
Plymbridge Distributors Ltd., Estover Road, Plymouth, PL6 7PZ,
United Kingdom

ISBN 963-9116-71-8 *Paperback*

Library of Congress Cataloging in Publication Data
A CIP catalog record for this book is available upon request

Printed in Hungary by Akaprint

*To all those who, living in dark times,
believed in freedom and made it possible*

Table of Contents

List of Tables

Preface and Acknowledgements

The tenth anniversary of communism's collapse in Eastern Europe offers academics, the media, policy-makers, and the surviving former "new men and women" an opportunity to contemplate the first postcommunist decade's illusions, expectations, and balance sheet and to speculate on the years to come. This exercise is simultaneously exhilarating and sobering, nostalgic and anxious, passionate and lucid. Ironically enough, these short-term retrospective and prospective ruminations seem more likely at this point than any comprehensive examination of communism's natural history; a process similar to Germany's *Vergangenheitsbewältigung* has yet to start in earnest, although fragmented memories—both individual and collective—are currently being rescued and worked through, while topics such as the intellectual history of communist ideology, the comparative study of the Gulag's international avatars, the reconstruction of everyday life under state socialism enjoy growing scholarly attention.

As its title indicates by means of an Arendtian reference, this book examines the revolutions of 1989 and their aftermath from a dual perspective, looking back and thinking forward, spanning ten years of the recent past and ten years of the immediate future. To do so, we invited a number of outstanding scholars and public intellectuals that have been interested and/or involved in the roots, unfolding, and legacies of 1989 to engage in a critical assessment of their objects of expertise.

To make sure that the resulting volume would be more than just a collection of excellent papers, we started the whole project by putting together a conference, held in Budapest at the Central European University from 26 to 29 March 1999. Early drafts of the chapters included in this book were presented and thoroughly discussed at that lively public debate, with the exception of Ivan Vejvoda's text; due to the war in the former Yugoslavia, the author was unable to attend. Other conference paper-givers are unfortunately absent here: Ivo Banac, Daniel Chirot, János Kis, Gáspár Miklós Tamás. However, their contribution to the debates, alongside those of the panel moderators—including John Lampe and Alfred J. Rieber—enhanced the quality of the overall intellectual exchange. The book's final chapter eloquently captures the atmosphere of the conference, while the other individual contributions preserve, beyond the somewhat definitive touch of all substantially rewritten presentations, much of their original polemical, provocative, tentative edge. Readers will also notice that the editors, while doing what they were supposed to do, refrained from pushing for artificial consensus or superficial homogeneity; for instance, as most terminological variations stem from full-fledged theoretical, methodological, ideological stances, frequently used notions as well as the names of the region(s) covered by this book have not been standardized. What keeps the book together is, the editors hope, a common quest for the meanings of what 1989 epitomizes and symbolizes.

The conference went beyond the routines of academic gatherings in some other ways. Opened by Josef Jařab, then the Central European University's Rector and President, and Gábor Demszky, Budapest's Lord Mayor, it was prefaced by a media panel introduced by former U.S. Ambassador to Hungary Donald Blinken, moderated by Kati Marton, and featuring U.S. Ambassador Richard Holbrooke; Flora Lewis, senior columnist of the New York Times Syndicate; R.W. Apple, Jr., chief correspondent for *The New York Times*; Barrie Dunsmore, former diplomatic and senior foreign correspondent for ABC News; James Carney, political correspondent for *Time*; and György Bolgár of Hungarian National Radio. Other academics, public intellectuals, politicians, diplomats, journalists, and students, including U.S. Congressman Tom Lantos, took active part in the three-day discussion. The epilogue was contributed by Timothy Garton Ash, who undertook the mighty task of wrapping up the conference's explorations, and by Árpád Göncz, president of Hungary, himself an embodiment of the 1989 spirit, who reflected memorably on communism's downfall, on its origins and consequences.

The conference, sponsored by Central European University and the University of Maryland's Center for the Study of Post-Communist Societies, was generously underwritten by the Peter Gruber Foundation, the U.S. German Marshall Fund, and the United States Information Agency. The book's publication is also supported by a grant from the Peter Gruber Foundation. Our gratitude goes to these institutions and to the people working with them.

The book's speedy production would not have been possible without the painstaking, competent editorial assistance provided by Christine S. Zapotocky and without the professionalism and understanding of the team at CEU Press. Let them be thanked here once more.

And finally, throughout the two years of on-again, off-again work on the whole project, our respective wives, Mona Antohi and Mary Sladek, have been, as always, helpers, critics, and advisers. We thank them wholeheartedly.

Sorin Antohi
Vladimir Tismaneanu

I Meanings of 1989: Present Significance of the Past

1   *Between Past and Future*

AGNES HELLER

With the exception of the moments of our birth and our death we are always "between past and future". Our acts are not only oriented toward the future, they are also motivated by an image of the future; recollection is not only oriented to the past, it is also motivated by the image of the past. Since one acts in the present and recollects from the present, recollection is also motivated by the image of the present and of the future, and action by the recollection of the past. There is a commonplace that—contrary to many other commonplaces—is blatantly untrue; that is, the commonplace that the past is necessary because it cannot be changed, only recollected, and that the future is free, for one can shape it according to one's choice and will. This commonplace is the application of positivist conceptions of nineteenth-century natural sciences to history and to the human condition in general. It is based on the identification of causal determination and necessity, on a tautology that claims that if sufficient reasons existed for something to happen, it happened by necessity, and if something happened, there were always sufficient reasons for it to happen. Still, it could have happened otherwise, and in this sense it was not necessary, for the determining causes are normally entirely heterogeneous. They are like dice thrown from unrelated dicecups. Human will and determination are also dice of a particular dicecup of a particular throw. Moreover, past events could not only happen otherwise, but they are also constantly changed, since every act of recollection modifies them. One can tell the same story in a thousand different ways.

And what about the freedom of the future? This is as questionable as the necessity of the past. True, the future is free insofar as it cannot be recollected. It is open, for many dicecups still wait to be thrown, among them the cup that is governed by human will and decision. Still, there are dicecups from which the dice have already been thrown. These cups entail the general conditions for the future of the present: for example, that a person has been thrown by the accident of birth in such-and-such a year in such-and-such a country, place, et cetera. Every individual is thrown into the world by accident, yet it is in this world that one has to grow, to act, and to decide. Freedom, however, has an entirely different status in the modern world than in all preceding ones. In a nutshell: modern individuals are thrown into a world that is founded on freedom. Yet freedom is a foundation that does not found. As a result, individuals themselves have to contribute to limiting their own conditions for their own actions.

This conference is not just entitled "between past and future", but also points at a certain period of time of exactly ten years—the years between 1989 and 1999. Whose past and whose future are we discussing? The past and future of Central-Eastern Europe, or more precisely, the past and future of the so-called Central-East European *new democracies*. They are also frequently referred to as *posttotalitarian* states and societies, an expression that was formerly applied, in my mind wrongly, to the paternalistic variant of totalitarianism. Both "new" and "post" are temporal expressions; they indicate societies that come into being after a certain past, having left that past, and having embarked upon something new. Yet there remains a difference in meaning if one speaks of posttotalitarian societies or new democracies. Both expressions indicate that a new kind of society was born roughly ten years ago. But the expression "posttotalitarian" emphasizes the relationship of these societies to their past; they were born after a totalitarian state and society. Yet the description is not indicative of the future. If one speaks of new democracies, one places the social and political entities in question exactly between past and future. They are new, and essentially different from the past, because they are democracies. The term posttotalitarian defines the identity of the main sociopolitical situation; it suggests that the throw from the dicecups of the main political and social institutions is still pending, that certain conditions for the future of the present are not yet in place. The term new democracies suggests that the dice from the dicecup of the main political institutions have already been thrown, that certain fundamental conditions for the freedom of political actions are set.

Every new democracy is between past and future. This conference speaks of new democracies that are posttotalitarian and are situated in the center, or eastern center, of Europe. The topic itself entails a certain interpretation of the past and a certain way to presuppose conditions of the future. First, to speak of countries and nations between past and future as "new democracies" places emphasis on the political factor—it is a political identification. If one says new democracies, one means that the past and the future are entirely different. The past is nondemocratic; the future is democratic. In relation to the past one gives account of a rupture;

in relation to the future one presupposes continuity. The new democracies are newborn, without a proper time of pregnancy, but rather only a short period of incubation.

In traditional political terms one can rightly speak of revolution when referring to the experience of these countries. Political revolution is not identified by an uprising or by acts of violence. It is simply a change of sovereignty. New democracies are based—at least roughly, whether one likes the expression sociologically or not—on popular sovereignty, whereas totalitarian states are based on party sovereignty. It is legitimate to neglect this considering that there were many variants of totalitarianism, from terroristic to paternalistic, for even the most paternalistic version—the Hungarian—was grounded in party sovereignty. Pluralism existed, yet the party decided how far it could go. Popular sovereignty, a multiparty system, periodical elections, a parliamentary system, representative government, civil rights, human rights, and so on—these institutions in these states stand for something entirely new. The term new democracy, which indicates that there has been a total political break with the institutions of the past, speaks also of the expectation of continuity in the future. The countries of Central-Eastern Europe are new democracies now, yet they will mature as time progresses. Perhaps after another ten years, no one will speak anymore of new democracies, at least not in reference to the Central-East European states.

One may view these new democracies, between past and future, from two perspectives: first, in relation to their past, and second, in relation to their future. In the spirit of my introductory remarks I will formulate the question as such: Can the past of the new democracies be understood as necessary, is their future free?

The question is put in such a way that there can be no misunderstanding. The temporal terms "past" and "future" are not employed here in the spirit of the grand narrative. By past, I mean not the bygone ages, and by future, not a utopian vision of something beyond our horizon. By past, I mean the past of the present; by future, the future of the present.

Was the past of our present necessary, just because it happened the way it happened? I do not think so. There were conditions already thrown, but there were still—if not continuously, at least sometimes—other dicecups, the throws of which had several potential outcomes. For example, the hopes of many Russians for the end of the terror in 1945 and of Hungarians for liberation in 1956 were not entirely absurd. The Soviet system could have collapsed in 1956 as easily as it could have survived the year 1989. The throw of the unrelated dicecups was against us in 1956 and for us in 1989. That the Soviet regime collapsed in 1991 was in this sense a contingent event. One could say that these considerations are just ontological games and entirely without any practical relevance. One cannot write alternative history—or rather, one cannot write alternative history on the ground of "what would have happened if"; yet one can indicate alternatives in history, not just for theoretical but also for political—and perhaps sometimes even for ethical—reasons. In Hungary, for example, one has encountered and can still encounter nostalgia for the past, reinforced by anticapitalistic rhetoric—we are told how well people lived in the last years of the Kádár regime, and how the West has destroyed the progress made at that time. One could ask: What would have happened if the revolution of 1956 had been successful? Our standard of living was at least equal to that of Austria at the time. Who destroyed the livelihood of the Hungarian people?

As individuals constantly change their own past, so do social actors, trends, and ideas. East European actors change their past in recollection, historiography, and political ideology. Conflicts of the present and prognoses for the future of the present are also intimately connected with the interpretation of the past.

As far as politics and economics are concerned, the new democracies of Central Europe now exclusively refer to the single-party system and the state-controlled command economy in the past tense—these institutions no longer exist. Single-party systems became extinct ten years ago, and state-controlled economies gradually withered during the ten years between past and present as market economies and private property replaced them. Yet the question is constantly raised, and not without reason, whether or not the past is still in the present—and if yes, how.

This question implies several subsequent questions. First, can one speak of the completion of systemic change (*rendszerváltás* or *rendszerváltozás* in Hungarian) if the former social and economic elite remains in place? Second (and this question is not entirely unconnected to the first), can such systemic change be accomplished without simultaneously altering attitudes and mentalities? Third, is the past in the present only the future of the previous system, or does it entail something else, more, and different (such as traditions, ways of life, cultural priorities, and spiritual aspirations)? Needless to say, questions about the past in the present and the answers to those questions substantially influence questions concerning the future of the present—ideas, strategies, options, wishes of political and social actors—that is, the outcomes of the rolls of the dice.

I mentioned traditions. Traditions are past-oriented, but the past is not entirely homogeneous. Although there were times in the histories of totalitarian systems during which societies seemed to be entirely homogenized, totalitarian regimes had their own past—their own pre-Soviet past, which they continued to carry in their present—that is in our past. Those traditions have also lived on, though in many instances in altered form. What happened with this past in the present tense of new democracies?

At this point, I need to say a few words about modern imagination. Modernity is fragmented, and modern imagination is not homogeneous. I make a rough distinction between two main tendencies in modern imagination with their respective institutions of imagination: technological imagination and historical imagination. Technological imagination is entirely future-oriented. In the spirit of technological imagination, the newest is always the best—be it the newest invention, the newest prototype, the newest discovery, the newest fashion, the newest book. The spirit of the technological imagination is the spirit of progress, the betterment of society. Every conflict is a sign of malfunction and is related to a problem that needs to be solved, especially social problems. Technological imagination is future-oriented, optimistic, and rational. Science, the dominant worldview of modernity, shares the spirit of technological imagination and is the offspring of it. In contrast, historical imagination is past-oriented and tradition-oriented. In the historical imagination the oldest—buildings, paintings, families, histories, and historical claims—is normally also the best, the most beautiful, and the most valuable. The most valuable traditions are those of bygone times. Historical imagination is frequently employed ideologically; for example, in the Balkans today, every ethnic or national group legitimizes its claim for territory with history, with historical past. Nationalism and racism are deeply rooted in historical imagination. However, it would be unwise to conclude that historical imagination is dangerous; without it there is no poetry, religion, ethics, ceremonies, symbols, allegories, holidays. Neither would hermeneutics exist. Without historical imagination problem-solving would entirely take the place of meaning-rendering. Additionally, though historical imagination provides modern wars with ideologies, technological imagination provides them with weapons. One can also refer to historical imagination as romantic in a broad sense and conclude that two kinds of enlightenment—historical enlightenment and technological enlightenment—are fighting a constant battle in modernity.

I needed this short detour to make the following point: In Central-Eastern Europe between past and future, during the first ten years of the new democracies, the fight between historical and technological imagination has been brought to the forefront. It stands to reason why. In a single-party system, a unified ideology dominates that synthesizes historical and technological imagination. According to Marxism, universal progress is caused by the development of forces of production and their clash with the relations of production, and after achieving proletarian liberation from the straightjacket of capitalism, the modern forces of production will be successfully controlled and developed *ad infinitum* by socialism and communism. Needless to say, in this scenario technological imagination contains historical imagination, and vice versa. Since a dominating ideology no longer exists, the unity of the two imaginary institutions is past and gone. New democracies also have been normalized in this respect. In a democracy, which breeds the pluralism of opinions and views, historical and technological imagination frequently collide, sometimes even within the same individual's soul.

There are some areas in all the new democracies in which historical and technological imagination clash. Since my experience is Hungarian (and I think that in Hungary this conflict is tougher than in some other new democracies), I limit my examples to the Hungarian case.

Let me return for a moment to the presupposition that the future is free. I have already stated that this is not entirely the case, for the throw from unrelated dicecups is never simultaneous. Several dice have already been rolled—for example, had the Hungarian revolution succeeded in 1956, the economic and social conditions for the new democracy would have been entirely different. The new democracies of 1989 were thrown into circumstances that now provide the conditions for free action, yet also put limits on several decisions and actions. Some of those conditions have nothing to do with the matters I am going to discuss, but others do.

There are no natural social or political systems in the sense that no social or political system is more adequate to human nature than any other. However, the individual is a fairly elastic animal and can adopt various life strategies, ways of acting and thinking. What was not natural yesterday may be natural tomorrow. But it takes time to adjust, and every adjustment is readjustment. How fast one can adjust depends on several circumstances, but primarily on how partial or total the readjustment needs to be.

In the new democracies adjustment is partial, for one has to adjust from the requirements of nondemocratic and economically noncompetitive—yet already modern—social and political systems, to other, differently democratic and economically competitive, social and political systems. Although the readjustment is partial, it still needs time and cannot happen as abruptly as the change of political institutions and economic systems themselves. One can perhaps import the wording of a democratic constitution and can introduce fair laws in a short time, but one cannot produce law-abiding citizens. One can privatize enterprises, but one cannot introduce the entrepreneurial spirit from one day to the next.

Fifty years ago, between 1948 and 1949, the people of Central-Eastern Europe had to readjust to the introduction of the Soviet system.

The adjustment occurred under constraint and with fear. But up to a degree it happened. Yet, at least in matters of daily life, a whole generation (or rather two generations) adjusted and accommodated itself (or themselves) to the given circumstances, and afterwards to the paternalistic version of the single-party system. Seemingly inconsequential issues are far from being inconsequential: how to get an education, how to get a job, how to find an apartment, how to go on vacation, how to visit a doctor, how to get to a hospital. Ten years ago, very abruptly, the unpopular but familiar world collapsed; individuals had to learn new rules to new games. Some learn with ease, some with difficulty, and others not at all. A part of society will be absolutely lost, particularly because certain workplaces are disappearing due to contemporary technology; there is a loss of human value. If one looks at this development from the viewpoint of technological imagination alone, one could conclude that everything has its cost, and one must pay the price of progress. The spirit of progress requires adaptable individuals, for they are the ones on whom the future hinges.

Historical—or romantic—imagination does not accept this argument; rather, it avers that one should not pay the price of progress. What is progress, anyhow? If the lifeline of a nation is cut, and whole social strata become impoverished, useless, and perhaps homeless, there cannot be progress. Many of those who assume the attitude of historical imagination place more emphasis on the importance of life than on freedom. Technological—or rationalistic—imagination nowadays is universalistic in Central-Eastern Europe (though not at all times and not everywhere). This is understandably so—technology binds and bolsters the world: all computer engineers speak the same language, and the economy is global. Romantic imagination is more traditional; it prefers to speak the mother tongue. It fears that succumbing to universal—that is, global—intercourse threatens the survival of specificity and individuality. It wants to protect national traditions from the intrusion of the international market, particularly from the global media and the Americanization of culture. It also wants to protect certain features of daily life, such as the traditional family.

Historical imagination can pave the way for fundamentalism, but it is by no means always and in principle fundamentalist. Moreover, technological imagination also can evolve into a kind of fundamentalism. The conflict between technological and historical imagination is present in all modern societies. The specificity in Central-East European societies is, however, that the conflict is carried out under the burden and pressure of adaptation. Technological imagination enforces rapid adaptation; historical imagination supports resistance or makes the case for the deceleration of the process of adaptation.

But adaptation is also heterogeneous, as is resistance against it. To what does one need to adapt in the time between past and future? To democracy; to the rule of law, including civil and human rights; to a market economy, including the global market; to the latest technology. Yet these institutions rarely require direct adaptation; rather, adaptation occurs through the filters of everyday life and behavior—the so-called inconsequential, yet not so inconsequential, issues that I already mentioned: how to seek employment; what school to choose for one's children; whether or not to bribe the police officer, civil servant, or official in order to get something that is legal, but takes ages to be achieved through legal means; to protest or not to protest if facing injustice; to speak out in defence of one's own case or for the case of another; to hire personnel based on professional qualifications or on political connections. For example, in the current present, efficiency is necessary, but the individual is often faced with a choice between the moral and the practical. An additional conflict exists: the ramifications of one's actions based upon those that are familiar in the past. Freedom of speech is now practiced, but one may not exercise this right, being afraid that the specter of the past will appear in the present. To sum up, the past remains present— and limits the present—in at least two different ways: first, in the preservation of traditional attitudes and behavior, which adjust to new circumstances in a Hegelian way; and second, in the fear of both the ghosts of the past and of the risks of the future.

The past has a strong presence in intellectual life as well. Central-East European societies have been fairly apolitical, precisely because everything—or at least too much—was politicized. Art, education, and the economy were political matters. Now that totalitarianism, even in its paternalistic version, is past and gone, the apolitical character of totalitarian society survives in the minds of average citizens. They are contented with—and are even proud of—not caring about politics, far more than is desirable for a healthy democracy. In contrast, intellectuals became overpoliticized in the old regime, and the old tendency remains in force; they regard everything as a matter of politics. To complicate matters, everything is regarded as a matter of party politics. Public life is divided along party lines, especially in Hungary, and the sympathizers of a party behave as if they were party intellectuals in the historic sense. The old distinction between the so-called constructive and destructive criticism has not withered.

Until this point, I have discussed briefly the past of the present and the past in the present. Now I briefly turn to the future of the present and the future in the present.

Let me stress again that as the past is not entirely necessary, the future is not entirely free, for there are constraints; there is a finite space for action to change things. It is of the greatest importance in the new democracies to determine where those limits are and what constraints exist. Constraints cannot be described in terms of necessity or determination; they are the framework, the limit, on the space for free action while preserving the freedom of action. In the new—yet not quite established—democracies, great uncertainty prevails concerning the establishment of free space; yet to accept a limit or a constraint does not mean to resign freedom. One can assume—though nothing is certain—that those constraints are presently immovable because they do not seem to be movable by actions within the new democracies, but nothing in the world is absolutely immovable. When one uses the term new democracies, the word "new" is the attribute of democracies. It does not add to the essence of the thing but does not detract anything from it either. New democracies and old democracies are democracies all the same. Sometimes the new institutions are even more democratic than in traditional democracies. How can one then explain the feeling, which has been expressed many times by several intellectuals, that this democracy is somehow not "real"?

I have already mentioned one of the reasons. The institutions are in place, yet the attitudes necessary to maintain these institutions are sometimes absent. Yet there is another reason. In totalitarian times, even during its paternalistic period, Central-East European intellectuals viewed democracy in a rosy light. It stood for the perfect political order. Yet a political order is by definition imperfect. By realizing that the new democratic order is imperfect, the answer is readily at hand: it is not democratic enough. To balance those inflated expectations, one could perhaps refer to Churchill's well-known *bon mot*: democracy is a fairly bad political institution, yet still the best ever invented. One could add that it is the best for a very simple reason—modernity can best reproduce itself within the framework of democracies, for the institutions of liberal democracies have the greatest potential to secure the freedom of the individual. This freedom is *relatively* stable, first because freedom of the individual does not depend solely on the political order, but on society and on the institutions of the intimate sphere as well; and second—and this is the gist of the matter—because democracy is an imperfect political order, as all political orders are.

Although the grand narrative was rejected by Central-East European intellectuals a few decades ago, its vestiges are still lingering in their imagination, first and foremost in the foible for the metaphysical category of perfection. Where there is perfection, there can be neither action nor criticism, yet irritation for imperfection remains. Only where there is unjust distribution can one make a case for distributive justice; only where many things are wrong can one make the case to set it right. Democracy opens the door for making such claims; it opens the territory of future-orientedness in politics, for the not-yet. Democracy, while offering space for the dynamics of modernity, gives the future-orientedness in politics an ontohistorical foundation.

Thus, *the future of the present presupposes the future in the present.* Democratic institutions are the embodiment of the future in the present, for they offer the opportunity not just for future-oriented action, but also for future-oriented negation. Yet future-oriented action, and future-oriented negation, too, must have limits; they must be limited by certain conditions. Liberal democracy is an institution that freely sets the limits to its own freedom.

I earlier mentioned economic constraints, including the constraints of the global economy. Economic constraints are relatively or partially external to the modern state, just as many other institutions of technological imagination, such as science; otherwise they could not be universal. An external limit is not self-limitation, although it can be related to self-limitation. The legal order is self-limitation; human rights are self-limitations. That freedom itself is based on self-limitation is as old a wisdom as the idea of liberal democracy. But old wisdoms also need to be repeated sometimes.

Let me return to a short sentence I formulated close to the beginning of this paper: The modern world is grounded on freedom. But freedom is a foundation that does not found. As a result, the modern world is unfounded; it needs to found itself, it needs to give itself its own foundation. For without a foundation there is no theory, no world and, of course, no politics. The foundation is the *arche*, the final and ultimate principle, on which other principles need to be measured, to which other principles need to have recourse. Without grounding, one will enter a chain of determination without end. And since this does allow for a political order, there will be a nondemocratic order.

One of the greatest political inventions of modern times is the kind of constitution that works as a political foundation. It is not a natural foundation, for as the name suggests, it is constituted; yet after having been constituted, it becomes quasi-natural. In the modern world, freedom can be founded if the constitution is behaving like the *arche*, the fundament to which all laws have to take recourse. Further, the legitimacy of actions taken and decisions made for the future from the vantage point of the future can be limited by this foundation alone. The foundation can also be modified, but it is better to modify it infrequently. It is not the most important matter whether the foundation is a written constitution or not, but that individuals are aware of the limits of contestation and that the future of the present is a future within this limit. The constitution and the spirit of the constitution, as Montesquieu once said, is the foundation of modern democracies.

The ten years between 1989 and 1999 were indeed the years between past and future. What was at stake was learning how to live constantly and continuously between past and future: how to cope with the tension between historical imagination and technological imagination; how to accept life in a state of uncertainty, in the process of constant trial and error, in contingency and freedom which sets its own limits. One adapts to a transitory period when one discovers that it is not a transitory period, because modernity is not to be understood as a transitory period that finally leads to an earthly paradise. The possibility for betterment always exists. The present always can be better than it is. But even if it will be better, and should be better, there always will be suffering, nuisance, injustice, and pain. And there will be losers. This is not transitory. Modernity does not enjoy a privileged position in history.

Still, the new democracies of 1999 have reason to celebrate. Traditional novels end with weddings: lovers divided by tough luck, conspiracy, and misunderstanding finally meet each other before the altar and on the nuptial bed. Very rarely does the author offer the reader a look into the lives of the married couple ten years after. For ten years of marriage after the happy day of the wedding would show that nothing happens exactly as expected; it would show disappointment, quarrels, sadness, moments of regret, and nostalgia for the honeymoon. And still, this is real life—engagement is just a preparation, and the wedding is a happy moment that shines beautifully in our memories. This has also happened in the new democracies. There were weeks of jubilation, of passionate hugs and enthusiastic intoxication, but now the Central-East European countries have already been married to liberal democracy and the market economy for ten years. These ten years could not have matched those dreams. Those who were promised the rose garden were cheated or were mistaken. Rose gardens on earth exist only in the totalitarian mind. Yet things can be better than they are, and they should be better.

One can celebrate the first decade, the first essential anniversary, with a promise: to make the marriage work with less suffering, less pain, less remorse and also with less nostalgia—but not with fewer quarrels. Because without altercation there cannot be a good marriage between free and independent minds.

2 On Two Models of Exit from Communism: Central Europe and the Balkans

JACQUES RUPNIK

Ten years after the collapse of the Soviet empire one thing seems clear: the word "postcommunism" to describe the variety of its offsprings has become almost irrelevant. What indeed is the common denominator of Hungary and Albania, the Czech Republic and Belarus, or Poland and Kazakhstan? The fact that they used to share Soviet-style communism is hardly relevant for understanding the vastly different itineraries of the democratic transition in each. Indeed, if one looks today at the landscape after the battle, one is struck by how different the outcomes of the democratic transitions have been in Central and Eastern Europe. Among these situations, certain patterns, however, do appear. A new political geography of formerly communist Europe is emerging: Central Europe is back (the so-called Visegrad group, the Baltic countries, plus Slovenia) as the real "success story" of the democratic transition; the Balkans have often been "derailed" by the priorities of nation-state building or undermined by the legacies of communism and economic backwardness; Russia, in search of a postimperial identity, is teetering on the brink of economic disaster and an impossible restoration of the *ancien régime*.

In his *Essay on the Revolution in Europe*,[1] published shortly after the collapse of the communist system (and still the best guide to the decade that followed, compared to the hundred volumes of "transitology" that western political science tried to placate on the unfamiliar realities of the "other" Europe), Ralf Dahrendorf identified three interlocking areas of change with different "time tables": political democracy and the rule of law (six months), the conversion to a market economy (six years), and the emergence of a civil society (sixty years). One of the major challenges of the transition is precisely the management of time—the combination of three mutually interdependent areas of change with very different time spans. It can be argued almost a decade later that in Central Europe this management of time by the new political elites has on the whole reached its prime goals. Parliamentary democracy has been established as the only game in town—that is, the creation of a constitutional framework and political institutions that are seen as legitimate by all political actors; the formation of a relatively stable party system that allows for smooth alternation in power—everywhere in Central Europe. A market economy has been established with more than half of the gross national product produced in the private sector and over three-quarters of trade now conducted with Organization of Economic Cooperation and Development countries. A civil society is developing with both its economic dimension (emerging new strata of entrepreneurs) and its networks of nongovernmental organizations (for example, over twenty thousand voluntary associations were formed in Poland in the 1990s).

This picture contrasts not only with that of the former Soviet Union (the Baltics being the exception to the rule), but also with the Balkans, the most extreme case of a "derailed" transition being, of course, former Yugoslavia (the most advanced in the reform of communism before 1989 and the last in the democratic exit from communism after 1989) because of the war and the break-up of the federation into several successor states, the legitimacy and the viability of which are still being questioned. The legitimacy of the territorial framework clearly remains the first prerequisite for a democratic transition. The redefinition of the role of the state also concerns the capacity to implement the rule of law. In this perspective, to speak of a "crisis of the state" is a euphemism for describing the situation in Albania, torn between conflicting regional and political factions. Just as President Berisha was forced to step down by an armed insurrection in 1997 only days after his reelection, so his successor and rival Fatos Nano resigned in 1998 after Berisha mounted a campaign of violent unrest.

To be sure, the situation in the Balkans should not be seen solely through the prism of the Yugoslav war and ethno-nationalist conflict. And there have been encouraging developments over the last two years in both Bulgaria and Romania. In the former, the winter of discontent (1996–97), culminating in the ransacking of Parliament, forced the incompetent and corrupt ex-communist government to step down and call an early election that opened the way for much delayed economic reforms. In Romania, a belated yet smooth alternation in power ("We have lost seven years," said President Constantinescu when taking over from Iliescu) saw the ex-communists replaced by a right-wing coalition, which after three years in power has produced little in terms of reform—a wasted opportunity (unlikely to return) to use the trade-off between political gains and economic losses for giving the democratic transition a fresh start.

If the contrast between Central Europe and Southeastern Europe can be summed up as that between democratic consolidation and the rise of "illiberal democracies", then Bulgaria, Romania, and Slovakia are in an intermediate position, moving from the latter to the former.[2] This differentiation through the transition process (rather than through geopolitical design) has important foreign policy implications. The double enlargement process of the North Atlantic Treaty Organization (NATO) and of the European Union (EU), both of which stress democratic conditionality, imperfectly reflect this differentiation. One can, of course, point to the inconsistencies of leaving Slovenia or the Baltic countries out of the first round of NATO enlargement or be concerned that Slovakia or Romania have the possibility to rejoin the "first circle" of EU enlargement if the recent departures from authoritarianism are confirmed. But it is the outcome of a decade of democratic transition and the related differentiation between the "ins" and the "outs" of enlargement of Euro-Atlantic institutions that is shaping the new political geography of postcommunist Europe.

There is, of course, no single causal explanation to account for this process. We can only point to a combination of factors, explanations or hypotheses that can be helpful in making sense of the current state after a decade of democratic transition. It is only if the six hypotheses proposed here produce a convergent picture that one might be in a position to suggest a correlation between them, a common denominator.

The Legacies of Communism

More than the actual character of disintegration of the old regime and the transfer of power in 1989 (gradual or sudden, negotiated from above or imposed from below and from abroad), which is important in the early stages of the transition, it seems that in a long-term perspective it is the legacy of communism, the nature and depth of its imprint on society, that is relevant. One can, in this respect, point to the fact that some of the harshest and longest periods of totalitarian domination in the post-war period concerned the Balkans—Albania, Bulgaria, and Romania—whereas a greater degree of reform and accommodation was characteristic of the post–1956 regimes in Hungary and Poland. The contrasting case of Yugoslavia since the 1960s and that of "normalized" Czechoslovakia since the 1970s show the limits of such a generalization.

The contrast between Central Europe and the Balkans is relevant, however, if one examines the nature of the crisis of the communist regimes. Communism in Central Europe experienced three major crises—the 1956 Hungarian revolution as well as the events in Poland, the 1968 Czechoslovak reform movement, and the 1980–81 Solidarity movement in Poland—that posed in different ways the issues of democracy and civil society; and only in a second phase (under growing external constraint), that of national independence. The three major crises of communism in the Balkans (Tito's break with Stalin in 1948, Hoxha's swing in allegiance from Moscow to Peking in 1961, and Ceauşescu's 1968 bid for independence) all stressed the autonomy of the national communist apparatus vis-à-vis Moscow while reinforcing the totalitarian features of the regime.[3] The origins of the rebirth of civil society in Central Europe go back to these three major crises as well as to the dissident movements of the 1970s and 1980s. The origins of "nationalism as the supreme stage of communism"—to use Adam Michnik's phrase—in the Balkans owes a great deal to the legacies of Ceauşescu, Hoxha, and Tito. Similarly, the emergence of alternative political elites during and in the immediate aftermath of 1989 in Central Europe owes a great deal to the existence of organized democratic opposition movements that were lacking in Southeastern Europe, where all of the first free elections were won by the ex-communist parties.

Market and Civil Society: "No Bourgeoisie, No Democracy"

Barrington Moore's famous phrase concerning the social origins of dictatorship and democracy[3] provides a second clue for a comparative assessment of the democratic transition in Central and Eastern Europe. There were, of course, differences due to the uneven level of economic development dating back to the precommunist period (Czechoslovakia ranked in the top ten in gross national product per capita after World War II) or due to the degree of economic reform pursued in the decaying phase of communism (Hungary and Poland were clearly the frontrunners, while Bulgaria and Romania, for reasons of ideological orthodoxy, lagged behind). But the most striking contrast is between those that after 1989 embarked on radical market reforms (known as "shock therapy" in Poland) and those that chose gradualism or simply the postponement of market reforms and privatization (Bulgaria and Romania).

The results are fairly clear in terms of the size of the economy in the private sector, but they are also evident in foreign trade, in growth rates, and last but not least, in the level of foreign investment (nearly half of direct investment in Central and Eastern Europe went to Hungary alone; ninety percent to Hungary, the Czech Republic, and Poland). There are almost one million registered private entrepreneurs in the Czech Republic and over eight hundred thousand in Hungary, both countries with populations of ten million. The emergence of new middle classes is also related to the breakthrough of the "information revolution" and the formidable expansion of the service sector—that is, areas where "human capital", or levels of education and ability, are rewarded. (Before 1989 less than a third of Czechs considered that education was related to success. They are almost two-thirds today.) The development of these middle strata as well as the conversion, through the privatization process, of part of the old nomenklatura into the new bourgeoisie provided the backbone for market-oriented changes in the economy.

They are also related to the development of a civil society without which, as Dahrendorf argued, the democratic transition would not be sustained. The term has undergone numerous definitions in Central and Eastern Europe over the last twenty years. It emerged in the late 1970s in the dissident movements' attempt to shift their approach from the powers that be and their ideology to the self-organization of society. But this concept of an alternative society (the "new evolutionism"[4] as Adam Michnik called it in 1976, or a "parallel polis" as Václav Benda put it in 1978) under the circumstances had more of a moral and political content: a unifying moment for society's opposition to totalitarianism.

After the collapse of communism the concept acquired new meanings relevant for the democratic transition. Two main definitions seem to have developed. The first, prevalent in Central Europe among "liberals on the right", tended to identify the concept with the above described economic revolution. This is civil society as *Bürgergesellschaft*. The market economy is the priority from which everything else will follow. Indeed, in Václav Klaus's thinking there was simply no place for the notion of "civil society"—between the individual and the state there is need for little else except the market.

In the second definition of civil society, prevalent among "liberals on the left", the term is almost completely divorced from the market economy and is largely identified with the so-called "third sector"—that is, nongovernmental organizations (NGOs). This is a view of civil society as distinct from both the state and from the market, and much closer to the old dissident discourse on the subject. The NGO is by definition almost doubly pure: it is corrupted neither by power (that is, politics) nor by the market (that is, money). Civil society, according to the former concept, is more developed in Central Europe; the NGO sector has been relatively more important to the transition in Southeastern Europe, where it often compensates for the weakness of both the middle class and the political opposition to semi-authoritarian rule (Romania under Iliescu or the former Yugoslavia). The case of Slovakia, which since 1993 seemed to drift away from the Central European model, has recently shown how effective the "third sector" can be in mobilizing society and helping the opposition to overcome the "democratic deficit".

The Rule of Law and the "Habsburg Factor"

The development of the rule of law is no doubt a crucial element in the success or failure of the democratic transition. Whatever the various other merits or policy implications of the recent debate about "illiberal democracies", this much has been established by the last decade in post-communist Europe. Again, even though generalizations are also exaggerations, the rule of law, constitutionalism and the existence of an independent judiciary are undoubtedly more developed in Central Europe than in the Balkans. In searching for an explanation we can, of course, take into account political circumstances or the degree of openness and adaptability of the new elites to western models of the separation of powers.

There is one factor, however difficult to use, that deserves to be mentioned in this connection: the legacy of the Austrian (as opposed to that of the Ottoman) empire. The Habsburg empire was certainly not a liberal democracy on the British model, but nor was it an autocracy like tsarist Russia. It was a *Rechtsstaat*—that is, a state run by the rule of law. Indeed, the whole of Austrian turn of the century literature (from Musil and Roth to Broch and Kafka) is dominated by the question of law, the tension or conflict between legitimacy and legality. This tradition of the rule of law that has been shared by several Central European successor states has survived (albeit in a distorted and transformed manner) the demise of the empire in terms of legal scholarship, administration, and more generally, political culture. It was rediscovered already in the last phase of decaying communism by self-limitation of the powers that be and by the opposition challenging their rule not in the name of the ruling ideology but in the name of accepted domestic and international legal commitments. The 1990s have largely confirmed the trend that acquired major significance in the European Union's assessment of accession prospects: the capacity of the candidates not just to adopt EU norms in their legislation, but also to implement them and enforce them. The contrast between Hungary and Romania with regard to the rule of law is an obvious case in point. The cases of Slovakia and Croatia are toned down, but do not invalidate the general argument.

Nation-state Building and "Homogeneity"

The return of democracy in 1989 was inseparable from the return of the nation: popular sovereignty and national sovereignty became indistinguishable. In this, 1989 followed in the footsteps of 1848 and 1918—the idea that the nation-state is the natural and most favorable framework for democracy. The demise of federalism inherited from communism (Czechoslovakia, the Soviet Union, Yugoslavia) seemed to confirm this conviction. But the link between national sovereignty and democracy can work both ways, as we have seen in the former Yugoslavia. This is a classic dilemma described by the Hungarian political thinker István Bibo at the end of World War II in his essay *The Misery of the Small Nations of Eastern Europe*: "Fascism exists in germ everywhere where, following a cataclysm or an illusion, the cause of the nation separates from that of freedom..."[5] This fear to see freedom and democracy "threaten the cause of the nation" has been historically one of the major impediments to the democratic graft in the area between the two wars and has no doubt been an important factor in the sidetracking of the democratic transition after 1989 in the Balkans and in Eastern Europe (in former Yugoslavia and in the former Soviet Union; less so in the Czechoslovak divorce, where there were no conflicts between the two protagonists over borders and minorities). Nation-state building takes precedence over the democratic transition and the rule of law.

One hypothesis concerning the lesser importance of the national question in the democratic transition in Central Europe is that it is relatively more homogeneous than Southeastern Europe (and where it is not, as in Slovakia, is precisely where we saw the single most important failure of the transition in Central Europe). Poland today is a homogeneous state (compared to the prewar situation, when a third of the population was composed of minorities). The dream of the nationalist right of the *Endecija* came about with the help of Hitler and Stalin under communism. The same is true in the Czech Republic, without Jews, Germans, and now even Slovaks. Alone at last! Slovenia is the only ex-Yugoslav successor state where the democratic transition fits into the Central

European pattern; it is also the only one that does not have a significant minority problem. In short: What is the difference between Central Europe and the Balkans? Fifty years. The major difference between Central and Southeast Europeans is not that the former are more tolerant and pluralistic, but that their "ethnic cleansing" was completed half a century ago, whereas in the Balkans the process of "homogeneous" nation-state building is still under way (after Greater Serbia and Greater Croatia, making the viability of Bosnian democracy a dubious proposition, the Albanian question is on the agenda, as the conflict in Kosovo tragically reveals). This, as Ernest Gellner put it, is meant as a description, not a prescription.[6] It would be absurd to suggest that ethnic "homogeneity" is a prerequisite for democracy. Yet the contrasting situations in this respect of Central Europe and the Balkans account, at least in part, for the different fates of the democratic transition in the two areas.

The Cultural Backbone of Democracy

This has been one of the oldest—and also one of the most used and abused—arguments about the cultural factors of democratic polity. It goes back, of course, to Max Weber's classic thesis about the Protestant ethic and the spirit of capitalism. The question therefore would be: Looking at the balance sheet of the democratic transition in Central and Eastern Europe, is there a case for pushing the thesis one notch further— is there a correlation between the success of democratic transition and consolidation and western Christendom (Central Europe) or, conversely, between the difficulty of democratic (and market-oriented) change and Orthodoxy? The argument revolves around the issue of the separation of the spiritual and of the temporal in Central Europe—the merger or subordination of the church to the state (and the close identification between religion and ethnicity) in the Orthodox lands as a major handicap in the emergence of a democratic public space and of a civil society.

The Weberian question has however become loaded since Huntington's thesis concerning the "clash of civilizations" (which has many ardent disciples in the Balkans), which has been used and abused in the interpretation of the recent war in Bosnia and more generally in discussing the western democracies' international agenda after the cold war. Fortunately, we had Slovakia and Croatia (as well as encouraging developments in Bulgaria and Romania) to disprove Huntington's thesis.[7] Yet Slovakia is returning to the Central European model since Meciar's defeat in September

1998, a possible source of inspiration for Croatia as it comes to the close of the Tudjman era. All one can do in the face of a politically very loaded debate is both to refuse cultural determinism (especially reduced to its religious dimension) as misleading or politically dangerous and also to avoid, out of moral concern or political correctness, turning Max Weber's classic sociological question into a political taboo.

The International Environment

The international and regional environment also helps to account for the different fates of the transitions to democracy in Central Europe and in the Balkans. It can be argued that, in a historical perspective, the post–1989 Central European environment thus far has been exceptionally favorable to the democratic transition (although it remains to be seen how long this environment will last):

1. Russia is weak and inward-looking, and its sphere of influence is shrinking. (How near is the near abroad? is the question Central Europeans ask concerning Russia.)

2. Germany is reunited and economically powerful, but democratic and anchored in two western institutions, NATO and the EU, both of which create an appropriate, more balanced framework for Germany's relations with its eastern neighbors.

3. There are no significant regional conflicts between states in the region, a major difference with the interwar period marked by what Hugh Seton-Watson called a "private civil war" over the legitimacy of borders or the fate of national minorities. Hungary has signed treaties concerning these issues with its two neighbors, Slovakia and Romania. Poland was prompt to recognize Ukrainian and Lithuanian independence and acts as a stabilizing and democratizing actor vis-à-vis its eastern neighbors. Even the Czechoslovak divorce (unlike the Yugoslav breakup) was a velvet one. All three factors are unprecedented in the modern history of Central Europe and contrast with the relative instability of the Balkans connected with the wars of succession in the former Yugoslavia, the collapse of the Albanian state at the very moment when war and ethnic cleansing returned to Kosovo, not to mention the latent Greek-Turkish rivalry in the region.

These differences are reinforced by the prospects of "Euro-Atlantic" integration, the Central European code word for the double enlargement of NATO and the EU, which has been the prime foreign policy objective of the new democracies. Both institutions insist on democratic conditionality and, as the Slovak case showed, they mean it. Paradoxically, it is NATO that tends to be perceived in Central Europe as a "value-infused institution" (A. Smolar) whereas the European Union tends to be identified primarily with economics and a legal framework. However, when looking for inspiration as far as institutional design is concerned, it is mainly in Western Europe that the new democracies tended to find plausible models. The conversion to the market economy was largely influenced by American free marketeers (such as Jeffrey Sachs, the mentor of Poland's Leszek Balcerowicz, or Milton Freedman for the former Czech prime minister, Václav Klaus), but the German political model seemed most influential in Central Europe: the constitutional court (Hungary or the Czech Republic owe a great deal to the Karlsruhe model), the parliamentary system (preferred to presidentialism French-style, which has many disciples in Southeastern Europe), and the electoral system (proportional representation or a mixed system).

Ten years after the fall of the Berlin Wall it seems that for both major institutions identified with western democratic values, the priority toward Central Europe is integration, whereas toward the Balkans it is intervention (or containment). No Balkan country features in the planned enlargement of either NATO or the EU. A possible second wave of NATO enlargement could concern Slovenia, Slovakia, and—who knows?—Austria, thus giving further geopolitical coherence to the process. It remains to be seen, on the other hand, what the impact of nonenlargement will be on the democratic transition of countries "in between," such as Romania and Bulgaria. Clearly, the differentiation between the "ins" and the "outs" of the enlargement process is a consequence of the democratic transition so far, but it is also a factor that could contribute to undermining it precisely where it is most fragile. The Central European success story should not be helped by a new "iron curtain" built vis-à-vis Eastern or Southeastern Europe. It is therefore of utmost importance for the future of Central Europe's integration in the EU that Europe's democratic project shapes the borders of the union, and not that preconceived historical or cultural borders shape the project.

Notes

1 Ralf Dahrendorf, *Essay on the Revolution in Europe* (London: Chatto, 1990).
2 F. Zakaria, "The Rise of Illiberal Democracies," *Foreign Affairs* 1 (1988). François Fejtő was the first to point out the paradoxical attempts at emancipation from the Moscow fold among the most hard-line regimes in his *Histoire des démocraties populaires* II (Paris: Seuil, 1969), 1953–68.
3 Barrington Moore, *The Social Origins of Dictatorship and Democracy* (Cambridge: Harvard University Press, 1971).
4 Adam Michnik, "Le nouvel évolutionnisme," in *Varsovie-Budapest 1956, la deuxième révolution d'Octobre* eds. P. Kende and K. Pomian (Paris: Seuil, 1976).
5 István Bibo, *Misère des petits États d'Europe de L'Est* (Paris: l'Harmattan, 1988), 128.
6 Ernest Gellner, Conclusion to *Le Déchirement des Nations*, ed. Jacques Rupnik (Paris: Seuil, 1995).
7 Samuel Huntington, "The Clash of Civilizations," *Foreign Affairs* 72 (Summer 1993): 22–49.

3 *1989 as Rebirth*[1]

KAROL SOLTAN

The events of 1989 were *not* a revolution (neither liberal, nor self-limiting, nor velvet, nor anti-revolutionary). They were *not* simply reforms or restoration. They *were* a rebirth,[2] and rebirths (not revolutions, as Marxists would have it) are the locomotives of history.

It is symptomatic of the uniqueness of these events, and the inadequacy of contemporary social science and political theory, that we still argue not just about the causes, consequences, or significance of them, but about what we should *name* them. Of course, the naming itself has little importance. We must find a satisfactory framework for understanding such events. The most revealing name will naturally emerge when we find an appropriate framework.

There is now a large literature on the meaning of 1989,[3] but I don't think an adequate framework has been found. The proposal I sketch in this chapter centers on a broadly "constitutionalist" conception of modernity. According to this conception, the politics of modernity is deeply and permanently bipolar, a battle between creative and destructive power, between a civic politics (building, protecting, and improving complex institutional structures) and a politics of war between revolution and subversion. The great rebirth that occurred in 1989, while a victory for civic politics, did not end bipolarity; it only ended the distinctive and rather well-articulated form of bipolarity that characterized the cold war.

Constitutionalist Conception of Modernity

Constitutionalism is a big and awkward word, which we do not use much.[4] And when we do, we give it a narrow and technical meaning. For some, it refers to the art of writing and interpreting legal texts known as constitutions. But legal texts called constitutions can be pure fictions, as

Stalin (among others) demonstrated. Constitutions as legal documents matter when they have real effect, when they determine, or at least significantly influence, the main features of a political system. We have then a political system restrained by law. A still more meaningful conception of constitutionalism is not narrowly legal, but more broadly political. It refers to the art and science of designing political institutions, creating in the process the capacity to achieve collective purposes, but also restraining those institutions by the rule of law.

I would like to suggest a "constitutionalism" that is broader still: a perspective on modernity, politics, and human interaction. According to this conception the central battle of modern politics and (underlying that) the central battle of human interaction in general is the battle between creative and destructive power. We live in an inherently and unavoidably bipolar world. We should not be neutral in that battle; we should promote creative power and limit destructive power. We can see the events of 1989 as a major victory for politics on the creative side, which we can call civic politics, and the defeat of communism, the most fully organized form of destructive politics yet invented, centered on a revolution imposed from above using the full coercive apparatus of the state.

According to this broadly constitutionalist view, there is a big story of modernity, but it is not anything like the big story of inevitable liberal progress or inevitable progress toward communism (via a sequence of revolutions). The direction of history does not seem inevitable at all; in fact, it is very difficult to predict. But the battle between civic and destructive politics does seem inevitable; it is a battle of creative power (creation of new institutions, new capacities to improve the world) against the forces of destruction and degradation.

A more conventional view of modernity neglects the forces of destruction, decay, and death. According to this view, modernity lifts the chains of inevitability that bind all premodern, traditional societies, dramatically expanding the scale and depth of human design as opposed to organic growth or evolution. The world increasingly does not impose itself on us. We make it ourselves, though we do not make it "as we please". In the institutional sphere, legislation (made law) replaces found law, and our lives are increasingly governed by formal, special-purpose organizations. In the human sphere we see the spread of various forms of education (schools, therapy, counseling), organized efforts to design the furniture of our minds. In the material sphere we see the development of technology and machines, accompanied by the shift of human life from a natural to a constructed environment (the city).

According to this view, modernity is characterized not simply by the growing scale but also the greater "depth" of design, as seen in the increasing importance of second order design. Let me give two examples. In the institutional sphere second order rules are rules governing the making of rules. They are the chief distinguishing characteristics of modern legal systems (in contrast to systems of customary law), in which they take a broad range of forms, including constitutional and contract law. They are the foundation of the legal-rational forms of authority about which Weber writes. In the material sphere, second order design involves the design of objects for the production of objects and constitutes the foundation of the industrialization of the world.

The constitutionalists, as I imagine them in this essay, claim that this picture of modernity is radically incomplete, missing a crucial ingredient. Modernity does indeed lift the chains of inevitability, but in doing so it liberates both creative and destructive forces, both design and destruction. So modernity is characterized by the increasing scale and depth of the battle between the creative and destructive forms of power.

We live in a permanently bipolar world. Keeping this thesis really in mind has deep consequences. It allows us to live our lives, allocate our energies, and choose our politics in a way that recognizes the pervasiveness of evil and the inevitability of death. Those who are forgetful of death and who think evil is somehow a temporary and avoidable burden will necessarily seem to lack seriousness. They will seem adolescent.

The intellectual and motivational sources of communism were in many ways adolescent in just this way. But in giving organizational form to human destructiveness, communism appears to have also provided an opportunity for the development of a more deeply constitutionalist mentality. This mentality often (as in this case) has grim allies. The intimate experience with the destruction of matter and spirit produced by communism was one such ally. The development of nuclear weapons and increasing environmental destruction are additional allies. To understand the constitutionalist mentality, it is best to turn not to the technicians of constitutional law and political theory, who will tell us only how to put routine limits on the destructiveness of ordinary states, but to the anticommunist opposition, who have experience with the most elaborate forms of political and social destructiveness (though more pathetic than vicious toward the end).

The Civic Style of Politics

We can extract from the political thought and practice of the anticommunist opposition a distinctive civic style of politics and an ideal of *civic* society.[5] The concept of citizenship usually refers to a form of membership in the state and its associated set of rights. But citizenship can also be understood in a less law-bound and state-centered way, as a form of loyalty to any institution or group and a mentality associated with that loyalty. The anticommunist opposition developed the idea of civic society as an alternative to more state-centered strategies of reform. The idea of citizenship implicit in it had little to do with the state. It did have something to do with a more general form of loyalty to society.

A society of citizens is a society of people pursuing a variety of projects, improving in a variety of ways the world around them, without much direct concern for the state. The civic attitude they express combines a willingness to sacrifice in defence of the object of loyalty with a willingness to sacrifice in the reform and improvement of that object. This loyalty of a citizen, who combines efforts to defend and to improve, can be contrasted with the loyalty of a *subject*, who defends but is unwilling to criticize. This would have been the loyalty of a perfect socialist individual, if such a creature had been created. It can also be contrasted with a variety of attitudes that have nothing to do with loyalty: the mentality of a subversive aim to destroy or at least degrade its object and the mentality of the manipulator, or as the Polish philosopher Jozef Tischner's "beggar-thief," who sees in the world nothing but instruments to be used without limit as means to achieve one's own purposes. Real socialism produced many beggar-thieves, some subversives, and a few good subjects. The aim of the opposition was to promote a more civic attitude.

The civic perspective can be divided into general political and intellectual inclinations on the one hand and specific institutional design and policy development skills on the other. The anticommunist opposition had no reason or opportunity to develop the latter, given the assumption of the continued survival of communism. The general political and intellectual inclinations they *did* develop, though, bear a striking resemblance to those we recognize as requirements of complex institutional design in a bipolar world:

1. They promoted two kinds of "social arts": the art of separation[6] and the art of combination. Society needed to be separated from the state, and various aspects and elements of society needed to be kept separate from one another. The blended and homogenized "fish soup" of communism needed to be transformed back into a vivid and complex aquarium. The construction of complex institutional wholes requires the art of separation so that the identity of the various parts can be maintained. But it also requires the art of integration so that the parts can be made to work to-

gether. And the opposition also worked to reconstruct the broken forms of horizontal social solidarity.

2. They had a preference for ideological hybrids and for the political center. Civic politics balances two concerns, those of security (protection, maintenance) and those of improvement (progress, reform). We might call this a form of progressive conservatism. But in Poland, at least, another term became popular, vividly expressing the widespread skepticism about the extremes of the political spectrum and about what passed for consistency in politics. Many in the anticommunist opposition signed up to Leszek Kołakowski's liberal socialist conservative manifesto.[7] Their political ideology was liberal, but it was *hyphenated* liberal—it was a hybrid, unapologetic about its political syncretism. So the events of 1989 were not a liberal revolution, in part because they were not a revolution (they were more moderate than revolutions), but also because they were more hyphenated and syncretic (and hence more inclined toward the ideological center).

3. The anticommunist opposition rejected the idea of large-scale social experiments. They preferred the incremental and the well-tested. They tended to accept some version of a Popperian style of critical rationalism and the idea of an open society. The rebuilding of the aquarium was going to be a decentralized and incremental task, in which much room had to be allowed for learning and error correction.

4. The oppositionists were quite conscious of human imperfection in all its many aspects. They had all around them evidence of what can happen when one forgets about human frailty. Their political thought was ever mindful both of human cognitive limits and of the pervasive danger of destructiveness. They thought a great deal about how to prevent an anticommunist revolution. And in a deeply constitutionalist spirit, they inclined toward self-limitation, both in the choice of means (nonviolence) and in the choice of ends. So they supported the rule of law as an ideal for the state and a Gandhian-style, self-limiting social movement for the opposition to the state.

5. They revived not only the idea of a civic (or civil) society, but also the ideal of an antipolitical politics of truth. The politics of truth can take a variety of forms. For the critical intelligentsia and public intellectuals, this mostly means speaking truth to power. For the great nonviolent and self-limiting social movements of the twentieth century (Gandhi, Martin Luther King, Solidarity), it is best expressed in Gandhi's term *satyagraha*, or truth force.[8] In the constitutionalist tradition it has taken the form of natural law,[9] with its claim, in slogan form, that truth can be the source of law (*veritas facit legem*). Modern natural law incorporated as its centerpiece a commitment to some form of a universal charter of

rights. And that commitment, too, was prominent in the fight against communism.

The events of 1989 were marked by this combination of features found in the political thinking of the anticommunist opposition. Most oppositionists did not make successful transitions to government officials, civil servants, or parliamentarians. But the general principles of their political thinking were nonetheless a significant element in defining the distinctive qualities of those events.

1989 as a Rebirth

The events of 1989 were profoundly antirevolutionary, so they cannot be called revolutions. Yet they were also clearly not part of the routine of politics the way "reforms" are. They were more dramatic, radical, and involved changes too deep for this simple category of ordinary politics to be applicable. So commentators have coined new words (refolution) or paradoxical combinations (antirevolutionary revolution) to describe these events. Neither strategy is likely to be helpful in understanding the distinctive quality and significance of what happened. We need a more adequate alternative.

In light of a constitutionalist interpretation of modernity and of politics, we should see these events as a *rebirth*. For a constitutionalist, rebirths (and not revolutions) are the locomotives of history. The chief source of hope in politics is not the inevitability of progress or of the final triumph of the socialist revolution. The main source of hope is the possibility of rebirth, a reversal of destruction. The collapse of communism in East Central Europe is a vivid and dramatic illustration of such a reversal.

Historians, political theorists, and social scientists have spent many years honing the concept of revolution and clarifying its various subtypes. We need to get started on the idea of rebirth. Let me suggest that a pure case of rebirth (a kind of ideal type) would have the following three distinctive features:

1. rebirths restore some form of continuity with the past, reversing destruction or decay;
2. they are distinguished by the level and form of activity they involve—there is an unusually high level of plural and incremental improvement;

3. they are periods permeated by social energy and passion, in which sacred values are taken seriously. They momentarily reverse, in a way, the disenchanting tendencies of modernity.

Restoration of Continuity

Revolutions are breaks in continuity (in addition to displaying other characteristics, of course). In this, rebirths are the opposite of revolutions; they restore continuity. Yet the reality of actual revolutions is more complex. Their appeal to the political imagination is certainly due in part to a dramatic break with the past, but it is also due to the element of rebirth that often accompanies revolution. The early revolutions of the modern era were seen largely as restorations. Cromwell fought for the restoration of "ancient English liberties". The French Revolution in its early phases was also largely a fight to restore old rights and privileges. The word "revolution" originally had *return* as a central element of its meaning. So introducing more systematically the contrast between rebirths and revolutions will probably also require us to rewrite the history of revolutions.

If revolutions are the locomotives of history, then the key events of history are breaks in continuity. Modern civilization is a product of a fundamental *break* with the past or perhaps a whole series of such breaks. If rebirths are the engines of history, then the fundamental events are restorations of continuity, not breaks. The basic model is the Renaissance, which centered on a restoration of continuity with various elements of ancient culture and politics, whether real or imagined.

Enlightenment critics, convinced that a fundamental break had occurred between the ancients and the moderns, accused the Renaissance of ancestor worship. However, no one with even the most superficial acquaintance with Renaissance culture—its writing, its painting, or its architecture—could possibly reduce it to ancestor worship. The critics failed to make the important distinction between restoring the past (or worshipping it) and restoring *continuity* with the past. The Renaissance did only the latter.

The same distinction is also fundamental to understanding the events of 1989. Efforts to restore the past—as it actually was before the communist episode, with its borders, political systems, political parties, and ideologies—were quite weak in 1989. This was not a restoration, but a rebirth. It centered on civic loyalty, not the loyalty of a subject. Civic loyalty aims to improve its object as well as to protect and maintain its continuing identity. The loyalty of a subject is different: it expresses itself only in the protection of its object as it is. A subject attempts to maintain and restore the past *without change*. A citizen maintains or restores *continuity* with the past, allowing for change and even insisting on it. This contrast may not sound very substantial on paper, but it marks the difference between the democratic politics of civic societies and the fundamentalism that now feeds contemporary forms of destructive politics. Few contrasts have greater practical significance.

Plural Improvement

In addition to being a break with the past, a revolution introduces change that is both large scale and novel (capitalism is replaced by communism, for example). We can often identify the revolution's program, even if it is rarely carried out exactly as planned. Rebirths are different in every way. They are periods of great activity, but involve many individuals and groups engaged in their own projects, largely independent of all the others. There is for the most part no central program, and most of the change is incremental.

Rebirths, unlike revolutions, take into account the basic law of social change, the foundation of which lies in inescapable human ignorance. This basic law tells us that large-scale improvements are more likely to succeed when they are not innovative, and innovative improvements are more likely to succeed when they are incremental. The great revolutions were efforts to introduce large-scale and innovative change. They were not likely to succeed as intended, and for the most part they did not. Rebirths substitute a combination of large-scale change that is not innovative, for example, establishing the conditions necessary for a rebirth, as we saw in 1989, and many small-scale innovative improvements.

The large-scale change can be achieved, as we saw in 1989, by a combination of pressure from self-limiting mass social movements and "round table agreements". Incremental innovations are the work of civic society and the market. This combination constitutes, I would suppose, the core "methodology" of rebirth. It is a methodology that recognizes the conflict we face between scale and novelty when we want to change the world, a conflict due to our basic ignorance. The revolutionary tradition, based as it is on a stronger *faith* in reason, has trouble recognizing this conflict. It has been tempted by the illusion of a complete and deep understanding of social life and history (as contained, say, in Marxism-Leninism), with which the conflict would disappear and great revolutions, however destructive, could at least achieve their ends.

Re-enchantment

Rebirths, and revolutions as well, are full of energy, exuberance, and passion. People are willing to do what they wouldn't think of doing at other times. They go out on the streets to protest. They organize committees and councils. They form new groups and organizations. They do not act out of cold calculation of interests, but out of internal necessity moved by higher ideals. These are periods during which, in small ways and large, people are willing to risk or to sacrifice their lives. And historically this also has meant that people have been willing to risk and sacrifice the lives of others: revolutionary passions led to revolutionary violence.

This century provided many examples of such turns of events. It has made many people suspicious of all forms of passion and all forms of great sacrifice as somehow tainted by violence. Let us be bourgeois and civil instead, they say. They reject anything that smacks of the heroic because of its association with violence. They turn, with Richard Rorty, to a postmodern bourgeois liberalism, or to a fully disenchanted civil society: a true *bürgerliche Gesellschaft*, which seems to me quite a bit less than a society of citizens as conceived by many in the anticommunist opposition.[10]

But the twentieth century has also provided an alternative upon which the anticommunist opposition drew. We associate it most fully with Mohandas Gandhi. The basic invention amounts to this: It is possible to have an effective form of politics in which willingness to risk and sacrifice life can be combined with a firm *un*willingness to risk and sacrifice the lives of others. This discovery was an essential ingredient of the political thinking of the anticommunist opposition; sacred ideals did not have to be abandoned. And commitment to them need not make one dangerous. Gandhi and Martin Luther King Jr. proved this to be true, and Solidarity proved it again. Heroic virtues that for ages have been associated in politics with violence and destructiveness, with war and revolution, can be constitutionalized. Rebirth can perhaps finally also mean rebirth of the most sacred ideals without a turn toward violence, which a Gandhian "political methodology" would now block.

There was something profoundly new and hopeful about the events of 1989, even if (or perhaps because) they did not introduce (nor did they aim to introduce) any regime of a completely new type. Activation of energies in politics and in other forms of human activity requires hope. In modern politics the deepest source of hope traditionally has been faith in the inevitability of progress. Some believed in the inevitable triumph of reason, others in the inevitable triumph of the socialist revolution.

This form of hope turned out to be both misplaced and dangerous, and for a long time now nothing has been found to replace it. The events of 1989 suggest a new deep source of hope, the basis of which is not the inevitability of progress but the reversibility of destruction. It is striking, therefore, that these events were followed not by enhanced hope, but by a deep and widespread disappointment.

The Disappointment of 1989

The years 1989–91 saw the collapse of communism as a serious global alternative and as the victory of civic politics over the remnants of the twentieth century's main form of destructive politics. It was a period of great—though ambiguous—rebirth; it was a combination of triumphs and defeats, the exhilaration of victory and deep disappointment. The disappointment had at least two sources, based in what the events of 1989–91 were not.

First, they were not a permanent defeat of the politics of destruction, but just one of its forms. So disappointment emerges as we face the politics of destructiveness being reconstituted into new forms, more warlike and energetic than communism had been for a long time. War returned to Europe, and in most of the places where it has been avoided, new forms of aggressive politics have emerged. But no one should have expected that the destructive aspect of politics would somehow evaporate together with communism.

The second source of disappointment has been in some ways more subtle. The social movements that were triumphant over the revolutionary form of destructive politics turned out to be helpless in the face of a fully disenchanted modern civilization with its consumerism, technocracy, and cynicism. The sovereignty of the communist party was replaced by the sovereignty of money. Or, if you are a true cynic, it was replaced by the sovereignty of "real things": money, power, and sex. The heroic element, centered on the Gandhian idea of a self-limiting social movement committed to truth and love, to *satyagraha* and *ahimsa*, disappeared almost without a trace. And this (almost) disappearance has been quite painful, especially in Poland where Solidarity had deep roots.

But the events of 1989 were not just events of local significance, and so perhaps the disappointment is premature. They also transformed the global organization of power and ended the cold war. And the world keeps changing in ways that suggest that the rebirth of 1989 may yet turn into a harbinger of a more global rebirth, transforming modernity from a civilization centered on a break with the ancients and on revolutions to one centered on the Renaissance and rebirth. It is not anything one could predict, but it is perhaps a possibility.

In fact, ideas that were central to the anticommunist opposition are showing up all over the world. It seems that almost everybody now favors the strengthening of domestic civil society as an important bulwark against the coercive state and as an instrument for decentralized reform. We also increasingly recognize the importance of a global civil society with its interconnected worldwide network of nongovernmental organizations fighting to protect human rights, to defend the environment, to limit corruption, and so on.[11]

Conservative liberal socialism used to be a quaint—and moderately ironic—political formula that only people connected to the anticommunist opposition would love. Leszek Kołakowski, when he first put forward his conservative liberal socialist (CLS) manifesto, felt certain that a CLS International would never come into being. It is not so clear any more.

We see a rush to develop a principled politics of the center, one that doesn't simply search out the median voter to win elections; hence, political hybrids are taken with new seriousness. Officials of the Catholic Church, from Pope John Paul II and Cardinal Joseph Ratzinger down, talk of the need to incorporate certain key aspects of liberalism into Catholic social doctrine,[12] which was already quite open to conservative and socialist thinking. So CLS seems to have a bright future among the Catholics of the world. CLS is also alive and well in the communitarian movement in the English-speaking world, which is liberal as well as communitarian and whose communitarianism carefully incorporates both conservative and socialist impulses. The Third Way of Clinton, Blair, and Schröder is not yet quite CLS in power, lacking an explicit conservative component, but it may be as close as one can come in a political system dominated by two parties.

These two examples are changes on the surface of political thinking and practice. But there are also intellectual changes that address the larger issue of the kind of modern civilization in which we want to live. There are various efforts to revive the Renaissance, to go to the roots of modernity in order to free us from some of the grim legacy of the seventeenth century: Cartesian rationality, the logic of which drives revolutions (destroy first, build later); contractarianism in political theory, which in many ways reinforces this Cartesian logic; and the Westphalian system of sovereign territorial states, within which the destructive power of states can be limited only domestically.

The Renaissance revival projects with which I am familiar cover a broad range of politics, society, and culture. They include:

1. a broader front of attack against the Cartesian formulation of rationality and against Descartes in general; the well-known works of the critical rationalists, such as Popper and Hayek, are now joined by Stephen Toulmin's effort in *Cosmopolis* to undermine the main Cartesian aspects of modernity by elaborating on some late Renaissance intellectual trends, visible especially in the work of Montaigne;[13]

2. the new republicanism in political theory,[14] which establishes continuity with the civic humanism of the North Italian Renaissance as a way of fighting the contractarianism that has its modern roots in the seventeenth century (Hobbes and Locke);

3. the "Romanian Chicago School" in the study of religion,[15] which attempts to establish continuity with the program of the Platonic Academy in Florence and the works of Ficino and Pico della Mirandola, searching for deep structures of the experience of the sacred, independent of differences in creed and dogma;

4. efforts of the social potential movement in the United States to bring about some sort of a new Renaissance, promoted in the cultural and political journal *Utne Reader*, among others;

5. efforts to rethink the global system of international relations in a way that abandons the assumptions that have come to be associated with the Treaties of Westphalia. Instead of a system of sovereign territorial states, something more complex should emerge, based in part on a thorough revision of what we mean by security[16] and development, and which institutional system can best guarantee both. In discussing these changes, some have used the term "a new medievalism",[17] but they do not mean a return of the Dark Ages (although that, too, is a possibility). They mean a system like that before the Treaties of Westphalia; a return to the Renaissance.

All these efforts to re-establish continuity with the Renaissance can also be seen as ways to redefine the meaning of modernity. We see an effort here to abandon an idea of modernity in which the state and revolution are the main players. Its basic image was set out by Descartes: modernity must first destroy what it has inherited from the past in order then to be able to design a new world *ex nihilo*, using in the case of social design the device of a contract or the strategy of revolution. This kind of modernity requires a fundamental break with the past. And a revolution, taking over the state and using its coercive apparatus, is the most powerful instrument to achieve this goal. Communism was the high point of modernity understood in this way.

The constitutionalist alternative proposes a different picture: a complex institutional design that limits the destructive capacity of the state but promotes its capacity to make the world better and protects the capacity of other agents both to make the world more secure and to improve it. And the main locomotives of history are not revolutions breaking continuity with the past, but rebirths that re-establish this continuity. The real origin of modern civilization is not in the break between the ancients and the moderns that much of the Enlightenment promoted, but in the Renaissance effort to re-establish continuity with the past. In a modernity that celebrates breaks with the past, the rebirth of 1989 is at best puzzling. But in a modernity that re-establishes continuity with its symbolic origins in the Renaissance, the events of 1989 can be celebrated as exemplary: in them more than anywhere else we see revolution replaced by rebirth.

Notes

1 I presented an earlier version of this chapter as a paper during the conference "Between Past and Future" at the Central European University in Budapest and as a lecture during a summer school organized in Timişoara by the Open Society Institute and the Center for the Study of Post-Communist Societies, University of Maryland. I would like to thank especially Jeffrey Isaac and Bartlomiej Kaminski for their comments.

2 György Konrád, *Antipolitics* (New York: Harcourt, Brace, 1995); Václav Klaus, *Renaissance: The Rebirth of Liberty in the Heart of Europe* (Washington, D.C.: Cato, 1997).

3 Bruce Ackerman, *The Future of Liberal Revolution* (New Haven: Yale University Press, 1992); Andrew Arato, "Interpreting 1989", *Social Research* 60 (1993): 609–46; Ralf Dahrendorf, *Reflections on the Revolution in Europe* (New York: Random House, 1990); Francis Fukuyama, "The End of History?" *The National Interest* 16 (Summer 1989): 3–18; Francis Fukuyama, *The End of History and the Last Man* (New York: Free Press, 1992); Jeffrey Isaac, "The Meaning of 1989", *Social Research* 63:2 (1996): 291–344; Ken Jowitt, *New World Disorder: The Leninist Extinction* (Berkeley: University of California Press, 1992); János Kis, "Between Reform and Revolution", *East European Politics and Societies* 12 (1998): 300–83; Ulrich Preuss, *Constitutional Revolution* (Atlantic Highlands, N.J.: Humanities Press, 1995).

4 Mircea Elkin and Karol Soltan, eds., *A New Constitutionalism* (Chicago: University of Chicago Press, 1993); Jon Elster and Rune Slagstad, eds., *Constitutionalism and Democracy* (Cambridge: Cambridge University Press, 1988).

5 Jean Cohen and Andrew Arato, *Civil Society and Political Theory* (Cambridge: MIT Press, 1992); Václav Havel, *Living in Truth* (London: Faber and Faber, 1987); György Konrád, *Antipolitics*; Marcin Krol, *Liberalism Strachu czy Liberalizm Odwagi* (Krakow: Znak, 1996); Adam Michnik, *Szanse Polskiej Demokracji* (London: Aneks, 1984); Aleksander Smolar, "Revolutionary Spectacle and Peaceful Transition," *Social Research* 63 (1996): 439–64; Jerzy Szacki, *Liberalism after Communism*

(Budapest: CEU Press, 1995); Vladimir Tismaneanu, *Reinventing Politics: Eastern Europe from Stalin to Havel* (New York: Free Press, 1992).

6 Michael Walzer, "Liberalism and the Art of Separation", *Political Theory* 12 (1984): 315–30.

7 Leszek Kołakowski, "How To Be a Conservative Liberal Socialist", *Encounter* 51:4 (1978): 46–47; Marek Leszkowski, "Glowne Nurty Solidarnosci", *Kontakt* 1:8 (1982): 7–10.

8 See for example, Bikhu Parekh, *Gandhi* (Oxford: Oxford University Press, 1997).

9 See A. P. d'Entreves, *Natural Law* (London: Hutchinson, 1951).

10 Ernest Gellner, *Conditions of Liberty* (London: Penguin, 1994); Michael Ignatieff, "On Civil Society", *Foreign Affairs* 74:2 (1995): 128–36.

11 Jessica Mathews, "Power Shift", *Foreign Affairs* 76:1 (1997): 50–66.

12 Maciej Zieba, *Po Szkodzie? Przed Szkoda?* (Krakow: Znak, 1996).

13 Stephen Toulmin, *Cosmopolis* (Chicago: University of Chicago Press, 1992).

14 J. G. A. Pocock, *The Machiavellian Moment* (Princeton: Princeton University Press, 1975); Ronald Terchek, *Republican Paradoxes and Liberal Anxieties* (Lanham: Rowman and Littlefield, 1996).

15 Mircea Eliade, *The Sacred and the Profane* (New York: Harcourt, Brace and World, 1959); Mircea Eliade, *the Myth of the Eternal Return* (Princeton: Princeton University Press, 1971); and Ioan Couliano, *Eros and Magic in the Renaissance* (Chicago: University of Chicago Press, 1987).

16 Emma Rothschild, "What is Security?" *Daedalus* 124:3 (1995): 53–98.

17 Stephen Kobrin, "Back to the Future: Neomedievalism and the Postmodern Digital World Economy", *Journal of International Affairs* 52 (1998): 361–86.

4 *1989 and the Future of Democracy*

JEFFREY C. ISAAC[1]

What is the future of democracy? And, in a vein only slightly less gran-diose, what is the relationship between this future and what has come to be called "1989"? As we approach the millennium it is tempting to ad-dress our subject in a millenarian fashion. Indeed, the subject seems to invite such an approach. For the velvet revolutions of 1989 were surely world historical events—even if, as Jürgen Habermas put it, they were "rectifying revolutions", reiterating classical themes of liberal democ-racy.[2] The overturning of communism, first in Eastern Europe and then in Russia, signified the death of revolutionary Marxism and transformed the political geography of Europe and, indeed, the world. The year 1989 seemed to inaugurate a new world, or at least a new world order.

This at least was the message of Francis Fukuyama's much-cited "The End of History", which echoed the western media in proclaiming the global advent of liberal democracy.[3] The postcelebration hangover was not long in coming. The so-called "Fukuyama thesis" engendered powerful criticism from liberal skeptics like Samuel Huntington and Jean-Francois Revel, who insisted, in Huntington's words, that "to hope for a benign end of history is human. To expect it to happen is unrealis-tic. To plan on it happening is disastrous."[4] Fukuyama himself voiced reservations, first in a series of qualifying follow-ups, then in his next book, *Trust*, which gives voice to a widespread concern among liberal writers that liberal democracy is not faring well in the world, even in the places formerly known as the "free world".[5] This skepticism among lib-eral public intellectuals is mirrored in the burgeoning political science subfield of "transitology", which takes as its premise the problematic character of democratic transition and consolidation.

This brings us back to our question about "1989 and the future of de-mocracy". We know that "1989" is not in any simple sense a story of the ascendancy of freedom or democracy. We know that the record of the postcommunist countries is varied: in Central Europe (the Czech Republic, Hungary, Poland, Slovenia) and the Baltic states (Estonia, Latvia, Lithuania) versions of liberal, capitalist democracy have been instituted; in Russia and certain European parts of the former Soviet Union—Belarus, Moldova, Ukraine—quasi electoralist, authoritarian regimes have been established on the basis of a new kind of primitive accumulation and gangster capitalism; and in the Transcaucasus (Armenia, Azerbaijan, Georgia) and Central Asia (Kazakhstan, Kyrgystan, Tajikistan, Turkmenistan, and Uzbekistan) communism has given way to smoldering ethnonationalist conflict, civil war, and dictatorial government.[6]

Thus 1989 had a bright side—so to speak—and a dark side. These are two sides of the same coin. It is disingenuous to concentrate on one at the expense of the other. The structure of this conference is true to this insight. Far from celebratory, the conference has adopted a tone that is cautious, skeptical, and incredulous about the prospects for democracy in the wake of 1989. Following Tony Judt in his new book, *The Burden of Responsibility: Blum, Camus, Aron and the French Twentieth Century*, we might say that the tone of the conference is Aronian: calm, detached, realistic, determined to generate reliable causal accounts that might produce tentative predictions and inform intelligent policies that advance liberal democratic values.[7] This is as it should be. The production of such knowledge is surely one of the most important vocations of the intellectual-as-scholar.

While in what follows I will not abjure such a posture entirely, I want to sound a different theme, a Camusian theme. I want to prick our consciences and prod our thinking by pursuing the question of "1989 and the future of democracy" in a slightly different and deliberately provocative way—by focusing my attention not on the subject of velvet revolution but on the subject of "Bosnia" and its meanings. I want to do this to emphasize some of the profound challenges confronting democracy today, but also to underscore the continuing importance of creative thought and action on behalf of democratic values. Having done so, I will briefly adopt a more Aronian posture, suggesting some lines of democratic inquiry and experimentation appropriate to the challenges of the next century.

The Meanings of Bosnia

Bosnia is a place in the heart of Europe. What can it mean to speak of the "meanings" of a place? It all depends. In some contexts to speak of the meaning of a place is clearly to succumb to a kind of political romanticism, to appeal to collective passions, and to invoke associations in a hyperbolic manner. In this way, for example, "remember the Alamo" can be seen as incitement to action against the Mexicans. There are good reasons to be suspicious of the idea that profound meaning can be derived from an evocation of place, for this idea is often invoked for pernicious and chauvinistic purposes; think, for example, of the historical meanings attached to Kosovo by Serbian nationalists. But there are certain situations in which a place-name can come to symbolize something more than mere sentimentality or resentment, something historical and profound. "Auschwitz" was such a place-name for the generation that survived World War II. In many ways, I think "Bosnia" is such a place-name for us—we who inhabit advanced industrial societies and who believe ourselves to enjoy the fruits of civil and political freedom and enlightenment.

When the history of twentieth century political thought is written, the decade of the 1990s will claim credit, among other things, for a unique and distinctive contribution to the lexicon of politics: the concept of "ethnic cleansing." Bosnia is the site of this philosophic innovation. It is not as if the activities to which this concept is linked are novel. To the contrary, they have become chronic features of our political landscape in this century. And yet, as linguistic philosophers tell us, the invention of a concept is the enactment of a world. What is this world that has been enacted—that is being enacted—in Bosnia, and what is its significance for thinking about democracy in our time?

If in other parts of East Central Europe the demise of communism liberated democratic oppositions and helped to set in motion a process—for good and ill—of political and economic liberalization, in Yugoslavia it had the effect of setting in motion a process of rapid and precipitous political implosion. The republics of Bosnia, Croatia, and Slovenia quickly declared their independence and moved toward secession. Anxious Serbian ethnic minorities within these areas recoiled in fear; and into this political caesura stepped Slobodan Milosević, the Serbian ex-communist dictator of Yugoslavia, who used the crisis as an opportunity to enforce the political project of a "greater Serbia". A thorough and detailed account of events and causalities is beyond the scope of my argument here. The unfolding of events was no doubt complicated; political corruption, vice, and violence were practiced in many forms by many parties to a conflict in many ways complex. But I think it is possible nonetheless to offer a thumbnail sketch of the inhumanity in question, and for this one can do no better than to draw on David Rieff's impassioned *Slaughterhouse: Bosnia and the Failure of the West.*

> "This is what happened. Two hundred thousand Bosnian Muslims died, in full view of the world's television cameras, and more than two million other people were forcibly displaced. A state formally recognized by the European Community and the United States...and by the United Nations...was allowed to be destroyed. While it was being destroyed, United Nations military forces and officials looked on, offering 'humanitarian' assistance and protesting...that there was no will in the international community to do anything more. Two successive American Presidents, one Republican, the second Democratic, declared over and over that they represented the last remaining superpower and yet simultaneously insisted that they were helpless....And this was not, as so many pretended, the result of some grim, ineluctable law of history, but rather a testimony of specific choices made by those who governed the rich world and by civil servants who administered the international system that they had created."[8]

The Bosnian "civil war" began in the summer of 1991. It was brought to an official end only in the summer of 1995, when the Dayton Accords brokered by the United States ratified the independence of Slovenia and Croatia and the *de facto* partition of Bosnia. In the intervening years a brutal war of "ethnic cleansing" was waged by Bosnian-Serbian forces against the Muslim population of Bosnia. Towns and villages were depopulated and destroyed; mosques and cultural institutions were systematically pillaged and razed; a policy of mass rape was practised against Muslim women; a network of concentration camps was set up throughout those parts of Bosnia captured by Bosnian-Serb forces; and a campaign of terror and mass murder—a campaign of genocide—was undertaken against the Muslim population. It complicates the picture, but in no way mitigates the horror or minimizes the enormous responsibility of Milosević and his Bosnian-Serbian allies, to point out that the Croatian dictator Franjo Tudjman also organized a reign of terror, albeit on a smaller scale. Many people of all "ethnic" identifications suffered, as did many more who lacked a clear ethnic identification altogether. But none suffered more than the Bosnian Muslims, who were "cleansed" by Serbs, harassed by Croats, and helped by no one. While the Dayton Accords brought an official end to these atrocities, the "peace" that has been established is an uncertain one. Fear and resentment persist. Injustice goes unpunished. Paramilitary militias remain armed. The Bosnian Serbs remain in control of much of the territory and the property that they conquered and forcibly expropriated. And their leaders—Radovan Karadzic, Ratko Mladic, and numerous others—remain utterly unpunished and at liberty in spite of the fact that they have been indicted as "war criminals." These facts are beyond question.[9]

But the questions we must raise are in regard to their meaning: What do they signify? What lessons can we draw from them? What are their implications for thinking about democratic politics or about politics in general? There is, of course, no single or easy answer to these questions. Indeed, these are matters about which commentators are sure to argue for years to come as events continue to unfold. Yet I think some tentative answers are possible.

The most important point to make about events in Bosnia is that there is no reason to consider them as aberrations. Francis Fukuyama recently contended that such events are entirely "marginal" and in no way signify that liberal democracy has "plausible ideological competitors". As he writes: "more extreme nationalist states like Serbia that violate fundamental liberal principles of tolerance have not fared well. Because populations are not homogeneous, their emphasis on ethnic purity leads them to conflict, war, and destruction of the economic basis of modern power. It is thus not surprising that Serbia has failed to become a model society for anyone in Europe, East or West...Although ethnic conflict is a severe threat to democracy in the short run, there are a number of reasons for thinking that it will be a transitional phenomenon."[10]

This is a strange remark. The description of Serbia as "intolerant"—rather than, say, brutally repressive or genocidal—is a striking understatement. And what does it mean to say that ethnonationalist ideology does not represent a "plausible" ideological competitor of liberalism? A great deal hinges on the meaning of the term "plausible". For Serbian nationalist ideology surely has fared quite well in achieving its objectives. Bosnian Serbs control Bosnian territory. Milosević continues to rule Yugoslavia with an iron hand. As I write, Serbian police, paramilitary and military units continue to oppress, brutalize, displace, and kill hundreds of thousands of ethnic Albanians in Kosovo, all the while thumbing their noses at the demands of the United Nations, North Atlantic Treaty Organization, and the United States for a cessation of the violence. Serbia may not have become a spiritual model for the West, but it is nonetheless the case that the West has demonstrated little difficulty accepting, indeed *de facto* ratifying, its violation of "fundamental liberal principles". It is hard, then, to view Serbian aggression as "marginal" or "temporary". In any case, what proves to be "temporary" can be nonetheless utterly serious and indeed deadly, as was witnessed during the Thousand-Year Reich, which lasted roughly twelve years. So I would suggest that "Bosnia" is more serious than Fukuyama's comment—a comment that nicely mirrors western complacency—implies.

Many meanings can be attributed to the destructive and violent scenario still being enacted in Bosnia and even more violently in Kosovo. Among them four stand out. And contrary to Fukuyama, they implicate some general and disturbing realities that those serious about democracy cannot afford to gloss over.

1. First, the Bosnian debacle can be seen as a symptom of a broader crisis in international relations in a postcolonial and postcommunist age, a "foreign policy" crisis of tremendous proportions that tests the resources of liberal democratic states and their strategies of promoting a more organized and "liberal" world order.[11] The downfall of communism in Europe has let loose what Daniel Patrick Moynihan has called a pandaemonium of destructive forces, of which the Bosnian civil war is only one example.[12] While this crisis has not occupied center stage of either western media attention or political science scholarship, similar ethnonationalist conflicts have broken out throughout the ex-communist world—in Nagorno-Karabakh, Kosovo, Georgia, the Crimea, and in Chechnya, a human rights disaster of the first order that seems, like most things, to have faded quickly from public view into the oblivion that is historical memory in our time. But such hostilities are not limited to the ex-communist sphere. Similar conflicts are unfolding in Turkey and Iraq (and, though better repressed, in Syria and Iran), where Kurds are struggling for independence, a struggle that has recently made its appearance in the very heart of Europe; in Afghanistan; in Palestine; and throughout Africa.[13]

What has any of this to do with democracy? Aren't these events taking place in the nondemocratic parts of the world? Don't they testify to the value of and the need for democracy? Perhaps they do, but they also testify, contra Fukuyama, to how marginal democracy is in our world today.[14] Since the end of the eighteenth century, western humanists have envisioned a world of ever increasing cosmopolitanism, humanitarianism, legality, and self-government. And yet at the dawn of the next century, we confront a world that gives the lie to these expectations. More than thirty years have passed since Jean-Paul Sartre, in his notorious preface to Frantz Fanon's *The Wretched of the Earth*, wrote of the "inhumanity" of this European humanism, "stained with blood". But Sartre credulously wrote in the name of a more "authentic" humanism, a humanism of oppressed peoples—Third World peoples and national minorities—who would rise up against European neocolonialism and free themselves from oppression, who would make real the humanist impulses which are only given lip service by western imperialism.[16] We now know that this "humanism" was no more plausible than the one it so sneeringly disparaged.

The postcolonial and postcommunist world is a world of tremendous violence and profound chaos, destruction, and despair. As the journalist Robert D. Kaplan reports in his powerful *The Ends of The Earth: A Journey at the Dawn of the 21st Century*, the vast majority of the world's population today live amidst relentless disease, environmental devastation, soil degradation, population explosion, and grinding poverty and is subjected to ever present violence and political perdition.[15] It is of course important not to overgeneralize. Each situation is unique. Each political crisis presents its own possibilities. Bosnia is not Burundi; is not Burma. And yet, in different ways, each of these places is beset by intractable problems thrown up by a postcolonial world. They testify to the disorder of this world and to its recalcitrance toward democratic values and democratic political forms. The point is not that western liberal democracies are complicit in these problems, though they are complicit by virtue of their economic and diplomatic ties and their significant role as arms suppliers, a factor that deserves much more attention than it receives. It is that, at the very least, the "Bosnias" of the world defy democratic expectations and stand as a severe reproach to them. In the long run, these reproaches may pass from the scene, though it is surely more likely that they will not; but in the long run, as Keynes famously quipped, we are in any case all dead.

2. But "Bosnia" symbolizes more than a kind of moral or spiritual reproach to democracy, as a barrier beyond which democracy seems unable to pass. For if one feature of the world in which we live is the ever-presence of suffering, displacement, and violence, another is the utter porosity of the borders, literal and figurative, that keep these problems "there" rather than "here". In this deeper sense "Bosnia" can be viewed as the "future" of democracy in those very places where it seems to flourish. For the dynamic of persecution and dispossession is not, and cannot be, safely quarantined "over there". It is here, within our societies and within ourselves. What do I mean by this?

First, that Bosnia is here, within liberal democracy, because the Bosnians themselves are here. The world is currently experiencing a refugee crisis of truly "global" proportions. According to the Office of the United Nations High Commissioner on Refugees, in 1997 alone twelve million people—more than thirty-two thousand people every day—were forced to leave their countries for fear of persecution and violence. This is a conservative estimate. It does not include those millions who were forced to leave their countries under exigencies that do not "officially" qualify as politically violent. And it does not include the more than ten million others displaced within the borders of their own countries. According to a recent United Nations survey, "roughly one in every 130 people on earth has been forced into flight."[17] This is an incredible statistic.

Where do these people go when they are forced to leave their homes, those places in which, however tenuously, they have long resided and labored? They go elsewhere, abroad. They leave "there," wherever "there" is, and come "here". The Bosnian "ethnic cleansing" alone displaced two million people. Many wound up in concentration camps. Some found refuge in Slovenia, or Croatia, or even in Belgrade. Hundreds of thousands made their way to Western Europe, to democratic societies like Austria, Germany, Italy, or Switzerland. They became refugees in the heart of "civilized" Europe, resident aliens of liberal democratic nation-states. In this regard they share the fate of millions of others—Arabs, Africans, Asians, Latin Americans, Mexicans, and Turks—ethnic minorities who have changed the demographics of western liberal democracies and introduced a series of challenges vaguely registered by the concept of "multiculturalism". The challenges are immense. To what extent should these ethnic peoples be allowed, and to what extent refused, entry into western liberal democratic countries? To what extent should their cultures be assimilated; to what extent granted legal recognition? To what extent are they entitled to the forms of welfare benefits provided for citizens? To what extent are they, as subjects of the law and in many cases residents and productive members of the economy for generations, entitled to the full rights of citizenship itself? There are no easy answers to these questions, nor is there any reason to think that such questions can be answered a single way at all times and in all places, but if liberal democracy is to remain a viable form of government anywhere, it will increasingly be compelled to answer them and to do so in ways that remain true to core liberal democratic values of equal respect and political fairness.[18] Liberal democratic regimes have not, until now, proven themselves up to this task, a failure that is only likely to become magnified with the passage of time and the further straining of civic resources. "Bosnia" is here, then, in the sense that the problems of the rest of the world present themselves to liberal democracies not simply as problems of "foreign" but of "domestic" policy, as problems of managing conflict and constituting political identity in an increasingly pluralistic and increasingly fractious world.

But if Bosnia is present in liberal democracy as a challenge of multiculturalism, it is also present in another, more insidious sense—as a spirit of ethnonationalist exclusionism and political resentment that is becoming increasingly prevalent in liberal democratic societies. We do not have to go all the way with Hans Magnus Enzensberger's *Civil Wars* to recognize that public life in what used to be called "the West" has become increasingly acrimonious and that the kind of arrogance, meanness, and cruelty characteristic of the Bosnian genocide has become, in much smaller doses to be sure, a staple of the civic culture of liberal democracy.[19] The impressive electoral showings of Jean-Marie Le Pen's National Front in France are just one example of this; the significant growth of neofascist or neo-Nazi movements and parties in Austria, Eastern Germany, and Italy is another. The anti-immigrant sentiment that has spread throughout Western Europe and the United States is a sign of pervasive insecurity and fear on the part of "native" populations who are experiencing the effects of economic dislocation and fiscal austerity and who jealously guard the national patrimony through which they can vicariously derive a sense of security and belonging.[20] The emergence of right-wing populist movements that play upon ethnic and racial divisions to constitute—and enforce—an antiliberal vision of homogeneous communities represents a significant challenge to liberal democracy that has assumed increasing prominence on the political landscape. Equally significant are the uprisings of aggrieved minorities that increasingly dot the political landscape, from African-Americans in Los Angeles and St. Petersburg to Algerians in Paris, to Turks in Berlin. Responding to economic inequality and cultural marginality, these groups often project their own forms of fundamentalism that are no less hostile to the normal workings of liberal democracy.

Here we can think of "Bosnia" being present among us in an even deeper ethical, and perhaps metaphysical sense: as the challenge of otherness in general that has exploded onto the political arena in recent years. "Multiculturalism", after all, is not simply about the toleration or public recognition of ethnic, racial, or national groups. It is about a complex set of ways in which political identities are currently being contested, about the veritable explosion of a cultural politics centered around identity that has taken place since the 1960s. The problem of Bosnians among us is a problem of dealing with (literal) "strangers" and of dealing with the hostility that these strangers bring out in society; it is also a problem of how to deal with and to process strangeness itself, how to envision and to regulate the contestation of gender identity, sexual identity, racial identity, the human relationship to the nonhuman world ("ecology"), and, indeed, how to deal with the complex identities, and conflicts that reside in the soul of each individual human being. As Julia Kristeva puts it: "Strangely, the foreigner lives within us: he is the hidden face of our identity, the space that wrecks our abode, the time in which understanding and affinity founder. By recognizing him within ourselves, we are spared detesting him in himself. A symptom that precisely turns 'we' into a problem, perhaps makes it impossible. The foreigner comes in when the consciousness of my difference arises, and he disappears when we all acknowledge ourselves as foreigners, unamenable to bonds and communities."[21]

"Bosnia," then, is also a sign of the complexity of both the social and political world and the inner world of the individual, and of the need for liberal democratic citizens to generate the ethical and political resources to grapple with this world in all of its complexity. Here, too, their performance at present leaves little cause for optimism.

3. This leads me to a third meaning of Bosnia, as a sign of a moral crisis of humanism itself. By insisting that Bosnia is a sign of moral crisis, I mean that the very fact that the genocide could be carried out constitutes an instance of egregious ethical irresponsibility and that the abdication, if not complicity, of the rest of the world—especially the so-called advanced and "civilized" world—in the face of so glaring an atrocity symbolizes an even more profound failure of ethical responsibility in our time. The Bosnian debacle took place for four years within our very midst. It took place before our very eyes, as the bloodshed and displacement was broadcast nightly and indeed virtually instantaneously on CNN to every corner of the globe.[22] We citizens of advanced liberal democracies knew that it was happening. And yet we—and the agencies of intellectual enlightenment and political empowerment that supposedly represent us—did virtually nothing to prevent it from happening or to stop it once it began. This is what David Rieff means when he writes about the "failure of the West": a failure to name the genocide as genocide, and a failure to act on the refrain of "never again" that has so frequently been invoked in the wake of the Holocaust perpetrated by the Nazis a little over a half-century ago.

Like the events in Bosnia themselves, this failure is an accomplished fact. What does it mean to call it a profound crisis of ethical responsibility? Ethical responsibility is a complicated thing, something that philosophers, novelists, and poets have wrestled with for centuries. Suffice it to say that it has long been a presumption of our modern, "enlightened" societies that a certain conception of ethical responsibility is enabled by the institutions of liberal democratic self-government: that to be responsible is to be able to perceive what is going on around you, to make certain judgments about the rights and wrongs in which you are implicated, and to be capable of taking some kind of action within the limits of your power to restrain wrong and to abet right. It has long been believed that liberal democracy is uniquely hospitable to such ethical responsibility because of its freedom of expression, its freedom of the press, its forms of universal public education, its independent judiciary, and its system of responsible and deliberative self-government. And yet "Bosnia" puts the lie to such beliefs. Of course these events are not the first time the lie has been put to them. Indeed, in many ways the history of twentieth century politics can be viewed as an extended narrative about the failure of these benign expectations in the face of violence and injustice. And yet "Bosnia" is significant—and striking—precisely because it has taken place in the heart of Europe, fifty years after our supposed moral luminaries asserted "never again", and in the very midst of a veritable euphoria about the defeat of communism and the triumph of a liberal "new world order" in which democracy was ordained to flourish.[23]

The fact that this could occur is partly due to the failure of nerve of political leaders reluctant to offend diplomatic protagonists or to inflame popular passions by calling genocide by its name. It is partly due to the failure of the mass media to educate and to outrage. Indeed, the freedom of expression long ago hailed by Jefferson and his peers as a guarantee of civic virtue proved itself in practice to promote mass confusion and cynicism.[24] "Bosnia" signals a failure of organized political response and of civic responsibility, but at an even deeper level it can be argued that it signals a striking evacuation of responsibility altogether, of the increasing prevalence of a callow indifference among citizens of the "free world" that simply masks itself as an exercise of freedom.

As a victim of Soviet persecution, the Nobel prize-winning poet Joseph Brodsky penned a poem called "The Berlin Wall Tune" to call attention to the oppressions and hypocrisies of communism. How ironic, then, that, but three years after the demise of communism, he would be moved to write a sequel, "Bosnia Tune", to call attention to the ethical debility of "freedom" itself. His words are apposite.

As you pour yourself a scotch
crush a roach, or check your watch
as your hand adjusts your tie
people die.

In the towns with funny names,
hit by bullets, caught in flames,
by and large not knowing why
people die.

In small places you don't know
of, yet big for having no
chance to scream or say good-bye
people die.

People die as you elect,
new apostles of neglect
self-restraint, etc.—whereby
people die.

Too far off to practice love
for thy neighbor/brother Slav,
where your cherubs dread to fly,
people die.

While the statutes disagree
Cain's version, history
for its fuel tends to burn
those who die.

As you watch the athletes score,
check your latest statement, or
sing your child a lullaby,
people die.

Time, whose sharp blood-thirsty quill
parts the killed from those who kill,
will pronounce the latter tribe
as your type.[25]

Brodsky's poem brilliantly captures the incredible, shocking juxtaposition of political murder "there" and absorption in the "commerce" of daily life "here". It also sharpens the sense that there are no "here" and "there", that we inhabit a single ethical universe, that the suffering "they" (and their killers) are "here", too, on our television screens, at our borders, and on our streets, firmly within reach, and yet we choose to ignore them. It is widely reported that accident victims who lose a limb will long after the event experience the limb as if it existed. Brodsky's poem seeks to induce in us a similar effect, of becoming palpably aware of something—ethical responsibility—by heightening the experience of its utter absence.

4. This ethical failure, as I have insisted, is an accomplished fact, and so—even more importantly—are the injustices that have been committed in part as a result of such failure. This leads me to the final significance of "Bosnia": what I will call, speaking loosely, the irremediability of injustice that it instantiates. Political theory is not only about justice. It is also about injustice, about identifying injustice and of remedying it, of righting (as far as possible) the wrongs that have been done. Just as the liberal democratic nation-state has long been

considered a form of government uniquely suited to regulating problems of conflict and to fostering an ethos of respect and responsibility,
it has also been considered a way of enacting and enforcing legality so
as to be responsive to the claims of those who have been wronged.[27]
That "Bosnia" is the site of horrifying wrong is beyond doubt. And yet
in what ways are the victims of this wrong being compensated? Who is
responsible for such remediation? Who is empowered to enforce it? Is
such remediation even possible?

"Bosnia" is a symbol of mass persecutio, violence and widespread
destruction. It is also the symbol of the profound difficulty—indeed, I
would suggest, the impossibility—of compensation. There is no remedy
for the losses. There is obviously no chance of bringing back the dead.
But it seems equally impossible to restore the property of the dispos-
sessed or to restore the dignity and confidence of those who have been
terrorized, raped, and incarcerated. And it appears that there is little political will to enforce any kind of justice for those most politically responsible for organizing and perpetrating such violence.[26] To the extent
that this is true, it is not simply the past that is poisoned, but the future as
well, for those who have suffered, but also, I would submit, for those
who stood by and continue to stand by, doing nothing to assist them,
incapable of offering rescue or remedy. In his famous "Theses on the
Philosophy of History", Walter Benjamin described "the angel of history" thus:

> "His eyes are staring, his mouth open, his wings are spread. This is how one
> pictures the angel of history. His face is turned toward the past. Where we per-
> ceive a chain of events, he sees one single catastrophe which keeps piling up
> wreckage upon wreckage and hurls it in front of his feet. The angel would like to
> stay, awaken the dead, and make whole what has been smashed. But a storm is
> blowing from Paradise; it has got hold of his wings with such violence that the
> angel can no longer close them. This storm irresistibly propels him into the future
> to which his back is turned, while the pile of debris before him grows skyward.
> This storm is what we call progress."[28]

Such a grim picture is, of course, one-sided; wreckage is surely not all
that our recent history has wrought. But wreckage is an absolutely critical part of the story of our contemporary history, a part that most political scientists and political theorists writing about democracy attend to all
too little.[29] The most powerful image in Benjamin's famous parable is
the image of a world irremediably torn, one which cannot be made whole
or restored to some balance or justice. "Bosnia" symbolizes this problem.
It symbolizes it juridically, as an instance of the incapacity of legal
authorities to bring the perpetrators of violence to justice, an inability

that only continues to fuel a cycle of fear, resentment, and hatred towards all possible violators. It symbolizes it politically, by virtue of the incessant waves of refugees it produces, continually uprooting peoples and taxing the fiscal and civic resources of liberal democratic states. And it symbolizes it ethically, as an expression of profound civic cynicism that helps to reinforce the growing sense that meaningful public action on behalf of justice or solidarity is impossible.

The Future of Democracy

Serious political analysts should avoid the temptation to overgeneralize about the future of democracy. If the record of history tells us anything, it is that democratic ideas have extraordinary staying power and can take many shapes. And yet it also tells us that these ideas don't travel on their own but require carriers, vehicles, agents, and also that they usually travel in hostile territory.

In our time democracy has principally taken a liberal and capitalist shape and has been carried by an assortment of agents that includes democratically oriented political elites and parties; global financial institutions (sometimes) like the International Monetary Fund and the World Bank; geopolitical powers like the United States, the European Union, and the North Atlantic Treaty Organization; and also a range of civic initiatives, trade unions, universities, philanthropic foundations, and voluntary associations that comprise what is sometimes called a global or cosmopolitan "civil society". It is important to acknowledge the success of this unstable coalition of forces in advancing democratic politics in parts of Central Europe and the Baltic states and in other parts of the world, from Argentina to South Africa. Insofar as liberal democracy has experienced these successes, then, of course, what I have called "Bosnia" in this paper is not the whole story. Or, as I put it above, 1989 has its bright side.

Yet the dark side is no less dark for this. There is reason to be concerned about the future of democracy in those places where the very idea of it is revolutionary, in those places where it recently has made its appearance, and even in those places where it has long rested securely (at least as long as 1945). New forms of globalization produce massive economic disruption, unemployment and underemployment, and the devaluation of labor. New forms of communication and mass media promote the banalization of public discourse and a growing sense that nothing is truly real and nothing truly matters. The relentless technological imperatives of capitalist "creative destruction" produce ecological devastation and increasing risk. Economic dislocation and political persecution engender pervasive ethnonational conflict and extraordinary global refugee flows. Each of these processes is severe; together they constitute an explosive mixture, a potent source of political resentment, and a serious challenge to liberal democratic values and governance.

The conventional institutions of mass democratic politics in the modern world—mass suffrage, parliaments, parties, the free press—have by no means outlived their usefulness. Indeed, they are indispensable to any meaningful conception of a free society. But in many ways these institutions are inadequate to the problems of the next millennium that I have taken "Bosnia" to symbolize. Democratic politics in the next century cannot dispense with conventional liberal democratic institutions. But if it is to generate civic confidence, to foster new forms of inclusion and recognition, and to promote solidarity and effective action across borders, then new institutions are needed as well: institutions that do not correspond neatly with conventional nation-state centered forms of mass participation, either because they constrain states in new ways or because they connect citizens and constitute new identities globally. What are these institutions?

1. Regional and federal structures designed to generate economic growth, collective security, and human rights. In Europe the most important of these is clearly the European Community and its adjuncts, the European Parliament and the Council on Security and Cooperation in Europe. These institutions are important because they embody, at least in principle, a more universalistic ethos, thus countering existing tendencies toward economic marginalization and ethnic exclusion. In addition, such institutions are important because they seem mandated, so to speak, by the new forms of economic globalization that defy the borders of sovereign nation-states. Such institutions are by no means intrinsically democratic. Like the North Atlantic Free Trade Agreement, they often institutionalize a regime of depressed wages and promote significant economic inequalities and environmental degradation. For this reason democrats should not uncritically embrace such institutions. Yet they have the potential at least to promote democratic values and transnational cooperation—particularly when pressured from below to do so—and they are, in any case, emerging amidst globalization whether we like them or not. Democratic theorists and democratic citizens thus have no choice but to attend to them, to critically analyze their functioning, and to envision new and more democratic ways in which they might function.[30]

2. Global institutions, such as the United Nations, but also judicial bodies like the Hague, the International Criminal Tribunals established

for the Bosnian and Rwandan genocides, the recently proposed International Criminal Court, and conventions such as recent agreements to ban land mines and child labor. Here too, such institutions are not necessarily democratic in either their structure or their consequence, though ideally they represent responses to democratically mobilized pressure on behalf of human security and dignity. But in principle they seek to promote human rights and civic pluralism, and they represent forms of cross-border cooperation that address some of the more egregious forms of suffering and injustice in our world in a way that liberal democratic nation-states are neither set up nor predisposed to do. For this reason such institutions must be at the heart of the democratic agenda of the twenty-first century. The challenge for political scientists is to investigate how such institutions function and how they might be redesigned to better promote human rights, civic solidarity, and democratic legitimacy in an age in which nation sovereignty is in many ways an anachronism.

3. New forms of institutionalized public discourse, such as the "truth commissions" that have become such an important part of democratic transitions in Central Europe, Cambodia, Latin America, and South Africa. Such commissions serve many functions—investigatory, quasi judicial, pedagogical, and political—and as such they necessarily embody tensions and present ethical, legal, and institutional difficulties.[31] Yet it is clear that such commissions represent an important institutional innovation of the late twentieth century that seeks to abet democratic transition through a civil process of public testimony and discussion. Distinctive features of these institutions, relating to the recollection of a violent recent past and the attribution of responsibility (and forgiveness) for such violence, make them particularly relevant for transitional societies emerging from authoritarianism and civil war—in other words, for most societies on the face of the earth. But in broader terms such commissions pioneer new forms of organized public discourse of relevance to established liberal democracies as well. Here I have in mind such things as citizen advisory boards, which have played a central role in the implementation of environmental policy in the United States; citizen round tables like the ones that emerged in the East German democratic opposition to communism, but continued to function—particularly in the East—after German reunification, promoting public discussion of environmental policy, immigrant policy, the treatment of strangers or "foreigners", and even economic development policy; and other ways of promoting a more "deliberative democracy", from town meetings to meditative polls. Such institutions, whether organized by the state, by philanthropic foundations, or less formally by citizens, cannot substitute the conventional institutions of liberal democratic suffrage, bargaining, and political representation. But they are indispensable adjuncts to

and complements to these conventional institutions, and they help to compensate for the legitimacy deficits currently experienced by liberal democratic states.[32] If there is a conventional wisdom these days among democratic theorists, it is that deliberation is a much-needed dimension of democratic politics that is currently in short supply. Much of this literature is merely exhortative, but among political philosophers and political scientists, there is a growing awareness that deliberation cannot be considered independently of the distribution of power and the organization of political institutions. Institutional innovation in this domain is thus a central item on the agenda of democratic politics in the next century.

4. Finally, there are the various initiatives and associations comprising what has come to be seen as an increasingly global civil society, such as *Medecins sans Frontières*, Amnesty International, Global Exchange, Helsinki Citizens' Assembly, the International Campaign to Ban Land Mines, Greenpeace, Oxfam International, and numerous others. Groups such as these have in many ways revolutionized world politics by vigorously promoting a new consciousness of human rights and global responsibility.[33] In so doing, they have drawn upon the ethos—and the organizational forms—of the democratic oppositions to communism in Eastern Europe, as well as upon the western "new left" and peace movements of the 1960s and 1970s. Yet there is a danger here of overgeneralizing about such groups and of exaggerating both their democratic character and their beneficial effects. "Civil society" has in many circles become a buzz word or slogan rather than a serious analytical category, deployed loosely to designate anything "nonstatist" as civic, communitarian, voluntary, and thus good. The fact is, if civil society is taken to comprise the associational sphere of social life situated between markets and states, then civil society is the site of both liberal and democratic activities and antiliberal and undemocratic ones. Civil society is distinguished by its plurality rather than by any particular political principles or convictions. It is not an agent or a collectivity but a space within which democratic political contestation can occur.

The groups mentioned above— *Medecins sans Frontières*, et cetera— are distinctive, and I would argue distinctively democratic, in the following ways: they are collaborative, associational activities animated by a sense of conviction about the importance of universal values; they are grass roots and improvisational efforts in which people "on the ground" create their own power through their own concerted activity and reach out beyond themselves to others differently situated yet bound by common interests; they represent efforts to respond to injuries, or effect change, or deliver assistance, that resist antidemocratic forces, whether these be authoritarian states, guerilla or paramilitary armies or warlords, or transnational corporations.[34] To say that such groupings are democratic is not to attribute to them converging tendencies or an overarching common project. While they have formal similarities and ethical affinities, such groupings are also usually distinguished by their partiality and by a certain improvisational style that resists incorporation into a broader unity.

Further, even these kinds of efforts—which by no means exhaust civil society, which also includes skinhead movements, paramilitary groups, and staunch economic libertarians opposed to any kind of public assistance whatsoever—are not without their limitations. David Rieff emphasizes this in his recent essay "The False Dawn of Civil Society", contending that "when we put our faith in civil society, we are grasping at straws". The discourse of civil society, Rieff claims, promotes a romantic, self-righteous antipolitics that reflects the hegemony of neoliberalism rather than any kind of democratic aspirations or values. "What has been misplaced," Rieff argues, "is the belief that a network of associations could accomplish what states could not...the suggestion that civil society can cope where nations have failed is, in fact, a counsel of despair..."[35] Rieff details the limitations of civil society associations: they are improvisational and weak; they rely on private philanthropic support and typically lack broad public or state funding; they are unaccountable to the broader democratic public; they are dwarfed by the problems of oppression, violence, and inequality against which they set themselves.

Rieff is correct on each score. Civil society associations like *Medecins sans Frontières* or Global Exchange are severely limited. Their remedial activity cannot substitute for remedial state action, and their civic agency cannot substitute for the democratic legitimacy that can be conferred upon states through the conventional liberal democratic process. But Rieff is incorrect to imply that such associations present themselves as substitutes for conventional democratic state action. Civil society politics is important today not because of a naïve libertarianism or because of a willful faith in voluntary activity, but because in many instances states either cannot or will not do the things that need doing, and because in other instances state activity is itself predatory and noxious. Civil society politics is central to the democratic politics of the next century because such a politics is necessary in the face of the failings of liberal democracy and national sovereignty in a truly global age. Such a politics is limited, but it is also powerful insofar as it seeks to promote civic participation, civic pluralism and human right, and to challenge chauvinism and inequality. But such a politics does not work in a vacuum, and it can succeed, even partly, only to the extent that it can exert pressure upon nation-states and their domestic and foreign policies and also work to shape the other forms of transnational political responsibility outlined above. Nongovernmental organizations have a crucial role to play not simply in constituting their own forms of community and activity but in making sure that institutions like the United Nations, European Union, and World Trade Organization are accountable, that they are responsive to pressing needs, that they in fact pursue policies hospitable to peace, civility, and human rights. To this extent, the kinds of democratic practices I have briefly sketched are not independent of one another. Rather, they represent complementary efforts to respond to the public problems of our time.

What, then, is the meaning of 1989 for the future of democracy? There is no single meaning. "1989" signifies the power of ideals and idealism, but also the power of cynicism and the cynicism of power. If it is possible to derive a grandiose lesson from 1989, it is not the end of ideology or the end of history, but it is perhaps the end of utopianism. Democrats can no longer place any faith in either the utopia of communist classlessness or the utopia of beneficent, progressive liberalism.[36] Communism surely was not the riddle of history solved, but neither is liberal, capitalist democracy. Jürgen Habermas titled a recent essay on the next century "Learning By Disaster? A Diagnostic Look Back on the Short Twentieth Century". In it he observes that "phenomena of violence and barbarism define the signature of the age", but he also maintains, against a relentless negativism that he associates with thinkers from Adorno to Baudrillard, that we have learned something from the disasters of the century.[37] The legitimacy of liberal democracy is one thing we have learned. The development of a global sense of responsibility is another. The question, he asks, is if a "cosmopolitan solidarity" is likely to become empowered and institutionalized.

This is the question I have been posing in this paper as well. The jury is not yet in on this question, and because it is not yet in, it is important for intellectuals, scholars, and citizens to be creative, indeed visionary, at the same time that they remain painfully attentive to the barbarisms of our world. Habermas's title is telling. For it is not from the accumulation of benign experiences that we have learned; it is from the repeated experience of disaster. Power, and not limit, has been the watchword of democratic thought in the modern world. But if the experience of the twentieth century has taught us anything, it has taught that vulnerability is as central to the human condition as is power, and indeed that human power creates new and more frightening forms of vulnerability. What we learn in the present and the future is thus not likely to usher in an age of freedom or prosperity or solidarity or all that is good. If we are lucky, though, it may help us limit or control the damage that we humans are so adept at producing. Such a rationale for democratic innovation hardly comports with the idealism so often associated by democrats with political change. But it may be the rationale most appropriate for the trying times in which we live.

Notes

1 The author wishes to thank the Lynde and Harry Bradley Foundation and the Open Society Institute for their support.

2 Jürgen Habermas, "What Does Socialism Mean Today? The Revolutions of Recuperation and the Need for New Thinking", *New Left Review* 183 (September-October 1990). See also Ralf Dahrendorf, *Reflections on the Revolution in Europe* (New York: Random House, 1990); and Bruce Ackerman, *Future of Liberal Revolution* (New Haven: Yale University Press, 1992).

3 Francis Fukuyama, "The End of History?" *National Interest* 16 (Summer 1989).

4 Samuel P. Huntington, "No Exit: The Errors of Endism", *National Interest* 17 (Fall 1989). See also Jean-François Revel, "But We Follow the Worse...", *National Interest* 17 (Winter 1989–99).

5 See Francis Fukuyama, "The Primacy of Culture", *Journal of Democracy* 6:1 (January 1995); Francis Fukuyama, *Trust* (New York: Free Press, 1995); Charles Meier, "Democracy and its Discontents", *Foreign Affairs* 73 (July/August 1994): 48–67; Arthur Schlesinger, Jr., "Has Democracy a Future?" *Foreign Affairs* (September/October 1997); and Thomas Carothers, "Democracy Without Illusions", *Foreign Affairs* (January/February 1997): 85–99.

6 See Jacques Rupnik, "Postcommunist Divide", *Journal of Democracy* 10:1 (January 1999): 57–62.

7 See Tony Judt, *Burden of Responsibility: Blum, Camus, Aron and the French Twentieth Century* (Chicago: University of Chicago Press, 1998).

8 David Rieff, *Slaughterhouse: Bosnia and the Failure of the West* (New York: Simon and Shuster, 1995), 22.

9 In addition to Rieff, *Slaughterhouse*, see the following: Roy Gutman, *Witness to Genocide* (New York: MacMillan, 1993); Peter Maas, *Love Thy Neighbor: A Story of War* (New York: Knopf, 1996); Alexandra Stiglmayer, ed., *Mass Rape: The War Against Women in Bosnia-Herzegovina* (Lincoln: University of Nebraska Press, 1994); Michael A. Sells, *The Bridge Betrayed: Religion and Genocide in Bosnia* (Berkeley: University of California Press, 1996); and Warren Zimmerman, "The Last Ambassador: A Memoir of the Collapse of Yugoslavia", *Foreign Affairs* 74 (March/April 1995): 2–20.

10 Fukuyama, "Primacy of Culture", 10.

11 See Susan Woodward, *Balkan Tragedy: Chaos and Dissolution after the Cold War* (Washington, D.C.: Brookings, 1996); Ken Jowitt, *New World Disorder: The Leninist Extinction* (Berkeley: University of California Press, 1992); and Bogdan Denitch, *Af-*

ter the Flood: World Politics and Democracy in the Wake of Communism (Hanover: Wesleyan University Press, 1992).

12 Daniel Patrick Moynihan, *Pandaemonium: Ethnicity in International Politics* (New York: Oxford University Press, 1993).

13 Especially notable is the genocide in Rwanda. See Robert Block, "Tragedy of Rwanda", *New York Review of Books* (20 October 1994): 3–8; Gerard Prunier, *The Rwanda Crisis: History of a Genocide* (New York: Columbia University Press, 1995); David Rieff, "An Age of Genocide: The Far-Reaching Lessons of Rwanda", *New Republic* (29 January 1996): 27–36; and Philip Gourevitch, *We Wish to Inform You That Tomorrow We Will Be Killed With Our Families* (New York: Farrar, Straus and Giroux, 1998).

14 For similar arguments, see Ken Jowitt, "Dizzy With Democracy", *Problems of Post-Communism* (January/February 1996): 3–8; and Charles Gati, "The Mirage of Democracy", *Transition* (22 March 1996): 6–13.

15 Tony Judt offers a cogent critique of this third-worldism in his *Past Imperfect: French Intellectuals, 1944–1956* (Berkeley: University of California Press, 1992).

16 Robert D. Kaplan, *The Ends of the Earth: A Journey at the Dawn of the Twenty-First Century* (New York: Random House, 1996).

17 For the most recent (1997) data, see the United Nations High Commissioner for Refugees web site at http://www.unhcr.ch/. For the quotation, see United Nations High Commissioner for Refugees, *The State of the World's Refugees: The Challenge of Protection* (New York: Penguin, 1993).

18 See, for example, Jürgen Habermas, "Citizenship and National Identity: Some Reflections on the Future of Europe", *Praxis International* 12:1 (April 1992): 1–19; Jurgen Habermas, "Learning by Disaster? A Diagnostic Look Back on the Short 20th Century", *Constellations* 5:3 (1998): 307–20. See also Tony Judt, "The Social Question Redivivus", *Foreign Affairs* 76:5 (September/October 1997): 95–117.

19 Hans Magnus Enzensberger, *Civil Wars: From L.A. to Bosnia* (New York: New Press, 1994).

20 See Michael Walzer, "Multiculturalism and Individualism", *Dissent* 41 (Spring 1994): 185–91; and William E. Connolly, *Identity/Difference: Democratic Negotiations of Political Paradox* (Ithaca: Cornell University Press, 1991).

21 Julia Kristeva, *Strangers to Ourselves* (New York: Columbia University Press, 1991), 1. See also Kwame Anthony Appiah, *In My Father's House: Africa in the Philosophy of Culture* (New York: Oxford University Press, 1992).

22 Maas reports a striking conversation with a traumatized, highly educated, and urbane Bosnian Muslim, who declared in desperation: "We are in the center of mass crimes, pogroms, and genocide. We didn't believe this would happen. This is the twentieth century. We are in Europe. We have satellite television here. Even today, when there is electricity, we can watch CNN. We can watch reports about our own genocide!" Maas, *Love Thy Neighbor*, 75–76.

23 See Stjepan G. Mestrovic, *The Balkanization of the West: The Confluence of Postmodernism and Postcommunism* (New York: Routledge, 1994); and the superb essays collected in Thomas Cushman and Stjepan G. Mestrovic, eds., *This Time We Knew: Western Responses to Genocide in Bosnia* (New York: New York University Press,

1996). The failure of memory involved here is also discussed in Alain Finkielkraut, *Remembering in Vain: The Klaus Barbie Trial and Crimes Against Humanity* (New York: Columbia University Press, 1992).

24 This is the point of Jean Baudrillard's essays "No Pity for Sarajevo", "The West's Serbianization", and "When the West Stands in for the Dead", in Cushman and Mestrovic, eds., *This Time We Knew*; see also Jean Baudrillard, *The Gulf War Did Not Take Place* (Bloomington: Indiana University Press, 1995); and Jean Baudrillard, *The Transparency of Evil* (London: Verso, 1993).

25 Reprinted by permission of Farrar, Straus & Giroux, Inc., on behalf of the Estate of Joseph Brodsky: "Bosnia Tune" by Joseph Brodsky. Copyright © 1992 by Joseph Brodsky.

26 See Judith Shklar, *Faces of Injustice* (New Haven: Yale University Press, 1990).

27 See Lawrence Weschler, "Enabling Washington: The Coming Crunch in the Hague", *New Yorker* (6 December 1996): 9–10.

28 Walter Benjamin, "Theses on the Philosophy of History", in *Illuminations*, ed. Hannah Arendt (New York: Schocken, 1969), 257.

29 Two notable exceptions are Jowitt, *New World Disorder*, and Vladimir Tismaneanu, *Fantasies of Salvation: Democracy, Nationalism, and Myth in Postcommunist Europe* (Princeton: Princeton University Press, 1998).

30 Timothy Garton Ash has argued that the European Community is in danger of forfeiting this political project through its singular commitment to free markets. See his "Europe's Endangered Liberal Order", *Foreign Affairs* 77:2 (March/April 1998): 51–65. In a more theoretical vein, see David Held, "Democracy: From City-States to a Cosmopolitan Order", in *Prospects for Democracy*, ed. David Held (Stanford: Stanford University Press, 1993).

31 On the dangers of confusing judicial and political functions, see Jurgen Habermas, "Working Off the Past" and "Replies to Questions", in *The Berlin Republic: Writings on Germany* (Lincoln: University of Nebraska Press, 1997). On the way these dangers have been navigated in postcommunist Central Europe, see Tina Rosenberg, *The Haunted Land: Facing Europe's Ghosts After Communism* (New York: Random House, 1995). On the general theoretical issues at stake, see Martha Minow, *Between Vengeance and Forgiveness: Facing History after Genocide and Mass Violence* (Boston: Beacon Press, 1998).

32 On these points, see Jürgen Habermas, *Between Facts and Norms: Contributions to a Discourse Theory of Law and Democracy* (Cambridge: MIT Press, 1996).

33 See Michael Ignatieff, *The Warrior's Honor: Ethnic War and the Modern Conscience* (New York: Metropolitan Books, 1997).

34 See Jeffrey Isaac, "Reclaiming the Wasteland: Thinking About Land Mines and their Eradication", *Dissent* 45:4 (Fall 1998): 67–72.

35 David Rieff, "The False Dawn of Civil Society", *The Nation* (22 February 1999), 11, 14.

36 See François Furet, "Europe After Utopianism", *Journal of Democracy* 6:1 (January 1995), 79–89; and Francois Furet, "Democracy and Utopia", *Journal of Democracy* 9:1 (January 1998), 65–79.

37 Habermas, "Learning By Disaster?"

5 Habits of the Mind: Europe's Post-1989 Symbolic Geographies

SORIN ANTOHI

Ten years after the revolutions of 1989, Eastern Europe appears to be anything but a bloc. Despite decades of Soviet-style homogenization, this region's historic structural differences are almost intact. But not quite intact—the already explosive ethnic, religious, social, and political interwar legacy has been complicated by mutant identities and boundaries produced by the practice of state socialism and proletarian internationalism, within and between the sisterly republics building the ultimate in sameness, Communism. The collapse of Soviet hegemony seemed finally, and happily, to bring back the "organic" dynamics of long-suppressed national histories, and of regional international relations free of Moscow's *divide et impera* pressure. But the momentous changes of 1989 proved that this "end of Utopia" or "rebirth of History" was extremely problematic, and definitely not an idyllic End of History—the latter being a mesmerizing popular cocktail combining Hegel, Kojève, Rand, and Disneyland.[1]

This paper has four parts: the first and longest, "Eastern Europe's Symbolic Geographies", examines several alternative, and sometimes conflicting, visions of the region's mental map, trying to evaluate the contribution of knowledge, power, and imagination to the making of an aptly dubbed "other Europe", or rather of several blurred "other Europes"; the second part, "Mimetic Competition and Regional Cooperation", looks at Eastern Europe's poor record of regional integration, at its internal tensions and conflicts, and suggests an interpretation based on the hard facts of history, and inspired by the theories of René Girard; the third part, "The Failures of Political Identity", reviews Eastern Europe's passage from multinational empires to ethnic utopias, and some current processes of subnational fragmentation; the fourth part, "European Integration?", discusses the postcommunist fantasy of continental homogeneity and some of the challenges facing the construction of an integrated, inclusive European system.

Eastern Europe's Symbolic Geographies

The fall of the Berlin Wall and the end of the Cold War produced a series of spectacular changes on the mental map of Europe. In order to understand them, one has to go back several decades, and ultimately more than two centuries.

In the bipolar discursive universe dominated by Churchill's metaphor of the Iron Curtain, a circular transfer from geopolitics to journalism to collective consciousness—and back—had been successfully completed: a radical East-West cleavage had been singled out from among the multitude of endemic and ubiquitous, dynamic divisions of our continent. An ideological, political, military, and increasingly epistemological-cultural fault line appeared to separate two rival, parallel worlds. It was a fault line and not a mere border, as the separation seemed to extend from the minds of people into ontology.

But there was something more dramatic to the post-World-War II map of Europe than this radical separation. The whole region stretching from the Atlantic strip (the Occident, *sensu stricto*) to the Soviet border was changing its structure, substance, and meaning: Germany, traditionally self-located in *Mitteleuropa* and almost obsessed with a *Sonderweg* that allegedly made her different from the West, was split into a Federal Republic engaged in a thoroughgoing process of Occidentalization, and a Democratic Republic that was drifting eastward, alongside the other Soviet satellites, some of which had been previously included in a loosely and often polemically defined Central Europe.

To most Europeans educated after 1945, the East-West divide, as well as its "Orientalist" logic, according to which everything situated more to the West was necessarily superior to everything situated more to the East, seemed both natural and eternal. As a matter of fact, that cleavage and logic corresponded to a mental map already sketched during the Enlightenment.[2]

Until the fifteenth and sixteenth centuries, Europe was envisioned as the juxtaposition of a civilized South, heir to the Greek and Roman world, and a barbarous North: in the last chapter of his *Prince*, Macchiavelli alluded to the invasion of Italy by the French king, Charles VIII (1494), as the coming of the barbarians, using much the same rhetoric as that used by St. Augustine one thousand years earlier to describe Alaric's hordes *ante portas*. From the eighteenth century onward, this symbolic geography was reformulated, and Europe's North-South "Orientalist" axis separating Barbarity from Civilization was redrawn as an East-West divide. Currently, a third formula combines an inverted North-South cleavage—with the Germanic, Protestant North being more "civilized" than the Latin, Catholic South—and the more recent East-West one, thus resulting in a complex diagram organizing the European space according—as it were—to a vernacular interpretation of Max Weber's "Protestant Ethic", from North-West to South-East.

Samuel Huntington's more recent vision of the clash of civilizations relates to this pseudo-Weberian reading of the world in the way Fukuyama's articles and book on the end of history relate to Kojève's introduction to the reading of Hegel.[3] The other name of South-Eastern Europe, the Balkans, is widely used as a synthetic term, even a cultural metaphor, meaning everything from underdevelopment to political fragmentation to tribal warfare to ethnic cleansing. Thus Eastern Europe's own "Orient" takes shape, according to the inner dynamics of "Orientalism".[4]

Responsible for this new continental architecture were *les philosophes*, first and foremost Voltaire. The operation was inspired, documented, and perpetuated by a wave of Western travelers to the East. The Comte de Ségur (ambassador to Catherine the Great, winter 1784–1785), the Marquis de Custine (almost half a century later), and others like them invented and imposed as a hegemonic discourse the paradigm of Eastern European otherness, a necessary ingredient in the modern construction of Western identity, and an essential element in the process of self-identification started in the East by the local elites. Quite naturally, both Westernizers and Autochtonists, both ideal-types dominating the intellectual, social, and political life of the region, were born under these circumstances. From the "Slavophile controversy" epitomized by Chaadaev to this day, these two radical identities—one resulting frequently in alienation through imitation, the other collapsing into chauvinism—perpetually bordering on a stigmatic ethnic identity obsessed with a perceived normative gaze of the West, remained the major effect of the Enlightenment construction of Europe.[5]

At the Russian border, at the latest, these noble travelers had the clear feeling that they were leaving Europe—Civilization—and entering the *Barbaricum*. A few decades later, at the beginning of the nineteenth century, the opposite feeling was experienced by the increasingly numerous East European travelers going West. The more they advanced into "Europe" and "Civilization", the more culturally shocked they were; on their way back home, they realized, much to their despair, how different, and backward, their countries were—compared to the West. These transcultural travelers—who sometimes seem to be time travelers— produced and disseminated a hegemonic discourse integrating, or rather (con)fusing, knowledge, power, and imagination, transforming the East-West difference into a durable and devastating stereotype.

For example, the American John Ledyard, a former companion of Captain Cook's, therefore someone who had experienced radical otherness and was likely to grasp the elements of European sameness beyond local differences (an educated person, he had the ambition of a *philosophic geography*), sighed with relief when he reached the lands inhabited by Poles on his adventurous way against the current, from Siberia to the West. Also at the end of the eighteenth century, the British William Coxe published his *Travels into Poland, Russia, Sweden and Denmark,* referring to these countries as the "Nordic Kingdoms of Europe", a sign that the Enlightenment's symbolic geography was not yet the only way of seeing the European space, and that local differences were not yet automatically arranged according to an "Orientalist" diagram. Meanwhile, the fictitious Persian aristocrat, Rica, in Montesquieu's *Persian Letters*, although a prisoner of the *bon sauvage* convention and as such an embodiment of the Western critique of the West, could still challenge the superiority complexes of the *Lumières*.

Some Romanian illustrations may be used to make a similar point: Wallachian boyar Dinicu Golescu's 1826 travelogue, documenting his amazed "discovery" of the West, is by and large an expression of admitted inferiority, although one combined with, and redeemed by, an appeal to imitation; Jules Michelet's transfiguration of the Danubian Principalities in his *Légendes démocratiques du Nord*, no matter how obliquely favorable to the Romanians, states their backwardness. Future politician D. Brătianu's statement addressed to his former teacher, Michelet, "now I know: where France ends, nothingness begins", is hardly a declaration of (symbolic) independence, but rather a formula that is reminiscent of the Duc de Richelieu's *dictum* at Hertza: *"Ici finit l'Europe"*.[6]

But the most difficult exercise in post-1989 European symbolic geography would be to reconcile the East-West divide, or its radical subcategories, Russia and the Balkans, with the cultural mythology of *Mitteleuropa*.[7]

For the Visegrad countries, the regressive Utopian fantasy of a Central Europe rooted in *K.u.K.* bliss, as expressed mainly by Milan Kundera's political texts of the 1980s, represented the way out of Soviet Eastern Europe.[8]

Nevertheless, Kundera's position, playing up an essentially imagined Central European specificity, explicitly or implicitly excluded others:

Russia, in order to dramatize the opposition of Central Europe and Eastern Europe, and all Southeast European countries, possibly in order to help the West in an effort to limit its moral dilemmas. Thus, in the name of liberty and historical justice, another historical injustice was being reproduced and reinforced: the double exclusion of those Communist countries (and, after 1989, of their postcommunist avatars) that are Southeast or East European, not Central European. The case of Poland, the easternmost country included in Kundera's Central Europe, is revealing for the symbolic manipulation of political space: although Poland's spatial pendulum has moved east in the twentieth century, symbolic Poland was still granted the status of a Central European country, despite the limited support of such a mental mapping among Polish intellectuals, who tend to prefer Eastern Europe as a self-ascribed geocultural and geopolitical identity.

Ironically enough, some of the countries affected by this double exclusion would not hesitate to exclude others whenever possible: Slovene and Croat authors would thus further exclude their former Yugoslavian counterparts; Serb authors would do the same with Bosnia, Kosovo, Albania, and Macedonia; Romania's first postcommunist foreign minister tried to show that Central Europe's eastern border was the river Dniester, thus "rescuing" his country, and Moldova, from their dismal East European place on the map. [9]

Ten years after 1989, shortly after the admission of Hungary, Poland, and the Czech Republic to NATO, and against the background of the wars in ex-Yugoslavia, Europe's symbolic geography seems to be more dynamic and blurred than ever.

Central Europe appears to have lost its attraction, and to be relapsing willingly into posthistorical routine. Most postcommunist Central Europeans hope that their *Mitteleuopa*, coming closer to Austria, will become just as prosperous and just as geopolitically boring. The Kunderian mythology of the region survives in the latter's margins, enjoying a provincial afterlife. From Hungarian and Czech authors, the cultural motif of *Mitteleuropa*, especially its emancipatory potential, migrates to Romanian, Slovakian, and Western Ukrainian writers and audiences. Consequently, the centrality of Central Europe is gradually supplanted by its liminality, while its fashionable relics become the Banat, Bukowina, Galitia, or cities such as Temeswar, Czernowitz, and Lemberg (to use their nostalgic German names, generally rejected by the present-day majority populations). [10]

The Balkans have come violently into the global media spotlight, with their perceived untamable negativity and otherness. They had almost vanished after World War II, when Greece had been assimilated by the West, Yugoslavia had escaped into the extraterritorial geopolitical realm of the "non-aligned" countries, Albania had entered its dystopian non-time and non-space, while Bulgaria and Romania had been assigned to the ideological-symbolic territory of Eastern Europe. Despite attempts to discursively water down the threatening otherness of the Balkans by the less loaded, almost politically correct phrase "Southeast Europe", media and popular usage is adamantly sticking to the "marked category". Maria Todorova, in an excellent sequel to her *Imagining the Balkans*, sums up the whole process:

> While, as a whole, the attention toward the Balkan region seems to have been motivated by the fear of contagion and the accompanying quarantine policies, as well as by the whole negative spectrum from devastating but at least passive derision to high-minded but activist punitive impulses, there have been also efforts to mark out the Southeast European (or Balkan) region as an object of genuine concern and compassion. But marking out is not an innocent act. Complex notions (like region, nation, race, gender, etc.) are socially constructed systems of marked and unmarked categories (…). The complex notion of Europe comprises both marked categories such as Southeast Europe (the Balkans), East Central Europe, Eastern Europe, and unmarked categories, e.g. Northwest Europe, Southwest Europe, West Central Europe.[11]

Thus Europe seems to have lost its East—"Eastern Europe" is less and less frequently used as a geopolitical category and it has been officially replaced in most state documents by "Central Europe"—to have purged its Center of its culturalist fantasies, and to have pushed further into Otherness the countries of the Balkans and of the former Soviet Union, with the exception of the Baltics. Alternative symbolic geographies have been suggested, especially in the process of the (re)invention of national and regional identities, but notions such as the "Carpathian Basin", the "Danubian Region", the "Black Sea Region" and the like have not gained sustained international attention.[12] Russia's rediscovery of its "Eurasian" identity, another shift in the post-1989 European symbolic geography, represents for some local public intellectuals and politicians the best reaction to the tacit new exclusion of that country from our continent. It is essentially a rejection of, and escape from, Europe, like other discourses that I describe as *ethnic ontologies*.[13]

The next sections of this chapter will also show that most projects of regional cooperation and European integration built upon such failed, or parochial and conflicting symbolic traditions fail as well.

Mimetic Competition and Regional Cooperation

In a number of controversial books published in the 1970s and 1980s, René Girard, a French-born literary theorist whose main teaching career is related to Stanford University, put forward the concept of *mimetic competition*, in the framework of a wide-ranging, sweeping theory of culture based on the idea that human communities, from the origins of mankind to this day, are rooted in, and based on, violence.[14] The perpetual transfer of an original, endless, circular, generalized violence into the regulated, limited, targeted violence of subsequent human communities by means of the invention and manipulation of exclusion mechanisms can be defined as scapegoating. By offering the scapegoat (the *ostrakon*)—somebody who is both an insider and an outsider—to the violence of the community, this fundamental exclusion mechanism breaks the circle of generalized violence, and offers collective life a stable foundation, at least for a while; of course, the mechanism starts again when new accumulations of circular violence threaten the cohesion of the community.

It is not my intention to elaborate on this model, as I do not follow Girard in some of his theoretical propositions, although his attempt to overcome and refute a number of established reductionisms (Freud and the Oedipus complex, classical theories of the sacred, and so on) is appealing and refreshing. Let us simply go back to the idea of "mimetic competition". According to Girard, desire is mimetic: I desire what others (or the Other) desire(s); consequently I, the object of desire, and the Other enter a kind of love triangle. This mimetic desire is something deeper, and stronger, than the mere desire to emulate models, the kind of relatively serene imitation implied by Plato's theory of *mimesis*. This is a conflictual type of imitation, the "acquisitive mimesis", the mimesis of appropriation: the desire to have as a (temporary, partial) replacement of the desire to be.

East European philosophers, literary critics, publicists, and politicians have had a lot to say about imitation in the last one hundred and fifty years or so, after the onset of inescapable processes of modernization in the region: for instance, Romanian literary critic and *spiritus rector* Eugen Lovinescu has advocated during the interwar period a thorough, systematic imitation of the West as the key to his country's development.[15] As a theoretical authority, Lovinescu used Gabriel de Tarde's "imitation laws", a version of the acculturationist/diffusionist principle according to which human civilization proceeds basically through imitation, be it conscious or not.[16] And indeed, in most countries of Eastern

Europe, modernization and development have often been, and still are, synonymous with Westernization, i.e. imitation. The whole series of disputes opposing Autochtonists to Westernizers tends to organize itself around questions and answers related to ideas such as foreign models, cultural/historical authenticity (i.e. consistency with local models, ideas, and experiences—often regressive, almost always imaginary), alternatives to the Western canon, local knowledge and creativity. In such arguments, historical facts and the social imaginary, statistics and wishful thinking, pragmatic opportunism and (the manipulation of) collective fantasies are inextricably interwoven.

The poor record of East European cooperation shows how mimetic competition is constantly disabling regional integration, and also how conflictual mimesis can disintegrate all cultural and political systems. Thus, "Orientalism" can acquire circular, and metonymic dimensions: circular, because it can be used almost irrespective of actual geography; metonymic, because it can be used at regional, national, and intranational levels. For instance, the tragic wars in ex-Yugoslavia have been prepared by "Orientalist" discourses by which Slovenes, Croats, and Serbs established the East-West divide on the Slovenian-Croatian border, on the Croatian-Serbian, or on the Serbian-Bosnian (or Serbian-Albanian) ones, respectively. These disputes have systematically used ethnic, linguistic, religious, and political "evidence", from the split of the Roman Empire to the Catholic-Orthodox schism to the superiority of Protestants (in Slovenia, a country with only a few Protestants, there has been much talk about a local "Protestant ethic") as compared to their Catholic, Orthodox, Muslim lesser enemy brethren.[17] Along the same lines, although in a considerably less violent key, one encounters an anti-Slovak Czech "Orientalism"; tensions between Bohemians and Moravian-Silesians have been added; the difficult integration of "Ossies" in the united Germany; Transylvania vs. *Regat* discussions in Romania; Ruthenian vs. Ukrainian debates. And so on.

The list of failed cooperative projects in Eastern Europe is too long to be remembered. Nevertheless, a few of them may be mentioned: the variable geometry of the two pre-World-War I Balkan wars, with their unpredictable, and unstable alliances; the "Green International" of peasant parties between the world wars; the collapse of the Little Entente, despite the important cohesive foundation of a common enemy/scapegoat, Hungary; the difficult cooperation between the countries of the Visegrad Triangle, now the Visegrad Four, most likely due to Václav Klaus's "Orientalist" vision of his neighboring partners; and CEFTA, which has to include alongside the Central European states their embarrassing Eastern counterparts. This summary does not include the integration projects suggested, or imposed, from outside Eastern Europe, such as the French federalist projects; the COMECON; the Valev Plan; and, more recently, the project of a Southeast European *Zollverein*. The current fierce competition for access in structures such as NATO, the European Union, and so on, is only the most recent example of an apparently endemic mechanism.[18]

Ten years after their *annus mirabilis*, the countries of the former Soviet bloc are focused on their individual trajectories, and are interested in their neighbors only to the extent that they perceive them as competitors for the limited resources of the West. The mimetic competition goes on.

The Failures of Political Identity

Another recurrent problem in Eastern Europe is the difficulty in establishing, and reproducing, political identities. After the fall of Austria-Hungary, most successor states were as multinational as the Double Monarchy, but chose ethnicity as a principle of political integration. And it was the ethnicity of the majority population that was imposed as a normative collective identity, sometimes by the very elites that had fought discrimination based on ethnicity before 1918. The Romanian case is quite typical: before Trianon, the Romanian Kingdom counted 8 percent minorities, while Greater Romania—that included Transylvania, the Banat, Bessarabia, and Northern Bukovina, regions with Romanian majorities, but with sizable ethnic minorities—jumped to 28 percent minorities. Instead of formulating a political contract for the new state, Romanian elites devised ever more radical Autochtonist definitions of ethnicity. The state engaged in very active Romanianization policies, thus betraying the spirit of the Paris Treaties, and the tolerant program of Transylvanian Romanian elites who, upon agreeing to join the Romanian Kingdom, had insisted that substantial minority rights be guaranteed.[19]

But even the post-Trianon Hungarian state engaged in increasingly chauvinistic policies, although its population—due to territorial losses and the success of post-1867 aggressively assimilationist measures—was theoretically homogeneous: the "pure" Hungarians turned against the recently Magyariazed minorities that had vitally contributed to the making of a controversial Hungarian majority, and "unmasked" them as alien. Overall, the interwar European *Zeitgeist* and political practices were not exactly favorable to non-ethnic political contracts, or non-ethnic collective identities.

After 1945, under Soviet control, the radical ethnic identities of the region, which had by and large degenerated into chauvinism, and had sometimes ruthlessly treated some minorities—especially the Jews and the Gypsies —, were suppressed in the name of proletarian internationalism, which regarded all expressions of ethnicity, or "national character", as dangerous bourgeois relics. For some years, it seemed that Eastern Europe was finally being straitjacketed into the moulds of political identity: Yugoslavism and Yugoslavia survived World War II in a Communist guise, despite the horrible experience of mutual atrocities and the continued *de facto* Serbian hegemony; the other interwar political identity based on real ethno-linguistic affinities and on Utopian federalism, Masaryk's Czechoslovakia, was successfully reassembled after years of separation; even Stalin's genocidal project of a melting-pot Soviet post-national identity was apparently yielding its first genuine results, boosted by the shared traumas of World War II, further forced migrations, interethnic marriages, Union-wide military service, educational, and occupational mobility .

Theoretically, East Central Europe's political identities were quite confusing: they retained elements of the federalist schemes invented by the underprivileged minorities of Austria-Hungary, from Palacky to Aurel C.Popovici, in which assertive *Risorgimento*-type nationalisms were tamed by imperial loyalty; also, the Stalinist "solution" to the nationality problem could not fail to remind one of the Austro-Marxist federalism rooted in Marx's idea (Renner, Bauer) that ethnic conflicts would disappear after the proletarian revolution, as all the other forms of false consciousness. On a huge scale, the Soviet Union offered the example of a new political contract that, while manipulating ethnicities and nationalisms (by changing borders, inventing languages and ethnicities, granting "autonomous" status to various populations, regions, and republics), was preparing the monolithic Soviet "nation".

After 1989, these political identities disintegrated, and a new ethnonational process of fragmentation began: Yugoslavism disappeared in wars that cruelly prove how artificial this political project has been; Czechoslovakia fell apart, and not only in a "velvet" way. And ethnic minorities are politically active everywhere, with ethnic political parties lobbying for different forms of autonomy, self-determination, collective rights, devolution, subsidiarity, federalism.

European Integration?

These phenomena indicate that European integration is not at hand. Since the problems associated with the Maastricht Treaty, the European single currency, the *acquis communautaire* and similar topics are constantly covered by Western media and scholarship, I would merely add a few Eastern European footnotes to this discussion.

The fantasy of a homogeneous European political, economic, social, and cultural space is painstakingly promoted in Eastern Europe by a number of international organizations, NGOs, and state institutions. Very often, the former issue optimistic reports on the prospects of at least selected East European countries to be granted membership in NATO and the European Union; so far, while Hungary, the Czech Republic, and Poland have become NATO members and are talking dates for their accession to the European Union, most East European states are included in structures clearly designed to appease, rather than integrate them: the Council of Europe, the European Parliament, the Partnership for Peace, not to mention the endless series of summit meetings, are not the *real thing*, and everybody knows it. In some East European countries, such as Romania, the discourse about Euro-Atlantic integration is enthusiastically appropriated by the postcommunist political leaders (people who otherwise have exceptional demagogic skills, refined by years in the Communist *apparat*): this has been a great way of silencing the Westernizers while they were not in power, or rather of confiscating the latter's virtually unique legitimating discourse.

Going "back" to Europe is however increasingly problematic, especially when the concrete problems are approached: economic reforms, infrastructure development, trade liberalization (the extension of the Western European common market to the East), adjustment of legislation, the reform of the military. As a matter of fact, East European governments and political parties do not always explain their constituencies what European integration is really about. This is why the least reformed postcommunist countries have the most "Euro-optimistic" populations: the *Eurobarometer* and other survey figures are telling—when less than half of the Hungarian and Czech national samples were supportive of the idea of European integration, over ninety percent of the Romanian population were ready to go for it. In principle, of course. When a group of Romanian pro-Western political annalists and lobbyists claimed that Romanians should wait for the success of European integration in order to establish closer links with Moldova, rather than choose a decisive course of action leading to the reunification with Romania, they received some praise only from a few Romanian idealists, and from many West-erners. The Romanian public opinion was shocked by the proposition, which amounted to the betrayal of the national interest even in the opin-ion of the Opposition.

On the other hand, the European Union cannot import East European regional conflicts. Basic treaties are behind schedule among the con-cerned countries: Hungary's interest in the fate of Hungarian minorities living in the neighboring countries, potential territorial and sovereignty disputes, the revival of nationalisms and irredentisms are major obsta-cles. When such treaties are eventually signed under Western pressure, as those between Hungary and Slovakia, or between Hungary and Ro-mania, they are not perceived by all as durable and are only supported by some in the hope that they will be denounced some day.

The continuing crisis in ex-Yugoslavia is definitely complicating Europe's post-1989 order, as it epitomizes the failure of much of what the idea(l) of Europe stands for. Just like the "spiritualization of fron-tiers", European integration is still ahead of us.[20]

Notes

1 The irony in this formulation targets the global vogue of the End of History concept, which reached even the popular media in the aftermath of Francis Fukuyama's best-selling articles and book. Hegel's themes (the end of history, the last man) have a vast bibliography; for the intellectual origins of their twentieth-century discussion, initi-ated by Alexandre Kojève, see Lutz Niethammer, *Posthistoire: Ist die Geschichte zu Ende?* (Reinbeck bei Hamburg: Rowohlt, 1989) (English edition: Verso, 1992).

2 I put Edward W. Said's term in quotation marks to signal a special usage referring to Eastern Europe, Europe's internal "Orient". Cf. Said, *Orientalism: Western Concep-tions of the Orient* (London: Penguin Books, 1978, 1995) (with a new afterword); for Said's reception and (attempted) instrumentalizations, see Gyan Prakash, "*Orientalism* now", *History and Theory*, 34 :3 (1995): 192–212; Sorin Antohi, *Imagi-naire culturel et réalité politique dans la Roumanie moderne. Le Stigmate et l'utopie*, translated from the Romanian by Claude Karnoouh and Mona Antohi (Paris-Montréal: L'Harmattan, 1999): 290–292 (the original Romanian version of the rele-vant chapter was published in 1997). In several articles, Milica Bakić-Hayden, some-times writing with Robert M. Hayden, has applied Said's concept to Southeast Europe and proposed a similar notion, "nesting Orientalism"; see Bakić-Hayden and Hayden, "Orientalist Variations on the Theme 'Balkans': Symbolic Geography in Recent Yugoslav Cultural Politics", *Slavic Review*, 51, no. 1, (Spring 1992): 1–15; also Milica Bakić-Hayden, "Nesting Orientalisms: The Case of Former Yugoslavia", *Slavic Review*, 54, no.4, (Winter 1995): 917–931. Larry Wolff, in his pathbreaking *Inventing Eastern Europe: The Map of Civilization on the Mind of the Enlightenment* (Stanford, Calif.: Stanford University Press, 1994), suggested yet another term for the

same notion: "demi-Orientalism" (p. 7), and demonstrated the links and similarities between it and parallel Enlightenment inventions, such as Hellenism and Africanism. Many of my historical examples of "Orientalism" in the text are borrowed from Wolff's erudite work. Maria Todorova, in several articles (especially "The Balkans: From Discovery to Invention", *Slavic Review*, 53, no. 2, (Summer 1994) and her excellent *Imagining the Balkans* (New York, London: Oxford University Press, 1997), offered another application of the concept to Southeast Europe, thus proposing "Balkanism". Similar notions, ultimately based on Foucault's reminder that knowledge and power are intricately related (cf. Foucault's theory of discourse), can be constructed to denote similar practices by which the West reworks its modern self-identity in (frequently ambiguous) opposition to other regions. Such practices tend to be hegemonic, metonymic, and holographic (i.e., they can be replicated indefinitely according to a *pars pro toto* generation principle), and palimpsestic (i.e., they overlap both spatially and chronologically). More generally, all self-identities tend to be organized around such spatial-temporal-historical-cultural discourses, which may be summed up as symbolic geographies.

3 But Huntington's metadiscourse is of course the tradition of *Kulturpessimismus*, as epitomized by authors such as Oswald Spengler and, in the English-speaking world, Arnold Toynbee.

4 Cf. Maria Todorova, "Hierarchies of Eastern Europe: East-Central Europe *versus* the Balkans", in [Association for Democracy in the Balkans], *Culture and Reconciliation in Southeastern Europe*, (Thessaloniki: Paratiritis, 1999): 11–65. This is arguably the best piece ever written on the interplay between several "Orientalisms", both Western and Central European. Todorova places what she calls "Balkanism" in all its contexts, including several Central European (negative, with rare exceptions, most remarkably that of Oscar Halecki's writings) (di)visions of Europe, such as the most famous one, Jenő Szűcs's essay, "The Three Historic Regions of Europe. An Outline", published in English in 1983 (*Acta Historica Academiae Scientiarum Hungaricae*, 29, 2–4, pp. 131–184; original Hungarian version, 1981).

5 The best work on the endemic enemy brothers, Autochtonists and Westernizers, remains Andrzej Walicki's *The Slavophile Controversy. History of a Conservative Utopia in Nineteenth-Century Russian Thought*, (Oxford: Oxford University Press, 1975) (English translation by Hilda Andrews-Rusiecka). For an analysis of ethnic stigma in Eastern, Central, and Southeast Europe, see chapter VI of my book mentioned in note 2, "Cioran et le stigmate roumain. Mécanismes identitaires et définitions radicales de l'ethnicité" (the original Romanian version of the chapter was published in 1994). For a link between Chaadaev's view of Russianness and the Soviet times, see Julia Brun-Zejmis, "Messianic Consciousness as an Expression of National Inferiority: Chaadaev and Some Samizdat Writings of the 1970s", *Slavic Review*, 50, no. 3, (Fall 1991) 646–658. In my view, ethnic stigma, originally an "Orientalism" internalized by the "Orientals", can develop into a "native category" through its instrumentalization by fractions of the local elites; thus, ethnic stigma is shared by Autochtonists (who repress and deny it) and Westernizers (who use it to call for imitation of, or emulation with, the West, as well as to maintain the boundaries of their in-group).

6 Golescu's work, *Însemnare a călătoriei mele*, is written by someone who, while fully aware of the West's superiority, recommends its systematic emulation. Jules Michelet, by placing the Romanian Principalities of Wallachia and Moldavia in the North, is following a largely pre-Enlightenment symbolic geography and offers an ambiguous image of the North (i.e., East): barbarous, but healthy, energetic, unspoiled, primitively virtuous, etc.—a Rousseauvian model for the seemingly exhausted, overcivilized post-1789 French nation. Brătianu, possibly in order to please his former teacher at the Collège de France, brings the hopeless distances between France and his native country to an ontological climax very similar to Chaadaev's extreme anti-Russian lines.

7 A comparison between the roles played by Russia and the Balkans, respectively, in the construction of both Western and Central Europe, would be instructive. Todorova's *Imagining the Balkans* could be supplemented with works on the images (or the "ideas") of Europe in the region, such as those contributed by the late Romanian scholar Alexandru Duțu on his country. An article by another Bulgarian scholar, Alexander Kiossev, provides a combination of (self-)irony, psychoanalysis, and cynicism: "Mitteleuropa und der Balkan. Erotik der Geopolitik. Die Images zweier Regionen in den westlichen Massenmedien" (*Neue Literatur*, Neue Folge, 1, 1992: 102–119), suggesting that the Balkans have been institutionalized in the Western media as Europe's subconscious; more self-irony, coupled with a devastating critique of the West's self-serving interest in post-1989 Eastern Europe, in Slavoj Žižek's much quoted essay on "Eastern Europe's Republics of Gilead", now in his *Tarrying with the Negative: Kant, Hegel, and the Critique of Ideology* (Durham: Duke University Press, 1993). Žižek gives the discussion a Lacanian twist: "Eastern Europe functions for the West as its Ego-ideal: the point from which the West sees itself in a likeable, idealized form, as worthy of love". For the Russian case, a good starting point is Iver B. Neumann's "Russia as Central Europe's Constituting Other" (*East European Politics and Societies*, 7, no. 2, Spring 1993); see also Neumann's *Russia and the Idea of Europe. A Study in Identity and International Relations* (London, New York: Routledge, 1996). Whoever attempts to write such books should probably start by reading Federico Chabod's splendid *Storia dell'idea d'Europa* (Bari: Laterza, 1965).

8 The whole construction of Central Europe as anti-(Soviet) Russia has been abundantly debated over the last two decades or so. Todorova's article on the "hierarchies of Eastern Europe", mentioned in note 4, is a good introduction to the matter, from a viewpoint that I largely share, including some historical *mises au point* (e.g., Friedrich Naumann's predecessor, Joseph Partsch; Szűcs's inspiration, István Bibó). To retrieve most elements of the controversy, see George Schöpflin and Nancy Woods, eds., *In Search of Central Europe*, (Totowa, N.J.: Barnes and Noble Books, 1989); Peter Stirk, ed., *Mitteleuropa. History and Prospects*, (Edinburgh: Edinburgh University Press, 1994) (especially Stirk's text, "The Idea of Mitteleuropa", pp. 1–35). In my text, "Kundera" is an oversimplification of a plurality of discourses, ranging from Tomas Masaryk's image of a "family of small nations" spread from Cape Horn to Cape Matapan, but excluding Germany, to various texts by Czech and Hungarian authors presenting Central Europe as a geocultural realm of widely shared high cultural practices and values, ethnic, linguistic, and confessional pluralism, tolerance,

nostalgic *joie de vivre*, sophisticated lifestyles, self-irony, black humor, and the like. Timothy Garton Ash has noted that the phrase "Eastern Europe" was used in negative contexts by Kundera, Havel, Konrád, while "Central Europe" and "East Central Europe" were used only in positive, affirmative contexts; Adam Michnik and other Polish authors departed from this stereotype. According to Jacques Rupnik, Poles state their Europeanness rather than their alleged Central Europeanness, possibly due to their understanding of *Mitteleuropa* as a German tradition (cf. Jacques Rupnik, *The Other Europe*, London: Weidenfeld and Nicolson, 1988, a valuable combination of symbolic geography, history, and geopolitics).

9 I discussed the ambiguities of Romania's symbolic geography in a chapter from my book mentioned in note 2, "Les Roumains pendant les années 90. Géographie symbolique et identité sociale". Romanian claims for inclusion in Central Europe are inherently ambiguous, and potentially self-defeating, since the only territories that have a record of Central European identity are Transylvania and the Banat, objects of Hungarian irredentism; by insisting on the Central European character of the two provinces, the other historic territories incorporated by the Romanian nation-state may appear under their "real" light, as fragments of Eastern Europe or Southeast Europe. Transylvanian authors of Hungarian (and, more recently, Romanian) ethnic descent who support the Central Europeannness of their region are "exposed" as enemies of the nation; the same thing happens with a Timișoara-based group of authors who try to "revive" the "true" Central European identity of the Banat, although their activity is cautiously packaged as a research project in cultural studies. An older article by Radu Stern and Vladimir Tismaneanu is still a good introduction to the context of these Romanian symbolic tribulations: "L'Europe centrale. Nostalgies cutlurelles et réalités politiques", *Cadmos*, 39 (1987).

10 Speaking of the post-1989 changes in Romania's symbolic geography, I suggested the notion of *geocultural bovarism* to describe the tendency to think that that country can symbolically leapfrog out of its real location and be a neighbor to France or Belgium (Romanians have a tradition of calling Bucharest "Little Paris", or Romania the "Belgium of the Orient"—the latter being inadvertently an "Orientalist" statement in itself). See my article quoted in note 9. I think this tendency is common to other cultures. It may be useful to remember how *Webster's Third International Dictionary of the English Language, Unabridged* (I use its 1965 edition) defines *bovarism* or *bovarysm*: "a conception of oneself as other than one is to the extent that one's general behavior is conditioned or dominated by the conception; *esp.*: domination by such an idealized, glamorized, glorified, or otherwise unreal conception of oneself that it results in dramatic personal conflict (as in tragedy), in markedly unusual behavior (as in paranoia), or in great achievement".

11 Maria Todorova, "Is 'the Other' a Useful Cross-cultural Concept? Some Thoughts on its Implication to the Balkan Region", *Internationale Schulbuchforschung/ International Textbook Research*, 21: 2 (1999) 170. I would add to the discussion of the Balkans the relatively recent trend, more obvious among Serbs during the wars in Yugoslavia, consisting in the proud, virile, bellicose showing off of the Balkan stigma; it is precisely the danger of contagion that is defiantly held against the West, an active version of the traditionally passive, "Orientalist", Balkan identity. Thus "the Balkani-

zation of the West" is the just revenge of the stigmatized, their way to respond to Western hegemony.

12 The "Carpathian Basin" is frequently used in Hungary, for obvious reasons, as the notion includes Transylvania. The "Danubian Region" is also popular in Hungary, as it includes even more territories lost by Hungary after Trianon; the possible non-conflictual meaning of the same phrase is brilliantly illustrated by Claudio Magris's book *Danubio* (Milan: Garzanti, 1986; English translation by Patrick Creagh, *Danube*, New York: Farrar, Strauss, Giroux, 1989). The "Black Sea Region" (whose historical traditions have been splendidly researched by the Romanian historian Gheorghe I. Brătianu in a pioneering book which almost shared the author's tragic fate) is even less successful as a cultural notion. Other (sub)national and regional symbolic geographies, such as "Balto-Skandia", related to the discourses on Eastern Europe, are equally reasserting themselves after 1989. For a good introduction to the revival of geocultural discourses, see David Hooson, ed., *Geography and National Identity*, (Oxford, U.K., and Cambridge, Mass.: Blackwell, 1994). The book can also serve as an introduction to the theoretical and methodological problems related to symbolic/mental/conceptual/cultural/historical/philosophical geography. Such problems were outside the scope of my text. For a discussion of territoriality and (post)modernity, see Stefan Immerfall, ed., *Territoriality in the Globalizing Society: One Place or None?*, (Berlin, New York: Springer, 1998); some sections of this text draw freely on my unpublished paper presented at the conference that inspired Immerfall's edited volume, held at the University of North Carolina at Chapel Hill in April 1996. I thank Stefan Immerfall and the other conference participants who have commented on that presentation.

13 Ethnic ontologies are complex discourses that try to "discover", describe, and interpret the basic ontological categories of the nation—indigenized counterparts of universals, from time and space to language and soul. Such a discourse is not easily understood if read by scholars of nationalism who do not have the necessary cultural-philosophical background in both the "cultural intimacy" (Michael Herzfeld) of the given cultures, and in the Western intellectual roots of that discourse (from *Völkerpsychologie* to anthropogeography to philosophy of culture). I have sketched a relevant research agenda in my chapter mentioned in note 9.

14 René Girard's most relevant books for this text are: *Violence and the Sacred*, translated by Patrick Gregory, (Baltimore: Johns Hopkins University Press, 1977) (original French edition, 1972); *The Scapegoat*, translated by Yvonne Freccero, (Baltimore: Johns Hopkins University Press, 1986) (original French version, 1982); *Things Hidden Since the Foundation of the World*, translated by Stephen Bann and Michael Meteer, (Stanford, Calif.: Stanford University Press, 1987) (original French version, 1978); the first, rather oblique, statement of Girard's theory, in his *Deceit, Desire, and the Novel. Self and Other in Literary Structure*, translated by Yvonne Freccero, (Baltimore: Johns Hopkins University Press, 1965) (original French version, 1961); more recent application to literary texts, *To Double Business Bound: Essays on Literature, Mimesis, and Anthropology*, (Baltimore: Johns Hopkins University Press, 1978).

15 Eugen Lovinescu's *Istoria civilizaţiei române moderne* was first published staring in 1924. The best edition of his *opus magnum* is that contributed and introduced by Z. Ornea (Bucharest: Minerva, 1997).

16 Gabriel de Tarde (1843–1904), *Les lois de l'imitation: étude sociologique* , (Paris: Félix Alcan, 1890). English edition: *The Laws of Imitation*, translated from the second French edition by Elsie Clews Parsons, with an Introduction by Franklin H. Giddins, (Gloucester, Mass.: P. Smith, 1962)

17 See the article by Milica Bakić-Hayden and Robert M. Hayden mentioned in note 2.

18 In a succint treatment of this topic, Jacques Rupnik was brushing a similarly disheartening balance sheet of regional cooperation: "Europe Centrale: Les atouts et les limites de la coopération régionale", *Pouvoirs*, 74, (1995): 183–189. He noted that the Central European were not taking advantage of the post-1989 chance of reconciling their Western culture, their Eastern politics, and their Central geography.

19 Cf. Irina Livezeanu, *Cultural Politics in Greater Romania. Regionalism, Nation Building, and Ethnic Struggle, 1918–1930,* (Ithaca and London: Cornell University Press, 1995).

20 Cf. Jacques Rupnik, "L'Europe dans le miroir des Balkans", *Transeuropéennes*, 12–13, (Spring-Summer 1998): 117–126. In his *After 1989. Morals, Revolution and Civil Society* (New York: St. Martin's Press, 1997), Ralf Dahrendorf gives a synthetic picture of the entire post-1989 order; the book's last chapter captures the shifting agendas and the difficulties of European integration: "From Europe to Europe: A Story of Hope, Trial and Error".

II Winners and Losers in the Great Transformation

6 *Independence Reborn and the Demons of the Velvet Revolution*[1]

ADAM MICHNIK

I.

To understand the history of Poland is to believe in miracles. Consider this: If you supposed in 1984 that in five years time Poland would regain its liberty and independence, you would really have had to believe in miracles. However, the Polish nation, Catholic and God-fearing, didn't really have faith in this miracle. After all, who among us at *Gazeta Wyborcza* thought back then that soon enough we would come to work in a large and important daily newspaper, respected both in Poland and around the world?

Yet who would confess to being a person of little faith? So we dispute among ourselves: Who, which political camp, what forces effected Poland's independence?

This is not the first Polish debate of this nature. Michał Bobrzyński, a conservative historian from the Krakow Stańczyk group, wrote in his *Dzieje Polskie* (Polish History): "The hand of Providence directing the course of history and avenging the crime of the partitions surpassed all hopes and brought us to the long awaited end. Although the clearer it seemed to my eyes, as to many others, the more I had to shy away from the truly hellish quarrels that flared up in Polish society over the question of which political group foresaw the final result and deserves credit for it. And which group should be condemned, perhaps because it strove for the rebirth of Poland via those paths which, under the circumstances, seemed to be the only ones possible."

Bobrzyński believed that "all Poles and all parties endeavored toward a single end, and that each of them deserves a portion of the credit, and that this should soothe the irritable camps."

Zygmunt Wasilewski, an intellectual of the National Democrats, viewed the problem in a completely different light. He was of the opinion that in the mid-nineteenth century Poland gave the impression of being an "immature nation; active, but unprepared for life. Such an impression must have been created by the lack of coordination between emotions and sensibility. Poland's enemies understood this well and knew how to manipulate influences in Poland in order to widen the chasm between these two elements. Freemasonry in this case played the role of a malevolent psychiatrist, pulling the Polish soul in two directions—either toward outbursts of emotion, or toward opportunistic appeasement of the authorities—preventing the Polish psyche from ordering itself, keeping it in a state of anarchy, so that Polish political thought could not be consolidated...

"It drove some to exclaim patriotic slogans in reckless movements which later drove others into the arms of the partitioning nations and, as a result, deepened the servitude and slave mentality...The secret of success of this last generation, which created the all-Poland democratic-nationalist movement, was that it first freed itself from the influences of covert international organizations, which to that point had held political divisions in their control."

Michał Sokolnicki, a well-known supporter of Piłsudski, categorically dismissed these explanations, however. He wrote:

"This new generation of Poles regards independence and the state as obvious, arising from nature itself, and in fact believes that it is impossible for it to be otherwise. Memory plays tricks on older people and there occurs a certain, I would put it, well-meant blurring of the facts. In good faith it seems that before the war there was no independence, but then at least everyone wanted it....An exacting analysis of prewar facts shows quite the opposite: a terrible moral decay of Polish national feeling in the last hours of their servitude. Two basic desires existed in Polish society at the time: the desire for peaceful prosperity and the desire to preserve nationality and religion....That is why it is laughable if the matter is presented as if before the war everyone wanted independence, but each person wanted it in a different way, or that a powerful current existed in a Polish society striving to regain its own statehood....

"Mr. Roman Dmowski in *Polityka polska* (Polish Politics) often relates that after 1906 he realized the reconstruction of the Polish state was something inevitable and imminent. He claims that as chairman of the 'Polish Circle' in the [Russian] Duma he filled, as he himself put it, the role of Polish minister for foreign affairs, and initiated the neo-Slavic movement with the aim of bringing the Polish cause to the international arena. The deceptiveness of these statements is obvious. There is not a shred of evidence to suggest that he was head of 'foreign affairs' in the 'Polish Circle' in St. Petersburg. Quite the contrary, the entire weight of evidence states irrefutably that Poles operated sincerely and consistently on the basis of the Russian state. This was their frame of reference, as proven by the very fact that they participated in elections to the all-Russian representative 'National Duma'—this was, after all, the first instance of voluntarily performing national duties toward Russia, and not merely following command...

"Independence as a [political] program sprang up in the last fifty years from very small groups of people, whom we will come to look upon with increasing distance and see in a more historical, that is synthetic, context. From this point one figure, one name will appear more absolutely. In the course of their work and endeavors, these people were isolated for decades within their own nation. The image of this labor and effort is one of constant struggle, in large part with society itself. It turned out that the overwhelming majority of the nation was mistaken, and only a handful of people held the truth....Righteousness and victory in the historical process remained with a scant few, against an enormous majority."

II.

Bobrzyński, Wasilewski, Sokolnicki—all of them were right, but none of them completely. Without a shadow of a doubt everyone, in some way, desired an independent Poland and everyone, in their own way, labored for it. But in all political camps there was no shortage of people with base morals and little faith, political opponents and hooligans, traitors of the national cause and troublemakers in the service of platitudes. But after all, they performed a miracle: Poland regained its freedom and every Pole has the right to a moment of happiness in the "recaptured garbage heap".

We at *Gazeta Wyborcza* were not and are not objective observers of Poland's struggles. We were and remain active participants in the debate on Poland.

We remember the times when we spoke the words of Sokolnicki, inciting praise for the active, though woefully small group that lit the spark of dissent against the dictatorship from March 1968 to the foundation of the Workers' Defense Committee (KOR). We recall the time when, during the difficult days of martial law we spoke the language of Zygmunt Wasilewski, proclaiming the reason of an active policy, though one imbued with geopolitical realism, and rejecting the idea of armed irredentism. And finally, we remember the time when we borrowed the discourse of Bobzyński, announcing the need for a "united Poland", where former adversaries can take pride in the patriotic achievements of their own political camp.

The Polish path to democracy, through negotiation and agreement, was cleared for us by the round table agreement. I consider the round table to be the most prudent political act in Poland's twentieth-century history. Almost no one believed in an agreement between the ruling communists and the anticommunist opposition. And yet, it became fact—without blockades and without execution squads, without even a single shattered window—Poland itself knew how to negotiate the path to freedom and independence. If a Polish patriot had caught the proverbial magic fish in 1984, what would his three wishes have been? First of all: that Poland would cease to be a dictatorship and become a democracy, without the dictates of the police, without censorship, without closed borders. Second: that the Polish economy would be rationalized, that the logic of the free market would replace the logic of command, distribution, and shortage, and that mounting debts be transformed into stable economic growth. And third: that Poland would be a sovereign country, that the Soviet military would leave Poland, that the Soviet Union would crumble, and that our country would be a permanent fixture in a democratic Europe.

"The word became flesh and dwelt among us"

Why did communism fall in Poland? Was it pushed by the election of Pope John Paul II and his memorable pilgrimages to Poland? Was it occasioned by the policy of the American presidents, Jimmy Carter and Ronald Reagan, who used human rights as the weapon of American politics against totalitarian communism? Did Mikhail Gorbachev, who in his desire to modernize the Soviet empire bring it about by dealing it a fatal blow?

Each of these factors had a very essential significance. But another factor was decisive: the fact that Poles wanted to dismantle the system of dictatorship, that those Poles who served the dictatorship knew how to negotiate to this end with those who rebelled against it.

III.

That was the "Great Polish Velvet Revolution". Like every revolution, ours, too, carried with it great hopes and brought great disillusionment. The authorities were disappointed—they were counting on the rationalization and modernization of the system and not on its fall. Solidarity was disappointed, relying on the coming of a time of "fame and glory"; instead there came a time of bitter denouncements, unemployment, "the war at the top", the cunning of the former nomenklatura, and the corruption of the new ruling class. In short, all of society was frustrated, believing that the end of communism would transform Poland into a country with American wages, a Scandinavian welfare system, and a work ethic dating from the time of First Secretary Edward Gierek. The expected manna did not fall from heaven, because it couldn't.

IV.

Actually, for us at *Gazeta Wyborcza*, manna did fall from heaven; our good fortune changed water into wine. We realized that the round table had been a great success: the democratic opposition won everything there was to gain at the bargaining table.

That which was meant to be the price paid for the legalization of Solidarity—that is, participation in elections to a compromise lower house of parliament (with just thirty-five percent of the seats available to the opposition)—those people at the round table turned into an instrument of revolutionary change. The contract lower house of parliament and wholly democratic upper house were formed after elections that won us a crushing victory.

I remember those times well. Victory demanded of us imagination, courage, and caution. It was a shock for everyone: for the communist party elite, for the Catholic Episcopate, and for us—the people of Solidarity. In order to move forward and effect a change in government from communist to noncommunist, it was necessary to compromise, avoid rocky ground, clear the minefield, steer clear of conflict with the natural enemies of democracy—the ministries controlling the police and military—and also with Moscow, at a time when nobody thought yet of the dissolution of the Soviet Union.

The government of Tadeusz Mazowiecki was formed, the first noncommunist government in the Soviet bloc. This government performed the historical task of decommunizing Poland. Ten years later we look back on that government and the people who supported it with gratitude. It was a government of hope. In the midst of desperate economic collapse, a government of consensus and unity was formed after years of internal conflict that was tearing the state apart. A government was in place to build the framework for freedom and sovereignty after years of dictatorship and subjugation. The government of Mazowiecki, Kuroń, Balcerowicz, and Skubiszewski knew how to negotiate with President Jaruzelski, with Gorbachev, and with politicians from democratic countries. This government initiated the historical "Autumn of Nations": the fall of the Berlin Wall and the velvet revolution in Czechoslovakia. And it was this very government and this prime minister that just a few months later became the targets of unforgivable attacks initiated by those who condemned separating the past with a "thick line" (closing the book on the past), those who demanded an "acceleration of democratization and vetting of communists" and "completing the revolution". At the head of this attack stood the symbol of Polish resistance, the Nobel Peace Prize winner and leader of Solidarity, Lech Wałęsa.

V.

Someone from KOR wrote in spring 1995:

"I was of the opinion that Wałęsa consciously aspired to a personal dictatorship, to become a 'sultan' of authority in the union, condoning autocratic decision-making on fundamental issues. I believed this process forebode the slow death of union democracy and I decidedly opposed it. At the same time I feared Wałęsa was liable to come to an understanding with the government at the cost of 'cleansing the union of his antagonists.' I would have considered this a betrayal of Solidarity. I was aware of Lech's significance. By putting himself on stage, Wałęsa satisfied the universal need for a charismatic leader, all-knowing and all-understanding, to lead the union to victory. This resulted in a large number of union activists relinquishing independent reasoning and political responsibility. In such a situation the capitulation of the charismatic leader would have been the same as the capitulation of the union. Even when criticized by moderates, Wałęsa was accepted by the masses. Geremek, Kuroń, Mazowiecki, and KOR activists were accused of conciliation—Wałęsa was untouched by mass criticism. He was able to model himself as a leader accepted by millions. Sometimes he behaved like the great leader of the nation (repeating Kościuszko's oath in Krakow), while on other occasions he played the role of an ordinary worker, an equal among equals, casting off stateliness in exchange for directness and humor. He had a wonderful, simple, and pithy language and a brilliant intuition. He faultlessly sensed the mood of those around him and could say what was expected of him. Poles felt that their leader was 'one of them', and at the same time the embodiment of their long-awaited success. There was greatness in him.

"I was afraid of Wałęsa. I feared his ability to juggle words and his skill in eliminating opponents. I was afraid of his compromises and his fascination by talks with the government. I feared his susceptibility to a conspiracy-Mafia interpretation of the world, and his circle in which I saw many trivial and incidental people. I feared his apprehension before distinguished persons and his constant repetition: I am Solidarity!

"I should at this point confess openly that I was mistaken in my overall evaluation of Lech Wałęsa. The leader of Solidarity Trade Union turned out to be worthy of this role. Overlooking certain lapses, Lech Wałęsa saved the continuity of Solidarity with his stature and consistency. Returning to work in the shipyard, commenting on the events of public life, he became an outward symbol of Polish resistance; a lighthouse sending out regular signals of faith and hope from Gdańsk to all Poland. Combining defiance with restraint, Lech won the Nobel Prize and the status of a universally regarded authority...

"Today, Wałęsa is without a doubt the symbol of Solidarity, though he holds no actual power: he does not have an executive body at his disposal and he does not allocate posts in the regional administration. Today Lech is in no position to stop actions which are considered necessary. That is why attacks on Wałęsa today have a completely different motive than before 13 December [1981]. These days it is not a matter of fighting for democracy within the union but, despite intentions, depriving Solidarity of its symbol and authority. Consequently, it would be regrettable to continue the pre-martial law polemics today, with their baggage of injuries and bitterness, instead of seeking agreement and meeting halfway..."

This is my profile of Lech Wałęsa: a man of brilliant intuition and shameless self-adoration, a natural political talent and arrogant autocrat, the godfather of Polish freedom and its unwitting destroyer. No one did as much for Polish liberty, and no one trampled so many priceless Polish values underfoot. At the same time, no one defended the market economy and prowestern orientation in Polish politics as fiercely.

Lech Wałęsa did not want to and could not wait. Is that why I still think of Wałęsa with a mixture of warmth and aversion, fear and admiration? He did not respect partners, he only recognized loyal courtiers. He craved presidential power the way a drug addict craves cocaine. But it wasn't the personality of the Solidarity leader that was the deciding factor in the "war at the top". The outcome was decided by the mood of frustration that led Wałęsa's attack on Tadeusz Mazowiecki's government to success. The philosophy of this government was based on consistent but cautious reforms, the most important of which was Balcerowicz's economic transformation, later known as "shock therapy". Mazowiecki wanted to neutralize all other social conflicts. However, these frustrations and conflicts were the natural outcome of the transformation. This is where the sense of the "thick line" came in—to give everyone the chance to work for a democratic Poland, instead of foundering in "hellish quarrels".

Wałęsa's genius, however, was based on his acute perception and articulation of popular dissatisfaction. Solidarity activists were frustrated: they expected the Solidarity union to become the new "leading power", appointing university rectors and directors, chairmen, ministers, and province governors. Disaffected workers felt they had won their freedom through strikes only to come face to face with the specter of unemployment. Catholics were frustrated, as they had expected that, after the fall of "Communist Poland", the time of a "Catholic Poland" would come. Those discriminated against under the dictatorship felt cheated, for they had anticipated compensation, but instead looked on as the communist party nomenklatura was enfranchised.

New governments want to be liked—they like to hand out money. But Mazowiecki's government stood by Balcerowicz's strict economic policy. Now we can plainly see that Poland owes its present prosperity to that decision. At the time, however, demonstrations were held under the slogan "Balcerowicz is the Dr. Mengele of the Polish economy". This sort of frustration is inherent in every revolution: after the heroic battle for liberty follows the struggle for power and profit. Then, as often occurs, the former dictatorship is replaced by the dictatorship of the revolutionary regime. Fortunately it turned out differently in the case of Poland.

VI.

Balcerowicz—a politician with an iron will and a great and revolutionary imagination—had harsh critics from the very start. They accused him of being ruthlessly devoted to monetary affairs and the inhumane rules of the free market jungle, of creating unemployment and lacking social sensitivity, of aiding the rich and ruining the poor. Balcerowicz, however, had powerful allies: Prime Minister Mazowiecki and Jacek Kuroń, the minister of the Polish poor; and galloping inflation was also on his side. In his favor, too, were the lack of alternative programs and a conviction that other types of therapy would fail. A parliamentary majority and a large part of the media also supported him.

We at *Gazeta Wyborcza* always backed Balcerowicz's policy. We had trouble with this. Most of us entered the epoch of freedom holding the deeply embedded ethos of defending workers' rights: their dignity, their rights, and their interests. The ideal of emancipating the workers, rooted in the socialist tradition and Pope John Paul II's encyclicals, was in direct conflict with Balcerowicz's policy. Instead of independent workers' authorities came privatization; instead of pay raises came price hikes and belt tightening; instead of social security came the specter of unemployment. We often asked ourselves: Are we not betraying our ideals? Ten years on we can look back and answer: No. We did not renounce our dreams; we only renounced our delusions. We believe, here and now, that there was no other road for Poland to take than the rocky path of Balcerowicz's shock therapy. Along this path—though littered with mistakes, inconsistencies, and scandals—Poland experienced an economic boom and social progress never encountered before.

We are aware that nothing is ever inevitable. The harsh logic of a market economy is often accompanied by the market's cold cruelty, the ruthless business mentality, the rigor of technocrats and the abasement of human dignity. In such moments we recall and will continue to recall that our ultimate goal is Poland's liberty and social freedom, to create a civic society in which everyone has the right to live with dignity. We realize that the free market is an inevitable part of transformation. But by no means should we consider the enrichment of some and the poverty of others to be the result of divine justice. On the contrary, we should keep a check on the rich and provide the poor with aid and the opportunity to escape their poverty.

VII.

Tough free market policy and rapid modernization led to a conservative backlash and populist reaction. In Poland populism came in various forms: from the success of Stan Tymiński in the 1990 presidential elections, through the harsh anticapitalist and anti-European pronouncements of many Church authorities, to the show of support for the Democratic Left Alliance (SLD) and the Polish Peasant Party (PSL) in the May 1993 parliamentary elections. Fortunately the SLD-PSL parliamentary coalition did not keep its campaign promises. The rate of reform slowed, but there was no return to a command economy. The populist-conservative reaction also took an anticommunist form, drawing from clericalism and ethnic nationalism. The voice of Radio Maryja was an extreme and perhaps the most dramatic articulation of these attitudes: fear of the unknown, of Europe, and of foreigners; ill-will toward ethnic minorities; the fear of being responsible for one's own life, of poverty, unemployment, uncertainty, drugs, pornography, and the sexual revolution.

In other words Radio Maryja voiced, often using crude and unrestrained language, the fundamental issues of those who felt wronged and frightened. It is to these people that the Solidarity leader from Ursus, Zygmunt Wrzodak, appealed when he fulminated against the "pink hyenas" from KOR. It is these people upon whom Switoń and Janosz called to plant crosses in the Auschwitz gravel pit and who, led by Andrzej Lepper, blocked Polish roads.

We have described crushed and unfortunate people in *Gazeta Wyborcza*, usually using journalistic language, but we have always declared ourselves—in the language of commentary—on the side of the reformers. We understood that a defensive backlash is a natural consequence of modernization. That is why we were for the policy of social dialogue, compromise, and the regulation of employer-employee relations by the law. At the same time we knew that where dialogue ends, the destruction of the democratic principles of the law-abiding state begins. We did not call for making the criminal code more stringent, but we appealed for the unstinting execution of the law toward those who flaunt it.

We understood the complex situation of the trade unions. They are always an irremovable element of the democratic order. By their nature, they make demands. In Poland the trade unions were a fundamental factor in the evolving battle for freedom and the rights of workers; they unwittingly became a conservative agent in the transformation from a controlled economy to a free market.

Conflict between a government with a policy of transformation and the trade unions that defend workers' interests is just as inevitable as compromise between the two is inescapable. Ten years of transformation have shown that Poland cannot be reformed without society's consent and that this consent can only be won through dialogue and compromise. We believe that a compromise on the economy is a priority because economic growth is the prerequisite for Polish achievement both at home and throughout the world. The economy should be a jointly guarded area, taken out of the framework of political conflict. But will that be possible in the "cold Polish civil war"?

VIII.

From the beginning, since 1989, we at the newspaper have supported a united Poland, a republic: a homeland for all its citizens, a state based on compromises and not on the domination of one political camp nor on a relentless battle and a never-ending settling of scores. We did not want Solidarity to become the new "leading power"; we did not want the once compulsory conformity to Marxism-Leninism and the Soviet Union to turn into conformity to the Catholic Church or western capitals.

We looked on with joy when Polish society regained its liberty and the Polish state its independence. We supported the rational policy of successive governments toward all of our neighbors and our own ethnic minorities. We were grateful that Poland was free of conflicts with national minorities and arguments with neighboring nations for the first time in its history. That was an accomplishment of Polish politics. But it did not come about without difficulties. We saw in other postcommunist countries how aggressive nationalism took the place of dominating communist ideology and how old demons returned. We saw how the bloody conflict in Yugoslavia was born, erupted, and lives on, where yesterday's communists were transformed into today's aggressive nationalists and former democrats spoke in the language of ethnic fascism. We also saw how Christian clergy blessed ethnic massacres. We saw how nationalism, born of communism and anticommunism, seized Russia and other countries of the former Soviet Union; with unease we listened to the outbursts of greater Russian chauvinism from Zhirinovsky or Zyuganov. We witnessed the bloody riots in Romania, the dissolution of Czechoslovakia, the burning homes of African refugees in eastern Germany. We saw all this, and we must do all we can to prevent similar scenes from being repeated in Poland. That would be the death of Polish freedom.

This is why we have warned and shall continue to warn against the discourse of national hatred and against the ideology of ethnic exclusivity. We have condemned and will continue to condemn the Polish-German conflict in the Opole area, the Polish-Ukrainian polemic around Przemśyl, the Polish-Belarusian problems around Białystok, and Polish-Lithuanian tensions in the Suwałki region. We have condemned the abuse of Romani. We have also warned against anti-Semitism, which stupefies Poles and blights Poland's image abroad. We agreed with Jerzy Turowicz, who wrote to Father Stanisław Musial: "Dear Staszek, I read your distinguished—and very important!—*Gazeta Wyborcza* interview with true admiration. You are one hundred percent correct when you write that nationalism and anti-Semitism are the great weaknesses of the Polish Church. That is why this Church cannot tolerate the [Auschwitz] gravel pit affair, Father Jankowski, or Father Rydzyk and Radio Maryja. It's true that more people in the Church are beginning to understand this (also thanks to you!), but there is still a long road ahead!"

Only by traveling this road can Poland's good name in the world be defended against damning generalizations.

We have been advocates of new relations among states and nations in Central and Eastern Europe. With this intention in mind we have printed many Russian opinions, including those of Russian democrats, to whom the world has much to be thankful.

It is an honor for us to call so many fine Russians friends of our newspaper. We also have reason to be proud because we are shedding new light upon the tangled history of Polish-Ukrainian relations. We consider work on behalf of Polish-Ukrainian reconciliation to be one of the great accomplishments of Polish politics, in which *Gazeta Wyborcza* has played a part. We believed that the most effective path to the West and to the North Atlantic Treaty Organization (NATO) and the European

Union to be internal stabilization, good neighborly relations, and an active regional policy. That is why we report extensively on the Czech Republic, Hungary, and Slovakia, on Estonia, Latvia, and Lithuania, and on Belarus and Ukraine.

We were aware that the prowestern option in Polish politics, which we always supported, also has its staunch opponents. We saw these adversaries among members of the former communist regime. For this reason we were thrilled to note every prowestern turn among Christian-National Union politicians, and the decidedly prowestern turnaround in the postcommunist Democratic Left Alliance. It was, however, the visit of Polish bishops to Brussels and their pro-European declarations that provided a true breakthrough.

IX.

From the very first issue, we at *Gazeta Wyborcza* had great respect for the Catholic Church. We recognized the tremendous role the Church played throughout Poland's history and its great contributions during the communist dictatorship and the round table. We admired the great cause of Pope John Paul II. Despite all that, and despite exercising caution in criticizing certain Episcopal declarations, we have often been accused of enmity toward the Church. We regarded and continue to regard these charges as unjust.

We never claimed to be a Catholic newspaper, though we always considered ourselves friends of the Church. We opine, in the words of Leszek Kołakowski, that

> "the Church is, as it were, on the dividing line between heaven and earth; it is both the depository of grace and the guardian of the law, it distributes invisible goods in the visible world....The power of Christianity does not manifest itself in theology nor in its monopoly on creating canons to regulate all areas of life. Its power is revealed in the fact that it can build barriers against hate in people's consciousness. In essence, mere faith in Jesus the Redeemer would be in vain and worthless if it did not carry with it the resignation of hatred, no matter what the circumstances; if after the words 'forgive us our trespasses' Christians did not have to go on to say 'as we forgive those who trespass against us'. This resignation from hating is the challenge Christianity presents which remains today. If a true Christian is only someone who fulfills this scripture, is a pupil of Christ, someone who doesn't run from a fight but is free of hate—how may Christians have walked and walk today on this earth? I don't know. I know neither how many lived in the Middle Ages, nor today. However many they number, they are the salt of the earth and European civilization would be a wasteland without them."

It is from this kind of Holy Scripture that we came to understand the Church. That is why we are disturbed by voices filled with hate and contempt, fired by the spirit of revenge and embarking on a crusade against those who think differently, and all this in the name of the Gospel and under the sign of the Cross. We were determined to show another side of Christianity and a Church of ecumenical faith and hope, compassion and dialogue, forgiveness and reconciliation. We were and are today people of dialogue but not of blind obedience, of criticism but not malevolence. Ours is the first daily newspaper to include a regular column on the Catholic Church and religion.

There was a time when working with *Gazeta Wyborcza* was viewed unfavorably by the Church. Therefore we wish all the more to thank all those people of the Church who offered us their thoughts, articles, and essays with courage and understanding.

A time of unjust criticism is, by its nature, a difficult test of loyalty. We never lost respect and admiration for the Church thanks to those who offered us friendship in moments of bitterness. It is hard to imagine Poland without Catholicism. The Catholic Church is deeply ingrained in Polish society. That is why the Church embodies simultaneously both the best and the worst of Poland. We were lucky in that we had the opportunity to associate with the best.

X.

Often we at *Gazeta Wyborcza*, and particularly myself personally, have been accused of being too soft on the perpetrators of the former regime. We have been criticized for not settling accounts and not taking part in vetting or decommunization, and as a consequence, of blurring the boundary between good and evil, truth and lies. One critic called this "a friendship pact with Cain".

The tenth anniversary of *Gazeta Wyborcza* seems a good occasion to respond to these accusations.

For many years we belonged to the anticommunist opposition. Many of us spent a good bit of time underground or in jail, on the margins of public life, discriminated against and humiliated. Our opinions and our friends were excluded from the debate on Poland and the shaping of its future. This continued for many years.

In the pages of underground newspapers we vehemently denounced the communist regime. Only in 1989, during the round table talks, did we acknowledge that there was a light at the end of the tunnel for Poland. Then we realized that the route to Polish democracy was to follow the Spanish way—that of evolution from dictatorship to democracy via compromise and national reconciliation. This approach assumes there will be no retaliation, no vanquishers or vanquished, and that future governments will be chosen by ballot. We did realize that we, members of the democratic opposition, KOR and Solidarity, were particularly winners. But from this moral high ground we rejected sweet revenge on yesterday's enemies. We said yes to amnesty and no to amnesia. This declaration meant casting aside retribution and exposing the whole truth. The historian, essayist, and artist were to pass judgement on our cursed past and not the prosecutor or investigator. We believed in the significance of this amnesty: for members of the right-wing National Armed Forces and the National Radical Camp, though they had much on their consciences, and for members of the Communist Party, who served the dictatorship for a variety of motives and with differing results. We judged that there must be a place under the Polish sun for all, because a broad spectrum of social harmony on these essential matters can only be built this way. Therefore, we wanted to see people of good will on both sides of the complicated Polish barricade. We wanted to uncover the complex truth of human fortunes, dramatically overturned in the course of successive twists, turns, and crises, caused by foreign aggression and native lies. We opposed the creation of a new historical myth for ongoing political polemics.

We understand the building of a democratic and sovereign state as a process of reconciliation, of bringing together "Poland Discordant": Communist Poland and Solidarity Poland. That is why we were against all attmepts at decommunization and vetting. We consider decommunization—that is, discrimination against former communist party activists—to be antidemocratic. We see the analogies between decommunization and post-Hitler Germany as misdirected. Gomułka, Gierek, and Jaruzelski were not the same kind of people as Hitler, Himmler, or Goebbels. They were dictators but not mass murderers, and to blur these definitions is wrong.

The Spanish transition to democracy fascinated us. We looked also to Chile, the Philippines, and South Africa, where yesterday's enemies took their places in a joint, democratically elected parliament. We consider it better to turn the numerous supporters of the "former regime" into proponents of democracy, independence, and market economy, and not their staunch enemies.

Naturally, we often wrote about the communist era while hardly disguising out heartfelt antipathy. But even while condemning the system and its practices—particularly the mixture of lies and violence—we attempted to understand those caught up in it. To put it in another, more

Christian way: We differentiated the sin from the sinner. For us a communist was not the embodiment of evil, the devil incarnate, Cain, or a criminal whose hands were stained with innocent blood. We did not want to demonize the supporters of the former regime, though we repeatedly wrote of the demonic nature of totalitarian dictatorships, nor did we want to "deify" the anticommunist opposition, though these were often our friends from Solidarity, the underground, or prison.

We often reiterated that people who had been in conflict for years created the interwar Second Polish Republic. What's more, they fought in opposing armies during World War I. Yet Poland's independence brought them together. We wanted to follow in their footsteps. We wanted, despite obvious biographical, political, and ideological differences, to seek that which binds.

This is where our resistance to vetting came from. Of course, we cared if communist informers became ministers, ambassadors, et cetera. However, we felt that the data held in security service files could not decide whether a citizen was suitable for work in government administration. We did not believe the secret service archives were an accurate source of information. These documents were used as instruments of police blackmail, to compromise those people who were inconvenient to the authorities. A prime minister wanting to know more about a coworker can examine the material, but it should not be used to create a political circus. It was with dismay that *Gazeta Wyborcza* reported on the "night of the long files" instigated by Antoni Macierewicz, minister of internal affairs in Jan Olszewski's government, who cast dark shadows on the good names of so many people who had contributed so much to Poland.

XI.

Political conflicts and disagreements were a natural part of the first decade of a democratic Poland. We just didn't want these conflicts to overstep the barrier of the "common good", of law and good manners. Thus, we followed Poland's unity in its accession to NATO with joy and looked on with unease at signs of the government exploiting legal loopholes. We were also unnerved by the special services' interference in tensions among political camps: forging documents that were to compromise politicians and incite arguments, accusations of "high treason" directed at the prime minister by his own minister of internal affairs and based on the flimsiest of evidence.

Increasingly, brutal political battles alarmed us: attacking the deputy minister of internal affairs for his willingness to surrender Silesia, suggesting that the president had connections with foreign agents, pelting politicians with eggs or splashing them with foul-smelling liquid.

We rejoiced at the triumphs of the Polish economy. We categorically rejected the theory that turncoats and thieves ruled Poland. Even so, we were disturbed by corrupt links between the political and business worlds, which we described in painstakingly detailed reports. We steered well clear of making groundless accusations, insinuations, and insults. However, no government, no department, and no political party could count on our unflagging support.

Reporting on Polish politics and taking part in Polish polemics, we realized that mere politics do not life make. We wanted, therefore, to create a newspaper that was sympathetic and helpful.

We brought democracy and human rights right down to the grass roots with, for example, the two-year "Give Birth Humanely" campaign that changed the face of Polish maternity hospitals. We demanded that staff show pregnant women respect and empathy instead of the impersonal or even boorish treatment often practiced. We championed uninterrupted contact with the newborn and the presence of family members at birth. We asked readers to send in letters and surveys rating maternity hospitals, on the basis of which we compiled guides and rankings. Both medical staff and authorities at first scoffed at the campaign, but just a few months later hospitals entered a heated race for a better place in the ranking. We effected a change in consciousness and the term "give birth humanely" entered everyday language. Specialists even believe that the rapid drop in the infant mortality rate was in some part thanks to the humanization of the birth process.

Gazeta Wyborcza also stepped in to defend the children of alcoholics and condemn domestic violence and violent television programs. We saved state orphanages by organizing a massive fundraiser, and we supported the creation of family-style children's homes. We encouraged readers to "escape from the housing projects" in our "Live Humanely" campaign.

Several times we directly lobbied for changes in the law. After the unexpected cancellation of the housing tax break in 1997, we collected thousands of signatures to urge the ombudsperson to appeal against the taxation bill. We covered the most difficult issues and those bound by social taboos, such as sex education and, recently, the moving series "Why a Hospice Shelter". The newspaper regularly tried to convince Poles to live healthier lifestyles—to quit smoking, eat properly, et cetera.

For years we have offered a steady stream of tax and financial advice, not to mention innumerable guides to construction, renovation, decoration, and buying an apartment in *Gazeta Dom* (Home Gazette) or buying a car in the *Auto-Moto* section. We also print sample tests to help students prepare for standardized exams. Recently, our coverage of social reforms has been very popular, especially as there is a lot of confusion surrounding the changes. The most popular series are "How to Get Medical Treatment in This Mess" and "Choosing a Pension Plan".

Readers are also quite attached to our local supplements. They include lost pet listings, tongue-in-cheek competitions for the biggest pothole, and hundreds of movie and theater ticket giveaways. Anyone can bid a fond farewell to a loved one in the obituary pages, and some of our twenty local supplements print pictures of newborn babies in the "Welcome to the World" section. The supplements chronicle city life and include amusing stories, such as that of the many month-long search for a warthog that escaped from the zoo.

The supplements always keep a watchful eye on the local authorities. The series of articles "Cities Inside-Out" published before the 1998 local elections was the first summary of the achievements and failures of municipal authorities. The supplements also got involved in the tussle over the rearrangement of Poland's regional administration map, organizing local referenda not only in those places threatened with losing their status as a province capital.

We have always been proud of our roots in the opposition, KOR and Solidarity. But we did not want to be either an organ of Solidarity or part of it. For we wanted to work for a democratic Poland and not for successive Solidarity union bosses or for any other political party. When Lech Wałęsa and the Solidarity national commission banned us from using the Solidarity symbol on our masthead, we painfully accepted the decision. Today we see it as a positive move—a trade union should be a trade union, and an independent newspaper an independent newspaper. The important thing is for the union to be wise and the newspaper absorbing and honest.

The first issue of *Gazeta Wyborcza* stated: "This newspaper has come into being as a result of the round table agreement, but we are publishing and editing it ourselves, and we are alone accountable.

"We do have links to Solidarity, but we intend to present the views and opinions of all society, of opposing trends."

Did we keep our word? We leave it up to our hundreds of thousands of readers to answer that question.

We believe that the prerequisite of our credibility is independence: political and material. We have built up this independence over ten years, receiving many complements and diatribes along the way. Today is a fitting time to thank both our critics and our friends.

XII.

For nearly two centuries Poles symbolized martyrdom and bravery in the eyes of the world, but the Polish state was called the "sick man of Europe", and the Polish economy was spoken of with contempt as *"die polnische Wirtschaft"*. Today the world sees not only Polish heroism but also the wisdom of Polish policy and the success of the Polish economy.

Today, Poland is no longer a lamentable object of pity in defeat, but respected, admired, and envied in victory. This is also a good moment to remind ourselves of the downtrodden: the unemployed and the homeless, those impoverished and wallowing in apathy, those who do not take part in elections but strike and block roads for fear of an uncertain tomorrow. All are an intrinsic part of Poland and Polishness. Their fate should be a matter of common concern. Our attitude toward the downtrodden is, we believe, an essential measure of contemporary Polish patriotism.

What does patriotism, for that matter, mean to us at *Gazeta Wyborcza* today? We looked on with aversion when Solidarity members requested compensation for the years they spent in prison and others demanded compensation for time spent in concentration camps. Both have a right to compensation, but we believe that patriotism consists in not taking advantage of all our rights, in being able to offer communism's debts to a free Poland.

That is our first instinct: to demand the truth and the righting of wrongs, while renouncing retaliation and veterans' privileges. Our patriotism is not a stick with which to beat those who have a different view; it is not to be used as a method of extortion by tossing around slogans about the homeland. What we need is common reflection for the common good. Our patriotism does not endorse any one political party to take possession of the state, be it postcommunist or post-anticommunist. Our patriotism is the firm conviction that Poland is the common homeland of all its citizens. Only the nation—meaning all the republic's citizens—can give the authorities a mandate. Any governing group that explains its right to rule through services performed in the past, no matter how great, is on the path to dictatorship. Our patriotism consists in opposing dictatorship.

It also consists of memory. We try to remember that Poland was lost in the past not only due to foreign aggression, but also to internal discord and the drive for personal interests and to an inability to compromise. The epitome of this was the *liberum veto*. This was not the height of liberty as claimed, but a channel for corruption and the cause of the fall of the Polish Republic.

We are glad that Poland's happiest decade in the last three hundred years also happens to be the best ten years of our lives. *Gazeta Wyborcza* is not only our contribution to this period, it is the contribution of a democratic and independent Poland in its entirety.

Notes

1 Excerpts from this chapter were printed in the 13 May 1999 edition of *Time*. They are reprinted here by permission of the author.

7 Between Idealism and Realism: Reflections on the Political Landscape of Postcommunism

MARTIN PALOUŠ

> "He has two antagonists: the first presses him from behind, from the origin. The second blocks the road ahead. He gives battle to both. To be sure, the first supports him in his fight with the second, for he wants to push him forward, and in the same way the second supports the first in his fight with the first, since he drives him back. But it is only theoretically so. For it is not only the two antagonists who are there, but he himself as well, and who really knows his intentions? His dream, though, is that some day in an unguarded moment—and this would require a night darker than any night has ever been yet—he will jump out of the fighting line and be promoted, on account of his experience in fighting, to the position of umpire over his antagonists in their fight with each other."[1]

I.

Almost ten years have passed since the revolutions of the late 1980s terminated totalitarian rule in Central Europe. Many things have changed radically in the meantime, but equally important as the shifts themselves is our perception of these changes and of their effects. The process of transition has been undoubtedly a great learning experience for all who have taken part in it. As far as the nature and scope of this process is concerned, however, in 1999 we seem to be less certain and less self-confident than we were at the beginning. We realize that maybe we are finding ourselves on the verge of, according to Samuel Huntington, a "clash of civilizations" but certainly not, according to Francis Fukuyama, at the "end of history". With the collapse of communism—the ideologues of which pretended to have discovered the universal laws governing the historical movement of human society and believed in their own capability to plan its "radiant futures" accordingly—human history has become largely mysterious again, and it is once more perceived as a story with an open end. The stability and rigid constellations that characterized Europe in the long decades of the cold war are now irrevocably gone, and we indeed regained freedom ten years ago. There is a price, however, to be paid for our liberation: a long period (forty years?) of flux, destabilization, and uncertainty.

In my paper I would like to argue that this epistemic deficit—the fact that we know that we do not know exactly where we are and in which direction we are heading—represents an essential and perhaps the most dynamic aspect of the politics of transition. It is true that we still believe that ten years ago we started our return to Europe after decades of "Babylonian captivity" and that we hope to join the European Union within four or a few more years. At the same time it is evident that our return to Europe is much more—or even something entirely different— than a mere "homecoming", because the "home" itself would have to change profoundly in order to absorb all returnees. If Timothy Garton Ash could announce in 1990 that what we were witnessing was the great victory of "old, well-tested ideas", there is no doubt today that this victory brought us to an entirely new, unprecedented situation.

The remarkable coincidence is that at the moment of this conference, convened to examine the lessons of the past decade that started with the collapse of communism in Central and Eastern Europe, the actions of NATO against the Milosević regime in Yugoslavia demonstrate very clearly profound and radical change, the "innocent" beginnings of which were celebrated in the streets of Budapest, Prague, Warsaw, and elsewhere during the *annus mirabilis* 1989. But it also shows how difficult and even painful it can be to understand the weight and impact of actual historical events. It seems to me that when the bombs were dropped on Belgrade and other Yugoslav cities by NATO pilots, the process of transition reached a critical point, illuminating the whole postcommunist landscape and forcing us to rethink what is going on around us and what is really at stake. If the year 1999 was originally planned as the year of celebration of the European revolutions of 1989, when "truth and love triumphed over lie and hatred", we cannot fail to see under the given circumstances that the past decade had not only its "happy" beginning but also its "tragic" end.

What I would like to suggest is that the whole period between 1989 and 1999 can be divided into three different phases introduced and characterized by specific events. What is the place of these events in our understanding of the politics of transition? Is there any rationality behind them? Or were they entirely unpredictable and triggered by coincidence?

Can we interpret them as a chain of steps tied together by some inner logic? Did they just happen, come unexpectedly, or were they bigger than the intention that might have led to their ignition? Is it not exactly here in these questions, which we have to leave unanswered, that lies the root cause of our current uncertainty and "epistemic deficit?" Is it not the proper historical understanding of events irreversibly changing our world that is at stake if we want to reconcile ourselves with the reality that ten years after our "revolutions" we still seem to be on the historical cross-roads, in the Arendtian gap between the past of the twentieth and the future of the twenty-first centuries?

II.

The atmosphere that prevailed in Europe immediately after the revolutions of 1989 swept away the totalitarian communist governments seemed to favor political idealists. The former dissidents became revolutionary heroes overnight. Shouting and singing crowds marched in the streets of Central European cities tinkling with their keys, ready to enthusiastically support the cause of Charter 77 with its ideas of human rights and "nonpolitical politics" (hitherto observed by the majority of the population with a lack of understanding and from safe distances), sending a clear signal that times were changing. The new politics was born from that spirit and was greeted and admired—as all innocent newborn children usually are—by almost everybody. The message sent to Washington by the new president of Czechoslovakia, Václav Havel, in February 1990 when he addressed a joint session of the U.S. Congress (which applauded more than twenty times during his speech) could not have been clearer: "The specific experience I'm talking about has given me one great certainty. Consciousness precedes Being, and not the other way around, as Marxists claim. For this reason, the salvation of this world lies nowhere else than in the human heart, in the human power to reflect, in human humbleness and in human responsibility."[2]

It is fair to admit, however, that not only the freshly liberated "post-totalitarians" but also the distinguished international community of the West were taken by the revolutionary idealistic spirit of renewal. The Paris Charter for the new Europe, signed in November 1990 by all heads of member-states of the Council on Security and Cooperation in Europe, solemnly declared that the cold war was over. The language of this document reflects very well the atmosphere of these "fair, well-spoken days". "Europe is liberating itself from the legacy of the past. The courage of men and women, the strength of the will of the peoples and the power of the ideas of the Helsinki Final Act have opened a new era of democracy, peace and unity in Europe."[3]

What happened in 1989 was truly a historical breakthrough. It was as if the world had become young again, full of hope, good will, and great expectations. The message of the epochal event we were all part of was clear and simple, and everybody seemed to know well what was at stake. The societies that had been kept closed for decades started to open again, and in this situation they could ask for and expect the helping hand of the democratic West. Practically all postcommunist states were well aware of the fact that the window of opportunity was wide open, and for both their foreign and domestic policies they set the same, or at least very similar, goals: the return to Europe, transition to the market economy, and democratization.

The Havelian vision, emphasizing the key role of human consciousness in world politics today—a position based on the spirit of the "resistance movements" of the 1970s and 1980s, such as Charter 77—was certainly inspiring and motivating. As a political program, however, defining not only the goals but also the instruments and ways to achieve these goals, it was insufficient. In order to identify and formulate all elementary agendas of the politics of transition more "realistic" approaches were needed. The work that was used as a basic source of inspiration, as a manual of political ideas for those who were charged with the enormous task of restoring (or building from scratch) liberal democracy in the postcommunist region, was undoubtedly Ralf Dahrendorf's *Reflections on the Revolution in Europe*, written in the form of a letter dated April 1990, "intended to have been sent to a gentleman in Warsaw".[4] "What does it all mean, and where is it going to lead (you want to know)? Are we not witnessing a process of dissolution without anything taking the place of the old and admittedly dismal structures?"

Dahrendorf sees his predecessor in Edmund Burke, who, two hundred years before him, sent a similar letter to a fictitious gentleman in Paris and articulated similar opinions concerning the revolution that took place in France: "Though I do most heartily wish that France may be animated by a spirit of rational liberty, and that I think you are bound, in all honest policy, to provide a permanent body in which that spirit may reside, and an effectual organ by which it may act, it is my misfortune to entertain great doubts concerning several material points in your late transactions."[5]

According to Dahrendorf, as far as European revolutions are concerned, nothing much has changed between 1790 and 1990. The central problems of postcommunist countries, returning after decades of Baby-

Ionian captivity to Europe, were apparently the ones that have occupied the minds of all modern European revolutionaries: How to provide a permanent body in which a spirit of rational liberty may reside? How to create, after an outlived "ancient" regime was displaced or simply fell apart, a new body politic? How to transform a profoundly negative force of revolution into the architectonic power of law making and city building? How to follow the U.S. rather than the French example in this matter and found a new political order without violence and with the help of a constitution?[6]

Dahrendorf, a determined enemy of all utopian visions and of all versions of system thinking in political matters, foreseeing "the conflicts between advocates of systems and defenders of the open society" in postcommunist politics, states unequivocally: "Neither Central Europe, nor social democracy, nor any euphemism for the 'middle way' must be thought of as a system, or indeed a Utopia, if liberty is what we want. The choice between freedom and serfdom is stark and clear, and it offers no halfway house for those weaker souls who would like to avoid making up their minds."[7]

Only after this first step is made and the existence of open society secured can "normal politics" emerge, where "a hundred options may be on offer and three or four usually are".[8] The relation and proper ordering of very different agendas in the process of transition, the correct sequencing of "constitutional" and "normal" politics, and the right choice and use of "republican remedies" that would be capable of making the government stronger, in Dahrendorf's account, are the key problems. The envisaged ideal schedule of transition to democracy develops, according to Dahrendorf, as follows. First comes "the problem of constitutional reform" that "takes at least six months".[9] Then "normal" politics bursts in, and economic reform must be executable within this environment.[10] The key, however, the lengthiest process, is the third problem—the emergence of civil society. "The third condition of the road to freedom is to provide the social foundations which transform the constitution and the economy from fair-weather into all-weather institutions capable of withstanding the storms generated within and without, and sixty years are barely enough to lay these foundations."[11]

There is no doubt about what Dahrendorf suggests as "remedies" to be used to protect the security of people and at the same time to keep their society open under the given circumstances. It is certainly not any sort of utopian vision of a "just" society—which in the last instance can only end up in "reigns of terror and virtue"—but free republican institutions. It is not the "pure ethics of conviction" of former dissidents turned into politicians, but the standard western political process (characterized by the rule of law, respect for unalienable rights, parliamentary democracy, and the market economy) animated by the "practical ethics of responsibility".[12]

It must be emphasized, however, that Havel's idealism and Dahrendorf's realism do not necessarily contradict each other. In fact, the disagreement between them only illustrates the elementary fact that an activist and an observer see the political processes from different, rather complementary, and not necessarily mutually exclusive perspectives. In his Burkean criticism of the "negativity" of the revolutionary spirit having the intrinsic tendency to transform its "pure ethics of conviction" into violence, Dahrendorf undoubtedly scores some points, but he is missing, in my view, the essential aspect of our recent revolutionary experience: the radical novelty and the lack of precedence of our current situation. The problem will become clearer when we deal with the role of civil society in the politics of transition. Here I will mention very briefly one reason why I prefer—with all due respect to political realism and the venerable tradition of liberal thought—Havel's revolutionary vision and not Dahrendorf's Burkeian conservatism.

The key question concerns civil society. For Havel civil society is not only a necessary condition for the functioning of democracy in the distant future but also something that must be recognized as already existent here and now; that, for instance, existed in the form of the "parallel polis" of Charter 77 for almost thirteen years before it was brought to the surface during the revolution; that has to play its crucial nonpolitical role within the context of the politics of transition. For Dahrendorf the emergence of civil society as a prerequisite for the successful "road to freedom" and as its necessary social foundation seems to be somewhat postponed and is presented as something that may only exist fully sixty years from now. The reason why Dahrendorf is somewhat reluctant to speak more positively about the ideas of civil society in the context of the revolutions themselves is obvious: It is his negative attitude toward what he calls "revolutionary utopianism". Civil society cannot be created by a revolutionary act; it must grow slowly. No proclamations, no political decisions, no legal acts or decrees, but only gradual uninterrupted development can bring its fundamental structures fully into existence. As the English know very well, maybe better than other nation, habits die hard and mentalities change slowly. That is why any impatience in this matter would lead posttotalitarians astray.

Nonetheless, what might be good advice and a healthy position during stable times that are favorable to evolutionary thinking and are backed by the idea of infinite progress do not necessarily work well in times of transition. Can we afford to think in such long-term historical perspectives when finding ourselves in the "gap" between past and future, in the middle of great historical change? What makes us believe that we will be given a sufficient amount of time for a successful transition? What should we do if some unexpected events lead us to arrive at the opposite opinion? Would it mean that the project of rebuilding the liberal order is doomed to fail or is simply incompatible with the situation in Europe and in the world at the end of the twentieth century?

III.

If the events that determined the character of the first phase of the post-communist transitions were the revolutions connected with the collapse of the totalitarian regimes themselves, then the beginning of the second phase was marked by the collapse of the empire. In December 1991 the Soviet Union ceased to exist and Yugoslavia disintegrated, resulting in the emergence of the first new independent states. With these events, according to Dahrendorf, the period of unifications terminated and was followed by the period of fragmentations. The political weather in Europe, bright and sunny after 1989, suddenly deteriorated. In fact, not only were some states falling apart, but the idea of a united Europe open to accept all returning posttotalitarians also started to evaporate in the new "climate". The concept of "virtuous" and "vicious" circles appeared in the debate on the politics of transition: "The more successful and 'virtuous' a country is in its transition to democracy and market economy, the more favorable are relations with the European institutions which in turn enhance democracy and contribute to prosperity...the countries which are less successful in the post-communist transitions for all sorts of reasons—be it economic hardships, social or political tensions or adverse international development—find themselves in...a vicious circle, being increasingly marginalized and separated or even excluded from the process of European integration."[13]

A new question was introduced in European political discourse concerning the new divisions emerging in Europe, new walls that were built to isolate the stable zone of European integration (to which the Central European countries were heading, according to their own conviction, firmly rooted in the traditions of "western civilization") from the irradiation of instability in some postcommunist regions—namely, in the Balkans and in the East. The European body politic was infected in these vulnerable areas by new dangerous diseases, and political "idealists" and "realists" naturally came with different medical prescriptions and therapies. The original consensus concerning the basic direction of the process of transition was broken, and the gap between the various "schools of transitology" grew wider and wider.

The second half of this chapter will deal with the test that international society has undergone while trying to resist the "Yugoslav virus", to use Adam Michnik's terminology. What must be mentioned first is the effect of the climatic change on the domestic postcommunist political scene, even in those "virtuous" countries. As an example I will take the Czech case because it offers a textbook example to illustrate traps and dilemmas of postcommunist democratization. Additionally, one also must take into consideration the fact that all discussions on the Czech political scene concerning the strategy of transformation—giving concrete "Czech" answers to the questions raised at the very beginning of the process by Dahrendorf—took place here against the background of the "velvet divorce": on 1 January 1993 Czechoslovakia was dismembered, and the Czech Republic and Slovakia came into existence.

The main and most influential opponent of Václav Havel on the Czech political scene, Václav Klaus, was the leader of the neoliberal Civic Democratic Party (ODS) which emerged as the strongest political unit from the revolutionary "Civic Forum". His aim from the very beginning was clear and simple: to formulate a "realistic" liberal alternative to the utopianism that, according to him, was the very essence of Havel's version of posttotalitarian politics. The arguments of Klaus—his criticism of the role of intellectuals in politics as promoters and disseminators of the "third way" thinking and his strong preference for "standard" western structures and strategies in addressing the problems of posttotalitarian politics—follow the lines of reasoning used by Ralf Dahrendorf. It was the Dahrendorfian version of western liberalism that made the Klausian political program both strong and weak at the same time; this model seemed to offer the best and shortest way from the dark communist past to the bright liberal-conservative future, yet it failed to do so in the end.

The Czech model of democratization, viewed at the time as a great success story and an outstanding example of "virtuous" transition, was characterized by several distinctive traits:[14]

1. neoliberal economics, rejecting the concept of the paternalistic welfare state and relying fully upon the omnipotence of market force;

2. transformation strategy as a practical application of the "turnpike theorem"; the main steps—the liberalization of domestic markets, the opening up of the Czechoslovak economy to world markets, and rapid privatization—were intended not to "build the capitalistic system" but to

unleash the spontaneous forces of the free market that were trusted to find the fastest way to an optimal situation;

3. spontaneous economic behavior as a first priority, unregulated and encouraged from the very beginning of the process of transition, and the belief that the speed of this process is more important than its legal purity—the difficulties of legal reform should not hinder the dynamic development of economics;

4. a strong and heavily centralized state administration (despite the rejection of state paternalism in economic matters), the existence of strong state institutions being the necessary conditions for successful passage through the uncertainties of transition;

5. belief in "standard" mechanisms of liberal democracy and in a technocratic or managerial concept of politics;

6. the articulation and representation of common positions and world views by political bodies (rather than the promotion of social dialogue and mediation of social communication);

7. contempt for all spontaneous activities of civil society, reborn from below, and mistrust of its intermediary bodies;

8. reliance that all political problems can be properly addressed and dealt with by political parties, that their structures and networks should serve as conduits to the decision-making mechanisms of a standard political system, that there is no room for the spontaneous activities of intermediary bodies of civil society, committed to the idea of "common good" in their not-for-profit oriented, yet (according to Klaus) "private" activities.

The consequences of the rejection of "the third way" by those who, with Václav Klaus, believed (or pretended to believe) "in [the] stark and clear choice between freedom and serfdom" and marked everybody who disagreed with them on this matter as "enemies" (or at least as "those weaker souls who would like to avoid making up their minds", to put the dilemma once more in the language of Dahrendorf) appeared only in the third phase of the process of transition. What already became clear in the second phase, however, was what made these postcommunist transitions essentially different from other, otherwise comparable processes of democratization (Latin America, Portugal, Spain, et cetera). Whereas previous transitions from autocratic regimes took place in the relatively stable international environment of the cold war, the recent reopening of closed societies after decades of communism was accompanied by profound destabilization of the international situation, when not only the postcommunist societies but almost everything was in flux. What we saw in Europe after communism, as Valerie Bunce clearly stated, was certainly not one transition, but rather a combination of domestic, regional, and international systems in transition.[15]

The collapse of regimes (state socialism, totalitarianism) in East Central Europe was accompanied, as I have already mentioned, by the collapse of an empire. What was at stake and what had to be taken into consideration was not only the possibility of successful transition from closed to open societies, but the fact that the events of 1989 seriously undermined the very foundations of some states and destabilized whole interstate systems in Europe. No doubt, the disintegrations of Czechoslovakia, the Soviet Union, and Yugoslavia in many respects are barely comparable. Their collapses were due to very different historical reasons, the catalysts and methods used were very different, and their dismemberments had very different outcomes and consequences.[16] What was, however, the common denominator of these events was the fact that in addition to the reopening of closed societies, another process was taking place as part of the transition, a process that implied an agenda counter to that of democratization: nation and state building.

The disintegration of three former socialist federations brought up one essential aspect of postcommunist politics. What came first under the test of the transition process was not so much a commitment to the ideals of open society or the market economy, but rather the firmness of constitutional foundations and the cohesion and viability of the political communities creating the state. Czechoslovakia, a state with a genuine democratic tradition, disappeared from the political map of Europe after more than seventy-four years of existence because its political representatives were unsuccessful in finding any other solution to the question of Czech-Slovak relations, which surprisingly emerged as the first problem of the Czechoslovak transition.

How can the differences among various examples of fragmentation be explained? Why was the Czechoslovak "divorce" so smooth and peaceful while the dismemberment of Yugoslavia resulted in a bloody war and ethnic conflict, the solution of which now seems to be extremely difficult if not impossible? Is it because of the different cultural legacies, the different histories, the different national mentalities and habits of Central European and Balkan nations? Has geopolitics played the decisive role here?

There is no doubt that it is nationalism, or ethnonationalism, that first should be discussed—and eventually blamed—for the horrors of the "low intensity wars", "ethnic cleansing" and "crimes against humanity" that occurred after the stable bipolar system in Europe collapsed and the newly liberated societies again began to address their statehood. Nevertheless, it must be clearly noted that there is much more here, and maybe something else at stake, than the reemergence of ethnicity that was suppressed by communist ideology and kept in a "frozen" state during the four decades of the cold war. New nationalists do not operate in a vacuum, and the reason why they were able to begin implementing—and eventually to succeed with—their plans must also be sought in the external dimensions of the problems of state transition and state-building: in the European situation after the collapse of communism, in the context of dominant European political projects and endeavors, in the general habits and practices of the European "*realpolitik*".

Should we not admit that the "mismanaged" state transition of Yugoslavia proved also that there is something wrong and obsolete not only with Yugoslavs, but also with the very foundations of European liberal order? Has not the Yugoslav tragedy problematized the very principles of European international law and politics? Does Europe still believe the old and honorable maxims according to which the transition of statehood is an event outside the realm of legal regulation?

States, as European jurisprudence believed at the beginning of this century, can neither "set laws for their own origin, because they must come into existence first in order to be able to create the law",[17] nor can they legislate their own termination. And international law, when the matter at stake is state sovereignty, also leaves us without guiding rules; it can only confirm what already exists and thus cannot be used at the moment of "legal revolution".[18] Since the domestic legal order is, strictly speaking, momentarily nonexistent, the legal force of the international community comes only *post festum* (a new state must be recognized by the other members of international community).[19]

Why then are we so surprised when observing the behavior of new posttotalitarian states and pseudostates as they pursue their "national interests"? Is it not, after all, in full agreement with the leading and generally recognized paradigms of international relations and interstate systems theory that violence and the use of force are consistent with the nature of the modern nation-state? And that they are always present, at least as a threat, as long as the state exists, and that this state "power" must be clearly recognizable and already active at the moment of its origin? Whether they are being born into or are on their way out of history, states are always tempted to use violence against the individuals who cannot be anything but stateless at the moment of state transition. We have been told not only by current warmongers, but also by all European realists that states simply protect their basic or vital "national interests" such as their right to exist and survive. So is it not then obvious that, first and foremost, "national interest" includes control over "ethnically cleansed" state territory? And is it not exactly such control that is considered by the international community to be the only condition *sine qua non* for international recognition?

Observing the horrors of the ongoing "low intensity wars" that erupted as a result of the collapse of the rigid, bipolar, cold war architecture in Europe, one has to conclude that there is something wrong not only with those posttotalitarian leaders who in their lust for power awakened the ghosts of nationalism, but also with European politics in general. The outbursts of transitional violence in the Balkans, Transcaucasus, and elsewhere are not only damaging these particular regions, but are undermining at the same time the very foundations of the European liberal political order. "The Yugoslav virus" not only caused the deaths of thousands of innocent people hit by the "epidemic" in these territories, but is also effective outside the killing zone. It demonstrates the inability of Europeans to act in concert towards these problems; it reveals not only how inefficient the existing institutions and mechanisms are when confronted with such crises, but also how precarious and uncertain the concepts and ideas are that are supposed to give us a clear and undistorted picture of such situations and make us capable of understanding them.

To sum up the task with which all those involved in European affairs have been charged vis-a-vis the Yugoslav experience, I can quote from an article published in 1996 by Zoran Pajič, the leading Bosnian expert in international law:

> "It is common knowledge today that the war in Yugoslavia, and in Bosnia Hercegovina in particular, has been a test of the credibility and future durability of the idea of 'European unity', as well as a test of the Organization for Security and Cooperation in Europe (OSCE) and of NATO. The two major world political organizations, the UN and the EU, have been exposed by and involved in the Yugoslav crisis from the very beginning, and their record has been controversial, to say the least. In order to be able to re-cover and re-habilitate itself after the Yugoslav experience, the world community will have to evaluate its policy and address a couple of very direct questions: 'why' and 'when' this case went so terribly wrong, and 'what' should be done in the future to 'save' the world from another 'ethnically cleansed peace process.'"[20]

The questions raised by Zoran Pajič in the middle of the enormous tragedy that befell Yugoslavia in the 1990s—a multiethnic state that had a "socialistic" government, but managed to do exceptionally well during the cold war period—and brought enormous suffering to all its nations seem to be of crucial importance indeed for our efforts to examine the lessons of the past decade, and I will return to them in the last part of this paper.

IV.

I take the starting point of the third phase of the transition process to be the Brussels summit of NATO in January 1994. I will focus on its European security debate as the dominant theme. What made this summit a particularly historic event is that the first decisive steps were taken leading to a profound change in NATO that brought us into a completely new, largely unexpected situation at the end of the 1990s. What was at stake is clear: the key defense organization of the West, created in spring 1949 (that is, in the initial stages of the cold war), which divided Europe for more than four decades, was to be transformed into an institution that under the new circumstances was capable not only of fulfilling the traditional tasks of collective defense, but also of meeting the new challenges connected with the possible need for "new missions". Of course, the London summit of NATO in June 1990 sent the first signal to its former enemies and offered them the possibility to "establish diplomatic liaisons" with the headquarters of the organization in Brussels. And since then, every NATO summit has advanced the security debate and approved the next step toward gradual rapprochement. One could say that practically all NATO's activities in the 1990s recognized the fact that the division of Europe was over and that one day NATO would have to go "out of area" if it did not want to end up going, as U.S. Senator Richard Luger once put it, "out of business".

Nevertheless, the January 1994 meeting in Brussels was a turning point: after difficult debate, which was initiated in fall 1993, it was decided that the postcommunist states of Europe would be invited to negotiate with NATO separately and to create a mutually acceptable program package called "Partnership for Peace". The result of the Brussels summit clearly shows how sensitive and even explosive this debated theme turned out to be and how much the security situation had changed since 1989. The lessons to be drawn from it can be summarized in two points:

1. The more the "post-totalitarians" returned to Europe, the more Europe itself returned to the tradition of *realpolitik*. The farther we were from the miraculous year of 1989, when the principles of open politics were rediscovered in Europe and solemnly restated as the firm foundations of any European political architecture of the future, the more often the word "interest" was heard in the domain of European international politics.

2. It is then not at all surprising that under these circumstances the most sensitive and the most important security question concerned the future

role of Russia. With Gorbachev's Soviet Union gone and with Yeltsin's Russia trying hard to gain recognition as one of the key players in the European political arena, an old problem reemerged in a new robe: Where does Europe end and where actually is the place of the largest country on the Eurasian continent in the present historical constellation? Gorbachev strongly believed in the idea of a "common European house". But times changed, and under Yeltsin's leadership Russian foreign policy experts elaborated an entirely new concept articulating basic Russian security (or national) interests, a concept that was unpleasantly reminiscent of the old Yalta language of "zones of influence", the "near abroad".

There is not enough space here to go into the details of the process that ended in spring 1999 with the first wave of NATO expansion or to follow step-by-step the evolution of all the clashes and interactions of that round of the security debate. What is remarkable, however, when one reads again various texts and documents that were prepared along the path leading to this decision, is the shift in European perception of the international situation and, as I have mentioned, the changes in language. On the one hand, the *Study on NATO Enlargement* published in September 1995[21] once more confirmed the basic creed of the political process after 1989: "With the end of the Cold War, there is a unique opportunity to build an improved security architecture in the whole of the Euro-Atlantic area. The aim of an improved security architecture is to provide increased stability and security for all in the Euro-Atlantic area without recreating dividing lines".[22]

To achieve this goal the principles of the Charter of the United Nations are recalled and a broad concept of security (embracing political and economic as well as defense components) is referred to again and again. What is to be erected is a new security architecture that must be built through a gradual process of integration and cooperation.[23] On the other hand, however, the text clearly reflects that the time of original unity is over and that the most important condition for the success of the principles preached in the post-cold war is due respect for "legitimate" security interests: "NATO-Russia relations should reflect Russia's significance in European security and be based on reciprocity, mutual respect and confidence, not 'surprise' decisions by either side which could affect the interests of the other. This relationship can only flourish if it is rooted in strict compliance with international commitments and obligations…and full respect for the sovereignty of other independent states. NATO decisions, however, cannot be subject to any veto or *droit de regard* by a non-member state, nor can the Alliance be subordinated to another European security institution".[24]

The security debate, which brought us first from Brussels to Madrid (where the Czech Republic, Hungary, and Poland were invited to join NATO) and then from Madrid to Washington (where a jubilee summit honoring the fiftieth birthday of NATO was supposed to accept the first wave of NATO expansion to the East, but then was overwhelmed unexpectedly by difficult agendas connected with the Kosovo crisis), is indeed illuminating. The "open door policy" of NATO and the scope and content of its "new missions", the new security architecture as an interplay of existing multilateral institutions, certainly will remain on the European political agenda for years to come. Nevertheless, one can say with certainty after Kosovo that the process of transition will continue in a radically new environment, because with the military action of NATO forces against Yugoslavia the world has changed again, and this change makes us aware—through all the difficult and often painful questions that the Kosovo crisis generated—that the game is not yet over and that we are confronted not only with the evil forces of the past (such as the ghosts of the Balkans, for instance), but also with other and possibly even more powerful demons—those which guard the gate to the yet unknown future.

There is one more aspect connected with the third phase of the process of transition that is worth mentioning. The experience of the populaces of the postcommunist countries with processes of democratization and economic reform has been silently accumulating for a couple of years. Originally, people were ready to discipline themselves, even to make sacrifices, to accept the fact that what followed after the collapse of communism would be a passage through the "valley of blood, sweat, and tears". At a certain moment, however—and I believe that this moment came around 1994—the atmosphere changed, and the posttotalitarian political experience itself became a more and more important factor in posttotalitarian politics. This experience obviously differs from country to country. Of course, there are some success stories, but there are also many failures. Those falling into the former category, as a rule, are benefiting from the positive effect of a "virtuous circle". Those falling into the latter, on the contrary, are finding themselves in a "vicious circle" and are trying hard to avoid their marginalization.

Stories from Russia are the most threatening in this context, and it is quite sad—but absurdly funny at the same time—to read what Stephen Holmes, a sarcastic American author who is one of the wittiest observers of the Russian transition, had to say about the mental disposition of ordinary people in order to understand what is going on in this time of transition.

"Finally, one of the most important but unappreciated shock absorbers has been Marxism itself. Luckily, the inhabitants of postcommunist countries were not mentally debilitated by Chicago economics, which does not have a single word to say about how capitalism begins. Instead they were blessed with schoolboy Marxism, which teaches, as a law of history, that capitalism begins with unjust seizures, slave-labor and brutal exploitation. The only people who are deeply shocked by (rather than merely angry or disgusted at) the profiteers and swindlers, conmen and shysters, robber-baron capitalists and ruthless pirates, are the American peace corps workers, who had never before heard wealth equated with theft. (The average Russian may not be able to define 'primitive accumulation', but he or she understands the general idea.) As everyone knows, Marx never explained in any detail how communist society was to be organized. But he did give a vivid and believable description of Manchester capitalism without rules. For the first time, therefore, the inhabitants of Russian and Eastern Europe can be actors in a Marxist play. For the first time they can be Marxists."[25]

Of course, not all cases of transition would lead us to these largely cynical, yet apt, observations, but it seems to me that both successes and failures, despite the different effects they obviously have on the populace, have something in common. In the third part of this paper, I mentioned the Czech Republic as an example of a postcommunist country that is doing reasonably well and is benefiting from the advantages connected with being a part of the "virtuous circle". It must be noted here that the third phase of transition also brought the moment of truth for this country and that its actual situation—both political and economic—is far from being satisfactory. What actually happened with us in the past decade requires very substantive reflection and genuine soul-searching.

Is it not true that the main problem all postcommunist countries have in common and are struggling with, regardless of their successes or failures, is openness, lack of precedent, and radical novelty of this situation? Is it not so that the most difficult aspect of transition is the fact that there are no models, no examples, no "old, well-tested ideas" to be used as credible guides to the "brave new world" of the twenty-first century? What should be done with the posttotalitarian political experience that has accumulated in the past ten years? What kind of "shock absorbers" consistent with the posttotalitarian perceptions of political reality ten years after—especially for those who for various reasons have become not winners, but rather victims and outsiders of the postcommunist transitions—can be recommended, if we still want to believe in Dahrendorfian liberalism and its ideals of the "open society"? In the last part of my paper, I would like to sum up my *tour d'horizon* through the political landscape of postcommunism and to answer at least some of the questions I have raised.

V.

I want to depart from the insight of Gabriel Andreescu, a Romanian scholar who already at the beginning of the 1990s drew attention to the problem of postcommunist "epistemological chaos",[26] to that peculiar state of mind that is in a way a decisive factor in the politics of transition. What at the beginning was perceived as a problem that should be solved by organizing education in western liberal democracy at all possible levels for the posttotalitarians, by teaching them how to behave in the Europe they were trying "to return to", turned out to be a more difficult and not easily resolvable question. As a matter of fact, the situation ten years later has not improved in many respects, but rather the opposite. "The epistemological chaos" is not contained any more in the postcommunist region, and in different forms it influences European and world politics in general.

In 1990 we were told repeatedly by prominent western observers of the events in East Central Europe that there was nothing particularly original in the revolutions of 1989: "With all the fuss and noise, not a single new idea has come out of Eastern Europe in 1989".[27] What happened here and what was greeted with great enthusiasm and joy was understood as a liberation, as a restoration of an already known and existing western liberal order. "The ideas whose time has come are old, familiar, well-tested ones. (It is the new ideas whose time has passed.)"[28]

In 1999, however, the overall picture of East Central Europe is definitely less rosy than it was ten years ago, and the role played by all these "old well-tested ideas" is not at all unequivocal and entirely unproblematic. Should we perceive the political processes in the postcommunist countries only as more or less successful "transitions to democracy?" Or is there much more at stake here; should not only the "westernization" of the East but also other transitions be taken into consideration? Should the collapse of communism be understood as the victory of the "old" western world over the hubris of utopias and the totalitarian deformation of "well-tested" European political traditions? Or should we see here at the same time the crucial moment in the historical process that started at the beginning of the twentieth century, the consequence of which is that both politically and spiritually, Europe lost its—until then—undisputed and indisputably dominant position in the world? Is the process going on in Europe after the collapse of communism a mere homecoming of "posttotalitarians" from their Babylonian captivity to the nice, prosperous, and safe haven of the West? Or is the current rapprochement of East and West in Europe taking place at a moment of profound crisis in European civilization, and Europeans cannot go, as they might like to, "back to the future" but find themselves in an entirely new, unprecedented, and thus unknown situation? Is it really "old, familiar, well-tested ideas" whose time has come? Is it not that, in the end, what is at the heart of our posttotalitarian problem is the lack of new ones?

What I am saying is simple: The collapse of communism could not lead to restoration and/or expansion of good old liberal European order, because this event has not only liberated East Central Europeans but also has changed irreversibly Europe's political identity. With all due respect for the venerable traditions of modern European liberalism, it is essential for our discussion to see the limitations of the liberal paradigm—to understand not only the similarities but also the differences between Europe before and after the ruinous attack on its identity by totalitarian ideologies.

The international system emerging after the disintegration of bipolar, cold war architecture is more open, more interdependent, and definitely less "Eurocentric". Multiculturalism, multiple identities, and antifoundationalism are not only fashionable themes in academic discourse today, but also create the context of current international politics. There is no doubt, however, that the "grand opening" of the postmodern market of ideas does not necessarily generate more political freedom and improved communication among nations. On the contrary, the result is the possibility of the emergence of new, culturally motivated conflicts, the possibility that humankind, after it got rid of totalitarian ideologies, may be heading into an era of the "clash of civilizations".[29]

The victory of old well-tested liberal ideas in the ideological conflict fueling the cold war cannot change the fact of the endemic "deficiency" of modern European civilization—the fact that modern liberalism, as one of its most important products, finds itself in deep crisis in the twentieth century. The ever more complex network of communication connecting nonstate actors across national boundaries makes it increasingly impossible for national governments to exert decisive control over the growing number of important political issues and curtails the possibilities of traditional liberal politics. The process by which vital decisions are made often remains entirely opaque to most ordinary citizens; it is not discussed, not understood, not present in the public domain. There is an increasing sense of insecurity and powerlessness among populaces. What can be observed practically everywhere in the West is an increasing democratic deficit. The whole game of politics becomes increasingly distant from the lives of ordinary citizens and has begun, as some commentators observe, to acquire a bogus air and a sense of a kind of "virtual reality".

Globalization and complex interdependence, the most important characteristics of the situation of humankind at the end of the twentieth century, not only have changed the very nature of world politics but also have introduced its negative, hidden agendas. International crime generating enormous amounts of money to be used to infiltrate and corrupt political elites; the growing vulnerability of populaces to extremist views, stressing nationalist and antiforeigner rhetoric of the most disreputable kind; the disintegration of basic social patterns and structures, that is, the "coming anarchy"[30]—these and other phenomena represent the dark side of our postmodern, increasingly globalized situation.

In his above-mentioned, seminal work on the recent wave of European revolutions, Dahrendorf advised postcommunist politicians "to go back to the 1780s, to the lessons of the great transformations of that time" and to use *The Federalist Papers* as an "unsurpassed manual of liberal democracy".[31] "The biggest threat to democracy in the times of transition and of disordered society, warned James Madison, is weak government. The key question is what 'republican remedies' can be used to make the government stronger; how the emerging open societies can be stabilized and protected not only against the forces of the 'ancient regime', but also against those new politicians who pretend to be the speakers of the people but in reality serve their own self-interest and seek to 'aggrandize themselves by the confusion of their country'."[32]

However, what kind of remedies can be recommended if we want to cope not only with the question of transforming a closed political regime and building a republican form of government but also with the problem of the newly emerging international system and new world order? There are two aspects in the dramatically changing realm of international relations that were underestimated in the *realpolitik* of the past and now should be taken into consideration much more seriously. First is the internationalization of human rights. The emergence of international mechanisms for their protection as a reaction to the unprecedented crimes committed by totalitarian regimes during World War II represents probably the most important change in world politics in the second half of the twentieth century. The demise of the bipolar system in Europe only accelerated and strengthened this development. The issue of human rights has now lost the dimension of ideological confrontation. The existence of international human rights law—which deals with the protection of individuals and groups against violations of their rights by state governments—has an ever increasing impact on the formation, self-perception, and practices of the international community. Respect for international legal norms, active participation in their creation, and involvement in the dialogue in which today's understanding of human rights is formed and codified become essential conditions for participation and interaction of nation-states with supranational structures, for the creation of a truly transnational human community.

A second aspect which has been seriously underestimated and underrepresented in international politics of the past is the phenomenon of transnational civil society—the fact that international society ceased to be limited by the societies of nation-states over the course of the twentieth century but now is also populated, as I mentioned above, by many nonstate actors. All efforts to cope with the tasks that transcend the limited, closed space of the territorial nation state—be they the various problems that require "global governance" or questions regarding regional arrangements and "integrative" frameworks—cannot be successful without active participation of the civic element. What is now at stake and is urgently needed—and all the conflicts we have seen emerging in the postcommunist world demonstrate this more than clearly—is a profound "democratization" of international relations. The political architecture to be designed and created after the stable bipolar system of the cold war disappeared cannot be invented by some "wise" post-cold war architects and imposed "from above". The new world order can be formed only when all activities "from above" are complemented "from below", all international institutions, mechanisms, arrangements, regimes can be successful and effective only when they are democratic—when they are open to all information, instigation, impulses, and initiatives coming from the grass-roots level, when they permanently act and make decisions while communicating with their international constituency. The current situation in Europe, the discussions surrounding the future European political architecture, namely, the enlargement debate of NATO and the European Union, more than clearly prove this point. Maybe the threat that is bigger to the current Europe than any external enemy is the frustration and the feeling of helplessness generated by the fact that no matter how skillful "professional" Euro-politicians and Euro-bureaucrats are, the Euro-debate monopolized by them could easily result in a dead end. If this were the case, what kind of future could our "old" continent expect?

One does not need to be Cassandra to predict that some scenarios might be quite murky or even catastrophic. If Europeans still believe that "universalistic" European civilization is worthy of preservation in the age of multiculturalism and globalization, they themselves have to have the courage to overcome the shadows of the past, to enhance and actively promote politics based on transnational communication. Because nothing else but open dialogue can be recommended as the best—and maybe the only possible—"republican remedy" in the sense of the Federalists, can make "global governance" stronger and keep that element of freedom, which is still the essence and real nature of our humanity, in emerging world politics.

Notes

1 The parable of Franz Kafka, used by Hannah Arendt in the preface to *Between Past and Future: Eight Exercises in Political Thought*, Hannah Arendt (Penguin Books, 1996), 7.

2 Václav Havel (address to Joint Session of U.S. Congress, Washington, D.C., February 1990), 43.

3 *Charter of Paris for a New Europe: A New Era of Democracy, Peace and Unity* (adopted by the Conference on Security and Cooperation in Europe on 21 November 1990), par. 2. Quoted in *Twenty-five Human Rights Documents* (New York: Center for the Study of Human Rights, Columbia University, 1994), 210.

4 Ralf Dahrendorf, *Reflections on the Revolution in Europe in a Letter Intended to Have Been Sent to A Gentleman in Warsaw* (Times Books, Random House, 1990), 4.

5 "Reflections on the French Revolution", *Selected Works of Edmund Burke* Vol. I (London: Methuen & Co.,1905), 14.

6 Hannah Arendt, "What is Authority", in *Between Past and Future: Six Exercises in Political Thought* (New York: The Viking Press, 1961), 140.

7 Dahrendorf, *Reflections on the Revolution in Europe*, 62.

8 Dahrendorf, *Reflections on the Revolution in Europe*, 35.

9 "The formal process of constitutional reform takes at least six months" (Dahrendorf, *Reflections on the Revolution in Europe*, 99).

10 "A general sense that things are looking up as a result of economic reform is unlikely to spread before six years has passed" (Dahrendorf, *Reflections on the Revolution in Europe*, 99–100).

11 Dahrendorf, *Reflections on the Revolution in Europe*, 100.

12 Dahrendorf, *Reflections on the Revolution in Europe*, 10–11.

13 Zdeník Kavan and Martin Palouš, "Democracy in the Czech Republic", in *Democratization in Central and Eastern Europe*, eds. Mary Kaldor and Ivan Vejvoda (London and New York: Pinter, 1999), 78.

14 Kavan and Palouš, "Democracy in the Czech Republic", 78–92.

15 Valerie Bunce, "Leaving Socialism: A 'Transition to Democracy'", *Contention*, 3:1 (Fall 1993): 35–42.

16 These processes might be puzzling in many ways and offer to political scientists a unique opportunity to rethink and reexamine their concepts and theories. The fact that Czechoslovakia, a state with a genuine democratic tradition, disappeared from the political map of Europe due to the collapse of communism is in a way paradoxical. The most important issue to be solved after the "dark ages" of totalitarianism turned out to be the question of relations between Czechs and Slovaks and not the agenda prescribed to the "post-totalitarians" by Ralf Dahrendorf. The cases of Yugoslavia

and the Soviet Union are, as I mentioned, different, but raise similar questions nevertheless.

17 J. Jellinek, *Všeobecná státoveda* (State Theory) (Praha: 1906), 208.

18 "Legal revolution" is a concept introduced by the "normative" school of Hans Kelsen. According to normativists, the legal order is equal to a set of legal norms derived from one "focal point", from one supreme norm that represents the genuine source of law. In the normativist paradigm one can clearly distinguish between the continuity of law—which persists as long as a certain focal norm (usually the constitution of a state) remains valid—and the discontinuity of law—which occurs when, due to the "legal revolution", it is replaced by the new one.

19 Strictly speaking, there is only one prerequisite generally accepted for international recognition: a state must exist—that is, have a certain territory with a certain population under the control of a government. Obviously there may be other requirements of the international community, but the principal question always remains—their practical enforcement. The European Union formulated these conditions for the recognition of new states in the context of the disintegration of Yugoslavia: the obligation to respect all provisions of the United Nations Charter, of the Final Act of the Helsinki Conference, of the Paris Charter; the obligation to respect human rights, including the rights of minorities and ethnic groups; the obligation to respect the inviolability of borders and the possibility of changing them only through peaceful negotiations; assuming all obligations in the sphere of disarmament and nonproliferation of nuclear weapons; assuming the obligation to resolve all questions of legal succession by the means of mutual agreement and arbitration.

20 Zoran Pajić, "Where Do We Go from Here?" in "Reflections on the State of Europe from the Perspective of Civil Society", *Quarterly* 17 (Summer 1996), 33.

21 *The Study on NATO Enlargement* (n.p.: September 1995).

22 *The Study on NATO Enlargement.*

23 *The Study on NATO Enlargement.*

24 *The Study on NATO Enlargement.*

25 Stephen Holmes, "Cultural Legacies or State Collapse", *Public Lectures* (Collegium Budapest, Institute for Advanced Study) 13 (November 1995), 25.

26 Gabriel Andreescu, "Violence and Transition Period" (paper submitted at the Prague Conference of the Helsinki Citizen Assembly, Spring 1992)

27 French historian Francois Furet, quoted by Dahrendorf, *Reflections on the Revolution in Europe*, 27.

28 English scholar Timothy Garton Ash, quoted by Dahrendorf, *Reflections on the Revolution in Europe*, 28.

29 Samuel P. Huntington *The Clash of Civilizations and the Remaking of World Order* (New York: Simon and Schuster, 1996).

30 Robert D. Kaplan, "The Coming Anarchy", *Atlantic Monthly* (February 1994), 44–76.

31 Dahrendorf, *Reflections on the Revolution in Europe*, 30.

32 First letter of Alexander Hamilton, *The Federalist Papers.*

8 Postsocialisms

VALERIE BUNCE

Introduction[1]

The purpose of this chapter is to survey the economic and political landscape of postsocialism, to account for the variable political-economic
trajectories of East-Central Europe and the former Soviet Union, and to
use these observations in order to address some larger questions in the
study of regime transition.

We can begin our survey by noting that there were several reasons to
expect similarities among the postsocialist countries. One was the seeming homogeneity of the socialist experience. This was a system, after all,
that was remarkably alike in its form and functioning, whether in the
Soviet Union or Eastern Europe. Indeed, the structural similarity of these
regimes was one reason why they all collapsed (albeit in varying degrees)—and did so at virtually the same time.[2]

Specialists on the region and on comparative democratization and
comparative economic liberalization have been engaged in a spirited debate about both the content and the importance of historical legacies for
regime transition and consolidation. While some have taken the position
that the past is less important than, say, more proximate factors, such as
the mode of transition and where these regimes are heading (as opposed
to where they have been),[3] none of these arguments challenge one essential point: State socialism presents perhaps the strongest case we have for
the power of the past. This is because the political-economic system was
a distinctive form of dictatorship, unusually invasive and regionally en-
cased. Moreover, it was long in place and was the heir to a well-
established authoritarian tradition (excepting interwar Czechoslovakia
and the abortive and even briefer experiences with quasi-democratic
forms of government elsewhere in East-Central Europe during the
1920s). Thus, if we give any credence to historical institutionalism, with
its emphasis on the power of the past in narrowing the range of alterna-

tive futures, then the commonalities of socialism and the timing of its end at the least should have constrained the range of possible postsocialist pathways.

The second reason to have anticipated little variance in postsocialist developments is more proximate to regime transition. It was not just that these regimes ended at roughly the same time; it was also that the larger world into which the successor regimes entered was remarkably consensual in its ideological messages. By the close of the 1980s, liberalism in politics and economics had become the hegemonic standard; few incentives and, thus, opportunities were available to countries to embark on other paths of development; and the international order, because of unprecedented consensus and the resources of international institutions, had become a very powerful influence on domestic developments. This would seem to have been unusually the case, moreover, where regimes were new, economies shattered, and states weak—as throughout the postcommunist world (and, for that matter, Africa).

Thus, the homogeneity of the socialist past and the homogeneity of the global political economy both pointed to the same prediction: the postsocialist regimes would resemble one another in form and functioning. However, the *content* of that resemblance was another issue, depending upon the emphasis placed on the regional past versus the global present and the extent to which either determinant of outcomes was read as facilitating or undermining capitalism and democracy.[4] Thus, there were those for which the scenario for postsocialism was gloomy, with images of disarray, despair, and despots, as the "civilizations" of liberalism and state socialism clashed with each other. However, the picture that emerged in other investigations was a rosy one. Here, the argument was either that certain elements of the socialist past were helpful to a liberal outcome or that the socialist past, while illiberal, was replaced decisively by a new order defined and defended by democrats and capitalists. In either event, Eastern Europe, it was assumed, was well positioned to join the West.

The Reality of Diversity

It has now been ten years since the collapse of socialism began in East-Central Europe. There have been, to be sure, certain commonalities among the postsocialist states. These include, for example, the distinctive socioeconomic profile of these states when compared with other countries at the same level of economic development (for example, unusually high rates of literacy and urbanization, along with an unusually egalitarian distribution of income, even some years into the transformation); the enormous economic costs of the transition to capitalism; continuing difficulties associated with the privatization of large state enterprises; considerable corruption accompanying the establishment of new forms of property and property relations (even, recently, in the Czech Republic, a country that was widely thought to be "deviant" in this respect); rising crime rates; slow crystallization of party systems;[5] substantial public dissatisfaction with the performance of political leaders and the newly created political and economic institutions; limitations in—if not the absence in some cases of—the rule of law (including a legal framework for economic activity);[6] and a working class that is weak, disorganized, and dispirited.[7]

These rough similarities aside, however, the dominant pattern of postsocialism has been one of *variation*, not uniformity. To take some economic extremes as illustrative: the ratio of the labor force in agriculture is fifty-five percent in Albania and five percent in Slovenia; Slovenia's income per capita is seventeen times that of Azerbaijan; Poland's gross domestic product (GDP) in 1997 was eleven percent larger than what it had been in 1989 (which was the strongest performance in the region), whereas the Georgian and Bosnian GDPs in 1997 were only slightly over one-third of their 1989 size; and foreign direct investment in postsocialist Hungary accounts for nearly one-third of all such investment in a region composed of twenty-six states.[8] On the political side (which is less easy to summarize with numbers), we can offer the following examples. Only five of the states in the region existed in their present form during the socialist era (Albania, Bulgaria, Hungary, Poland, and Romania); another three were states during the interwar period, but not during the cold war era (Estonia, Latvia, and Lithuania); and the remaining nineteen are new formations (though some of these, such as Serbia, have historical claims to independent statehood).

If we shift our attention from states to regimes, we see that the twenty-seven new regimes in the region represent the full spectrum of political possibilities. On one axis, we can compare regime form, where the range extends from fully democratic to partially democratic to largely authoritarian to fully authoritarian orders. On the other axis, we can look at the variance in "regimeness", or the degree to which there is a single regime in place with full institutional expression, settled borders, common identities, and public and elite compliance. Here, for instance, the contrast runs from Hungary, where neither the state nor the regime is in question, to Bosnia, where both are today subjects of considerable contestation.[9]

The postsocialist experience, therefore, has been one of significant economic and political variety. Indeed, this region seems to be a microcosm of the world, though a large one, since this area represents more than one-fifth of the world's land mass and about one-sixth of its states.

How diverse is postsocialism? What explains the variable political and economic paths the regimes in the region have taken? It is to these questions that I now turn. I will begin with the economic side of the equation.

Economic Variability

In Tables 8.1–3, I present some economic data that provide a comparative overview of postsocialist developments. The picture that emerges is, of course, one of remarkable diversity in such areas as level of development, size of the agricultural labor force, economic growth, income distribution, and implementation of economic reforms (or the size of the private sector in the economy and a combined measure that includes this along with liberalization of markets, foreign trade, and domestic prices).

A closer look at these tables (supplemented by some other data) reveals some important patterns. First, there is the disastrous economic performance of postsocialism, particularly in the early years. For example, the region's economies declined by an average of 7.6 percent from 1990 to 1992; the average economic "growth" of the region from 1989 to 1998 was −1.0 percent (a figure that would be even lower if we were to include very rough estimates of the Bosnian and Serbian-Montenegrin economies and, most recently, the impact of the current Russian economic crisis); it was only in 1997 that this postsocialist region first registered any economic growth (a whopping 1.4 percent); and only two countries in the region—Poland and Slovenia—managed to register actual growth in real GDP from 1989 to (projected) 1998.

These trends are all the more striking once we place them in a larger context. Here, it is useful to note the following. First, the economic decline of the region in the first five or so years of postsocialism was greater than that registered by economies during the Great Depression.[10] Second, if we take comparable years and comparable measures (or average annual GDP growth, 1990–1995, as measured by the World Bank), the economic growth rates for southern Europe (Greece, Portugal, Spain) and Latin America—two other regions undergoing democratization and economic reforms—were approximately three times as high as those registered for the postsocialist countries.[11] At the same time, the variance in postsocialist economic performance—or the contrast between 2.4 percent for Poland and –26.9 percent for Georgia—is far greater than that for Latin America—or the spread between 6.1 percent for Chile and –5.4 percent for Nicaragua.[12]

Table 8.1 Economic Development and Economic Growth

	GNP p/c (1995)	% of Labor Force in Agric.	Annual Rate of GDP Growth (1990–1997)	GDP Index 1997 (1989=100)	Growth in Real GDP, 1998	Proj. GDP, 1998 (1989=100)
Albania	670	55	–2.1	79.1	12	89
Armenia	730	17	–8.1	41.1	6	41
Azerbaijan	480	31	–10.1	40.5	7	43
Belarus	2070	20	–4.0	70.8	2	72
Bosnia	765	na	na	na	na	na
Bulgaria	1830	14	–5.5	62.8	4.5	66
Croatia	3250	15	–3.4	73.3	5	76
Czech Republic	3870	11	–0.4	95.8	2	99
Estonia	2860	14	–2.8	77.9	5	82
Georgia	440	26	–10.6	34.3	10	38
Hungary	4120	15	–1.1	90.4	4.3	94
Kazakhstan	1330	22	–6.3	58.1	2.5	59
Kyrgyzstan	700	32	–5.8	58.7	5.9	68
Latvia	2270	16	–5.8	56.8	5	58
Lithuania	1900	18	–8.9	42.8	5.5	45
Macedonia	860	22	–6.9	55.3	5	58
Moldova	920	33	–11.4	35.1	1	34
Poland	2790	27	1.6	111.8	5	117
Romania	1480	24	–2.2	82.4	–3	82
Russia	2240	14	–7.7	52.2	1.5	58
Slovakia	2950	12	–0.3	95.6	3	98
Slovenia	8200	5	0	99.3	4	103
Tajikistan	340	na	–10.3	40.0	4.4	39
Turkmenistan	920	na	–9.8	42.6	13.5	47
Ukraine	1630	20	–11.1	38.3	0	37
Uzbekistan	970	34	–1.7	86.7	2.0	89
Average	2111	21.6	–5.3	64.8	4.45	67.6

Sources: The World Bank, *World Development Report: The State in a Changing World* (Oxford: Oxford University Press, 1997), 214–215, 220–221; Grzegorz Kolodko, "Equity Issues in Policy-Making in Transition Economies" (Paper presented at the Conference on Economic Policy and Equity, 8-9 June 1998), 40; Martin Raiser and Peter Sanfrey, "Statistical Review" *Economics of Transition* 6:1 (1998), 248, 251. The figures for Bosnia, Tajikistan, and Turkmenistan are very rough estimates and may not be comparable to those for the other countries in this table.

Table 8.2 Economic Reform and Income Distribution

	Private Sector Share of GDP (1995)	Composite Economic Reform Score	Gini Coefficient, 1993–1995 (1987–1989)
Albania	60	6.7	na
Armenia	45	5.2	na
Azerbaijan	15	3.5	na
Belarus	45	3.0	28 (23)
Bulgaria	45	4.9	34 (23)
Croatia	70	6.7	na
Czech Republic	65	8.2	27 (19)
Estonia	65	7.7	35 (23)
Georgia	30	4.4	na
Hungary	60	7.5	23 (21)
Kazakhstan	25	4.1	33 (26)
Kyrgyzstan	40	6.1	55 (26)
Latvia	60	7.0	31 (23)
Lithuania	55	7.1	37 (23)
Macedonia	40	5.9	na
Moldova	30	4.9	36 (24)
Poland	60	7.4	28 (26)
Romania	40	5.5	29 (23)
Russia	55	6.4	48 (24)
Slovakia	60	7.3	19 (20)
Slovenia	45	6.2	25 (22)
Tajikistan	15	2.7	na
Turkmenistan	15	1.9	36 (26)
Ukraine	35	4.7	47 (23)
Uzbekistan	30	4.2	33 (28)
Average	42.6	5.5	33.5

Sources: Kolodko, "Equity Issues in Policy-Making", 18; M. Steven Fish, "The Determinents of Economic Reform in the Postcommunist World", *East European Politics and Societies* 12:1 (Winter 1998), 34; Nicholas Stern, "The Transition in Eastern Europe and the FSU: Some Strategic Lessons from the Experiences of 25 Countries in Six Years" (European Bank for Reconstruction and Development Working Paper, 18 April 1997), 19.

What I am suggesting, therefore, is that the new regimes in the post-socialist world are distinctive with respect to both their economic diversity and the overall severity of their recent economic downturns. However, this is not the only way in which postsocialism stands out. These countries are also unusual in three other respects, all of which testify, as did the costs of economic transformation, to the powerful impact of the socialist past. One is that the agrarian sector in these countries is very small, given the norm for all countries at a matching level of economic development. Another is that income distribution is (still) unusually equal, even when we allow for level of economic development.[13] Finally, there is the problem, unusually pronounced in the postsocialist context, of states that fail to provide a stable and predictable business environment. On the basis of a recent survey of local entrepreneurs in sixty-nine countries, the World Bank concluded that the Commonwealth of Independent States in particular stood out among the world's regions—i.e. East-Central Europe, Subsaharan Africa, Latin America and the Caribbean, the Middle East and Northern Africa, Southern and Southeastern Asia, and the countries of the Organization for Economic Cooperation and Development—in its failure to provide law and order, security of property rights, and predictability of both rule application and policy implementation (given, in particular, corruption, an unreliable judiciary, and unstable governments).[14]

Table 8.3 Annual Growth of Real GDP

	Entire Region	East-Central Europe and the Baltic States	Former Soviet Union (excluding Baltic States)
1990	−4.9	−6.8	−3.7
1991	−7.7	−10.6	−5.8
1992	−10.4	−4.2	−14.3
1993	−5.5	0.6	−9.3
1994	−7.1	3.4	−13.6
1995	−1.0	5.3	−4.9
1996	−1.2	4.2	−4.6
1997	1.4	3.2	0.4
1998	2.3	3.5	1.6

Sources: Raiser and Sanfrey, "Statistical Review", 251.

Tables 8.1–3 also illustrate several other characteristics of postsocialist variation. One is that there seem to be two distinct "regions" within the region. Thus, the economic profile of the former Soviet Union contrasts sharply with that of East-Central Europe, whether the focus is on adoption of economic reforms or on measures of economic performance. The Baltic states manage to bridge the two areas, given their relatively high economic reform scores, but their poor economic performance. Put simply, political leaders in the Soviet successor regimes have been less likely than their counterparts in East-Central Europe to introduce economic reforms, and the economies in the former Soviet Union have on the whole contracted far more sharply than the postsocialist economies to the West. The other and related consideration is temporal. While the recessionary effects of the economic transformation were undeniably large in the early years of postsocialism and, indeed, were of such magnitude that only one economy in the region managed to be larger in 1997 than it was in 1989, these effects seem to be, nonetheless, transitory in many instances.[15] Thus, for example, beginning in 1993, the East-Central European economies, when taken as a whole, began to grow, and they have continued to do so in subsequent years. While similar in overall pattern, however, economic performance over time in the former Soviet Union varies in its details. There, the economic downturn appeared later, and it has lasted a good deal longer. What seems to distinguish East-Central Europe (including the Baltic states) from the Soviet successor states, therefore, are three related factors: *whether* there was an economic reform, *how long* the economic slide lasted, and *when* the economy began to recover.[16]

Table 8.4 Economic Reform and Economic Performance

	Considerable to Moderate	Limited to None
	Albania	Armenia
	Croatia	Azerbaijan
	Czech Republic	Belarus
	Estonia	Bulgaria
	Hungary	Georgia
	Kyrgyzstan	Kazakhstan
	Latvia	Moldova
	Lithuania	Romania
	Macedonia	Tajikistan
	Poland	Turkmenistan
	Russia	Ukraine
	Slovakia	Uzbekistan
	Slovenia	
Average Reform Score	6.87	3.7
Average GNP p/c	$2542	$1189
Average Growth	−3.4	−7.6

Sources: See Tables 8.1 and 8.2.

Tables 8.1–3 also allow us to address in a limited way a question that has received considerable attention: the typicality of the Russian experience. On the one hand, Russia lies in many respects at the regional economic mean. For example, the Russian level of economic development is slightly above the regional average (or $2240 versus $2111),[17] as is the size of its urban sector; its economic reform score is slightly above average for the region as a whole, as is the private sector share of the economy; and its rate of economic growth is somewhat below the regional average for 1990–1997 (or –7.7 percent versus –5.3 percent). On these dimensions, therefore, Russia does not stand out as unusual. On the other hand, Russia does seem to be exceptional—at least by regional economic standards—in certain ways.[18] For example, the distribution of income in Russia, while typical of the region at the beginning of the transformation, is now unusually unequal (though more typical within the larger setting of countries at roughly the same level of economic development); foreign trade seems to play an unusually small role in the Russian economy; and Russia introduced economic reforms midstream, a rare example within the region.[19] The more common pattern in postsocialism has been to introduce significant reforms early (with a marked tendency for them to be sustained), to avoid such reforms, or to introduce piecemeal measures accompanied by significant and enduring political conflict.[20]

These three tables also illustrate some correlation among categories. In particular, there seems to be a modest relationship between level of economic development (as indicated by gross national product [GNP] per capita or, alternatively, by the size of the agricultural labor force) and economic reform score and a stronger correlation between economic reform score and economic performance. These correlations can be most easily seen once we group our countries into two categories: those with moderate to high economic reform scores (ranging from 5.9 to 8.2) and those with lower scores (from 1.5 to 5.5). Thus, as Table 4 indicates, the two groups present a clear contrast in terms of average GNP per capita, average size of the agricultural sector, and average growth. One should not, of course, read too much into these data—especially given recent changes in some of these cases with respect to economic performance and economic reform (as in, say, the Albanian case) and to the effects of choosing one cut-off point over another. However, at the very least we can observe that: (1) economic reform seems to have economic payoffs, especially following initial recessionary effects (which tend to be shorter in duration in reformed contexts); and (2) the more economically developed countries in the region seem to be more likely to implement economic reforms. A final conclusion is also warranted, especially in view of the differential capacity of these countries to attract foreign investment. Put simply: "them that has, gets".

Accounting for Economic Variability

Let us now shift our attention from description to explanation. Here, the key question involves identifying factors that seem to explain differences in economic reform scores among the postsocialist countries. In a recent and careful statistical study that takes a number of possible social, cultural, political, and economic factors into account (including some of the factors in Tables 8.1 and 8.2), Steve Fish has concluded that the single best predictor of economic reform in the postsocialist world appears to be the outcome of the first competitive election.[21] Put in more straightforward terms: Economic reforms were more likely to be introduced, implemented, and sustained if the former communists lost the initial election following the collapse of communist party hegemony. This seems to be the case, moreover, whatever the political orientation of the opposition and their constituency base, and if that opposition included former communists among its ranks. Here we can contrast, for example, three parties that were victorious in 1990 and that, after winning, introduced significant economic reforms: the Croatian Democratic Union, the Hungarian Democratic Forum, and the Czechoslovak Civic Forum/Public Against Violence. Where the former communists won the first postsocialist election, however, one of two patterns materialized: either economic reforms were introduced, but then were sabotaged (as in, say, Bulgaria), or they were never seriously considered or fully implemented (the dominant pattern represented in Belarus, Serbia-Montenegro, Ukraine, and much of Central Asia and the Transcaucasus). In the first instance, the former communists faced a highly competitive political environment and in the second, a less competitive one. Russia, of course, fits the first model, given its midstream and compromised economic reform and given the contrasting electoral outcomes for the parliament versus the presidency.

The statistical support for this argument is strong. However, the real trick is explaining the explanation. Put more directly: What is it about the outcome of the first election that affects economic reform? We could take the obvious route and argue that this is simply a question of interests and ideology. Thus, a liberal opposition with, by definition, no stake in the old order would prefer economic reform to the alternatives. When joined with an electoral mandate, desire for economic reforms was then combined with considerable capacity to carry through such reforms. And once the reforms were in place, they generated supporters that allowed the reforms to continue.[22] On the other hand, the former communists were illiberal, again by definition, and had vested interests in defending the old order. With an electoral mandate, they were able to combine resistance to such reforms with political power—though not usually at the level they once enjoyed, given a more competitive order and given often narrow or ambiguous electoral victories.

This argument is, however, problematic in several ways. One is that the liberal credentials of at least some of the victorious opposition forces are questionable.[23] At the very least, what was common to the winning oppositions was not a liberal ideology so much as an anticommunist project. This introduces an important consideration: whether we should see economic reform as a commitment to a liberal economy (though in many instances this was crucial) or, alternatively, as a powerful mechanism (one of several) to root out the old order. The latter interpretation makes more sense because it identifies a clear commonality among the politically successful opposition forces; it recognizes the diametrically opposed principles defining capitalism and socialism; it treats economic reforms, as a result, as a means of using the former to end the latter; and it resonates with the thrust of public opinion at the time when and in the places where these reforms were introduced.[24]

This interpretation is also superior because it helps account for some puzzling aspects of an exercise that plugs a classically economic interest argument into the postsocialist context: the absence of either classes or sectors with vested interests in a capitalist economy[25] and the obvious uncertainty of decision-makers regarding the benefits, political as well as economic, of embarking on the historically unprecedented transition from socialism to capitalism. Thus, just as there were few groups that could be confident about payoffs from the economic transition, so the economic and, therefore, political costs of such a transition, at least in the short-term, were unknown but logically high. Indeed, many of the very people who introduced these economic reforms were members of the Academy of Sciences—an overemployed and economically inefficient public sector that could expect to dwindle sharply in budgets (and, thus, in personnel) once economic reforms began to make their presence felt. What I am suggesting, therefore, is that the overarching commitment to either completing or forestalling the revolution begun in 1989 and the necessarily conjoined political and economic form of that commitment, rather than the economic interests of decision-makers and their political constituencies, seem to do a better job of making sense of this particular and peculiar context.

If we accept the argument that the core divide in the region was between those parties that had power and wanted to complete the revolution versus those parties that also had power but wanted to maintain the *ancien régime* (with a number of cases showing middling economic reforms and, not surprisingly, a rough balance between the two forces), then we are still left with some unanswered questions. One is why the opposition was so committed to destroying the socialist economy, even when that would seemingly entail considerable political costs, particularly in the short term—which is, after all, what democratic politics is usually about. I can suggest two factors that supported the rush to economic reform. One is the recent empirical record of capitalism versus socialism and the demonstrable success of both economic reforms and structural adjustment packages in other parts of the world (albeit often producing political turmoil in the process).[26] There was, in short, a widespread understanding that the preferable option, particularly in the medium and long run, was economic reform—an option that would generate in time both economic growth and political support.

The other is that the public in Hungary, Poland, then the Baltic states, Czechoslovakia, and Slovenia managed to express its support for ending socialism in two powerful ways. If the opposition did not digest this message when communist party hegemony ended (in many instances through widespread public protests), then they certainly must have done so when publics voted them into power. Thus, one could argue that where the opposition was victorious, it enjoyed not just a mandate to rule, but also an unusually clear message about what ruling should entail.[27] Both of these political assets encouraged decision-makers to introduce economic reforms while giving them the luxury of assuming—rare in democratic politics—that they had some political time to show economic results.

Thus, what mattered in these cases was that there was a national—and, indeed, nationalist[28]—consensus around policies such as economic reform that would root out socialism. This was also aided, of course, by the idealized understanding that the public in these states had of capitalism—an understanding that spoke of capitalist liberal democracy as the welcome and eagerly anticipated "other" of state socialism and that was reinforced by the underestimation (perhaps out of ignorance and perhaps for more self-serving reasons) of the costs of these reforms put forward by policy-makers and political activists.[29] In this sense, it was not so much economic interests as, I would argue, a variant of the *public interest* that produced these reforms and that rendered them politically tolerable as well. However, where such consensus was missing and where that translated into different kinds of electoral results, decisions about such reforms were influenced by the familiar considerations of self-interest. Just as the former communists favored a continuation of the old system in some form (or at least time to position themselves well in the event that a new order would evolve), so they quite rightly feared the economic and, therefore, political costs of moving in the other direction—with the political costs understood not just as the loss of their influence through privatization and deregulation of the economy, but also as political unrest. The understandable fear, therefore, was that economic reforms could very well undercut both their economic and political power—a process that was already underway as a consequence of the deregulation of their political hegemony.

This, then, leads to a final question: Why did the opposition forces win in a few cases and lose in most of them? Thus far, we have discussed economic reforms as a product of proximate influences—in particular, the interests, economic and political, and the resources, again economic and political, of the opposition versus the former communists. However, now we need to bring in the socialist past. It is not accidental (to borrow communist parlance for a moment) that the opposition won the first election in those countries where there had been sizeable, cross-class, and relatively consensual mass protests during the socialist era. These protests were sometimes considerable and sometimes only a few years prior to the end of communist party hegemony—contrasting here, for instance, Poland in 1956 and in 1980–1981, Hungary in 1956, Czechoslovakia in 1968, Croatia in 1971–1972, and Armenia in 1980 versus Slovenia from 1987 to 1991 and the Baltic states from 1988 to 1990. Moreover, these protests were sometimes directed solely at the regimes (as in the earlier Polish, Hungarian, and Czechoslovak cases, along with Czechoslovakia in 1989); primarily at the state (as in Croatia and Armenia); or at both (as with the Baltic and Slovenian cases, along with Czechoslovakia in 1968 and 1989). Whether focussed on the regime and/or the state and whether early or late in the evolution of state socialism, however, these protests, I would suggest, shared one characteristic. They created counterregimes- (and sometimes counterstates-) in-waiting. This meant that regime collapse could be quickly followed by new regime construction; that is, by a process wherein the old system was quickly and thoroughly deregulated, the opposition won the first elections handily, and the revolutionary momentum was continued through the introduction of thorough-going economic reforms.[30]

What I am suggesting, therefore, is that economic reforms were part of the revolutionary project, and that some countries—a minority in the region—were well-endowed because of their socialist pasts to carry through on that project once communist party hegemony ended. Other countries, however, had very different experiences during socialism and, thus, different political and economic capacities once communist party hegemony ended. In those cases the opposition was weak, there was little consensus regarding alternative economic and political futures (or much of a sense that alternatives were even available),[31] and the development of counterregimes had to occur *after* the collapse of communist party hegemony and, thus, in an environment that was more fluid and lacking the "discipline" of a system-in-place that identified a common enemy and that facilitated a consensus around "not state socialism," or capitalist liberal democracy. Thus, in some countries there were two well-defined alternatives in place, publics and oppositional elites could move quickly to embrace the liberal option once communist party hegemony ended, and the quick result was competition that was intraregime in form; but in most other countries in the region, alternatives lacked definition, support for these was fragmented, regime choice was hedged, and competition, as a result, was either prevented or took an interregime form.[32]

We can now conclude this discussion of the economic diversity of postsocialism by noting one theme that runs throughout these data and these explanations. That is, the variance in postsocialist economies and the ways in which this variance testifies not to the power of the present and future in structuring what happened after socialism but, rather, to the opposite: the power of the socialist past. In this sense, while the similarities of that past produced some commonalities in the postsocialist project, it was the diversity of the state socialist experience that was crucial in producing diverse points of economic and, it would appear, political departure.[33] State socialism, in short, remained important long after it exited from the political stage, and it functioned as both a homogenizing and as a diversifying force.

Political Diversity

It is far more difficult to provide summary measures of the political variations among postsocialist regimes. This is not just because power—the measure of politics—lacks the quantitative simplicity of money. The difficulty also lies in some other complications. One is that there is no consensus regarding the meaning or the measurement of the three most important aspects of politics that speak directly to the nature and quality of governance in the postsocialist world: political stability, state strength, and regime type (or the continuum ranging from democracy to dictatorship). Another is that each of these political indicators are multidimensional; their dimensions do not necessarily correlate and neither, for that matter, do the three indicators. For instance, while Kazakhstan is stable but not very democratic, Bulgaria is unstable but far more democratic; while Latvia looks quite democratic with respect to the provision of political liberties and civil rights, its exclusionary policies regarding voting rights for minority populations make it less democratic; and while Russia has a fully inclusive electorate and free and fair elections, the weakness of its state and the continuing war of laws between the center and the regions mean that elected officials there, particularly at the center, lack the capacity to translate public preferences into public policy and, therefore, to provide genuine accountability. Finally, there is some flux over time in country "scores" on these indicators, however they are measured. Thus, if we were to focus on the first years of the transformation, we might judge Albania, Armenia, and Kyrgyzstan as presenting an impressive democratic profile. However, subsequent developments in these three countries suggest that such a conclusion would have been premature or, at the very least, time-bound.

Perhaps the best way to begin our political assessment is to define some terms. Political stability, in my view, is the capacity of the regime (or the organization of political power) and the state (or a political entity defined by space and granted a monopoly in the exercise of coercion) to provide political order. It implies such characteristics as relatively unchanging rules of the political game that are recognized by all and inform the behavior of all, the existence of a hegemonic regime (as opposed to competitive regimes), governments that function effectively, and physical boundaries that are clearly defined and uncontested. Instability, therefore, is indicated by high levels of social disorder, secessionist pressures, contestation over the form of the regime, high rates of governmental turnover, and governments that cannot decide or, if deciding, cannot implement. Put simply then, instability testifies to the failure of a regime and/or a state to be hegemonic— or without competitors—and to function effectively.

The other aspect of politics that is of interest is regime type, or the contrast between democracy and dictatorship and the many variations situated between these two poles. There are, of course, many definitions of democracy.[34] Some focus on substance and others on procedures, some are detailed and others parsimonious, and some set a high standard that relatively few countries can meet, whereas others are less discriminating. For our purposes, we can follow the lead of Adam Przeworski by defining democracy as that system of governance that combines freedom, uncertain results, and certain procedures (a definition which, by the way, works for capitalism as well).[35] This implies three clusters of conditions. One is freedom, or whether members of the political community have the full array of civil liberties and political rights.[36] The second is if political results are in fact uncertain: that is, if politics is competitive and competition is institutionalized through parties that offer ideological choice, if elections are regularly held and are free and fair, if governing mandates are provisional, and, as a result of all these factors, if politicians are fully accountable to the electorate. The final category, procedural certainty, refers to the rule of law, the control of elected officials over the bureaucracy, and a legal and administrative order that is hegemonic and transparent, commands compliance, and is consistent across time, circumstances, and space.

Table 8.5 Freedom Rating

Free	Partly Free	Not Free
Bulgaria*	Albania*	Azerbaijan
Czech Republic	Armenia*	Belarus*
Estonia**	Bosnia**	Serbia-Montenegro
Hungary	Croatia*	Tajikistan
Latvia	Georgia**	Turkmenistan
Lithuania	Kazakhstan	Uzbekistan**
Poland	Kyrgyzstan	
Romania**	Macedonia	
Slovenia	Moldova**	
	Russia	
	Slovakia*	
	Ukraine	

Source: "The Comparative Survey of Freedom", *Freedom Review* 28:1(1997), 21–22. A single asterisk connotes a recent falling score in civil liberties and political rights, or both, and a double asterisk connotes a recent improvement.

Beneath these three aspects of democracy, therefore, are complex clusters of preconditions. Moreover, implied in this elaboration is a hierarchy of traits that distinguish among dictatorships (where not even the first or second conditions are met); incomplete democracies (or those countries that are free and competitive, but that lack, say, full political inclusion and/or certain procedures); and political orders that are full-scale democracies, or what has been variously termed "sustainable" and "consolidated" democratic orders (where all three sets of conditions are present).

We can now apply these definitions of stability and democracy to the postsocialist region. With respect to stability, we can assign these countries (with a great deal of trepidation, I must admit) to three groups: (1) highly stable countries, or where both the regime and the state are consolidated and in which government is reasonably effective (the Czech Republic, Estonia, Hungary, Latvia, Lithuania, Poland, Slovenia, and, arguably, Kazakhstan, Turkmenistan, and Uzbekistan); (2) less stable countries, or where regimes are not fully consolidated (often combining democratic and authoritarian elements), in which state boundaries are in some dispute, and/or in which governments lack the political (including constitutional) support, the ideological consensus, and the legal-administrative capacity to govern effectively (Azerbaijan, Bulgaria, Croatia, Macedonia, Moldova, Romania, Russia, Serbia-Montenegro, Slovakia, and Ukraine); and (3) unstable countries, or where the regime and/or the state are—or at least have been—in serious question (Albania, Armenia, Belarus, Bosnia, Georgia, Kyrgyzstan, and Tajikistan). We can certainly debate if some of these country assignments are correct—for example, if Kazakhstan, Russia, and Uzbekistan should be downgraded and if Georgia should, on the basis of recent developments, be upgraded.

However, whatever our different readings of these cases, one point of consensus would nonetheless emerge: The great majority of the regimes and states in the postsocialist region are not stable. This is hardly a surprising situation, given that only ten years at most have passed since the end of communist party hegemony and given, as well, the revolutionary character of postsocialism. By the latter, I refer to the fact that *all* the building blocks of politics, economics, and society—or, put bluntly, the state, the nation, the class structure, the economic regime, the political regime, and the relationship between all these and the international system—are in the process of being reformulated. What is more, these processes are happening simultaneously.

If we assess democratization in the region, we are on somewhat (but only somewhat) firmer ground. In Table 8.5, I summarize recent rankings by Freedom House with respect to the provision of civil liberties and political rights. What these data suggest is that the postsocialist countries vary from liberal to decidedly illiberal, but that one-third of the region (Bulgaria, the Czech Republic, Estonia, Hungary, Latvia, Lithuania, Poland, Romania, and Slovenia) comes reasonably close to the standards of well-established democratic orders. What the Freedom House measures also suggest is that the Latin American countries (including Central America and the Caribbean) are freer than the countries making up the postsocialist world (with an average score in Latin America of 2.5 and in the postsocialist countries of 3.7).

Attention to the second standard of democratization, however, lowers the number of robust democracies in the postsocialist world. As Philip Roeder has recently argued, at least on the question of electoral inclusion, the postsocialist states divide into three groups: those states that have fully inclusive electorates and thereby meet a necessary precondition for democracy (which describes most of the region, albeit at varying times during postsocialism); those states that exclude ten to twenty-five percent of the potential electorate (at various points, Albania, Georgia, Kazakhstan, Kyrgyzstan, Moldova, Tajikistan); and those that exclude (and consistently) one-quarter or more of the potential electorate (Estonia and Latvia).[37] When placed beside the Freedom House measures, these indicators of electoral inclusion suggest only a modest overlap. This leads to two observations. One is that democratization in the post-socialist context is a highly uneven process—not just across countries, but also over time and across dimensions. The other is that very few of the postsocialist regimes could be termed full-scale democracies—that is, fully inclusive and fully free. In particular, only the Czech Republic, Hungary, Poland, and Slovenia—or about one-seventh of the region—meet this very high standard.

The third dimension of democracy, procedural certainty, is harder to measure. However, the secondary literature suggests that this is a problem (albeit in varying degrees) in all of the postsocialist countries. This is not just because so many political institutions are new, but also because of the legacies of the socialist past (and, indeed, the past before that past). One of the underlying principles of state socialism, we must remember, was capricious decision-making and rule application, along with procedures that could be termed, at best, cloudy. Moreover, individual decision-makers mattered a great deal in a context where there were, in effect, institutions instead of institutionalization. All this was not accidental. These characteristics gave the communist party one more way to control society and, within the party-state itself, one more way for elites "above" to control—and through uncertainty, manipulate—elites "below" them. Furthermore, some of these countries suffer from poor constitutional design. The problem is partly that the new constitutions were often grafted onto their socialist era variants, and partly that constitutions, especially when enacted later rather than sooner, reflect the complex and tense distribution of power between the former communists and the opposition. Here, the Russian and Ukrainian cases are illustrative. As Peter Murrell recently observed for the former: "Russia has only half-succeeded in following Napoleon's dictum that the best constitutions are short and confused."[38]

These influences aside, however, one can still make a relatively clear distinction among the postsocialist countries. There seems to be a considerable gulf separating those few countries where procedures have managed to become relatively routinized and transparent—the Czech Republic, Hungary, Poland, Slovenia, and, perhaps, the Baltic states (despite the contrasting timing in constitutional adoption)—from the rest of the region, where the state socialist past has interacted with dramatic changes in recent years to produce an administrative, political, and economic environment that is unusually confused, capricious, ever-changing, and, therefore, highly unpredictable.[39] Indeed, this is precisely the picture that emerges for the Commonwealth of Independent States, in particular in the already noted 1996 World Bank survey of entrepreneurs in sixty-nine countries.

What do these exercises in political comparison suggest? Most obviously, they indicate that a majority of the regimes and states in the region are unstable and, at most, partially democratic. The regional norm, therefore, is not the Czech Republic, Hungary, Poland, and Slovenia. Rather, it is Russia, with its fuzzy state, its fuzzy democracy, and, to echo an earlier observation, its fuzzy property.

How can we explain these patterns? There are a variety of factors that, while logical and suggestive, do not seem to produce a robust explanation. For example, while all the stable and fully democratic cases are rich and homogeneous by regional comparative standards, some relatively rich states score low on both democratization and political stability (Croatia, Slovakia, and Ukraine) and some homogeneous states do the same (Albania and Armenia).[40] Moreover, state age is not all that helpful a factor, given, for instance, the inclusion of the Czech Republic and Slovenia in the group of stable and fully democratic orders. Finally, factors such as religion, imperial lineage (or inclusion in the Habsburg versus the Russian or Ottoman empires), and institutional design (or parliamentary government versus forms of presidentialism) do not seem to account all that well for these differences.[41]

There is, however, one factor that seems at least to correlate with democratization. That is economic reform.[42] Put simply, all of the robust democracies score high on economic reform (with an average score of 7.3); all the postsocialist dictatorships score quite low (an average of 3.2); and the remaining countries, or incomplete democracies, fall in between these two extremes with respect to economic reform. This introduces a question that allows us to combine the discussion on politics with that on economics and leads us to the final issue to be addressed in this paper: Why does democratization correlate with economic reform in the postsocialist context?

Democratization and Economic Reform

There are two reasons to expect that democratization and economic reform would go together in the postsocialist world. One is that all democracies have had capitalist economies. The other is that democracy and capitalism are based on precisely the same principles, albeit applied to different arenas of human activity: uncertain results combined with certain procedures.

However, alongside these arguments must be placed a series of others that tilt the balance in the direction of presuming tension, not compatibility, between democratization and the transition to capitalism. First, we must remember that capitalist economies have often coexisted—and quite happily—with dictatorial politics. Moreover, just as it would not be in the interests of accountable politicians to introduce painful economic policies (especially when they are courting fickle constituencies lacking strong party identification), so such policies could very well encourage massive popular protest that could, in turn, lead to democratic breakdown. This would seem to be the case particularly where, as in the postsocialist world, political institutions are new and weak and where semi-presidentialism offers the possibility, especially if publics are unhappy, of a sequence of deadlock, concentration of power in the executive's hands, and suspension of newly won civil liberties and political rights. This scenario describes, of course, Weimar Germany in the first half of the 1930s. Third, in the postsocialist context, vested interests in capitalism are, by definition and history, minimal. Finally, even if we were to doubt these arguments, we would still come face to face with trends in other parts of the world. In Africa, Latin America, and Southern Europe, there have been serious tensions between democratization and economic reform.[43] This is precisely why specialists in these areas have argued in favor of sequencing, whereby economic reforms are delayed until democracy is consolidated.

Why, then, do we see this robust and peculiar relationship in the postsocialist world? We can begin to answer this question by following up the argument presented earlier with respect to the impact of founding elections on either continuing or stalling economic and political regime transformation. If we assume that founding elections, like other elections, shape both the incentives and the capacity of policy-makers and, thus, the actions they take, and if we assume as well that the key question in the postsocialist context is one of either destroying or maintaining, to the degree possible, the old order, then it can be argued that a victory of the opposition forces would produce *both* democratization and economic reform and that the victory of the former communists would undermine both. In this way, then, precisely because of the elections and the context of state socialism, economic reform and democratization become an either/or proposition.

From this perspective, one of three possibilities would present itself following the end of communist party hegemony. Either a decisive victory by the opposition would "bundle" democratization and economic reform (as in the Czech Republic, Hungary, Poland, and Slovenia); or a decisive triumph by the former communists would foreclose both (as in much of Central Asia); or close elections, where either the former communists barely won or power was divided in its institutional loci between the former communists and the opposition forces (with Bulgaria representative of the former, and Russia and Ukraine representative of the latter), would produce a compromised, uncertain, and highly destabilized transition to democracy and capitalism.

What I am suggesting, therefore, is that proximate politics—or, in this instance, the outcome of the first competitive election—was, indeed, crucial. However, these elections were crucial precisely because of the heritage of the socialist past: that is, if that past had created a large and consensual opposition that could quickly become a powerful political player in a liberalized landscape or if that past had bequeathed a small and divided opposition that could not compete effectively with the former communists. Thus, proximate politics mattered precisely because the past mattered so much, even after, but also especially following, the deregulation of the communist party's monopoly.

However this leaves one remaining question: Why didn't publics in the Czech Republic, Poland, and the like, when faced with the terrible and unexpected burdens of reform, use the considerable and in some instances recently and successfully used democratic tools at their disposal to mount protests against the regime in particular and the liberal turn in economics in general? Of course, many did, though support for both democracy and capitalism remained high.[44] But they did so at different times, in different ways and, for the most part, at lower rates.

Here, we can note the following. First, the consensus that allowed the end of communist party hegemony to be followed by the decisive victory of the opposition in the first elections functioned in effect as a political honeymoon. Put differently, politicians were allowed the luxury, rare in a democratic context (but more likely with large mandates), of longer-term horizons. Second, consensus was built on a simple equation: Democracy and capitalism were the inverse of state socialism and, thus, highly coveted. Finally, as the data in Tables 1–3 indicate, the earlier and more complete the transition to capitalism, the shorter the economic downturn and the faster the return of economic growth. Quick capitalism, in short, generated more winners and faster, while at the same time dividing and demobilizing the losers.[45] In this way, then, fast track democracy and capitalism created a virtuous circle.[46] Where the economic and political revolution was stalled, however, the communist party's monopoly was also deregulated, but mass publics were deprived of democracy, while economic performance was far worse. In these contexts, publics were twice cursed, and the political-economic circle was vicious in form. This, in turn, generated substantial political instability.

We can now conclude this discussion by combining the economic and political sides of the postsocialist experience. Perhaps the best way to do so is to divide the region into five groups, based upon democratization, political stability, economic reform, and economic performance. The first cluster is composed of those countries—a minority in the region—that, with the victory of the opposition forces, moved quickly to democracy and capitalism, that have consolidated both in a remarkably short period of time, and that, following a relatively short-lived but dramatic recession, have proven themselves to be economically vital. The members of this group are the Czech Republic, Hungary, Poland, and Slovenia (with Lithuania a possible member, save a slower economic recovery). The next cluster is composed of those countries that also moved quickly to economic reform and democratization but that have failed to sustain either one and that are, as a result, unstable in both economic and political terms. The members of this group include Albania, Armenia, and Kyrgyzstan. The third group consists of countries where democracy is compromised, which has created considerable political tensions, but where economic reforms are in place and economic performance testifies to that fact. Here, I would place Croatia, Estonia, Latvia, and Slovakia. The fourth group evidences a "medium" score on economic reform, poor economic performance, and democratic orders that are relatively good on paper but severely compromised in practice—for example, by considerable political conflict at the elite level (accompanied by frequent elections and high rates of governmental turnover), by legal and administrative disorder, and/or by limited governmental capacity to enact and implement policy. Members of this cluster—the largest of the five—include Bosnia, Bulgaria, Georgia, Macedonia, Moldova, Romania, Russia, and Ukraine. The final group is composed of countries that are oligopolistic in the structure of their economic and political systems and that have managed to maintain (often with an early, liberalized interlude) significant ties to the state socialist past. Members of this group include Azerbaijan, Belarus, Kazakhstan, Serbia-Montenegro, Tajikistan, Turkmenistan, and Uzbekistan.

Conclusions

We can now step away from these detailed comparisons and draw some conclusions. First, the political and economic landscape of postsocialism is extraordinarily diverse and, it must be noted, ever more diverse over time.[47] Second, by regional standards, the exceptional cases are those that either represent substantial continuity with the state socialist past, not just in leadership, but also in political and economic structures, or those that have made the leap from state socialism to capitalist liberal democracy. The regional norm is to fall in between these two political-economic poles. Not surprisingly, this "neither here nor there" tendency—or hybrid regimes that combine democratic and authoritarian, capitalist and state socialist elements—has produced significant political instability and unusually poor economic performance (which in turn reinforces hybridization). Fourth, there seems to be a correlation between democratization and economic reform in the postsocialist world.

Finally, a repeating theme in this paper has been the powerful impact of the balance of power between the opposition forces and the former communists. Here, one of three possibilities has presented itself—and has shaped significantly subsequent economic and political developments. When the opposition was strong enough to win the first competitive elections handily, we see rapid and thorough-going economic reforms, the relatively quick consolidation of both democracy and capitalism, a quick return to economic growth, and substantial political stability. Where the former communists have maintained significant influence and the opposition has been small, weak, and fragmented, however, the story is one of limited (if any) economic and political liberalization and often relatively stable authoritarian politics. Finally, where the former communists and the opposition are in rough balance, democratization, like economic reform, has been partial. This has led in turn to disastrous economic performance and considerable political instability.

We can now step back from these conclusions and use them to address briefly several issues in the study of democratization. The first is the debate over the singularity of socialism and postsocialism.[48] As I have argued throughout this paper, the political-economic point of departure was unusual in postsocialism, as was the agenda of transformation. Moreover, these differences have translated into distinctive patterns of democratization and economic reform and, just as importantly, into different payoffs attached to the strategies of transformation. Thus, just as the postsocialist world by comparative standards is more urban and more economically egalitarian and features fewer democracies and higher economic costs attached to reform, so the postsocialist world demonstrates a correlation, not a trade-off, between democratization and economic reform. When combined with other data, we can argue that both economic performance and democratization are served in the postsocialist context by a decisive—rather than a partial—break with the authoritarian past. This contrasts sharply with the preference for bridging, particularly with respect to the political and economic cooptation of authoritarians, that figures prominently in the study of democratization in Latin America and Southern Europe.[49]

Another issue is the debate over long-term versus short-term influences on democratization. What this study suggests is that the authoritarian past is extraordinarily powerful not just in its many specific legacies, such as the presence or absence of markets, a democratic tradition, or a democratic political culture, but also in shaping both the proximate politics of the transformation and their influence in turn on subsequent economic and political trajectories. In this sense, proximate considerations are important, but can only be understood and documented by reference to the past. Just as importantly, that socialist past in some cases enabled and in most cases undermined the movement toward democracy and capitalism. The key was if a counterregime existed prior to the collapse of communist party hegemony. Where it did, the socialist past became an enabling point of departure for liberal orders. Where it did not, the transformation has been slower and more compromised.

This leads to the final issue: the interpretation of difference. Do the varying political and economic scores of the twenty-seven postsocialist countries suggest different trajectories or do they suggest different country locations along what is the same overall trajectory? Put another way: Are we looking at results that are locked into place for the foreseeable future, or are we merely looking at fast and relatively trouble-free transformations to democracy and capitalism versus slower, more troubled, and more detour-prone transformations? Ten years (at most) into this process is not enough time to answer this question. But I would suggest that, in our drive to generate categories and draw conclusions based upon comparative analysis, we not forget that such a question exists. Winners and losers in the race to liberalism, as in the experiences of capitalism and democracy itself, can be, after all, temporary outcomes—with winners in a better position, of course, to continue their successes. This is especially the case since the differences between the frontrunners and the laggards in the postsocialist world may reflect different endowments, different sequencing with respect to regime termination and the formation of ideological alternatives, or different processes by which democracy and capitalism succeed in becoming hegemonic projects. In this sense, the Russian route to democracy might be best understood first by waiting, and second by looking not at the "quick" democratization experience and the literature that has developed around it, but rather by returning to the older literature on democratization that treats this process as long-term and uneven in nature. Thus, Russia and others in the region that have not equaled the Czech, Hungarian, and Slovene success stories might do so with time. However, we should not fall prey to a teleological bias, as was the case for so long, for example, with modernization theory. Rather, what I am suggesting is that we be open to multiple outcomes, that we recognize the temporal constraints of our comparative vistas, that we view the laggards in the race to democratization and capitalism as countries that might very well be following the older and more circuitous route, and that we expand our theoretical horizons to include those studies that predate the current emphasis on quick democratization. Here, what is striking, to me at least, is that the chaos in Russia today looks remarkably like Europe in the early Middle Ages when, as Jenő Szűcs has noted,[50] the collapse of order, while extraordinarily costly in the short-term, was quite beneficial to the subsequent development of islands of autonomy. These islands, in turn, became over time the foundation for the rise of liberal thought and action and, thus, capitalism and later, democracy.

Notes

1 This chapter serves as the basis for a larger study, "The Political Economy of Postsocialism", that is forthcoming in a special issue of *Slavic Review* (December 1999).
2 See Valerie Bunce, *Subversive Institutions: The Design and the Destruction of Socialism and the State* (Cambridge: Cambridge University Press, 1999). Also see Steven L. Solnick, *Stealing the State: Control and Collapse in Soviet Institutions* (Cambridge: Harvard University Press).
3 For diametrically opposed positions on the influence of the socialist past, contrast, for example, Ken Jowitt, "The Leninist Legacy", in *Eastern Europe in Revolution*, ed. Ivo Banac (Ithaca: Cornell University Press, 1991); versus Adam Przeworski, *Democracy and the Market* (Cambridge: Cambridge University Press, 1991). For a summary of these arguments and others that propose competing influences on postsocialist developments (and that divide along the axes of optimism and pessimism), see Béla Greskovits, "Rival Views of Postcommunist Market Society" (paper presented at Cornell University, 5 October 1998) and Grzegorz Ekiert and Jan Kubik, "Patterns of Postcommunist Transitions in Eastern Europe" (paper presented at the Council for European Studies, Baltimore, 1 March 1998).
4 See especially Greskovits, "Rival Views".
5 On the Russian case, see, for example, M. Steven Fish, "The Predicament of Russian Liberalism: Evidence from the December 1995 Party Elections", *Europe-Asia Studies* 49 (1997): 199–220; Kathryn Stoner-Weiss, "Democracy in Disarray: Central Governing Capacity in the Provinces and the Weakness of Russian Political Parties" (unpublished manuscript, Princeton University, August 1998). But by some measures, Russian party identification at least does seem to be developing. See Joshua A. Tucker and Ted Brader, "Congratulations, It's a Party: The Birth of Mass Political Parties in Russia, 1993-1996" (paper presented at the annual meeting of the American Political Science Association, Boston, 3–6 September 1998).

6 See, for example, the results of surveys of entrepreneurs conducted by the World Bank regarding the stability and coherence of the economic environment within which they work.

7 See, for instance, Martin Krygier, "Virtuous Circles: Antipodean Reflections on Power, Institutions, and Civil Society", *East European Politics and Societies* 11 (Winter 1997): 36–88; Ekiert, "Patterns of Postcommunist Transitions"; Karen Dawisha and Bruce Parrott, eds., *Conflict, Cleavage, and Change in Central Asia and the Caucasus* (Cambridge: Cambridge University Press, 1997); Karen Dawisha and Bruce Parrott, eds., *The Consolidation of Democracy in East-Central Europe* (Cambridge: Cambridge University Press, 1997); Karen Dawisha and Bruce Parrott, eds., *Democratic Changes and Authoritarian Reactions in Russia, Ukraine, Belarus, and Moldova* (Cambridge: Cambridge University Press, 1997); Karen Dawisha and Bruce Parrott, eds., *Politics, Power, and the Struggle for Democracy in South-East Europe* (Cambridge: Cambridge University Press, 1997); David Ost, "Labor, Class, and Democracy: Shaping Political Antagonisms in Post-Communist Society", in *Markets, States, and Democracy: The Political Economy of Post-Communist Transformation*, ed. Beverly Crawford (Boulder, Colo.: Westview, 1995), 177–203; and Karen Dawisha, "Postcommunism's Troubled Steps toward Democracy: An Aggregate Analysis of the Twenty-Seven New States" (paper presented at the annual convention of the American Association for the Advancement of Slavic Studies, Seattle, Wash., 18 November).

8 These figures are drawn from the World Bank, *World Development Report: The State in a Changing World* (Oxford: Oxford University Press), 218–21, 230–31, 234–37, 242–47; Martin Raiser and Peter Sanfrey, "Statistical Review", *Economics of Transition* 6:1 (1998): 258.

9 See especially Valere Gagnon, "Bosnian Federalism and the Institutionalization of Ethnic Division" (paper presented at the Workshop of Nationalism, Federalism, and Secession, Cornell University, Ithaca, 2 May 1998).

10 See Béla Greskovits, *The Political Economy of Protest and Patience* (Budapest: Central European University Press, 1998).

11 See The World Bank, *World Development Report*, 234–35.

12 These figures were calculated from the World Bank, *World Development Report*, 214–15. For a discussion of the difficulties of estimating economic performance in the postsocialist context, see Kasper Bartholdy, "Old and New Problems in the Estimation of National Accounts in Transitional Economies", *Economics of Transition* 5:1 (1997): 131–46.

13 See the World Bank, *World Development Report*, 222–23. For example, while the average Gini coefficient for all those countries outside the postsocialist region that fall in the lower middle income category is 45.2, the postsocialist countries that are in that category, such as Belarus, Bulgaria, Kazakhstan, Lithuania, Moldova, Poland, and Slovakia, register Gini coefficients of 34.4, 30.8, 32.7, 33.6, 21.6, 27.2, and 19.5. The contrast is even more glaring for the upper middle income countries of the Czech Republic, Hungary, and Slovenia. While their Gini coefficients are, respectively, 26.6, 27.0, and 28.2, the remaining countries in this category average a Gini coefficient of 55.4.

14 World Bank, *World Development Report*, 5, 37. More specifically, the Commonwealth of Independent States led in unpredictability of changes in policies, tied with

the Middle East and Subsaharan Africa in unstable government, tied with Latin America with respect to insecurity of property, and led all the other regions in the unreliability of the judiciary and levels of corruption. One example of the "state problem" in the former Soviet Union is Ukraine, where both decision-making and policy implementation are sabotaged by a political structure that is unusually complex and that allows for remarkable overlap in administrative jurisdictions (see World Bank, *World Development Report*, chart on 85). For an insightful discussion of the Russian state and its failure to provide a stable and transparent economic environment, see Kathryn Hendley, "Legal Development in Post-Soviet Russia", *Post-Soviet Affairs* 13 (July-September 1997): 228–51.

15 There has also been a dramatic decline in inflation. While in 1992, the average rate of inflation in East-Central Europe and the Baltic states was 199.2 and 13,525 in the former Soviet Union (minus the Baltic states), the comparable figures for 1997 were 10 and 13.1, respectively. See Raiser and Sanfrey, "Statistical Review", 252.

16 For evidence on these points, also see Grzegorz Kolodko, "Equity Issues in Policy-making in Transition Economies" (paper presented at the conference on Economic Policy and Equity, Washington, D.C., 8–9 June 1998).

17 Of course, the recent downturn of the Russian economy suggests some care when making these generalizations. However, several other countries in this table also show significant problems in the past few years—most obviously, Albania and Bulgaria.

18 For instance, it has been argued that the Russian experience is unusual from the perspective of theories of democratization. See Richard Anderson, Jr., "The Russian Anomaly and the Theory of Democracy" (paper presented at the annual meeting of the American Political Science Association, Boston, , 3–6 September 1998). For a somewhat different perspective, see Philip Roeder, "The Triumph of Authoritarianism in Post-Soviet Regimes" (paper presented at the annual meeting of the American Political Science Association, Boston, 3–6 September 1998).

19 To this list can be added one other way in which the Russian experience has been distinctive: the alarming statistics on declining male life expectancy. While about one-half of the countries in the postsocialist region have registered a small decline in male life expectancy, the Russian decline is, even by that sad standard, unusually large. See Peter Murrell, "How Far Has the Transition Progressed?" *Journal of Economic Perspectives* 10:2 (Spring 1996): 38, table 3; and Timothy Heleniak, "Dramatic Population Trends in Countries of the FSU", *Transition* 6 (September/October): 1–5.

20 Russia incurred costs, of course, from introducing economic reform later in the transitional process. In particular, because dominant interests in the socialist era had the opportunity to redefine their economic and political portfolios in anticipation of reform, their interests shaped the course of the reform while contributing in the process to both unusually high levels of corruption and an unusually prolonged period of economic recession. On this argument see, for example, Dawisha, "Postcommunism's Troubled Steps", 21.

21 M. Steven Fish, "The Determinents of Economic Reform in the Post-Communist World", *East European Politics and Societies* 12 (Winter 1998): 31–78. For a similar observation, absent the statistical support, see Valerie Bunce, "The Sequencing of Political and Economic Reforms", in *East-Central European Economies in Transi-*

tion, eds. John Hardt and Richard Kaufman (Washington, D.C.: Joint Economic Committee, U.S. Congress, 1994), 49–63.

22 For example, as Steve Fish has noted, ninety-six percent of individuals that owned or worked in small, private businesses in Russia supported Yeltsin in the presidential run-off in 1996. Fish, "The Determinents", 67.

23 Here, I am referring, for example, to the Croatian Democratic Union (or HDZ). There, we might explain the decision to reform as in effect a continuation of the policies of the past—in a distant sense, the particular character of Yugoslav self-management, and in a more proximate sense, the Ante Markovic reforms. See, for example, Vojmir Franicevic, "Privatization in Croatia: Developments and Issues" (paper presented at the annual convention of the American Association for the Advancement of Slavic Studies, Seattle, Wash., 20–23 November 1997). When taken more broadly, this argument reminds us that we need to be careful about imputing causality when we observe that a particular outcome in time "2" is preceded by an event in time "1".

24 Denise V. Powers and James H. Cox, "Echoes from the Past: The Relationship between Satisfaction with Economic Reforms and Voting Behavior in Poland", *American Political Science Review* 91 (September 1997): 617–634.

25 It has been argued that the same problem exists in the Latin American context, where import substitution has produced few groups with vested interests in economic liberalization. The puzzle then becomes one of explaining the right-turn in economics. However, there is one recent argument that suggests that there were in fact built-in sectoral supports for economic liberalization. See Hector Schamis, "Distributional Coalitions and the Politics of Economic Reform in Latin America", *World Politics* 51 (January 1999): 236–268.

26 See, for example, John Walton and David Seddon, *Free Markets and Food Riots: The Politics of Global Adjustment* (Oxford: Basil Blackwell, 1994).

27 See, for instance, the public opinion data cited by David Ost, "Labor, Class and Democracy: Shaping Political Antagonisms in Post-Communist Society", in *Markets, States, and Democracy: The Political Economy of Post-Socialist Transformation*, ed. Beverly Crawford (Boulder, Colo.: Westview Publishers, 1995): 177–203.

28 It has been commonplace in studies of the collapse of regimes and states in the region to presume that nationalism describes the political agenda of minorities and not majorities, and that nationalist movements describe what happens when people mobilize to carve out autonomy or leave the state and not when they engage in similar behavior, but directed at regimes or the Soviet bloc. In my view, this is wrong-minded, since national liberation was as much the project of, say, Poland, as it was of, say, Lithuania during the time of regime, state, and bloc unraveling. See Bunce, *Subversive Institutions*.

29 See Ost, "Labor, Class, and Democracy"; Grzegorz Kolodko and D. Mario Nuti, "The Polish Alternative: Old Myths, Hard Facts, and New Strategies in the Successful Transformation of the Political Economy" *UNU/WIDER Project* (UNU World Institute for Development Economics: Helsinki, 1997).

30 The usual argument, of course, is the development of civil society. I have avoided this terminology for two reasons. One is that civil society means different things to different analysts (particularly if we include the ways this term came to be used in East-

Central Europe during the socialist era). The other is that a focus on civil society makes it hard to explain those cases, such as Czechoslovakia, where the regime's response to popular protest had been a repressive one. However, if we use large-scale protest as an indicator, these problems are reduced. Moreover, by speaking of regimes-in-waiting, the multiplication of regimes, and the like, we place the events of 1989 in the appropriate family of revolutionary processes. See Valerie Bunce, "The Revolutionary Character of 1989–1990", *East European Politics and Societies* (forthcoming 1999).

31 As Adam Przeworski once argued when analyzing the rise of Solidarity in Poland, regimes are in trouble once people begin to imagine alternatives. See "The Man of Iron and the Men of Power in Poland", *PS (Political Science)* 15 (Winter 1982): 18–31.

32 Vesna Pusic, for example, has made a persuasive argument that a major problem in the Balkans has been the sequencing between the deregulation of the communist party's monopoly and the formation of a viable opposition. See Vesna Pusic, "Mediteranski model na zalasku autoritarnih drzava", *Erasmus* 29 (January 1997): 2–18.

33 One study that recognizes the duality of the socialist past in this respect is Stephen Crowley, *Hot Coal, Cold Steel: Russian and Ukrainian Workers from the End of the Soviet Union to the Postcommunist Transformation* (Ann Arbor: University of Michigan Press, 1997).

34 For a sampling, see Robert Dahl, *Polyarchy* (New Haven: Yale University Press, 1971); Adam Przeworski, *Democracy and the Market* (Cambridge: Cambridge University Press, 1991); and Philippe C. Schmitter and Terry Lynn Karl, "What Democracy Is...and Is Not", *Journal of Democracy* 5 (1997), 1–27.

35 See Przeworski, *Democracy and the Market*; Dahl, *Polyarchy*; Valerie Bunce, "Stalinism and the Management of Uncertainty", in *The Transition to Democracy in Hungary*, ed. György Szoboszlai (Budapest: Hungarian Academy of Sciences, 1991), 46–70; Valerie Bunce, "Elementy neopredelennosti v perekhodnyi period", *Politichestkie issledovaniia* 1 (1993): 44–51.

36 As defined in detail by Freedom House. See "The Comparative Survey of Freedom", *Freedom Review* 28:1 (1997).

37 See Philip G. Roeder, "The Triumph of Authoritarianism in Post-Soviet Regimes" (paper presented at the annual meeting of the American Political Science Association, Boston, 3–6 September 1998), 7.

38 Murrell, "How Far Has the Transition Progressed?" 33.

39 This contrast reflects, most obviously, the degree to which the revolution that ended communist party hegemony was both liberal and full-scale. However, there is another historical factor that considerably predates even socialism; that is, whether these areas were influenced by Roman law or not. Where they were, the legal-administrative tradition is such as to recognize the possibility of a law-based state. See, for example, Jenő Szűcs, "The Three Historical Regions of Europe: An Outline", *Acta Historica: Revue de L'Académie des Sciences de Hongrie* 29: (1983): 2–4, 131–84. Also see Perry Anderson, *Lineages of the Absolutist State* (London: New Left Books, 1974).

40 Here, I am referring to those arguments regarding the impact of economic development on democratization and the greater difficulties that heterogeneous national set-

tings—or settings where the national and the state questions have yet to be resolved—have in creating stable and durable democratic orders. See, for instance, Martin Lipset et al., "Are Transitions Transitory? Two Types of Political Change in Eastern Europe since 1989", *East European Politics and Societies* 11 (Winter 1997): 1–35. It is interesting to note that, while it is true that the three "quick" democracies in the region that recently have become decidedly less democratic (Albania, Armenia, and Kyrgyzstan), it is also true that some of the richest democracies in the region have also backtracked in recent years (Croatia and Slovakia). Thus, there is some question whether economic development has so much impact on democratic sustainability, as argued in Adam Przeworski and Fernando Limongi, "Modernization: Facts and Theories", *World Politics* 49 (January 1997): 155–183.

41 See, for example, Fish, "The Determinents"; Alfred Stepan and Cindy Skach, "Constitutional Frameworks and Democratic Consolidation", *World Politics* 46 (October 1993): 1–22; Timothy Colton, "Super-Presidentialism and Russia's Backwards State", *Post-Soviet Affairs* 11 (April-June 1995): 144–48; Gerald Easter, "Preference for Presidentialism: Postcommunist Regime Change in Russia and the NIS", *World Politics* 49 (January 1997): 184–211; Valerie Bunce, "Presidents and the Transition in Eastern Europe", in *Presidential Institutions and Democratic Politics*, ed. Kurt Von Mettenheim (Baltimore, Md.: Johns Hopkins University Press, 1997): 161–176. As both Gerald Easter and I have argued, however, institutional design may not be the culprit so much as the politics—or the relative strength of the former communists versus the opposition forces—behind the adoption of parliamentary versus presidential government. Moreover, as Steve Fish has argued, what may really matter is presidential interpretation of presidential power in new democracies. See M. Steven Fish, "Reversal and Erosion of Democracy in the Postcommunist World" (paper presented at the annual meeting of the American Political Science Association, Boston, 3–6 September 1998).

42 See M. Steven Fish, "Democratization's Prerequisites", *Post-Soviet Affairs* 14:3 (1998): 212–47; Bunce, "Sequencing of Political and Economic Reforms".

43 See, for example, Thomas M. Callaghy, "Political Passions and Economic Interests", in *Hemmed In: Responses to Africa's Economic Decline*, eds. Thomas Callaghy and John Ravenhill (New York: Columbia University Press, 1993): 463–519; Henry Bienen and Jeffrey Herbst, "The Relationship between Political and Economic Reform in Africa", *Comparative Politics* 29 (October 1996): 23–42; Robert Kaufman, "Liberalization and Democratization in South America: Perspectives from the 1970s", in *Transitions from Authoritarian Rule: Comparative Perspectives*, eds. Guillermo O'Donnell, Philippe C. Schmitter, and Laurence Whitehead (Baltimore: Johns Hopkins University Press, 1986): 85–107; Jose Maria Maravall, "Politics and Policy: Economic Reforms in Southern Europe", in *Economic Reforms in New Democracies: A Social Democratic Approach*, eds. Luiz Carlos Bresser Pereira, Jose Maria Maravall, and Adam Przeworski (Cambridge: Cambridge University Press, 1993): 77–131; Stephan Haggard and Robert Kaufman, *The Political Economy of Democratic Transitions* (Princeton: Princeton University Press, 1996); Guillermo O'Donnell and Philippe C. Schmitter, "Tentative Conclusions about Uncertain Democracies", in *Transitions from Authoritarian Rule*, eds. Guillermo O'Donnell, Philippe C. Schmit-

ter, and Laurence Whitehead (Baltimore: Johns Hopkins University Press, 1986); Stephan Haggard and Robert R. Kaufman, "The Political Economy of Democratic Transitions", *Comparative Politics* 29:3 (April 1997): 263–83.

44 Ekiert, "Patterns of Postcommunist Transitions".

45 The losers were demobilized because a quick transition unsettled interests; because of the conflict between values, which were liberal, and interests, which were counter to the transitional project; and because people were caught in a tension between past-oriented interests, which were known but logically outmoded, and future-looking interests, which were unknown, but, given the pace of change, likely to be crucial. See Valerie Bunce and Maria Csanadi, "Uncertainty in the Transition: Postcommunism in Hungary", *East European Politics and Societies* 7 (Spring 1993): 240–75.

46 Here, I am drawing on the terminology used by Martin Krygier, "Virtuous Circles". The metaphor can be extended to include political stability as well. Thus, while democratization and the transition to capitalism imply state reduction, they also, when accompanying each other, could be said to strengthen the state as well, through the creation of new, serviceable, and increasingly effective institutions. On this point, see Hector Schamis, "Re-forming the State" (Ph.D. diss., Columbia University, 1994).

47 See Ekiert, "Patterns of Postcommunist Transition".

48 See, for example, Philippe C. Schmitter and Terry Lynn Karl, "The Conceptual Travels of Transitologists and Consolidologists: How Far to the East Should They Go?" *Slavic Review* 53 (Spring 1994): 173–85; Valerie Bunce, "Should Transitologists be Grounded?" *Slavic Review* 54 (Spring 1995): 111–27; Valerie Bunce, "Differences in Democratization in the East and South", *Post-Soviet Affairs* (Fall 1998).

49 See especially Haggard and Kaufman, "The Political Economy"; Terry Lynn Karl, "Dilemmas of Democratization in Latin America", *Comparative Politics* 23 (October 1990): 1–22.

50 Jenő Szűcs, "The Three Historical Regions".

9 Fighting for the Public Sphere: Democratic Intellectuals under Postcommunism

VLADIMIR TISMANEANU

> "Wherever knowing and doing have parted company, the space of freedom is lost."
>
> Hannah Arendt, *On Revolution*
>
> "I am convinced that the contemporary world, beset by so many threats to civilization and seemingly incapable of confronting these dangers, demands that people who understand something about this world and what to do about it have a much greater influence on politics. I was convinced of this even as an independent writer, and my participation in politics has only served to confirm it."
>
> Václav Havel, 1994
>
> "Democratic revolutions of oppressed and self-oppressing societies bring all manner of unsavory matters to light."
>
> György Konrád, 1989

In March 1996 a conference took place in Budapest on a fascinating topic: intellectuals between morals and politics. The organizers (from the Hungarian edition of *Lettre Internationale* and Collegium Budapest) asked the participants—among them many illustrious former dissidents of Eastern and Central Europe, as well as a number of western writers—to examine the role of the intelligentsia at the end of this century. Some of the participants insisted that the declining role of intellectuals in the East is only an expression of normality. Thus, the mayor of Budapest, Gábor Demszky, insisted that in Hungary not only former dissidents but also nationalist intellectuals have left politics. The view he expressed at the time was that the peaceful Hungarian revolution was over, and there was no need for any "teachers" or "fathers" of the nation. Adam Michnik echoed this theme and criticized many former dissidents who simply could not adjust to the new conditions of democratic normalcy. In his view: "the heroes fought for freedom, but do not love freedom." He gave the example of poet Zbigniew Herbert, whose radical anticommunism amounted to a deep distrust for the democratic values and institutions that allowed the former communists to return to power.

French philosopher Alain Finkielkraut spoke about a widespread melancholy, East and West. In his view our world was devoid of "great causes", a point echoed a few years later by historian Tony Judt when he spoke about the transition from a "highly politicized to a de-politicized world".[1] The moral lesson of dissidents (itself a "meta-narrative" of sorts) was not fully grasped and therefore swiftly jettisoned; more than a critique of the monopolistic Leninist regimes, the philosophy of civic emancipation advocated by Eastern Europe's critical intellectuals bore upon the fate of modernity and our understanding of the relationship between means and ends in the organization of social space. Perhaps the best brief description of the postcommunist condition was given by Bulgarian writer Ivan Krastev who said that when we speak about politicians in Eastern Europe today, we mean former communists, and when we refer to intellectuals we have in mind former dissidents. The question remains: Between lionization and vilification, what is the role—or better said, the responsibility—of critical intellectuals in these societies?[2] Is Václav Havel an incurably naïve and sentimental moralist when he calls on former dissidents to remain involved in politics? Or, resuming a question addressed by Agnes Heller and Ferenc Fehér, "How can one be dissatisfied in a satisfied world?"[3] Shouldn't they rather challenge, as Slovak writer Martin Šimečka movingly suggested, the "provincialism and stupidity" of the new authoritarian, populist, and ethnocentric movements in the region?[4]

The dissident as a hero turned out to be a political myth in Central and Eastern Europe, but the myth raised these societies to a higher level of moral self-awareness.[5] Since the collapse of communism, most former dissidents both opposed the restoration of the old regimes and defended the liberal principles of universal equality under law, even for their former jailers. This may have cost them electoral votes, but their consciences remained clean. Eastern Europe has a memory of despotism and political dissent that no other part of the world can claim. Precisely because they knew better than anybody else the nature of the old regimes, the humiliation imposed on the individual in the name of collective salvation, former dissidents are the proponents of a liberalism based on memory and caution.

The revolutions of 1989 were first and foremost revolutions of the mind, and critical intellectuals played the role of "revolutionary subjects". In the aftermath of 1989, an important transformation of identity occurred within this group: critical intellectuals converted into something that was long absent from East-Central (and arguably West) European experience, namely *democratic intellectuals.*[6] In the midst of the difficult transition, democratic intellectuals serve to remind society that no goal is so important as to justify the sacrifice of individual freedom. Non-Machiavellian political practices (what used to be called "antipolitics"), with their wager on pluralism, diversity, and the rejection of ascribed collective identities, will remain timely. The decline of the public intellectual, a phenomenon noticed both East and West, is not a sociological fatality. The ongoing tension between proponents of an open society and their rivals (a contradiction more salient, but not at all limited, to the postcommunist world) makes the role of democratic intellectuals as significant as ever.

Intellectual Daydreams under Communism

In the 1970s and 1980s it became trendy in some quarters to revere the Austro-Hungarian "Golden Age" with its real or invented cosmopolitan and tolerant traditions. Central Europe was ascribed with all the lost legacies of civility, cultural experimentation, scientific innovation, and individual rights within the rule of law. Although there were many contributors to the manufacture of this myth (Philip Roth's "Writers from the Other Europe" series and Nobel Prize winners Czesław Miłosz, Elias Canetti, and Isaac Bashevis Singer), perhaps the most eloquent soothsayer was Milan Kundera, whose "Tragedy of Central Europe" seemed to forever define the topography of the region. Central Europe, or to use Kundera's original metaphor, the "abducted Europe", was turned into a cultural myth, galvanizing both western and eastern intellectuals, from Susan Sontag to Danilo Kiš.[7]

As long as Central Europe remained a cultural (literary) myth, no one could attack the critical intellectuals of the Warsaw Pact countries for harboring political illusions.[8] Had they not dreamt about Central Europe, civil society, and antipolitics, about a universe of autonomy and diversity, they would have been condemned to spineless vegetation. By eulogizing civil society and Central European traditions, they proposed political and cultural archetypes, normative ideas fully opposed to the uniformity and stultification required by Sovietism, and they also ascribed special status to the critical intellectual as a moral "tribune". To use Polish poet Stanislaw Baranczak's inspired metaphor, critical intellectuals continued to "breathe under water" and to generate ideas and values for which they gained respect from less active individuals, the inhabitants of the "gray area".

These writers and dissidents were admired, if not always loved, by their countrymen. Even rulers were interested in their ideas, as newly opened communist-era archives bear witness. They were seen as moral heroes, though few would take the risk to publicly endorse their gestures. Dissidents risked their jobs, friends, and even freedom. The fact that these individuals were underappreciated in the mid–1990s should not make us oblivious to their prerevolutionary credentials. Critical intellectuals did matter under communism; as an ideocratic regime, communism took ideas—especially oppositional, alternative ideas—seriously. The ideal of growing civic activism from below allowed individuals to escape ubiquitous bureaucratic controls and engage in spontaneous forms of association and initiative.

Not so long ago, in the pages of the *New York Review of Books*, Timothy Garton Ash wrote poignantly about the uses of adversity and acquainted western readers with the main ideas that eventually subverted the Leninist order. A frequent visitor to the region, well-connected to every important person associated with Eastern Europe's cultural underground, Garton Ash did more than anyone to make the political writings of Václav Havel, Adam Michnik, and György Konrád well-known and valued in the West. Not only did he write about the region, but his essays were widely discussed and commented on by those whom he praised as moral and political heroes. Thanks to him (and to other writers like Andrew Arato, Neal Asherson, Tony Judt, John Keane, and Jacques Rupnik), dissidents were rightly seen as paragons of dignity within a morass of cynicism, duplicity, and conformity.

Then, suddenly, civil society became political reality. As communist regimes fell one after the other in the almost surreal revolutionary avalanche of 1989, there were no political counterelites to take over (Poland was somewhat of an exception). There was no full-fledged counterideology, unless we consider the generous calls for truthfulness, pluralism, and authenticity as political doctrines.[9]

Never before perhaps in human history have so many individuals been so swiftly and traumatically exposed to earth-shattering transformations of their whole existential world. All the ideologically imposed norms and slogans were exposed as lies. The hour had arrived, it seemed, for these societies to finally live in truth. But the revolutionary euphoria associated with the fall of communism was short lived, and discombobulation, frustration, and bitter disappointment have marked its aftermath. The moral polis heralded by Eastern Europe's dissident writers has not come true. Instead, there is noise, discomfiture, and a lot of nostalgia for the "good old days" of the past.

All established ranks, statuses, traditions, hierarchies, and symbols have collapsed, and new ones are still tottering and quite problematic.

Envy, rancor, and resentment have replaced the values of solidarity, civility, and compassion that once drove the East European revolutionaries. Long disguised by Leninist propaganda, inequality emerged as a shocking reality. As Polish sociologist Jacek Kurczewski noted: "Poverty is accompanied by envy, a feeling that becomes dominant in times of economic change. The feeling expresses itself not so much in a striving for communism, but in a defense of socialist mechanisms of social security under conditions of a capitalist economy and suspicion of everyone who has achieved success in these new conditions."[10] Greed, corruption, and abuses of power are all-pervasive, affecting all political parties, left and right. Thus, veteran Solidarity activist Bogdan Borusewicz wryly admitted: "We were convinced that when communism collapsed and the USSR fell apart, then the best people would step forward to rule well and honestly. It turned out that people remained people, and the shortcomings we were used to blaming on the system are simply embedded in each person, me included."[11] Much of the idealistic ethos of the revolutionary upheaval evaporated and left room for bitterness, suspicion, and paralyzing self-pity. In Poland and Hungary as much as in Romania or Bulgaria, contemplating the rise of the new bourgeoisie, overwhelmingly recruited from the communist economic nomenklatura, led to mass feelings of frustration. Instead of promises of emancipation and revolutionary change, many individuals are now sharing a psychology of helplessness, defeat, and dereliction.

Metaphysical Mud-slinging

The rampant indulgence in "metaphysical mud-slinging" indicates a temptation to dismiss the moral credentials of precisely those people who had championed dissidence under the late communist regimes. This resentful trend is intensifying further, and the return of former communists to government positions in Albania, Bulgaria, Hungary, and Poland exacerbates factionalism among former anticommunist forces. There is a contagious need to assign guilt and demonize those held responsible for the current troubles. Manichean visions are resurfacing in a world that seemed to have had enough of such dangerous temptations. Populist ideologies, radical mythologies of victimization and persecution, offer necessary alibis for new exercises in hatred and exclusion. History is often rewritten in order to accommodate self-serving national legends of heroism, and the calls for lucidity are denounced as harmful to the health of the ethnic community.[12]

Among those trying to assess the future of the postcommunist societies, two main schools have emerged. Optimists share a belief in the vitality and viability of liberal institutions and values, while skeptics despair at the host of former Leninists who have converted themselves into ethnocentric radicals, rabid chauvinists, clerical fundamentalists, fascists, and other varieties of antiliberals. The optimists see Central Europe quickly joining European structures, adopting and developing western values and institutions, and enjoying the benefits of market economies. Pessimists notice that privatization goes slowly and erratically, and its main beneficiaries are primarily the former communist hacks, ex-secret police officers, conmen, or mafiosi. Furthermore, they see political society in these countries increasingly marred by venomous hostility, pseudoprinciples, and the rise of irresponsible nationalist demagogues. For them, prospects for liberalism are dim in countries other than the relatively successful Central European triangle (the Czech Republic, Hungary, Poland) and the Baltic states.

Citizen-Scholars Needed

This discussion, which I deliberately oversimplify, contrasts those who think that it is high time for former dissidents and human rights activists to leave politics to the professionals with those who still see a pressing task for the democratic intelligentsia to advocate the needs and interests of civil society. In other words: Do intellectuals still matter in postcommunist societies?

Throughout Eastern Europe, intellectuals seem to have lost the war. Aleksandr Solzhenitsyn's long expected return to Russia provoked no soul-searching national debate on the country's past or present. Solzhenitsyn even went so far as to make public his decision not to vote in the December 1995 parliamentary elections because of his disgust with the dismal state of Russian politics. In the presidential election of June 1996, he lukewarmly supported Yeltsin, whereas Yelena Bonner, Andrei Sakharov's widow, and Sergey Kovalev, Russia's preeminent human rights activist, refused to vote for any of the leading candidates. It is hard not to feel sad, even desperate, at the political resurrection of so many former collaborators of the deposed regimes. The price of normalcy seems to be the institutionalization of oblivion. As French journalist Bernard Guetta asserted after the 1995 Polish presidential election: "The war is over. Poland has chosen a normal man for normal times. Everything is fine and it is very sad."[13] The pendulum has swung from the initial idealization of dissidents as prophets of truth, as the voice of the powerless, to the ongoing trend toward their dismissal and even vilification. The current prevailing view of dissidents as "losers" must be challenged. Their role and the values for which they have long stood are fundamental to the outcome of the ongoing political struggles.

It is the optimistic school that equates political normalcy with the end of political involvement of the East European intelligentsia. The problems of Central European democracies, they argue, should be analyzed and solved by professional politicians. Needless to add, where one can find these well-trained, skillful, and morally reliable individuals remains a mystery. Optimistic pessimists, like myself, take issue with this approach and wonder if the prospect of a political order rooted in morality is by definition doomed. It is thus disturbing to see that even some of the most articulate western analysts of the region have come to the conclusion that antipolitics is a failed project. If I refer more frequently to Garton Ash, it is precisely because I respect his acumen and perspicacity, his empathy for the moral dilemmas of these writers and philosophers, and because I ask myself: What happened that made him so distrustful of the same values he so eloquently cherished several years ago? Does he think that the political confrontation is over and that a constitution of liberty has indeed been achieved in these countries? Can one separate political participation from political critique? True, East European intellectuals briefly brought to power by the wave of 1989 were not always good politicians; they made some terrible mistakes. But should they now be banned completely from politics?

Precisely because of their independent position, their readiness to challenge the idols of the tribe, former dissidents remain vitally important. Building on their years of opposition to the authoritarian system in the name of human dignity, pluralism, and freedom, they can now shine their lanterns on hypocrisy, bureaucratic manipulation, and ideological conformity in present day politics. In early 1995, Garton Ash unambiguously wrote: "You do not have to be a president or a prime minister to change consciousness. In fact, you may stand a rather better chance if you are not."[14] Public intellectuals should thus resign themselves to their newly prescribed position of *spectateur engagé* (a hint to the memoirs of the late French sociologist Raymond Aron); however, whereas this detachment might arguably be justified in developed democracies, it is highly questionable that the new polities in Eastern and Central Europe can so easily dispense with the moral injections so needed during the transition.[15]

The intensity of the attacks against them, the vicious ironies and dismissive tones, suggests that their enemies understand this situation quite well. In fact, I propose that anti-intellectualism in postcommunist societies is intimately linked to antiwesternism and antiliberalism. The political setbacks of the dissidents are accompanied by widespread disaffection with delays in European integration of these countries as well as the lack of altruistic, decisive Western commitment to their economic recovery.[16] Many citizens in these countries expected the states of the European Community to act as quickly and as generously toward them as they had in the past toward Greece, Portugal, and Spain. Dissidents were the proponents of Western values, and as many people have come to resent what they perceive as Western indifference, these very intellectuals are held in contempt, accused of groundless idealism, utopianism, and wishful thinking. As their very existence is a constant reminder of how few really resisted communism, it becomes fashionable to discard their altruism. People have learned how to hate and scorn them.[17] This explains much of the reorientation of the Polish electorate in the November 1995 presidential elections. Poles have been disappointed with Western reluctance to speed up Poland's integration into Euro-Atlantic structures. One can thus notice in most of these countries a new wave of resistance to Western values and a mounting criticism of those elites directly associated with liberal choices.[18]

It was one thing to get rid of the old regime, with its spurious claim to cognitive infallibility, and a much more daunting task to erect a pluralist, multiparty order, a civil society, a rule of law, and a market economy.[19] Freedom, it turned out, is easier to gain than to guarantee. The events of 1989, unlike previous historical convulsions designated "revolutions", were not inspired by any systematic blueprint, by any plan for political or spiritual salvation. They were anti-ideological, antimillenialist, anti-Jacobin, and anti-Machiavellian. They did not proclaim the advent of the New Jerusalem, the Third Rome, the Empire of Reason, or the Republic of Virtue. Their leaders were not driven by an appetite for power or by utopian fervor. They were indeed reluctant revolutionaries who understood the perils of dogmatic hubris. For them, the ideocratic state was the devil incarnate, the imposition of a secular religion as the basis of politics, instead of contract or consensus.[20] This postmodern repudiation of any predictive teleology, of any world historical determinism, was both their moral strength and political vulnerability. It was the triumph of poetry over ideology or, if you prefer, of surrealism over realism.

From Prague to Berlin to Vilnius, philosophers, historians, journalists, poets, balladeers, jazz musicians, and rock singers became leaders—at least for a few days or months. As the ecstasy faded away, most dissidents were eliminated from the front stage, then blamed for all imaginable sins. The less impressive the anticommunist background of their critics, the shriller their voices. But again, does this mean that democratic intellectuals have ceased to influence the political process? What is then to be made of the key political role played in Poland by an outstanding medieval historian like Bronislaw Geremek, one of the main strategists of the 1989 round table agreements, later the chairman of the foreign affairs committee of the Polish parliament and the country's current foreign minister? Aren't former dissidents like Jacek Kuroń and Karol Modzelewski still significant voices in articulating political criticism and orienting the public debate?

Nowadays it is increasingly fashionable to lament the naïvety of critical intellectuals. They are chided for failure to establish a new set of values and for lack of nerve in confrontations with mounting populist waves. Instead, shouldn't they be held accountable in light of what they actually stated in their pre–1989 writings? Thinkers like Konrád or Michnik never claimed that they were interested in becoming leaders of their nations.[21] János Kis, the first chairman of Hungary's liberal and prowestern Alliance of Free Democrats, never saw himself as a national savior, but as a political philosopher. Dissidents have generally disliked collective emotions and refused the exploitation of individual charisma for political purposes. The main contribution of these intellectuals was to ensure the peacefulness of the revolutions. They wanted to avoid any form of Jacobin terror, and in this they fully succeeded. Their self-imposed mission was to continuously remind their fellow citizens of the values that inspired the revolutions, and therefore they consistently rejected the vindictive logic of mob justice.

1989 Redux

The revolutions of 1989 are now subject to all sorts of revisionism; even their moral roots are questioned. All kinds of bizarre stories are now circulated about what presumably happened in 1989: the end of communism was simply a gigantic hoax, a secret police operation, a grotesque masquerade engineered by factions within the former elite. Conspiracy theories abound in which the traditional reference to the "Yalta betrayal" is replaced by the new myth of "Malta", the December 1989 summit at which George Bush and Mikhail Gorbachev allegedly agreed on the future of Eastern Europe. This political myth has an all-explanatory power: it defines the source of evil, makes sense of the former communists' economic empowerment, and justifies civic demobilization. "Why fight when the end of the game is preordained?" many East

Europeans ask. Journalist Tina Rosenberg has noted: "What the world did not know about Malta, but about half of the Czechs I interviewed seemed to know, is that Gorbachev there had promised Bush to topple communism if the communists were given their nations' wealth and therefore retained power in its new currency."[22]

Perhaps these were not even revolutions, since so many of the former apparatchiks achieved success within the new order. Such disillusionment, in turn, creates anger and need for a scapegoat. Intellectuals are thus described as quixotic dreamers, unable to articulate pragmatic strategies of change. Their moral concerns are decried as proof of wimpiness. Former Czech prime minister Václav Klaus, a flamboyant free marketeer and staunch advocate of decommunization, is usually portrayed as a realistic, down-to-earth, and therefore successful politician compared to Havel, the tweedy intellectual. But the Czech case is in many respects unique, as it has shown little resurgence of the authoritarian populism overtaking Croatia, Russia, Serbia, and Slovakia. Moreover, in spite of his Thatcherite rhetoric, Klaus did not dismantle the social safety net inherited from the previous regime; under Klaus state spending in the Czech Republic remained at approximately fifty percent of the gross domestic product. His classical liberal agenda is a polemical device to contemptuously mock Havel and his supporters for comprising a "moralizing elite with perfectionist ambitions" and for their devotion to human rights and civil society.[23]

State Artists or State Jesters?

The main split in the region is not between communists and anticommunists, but between assertive nationalists (often allied with former communists) and the besieged liberal forces. The former denounce critical intellectuals precisely because they have refused to abandon their creed—their belief that truth has to be defended against all imperatives of *realpolitik*. They are again seen as troublemakers, sterile daydreamers with little grasp of the intricacies of the political game. Their calls for tolerance are turned down as dangerous to the survival of the ethnic community. In their post–1990 books, György Konrád and Václav Havel, intellectuals who most poignantly formulated the language of dissent, lamented the declining status of intellectuals in Eastern Europe. Both authors are struck by the ambiguities, disappointments, and pitfalls of postrevolutionary times. They look to their legacy of dissent as a wellspring of moral inspiration, and both see the memory of the communist experience as uniquely important for avoiding new mythological fallacies. Konrád and Havel have come to see many of their ideals scoffed, denied, and battered, but they still cling to their hopes of building states based on intellectual and spiritual values.[24] Their critics' ironies notwithstanding, they epitomize the need to preserve that peculiar East European social role: the critical intellectual as political activist, as defender of the values of modernity.

Even if one finds some of Konrád's reflections too sanguine, especially his belief that anti-Semitism will remain a peripheral trend in Hungary, one cannot but admire his enlightened vision of a liberated political community. Students of the transition will learn more from his writings than from countless arid, scholastic attempts to apply western concepts or mathematical formulae to a profoundly novel situation. The intellectual's main vocation is understanding, Konrád argues, and he sees this role as essential if politics is to have any meaning: "The intelligentsia is the keeper of legitimacies: it provides grounds for morality, argumentation for the law, exegesis for religion, allegories for ethics, and analysis for politics. In other words, intellectuals peddle clear consciences and guilty consciences."[25] Thanks to intellectuals, citizens can make fundamental distinctions between good and bad actions.

The causes of current confusion are based in the moral phenomenology of the East European intelligentsia. For decades this class was divided between those who accepted collaboration (Miklós Haraszti's "state artists") and those who rejected the pact with the communists (Leszek Kołakowski's "jesters"). Among the latter, there were many disenchanted Marxists. Breaking with the magic world of ideology and engaging in the rebellion of the mind, they discovered the force of critical reason. Under postcommunism, these intellectuals have tried new political forms and styles (civic forums, for instance), and they have voiced strong reservations about the conventional dichotomies in terms of left and right. Taking into account the growing crisis of ideologies and parties in the West, can one fault them in this commitment to moral values?

We cannot risk idealizing professional politicians who in this century have so frequently displayed both soullessness and thoughtlessness. It was, after all, the narrow-mindedness of Germany's political elite and its failure to detect the totalitarian nature of Hitler's party-movement that created the conditions for the Nazi takeover in 1933. Yes, intellectuals may err, but at least in the Central European case they invoke a heritage of heroic resistance to autocracy. They have, to paraphrase Hannah Arendt, a revolutionary tradition whose treasure hasn't yet been lost.[26] Thus, Konrád's call for a democratic charter, a nonparty civic initiative committed to the values of pluralism, is clearly linked to Havel's appeal for a spiritualization of politics. Otherwise, we are forever annexed to instrumental rationality, condemned to remain cogs in the wheel manipulated by anonymous, irresistible forces.

German sociologist Wolf Lepenies described intellectuals as "the species that complains".[27] At the same time, their complaints deny the frozen order of things and pierce the fallacious walls of immutable structures of domination. Democratic intellectuals are here to defend the political legacy of the Enlightenment against the new waves of atavistic passion, tribalism, nativist populism, and racism. Why did so many Westerners get excited at the moment of the antiauthoritarian revolutions of 1989 after all? Simply because a cohort of senile bureaucrats were kicked out of power?

The answer is surely more profound, and it is linked to the fact that the revolutions of Eastern Europe have rehabilitated the notion of citizen as the true political subject. Their main liberal component consisted of emphasis on the right of the individual to be free from state intrusion into his or her life.[28] This celebration of negative liberty was accompanied by an equally important focus on the revival of civic initiative and the restoration of substantive positive freedoms, especially the freedoms of association and expression.[29] The uprisings were the palpable expression of a need to reinvent politics, to insert values that transcend immediate pragmatic and ideological considerations into real life. Václav Havel's presence in the Prague castle is a symbol greater than his physical person enjoying (or abhorring) the presidential prerogatives. It is indeed miraculous that, out of the lowest levels of human destitution, out of the murky world of decaying Leninism, an experience of solidarity and civic fraternity could be restored. This is the deeper meaning of Havel's famous pledge in his presidential address on 1 January 1990: "I do not think you appointed me to this office for me, of all people, to lie to you."[30]

The struggle for this new politics is far from over. Because the stakes of the game played in Eastern Europe and the former Soviet Union are so high, the withdrawal of intellectuals from politics would be disastrous. The values formulated during the odyssey of dissent remain as urgent as ever: transparency of human relations, trust, and dignity. Marshall Berman is right that the 1989 revolutions have vigorously reconfirmed the philosophy of human rights as the basic intellectual foundation of modernity: "The hopes of 1989 will be harder to fulfill than the activists of that year believed. Yet those hopes refuse to die, and even their failures turn out to make them strong."[31]

Indeed, Eastern Europe's critical intellectuals first discovered the values of citizenship under conditions of mental subjugation and an unremitting onslaught on autonomy. Their memories (unlike those of their Western counterparts) are marked by opposition to ideological follies and social engineering. They know the full meaning of being unfree. They are not political greenhorns, for which they are often criticized by former communists. They may be reluctant to take jobs, but this is not because of lack of expertise. Their modesty should not be taken for incompetence, in the same way the former communists' arrogance should not be seen as professionalism. Insisting on the need for intellectuals to remain politically active, Havel referred to a former colleague who turned down his invitation to fill an important government position. The friend invoked the well-worn argument that "someone has to remain independent". But what responsibility is about is the opposite. Havel correctly pointed out that, if all democratic intellectuals would follow this escapist example, "nobody will be able to remain independent because there would be nobody in power who would make possible and guarantee your independence."[32]

Serbia, where the betrayal of the intelligentsia and its capitulation to populist adventurers has resulted in countless disasters, exemplifies Havel's theories. After all, we shouldn't forget that intellectuals can be as much proponents of human compassion as of venomous hatred. It was the Serbian intelligentsia that produced in 1986 the memorandum of the Academy of Sciences that, for all practical purposes, delineated the genocidal delusion of ethnic cleansing. But they did it as enemies of civil society, not as its most loyal supporters.[33]

With his reflexive, ironic, and less explicitly militant demeanor, Konrád may be the *spectateur engagé* that Garton Ash seems to favor. His ideas are gentle, his writings are extremely elegant. The problem is, however, can one counterpose Konrád to Havel? In fact, engaging in practical politics is more often than not a matter of personal psychology—some people are naturally disinclined to commit themselves to public service.[34] But this should not be presented as a sociological imperative. From Shelley to Michnik, writers have had a role in denouncing injustice and imagining a less immoral order.

Critical Intellectual Versus Clever Lunatic

Whom do the new postcommunist authoritarian groups and movements abhor the most? The democratic intellectuals, of course, eternally stigmatized as troublemakers, aliens, and Jews. But this scorn makes the "missionary" status of the East European intellectual valid again: critical stances toward chauvinism, despotism, and intolerance remain as important nowadays as they were a decade ago. Fully aware of the fragility of the newly established democratic institutions, Konrád captures this danger: "Our lives can be affected by a clever lunatic whose artistic forte happens to be mass destruction, the destruction of foreigners and his own kind, mixed. We are affected by the new collective identities that up and decide that they are incompatible with their neighbors and think nothing of killing to gain sway over them. In Eastern Europe these collective identities are particularly explosive. In their hysteria they feel surrounded by enemies and therefore in dire need of cleansing their ethnic-national-religious-linguistic-tribal ranks (a process that includes rewarding the politically loyal). While communist dictatorships wither on the vine, their internationalist ideology no longer viable, national dictatorships are blossoming."[35]

The long glorified "society", whose side dissidents took in their struggle against the communist state, turned out to be the source of much antidemocratic nostalgia and emotion. As Polish sociologist Jerzy Szacki put it: "Somehow, imperceptibly, a magnificent society, admired by the whole world, has turned into an unpredictable mass posing a danger to its own existence; it can be said, in its defense only that, for a long time, it was subjugated under communism."[36] Under these circumstances, intellectuals have to remain pedagogues, always watchful for the slide into new forms of barbarism. In what used to be Czechoslovakia, the Civic Movement (Havel's party) lost because it did not know how to explain to voters how difficult decommunization is and the dangers related to revolutionary justice. They refused to engage in lynchings and were widely perceived as soft on communism.[37]

Ironically, dissidents were punished for having failed to take revenge on their former tormentors. But this is exactly their moral lesson, and in the long run one can expect that people would realize the deep morality involved in the philosophy of forgiveness (which does not mean forgetfulness). Dissent fights for the survival of memory, and intellectuals have a special position in the organization of the difficult but inevitable confrontation with the past. After all, it was Russia's foremost intellectual, the physicist and human rights activist Andrei Sakharov, who fully engaged in articulating the liberal agenda for the burgeoning democratic forces in his country. Havel, Kuroń, Michnik, Sakharov, Zhelev—these names represent an international community of like-minded spirits opposed to atavistic collectivism and other trends inimical to an open society.

A Common Moral Voice in Society

Speaking to the PEN World Congress in Prague in November 1994, five years after the "velvet revolution", Havel boldly identified the purpose of this new chapter of antipolitics, adapted to the challenges of the post-cold war era, and called for a full commitment by intellectuals to the creation of open societies. They, the critical intellectuals, had been the ones who had debunked the old ideocratic regimes. Now their role, East and West, is to be moral critics of the existing order, which is always imperfect and calls for improvement.[38] They should not replace the prince, but complement him, and if need be, take him to task. Their role is not to withdraw in gratuitous contemplation or even celebration of the status quo. The discourse of rights, the defense of modernity's agenda against obscurantist reactionaries—this is what democratic intellectuals can and should do. Thus, they ought to, Havel argued, "gradually begin to create something like a worldwide lobby, a special brotherhood or, if I may use the word, a somewhat conspiratorial mafia, whose aim is not just to write marvelous books and occasional manifestoes but to have an impact on politics and its human perceptions in a spirit of solidarity and in a coordinated, deliberate way." As resolute defenders of the open society, they have to oppose the illusions of a presumed "third way", a theme espoused by leftists and rightists alike.[39]

Is this too much of an ambition? Will politicians listen to their suggestions? We don't know, but it would be proof of unjustified timidity to simply say that intellectuals should stay away from politics, that they are professional outsiders rather than insiders of the political game. Some authors think that, because of their different language and reflexive abilities, the role of intellectuals is to be moral critics of politics rather than involved actors. In such a view, the traditional roles of intellectuals in Eastern Europe (voice of the oppressed, priest, prophet, militant, ethical advocate, substitute politician, or even antipolitician) have fallen away with astounding alacrity. But, one may ask, have they? The struggle is not over in that part of the world, the battle over history continues, and democratic intellectuals remain crucially important for dispelling the new illusions and mythological chimeras. After all, this is true even in advanced democracies like France, Germany, or Italy, as demonstrated by endless and much-needed debates over Vichy, resistance, collaboration, historical consciousness, and memory in general.

It is true that parts of the original vision of civil society as defined by dissidents have become obsolete. Actual political choices have dissolved the previous suprapartisan vision of the moral countersociety. But, as

Aleksander Smolar writes, the new order cannot function democratically in the absence of determined civic engagement in favor of the values of private property and open society: "The civic principle is not just a principle of equality; it also creates the normative basis for the inner integration of civil society as well as its integration with the political system. The development of civil society, the consolidation of democracy, and the closer identification of citizens with state institutions—all these require counteracting the atomizing tendencies that the huge changes of recent years (however necessary and ultimately salutary) have set in motion."[40]

Ideas and patterns of resistance cannot simply vanish as figments of imagination. As Jacek Kuroń puts it, it is great ideas that shape world history.[41] The besieged legacy of dissent deserves to be defended, not ridiculed. It would be indeed preposterous to simply jettison its moral endowment only because nowadays it seems less appealing and less enthusing than a decade or two ago. Intellectual history evolves in cycles, and it is clear that these ideas will make a comeback, if only because the Western vision of public good and the current political structures seem themselves quite fluid. The issue is not to endorse antiliberal but more liberal ones. Indeed, as Philippe Schmitter argues: "Far from being secure in its foundations and practices, democracy will have to face unprecedented challenges. Its future...will be tumultuous, uncertain and very eventful."[42]

Intellectuals who enter politics—like the Czech Republic's Václav Havel, Hungary's Árpád Göncz, Poland's Jacek Kuroń, or Romania's Andrei Pleşu—need not become tainted. The choices may often be dramatic, even tragic, but this is not to say that politics is ontologically a sullying enterprise. Humans make it either pure or squalid.

To those who think that the dissidents' search for subjective freedom was just an isolated intellectual exercise, with no aftermath in the depressing world of postcommunist settlings of scores and moral turpitude, Konrád answers: "Modern East European humanism, which came out of the dissident democratic movements and matured by battling the strut, spasms, and hysteria of collective egos, has taken deep roots in our culture, and without it Hungary 1989 could not have taken place....[T]his year's peaceful revolutions—our own and the analogous ones in a number of Central and East European countries—have opened a new chapter in the history of European autonomy."[43]

This is indeed the major point: If the revolutions of 1989 restored the sense of morality in politics, if they offered the individual a sense of fraternity in the political rather than ethnonational community, then the current nationalist frenzy should be seen as a counterrevolutionary stage.

Thus, more than ever, democratic intellectuals are needed in politics if this most ancient human affair is to be a more hospitable place for truth, trust, and tolerance.

Notes

1 Tony Judt, "Beyond Good and Evil: Intellectuals and Politics at the End of the 20th Century", (paper presented at Tannen Lecture, Bloomington, Indiana University, 18 February 1999).

2 See András Bozóki, ed., *Intellectuals and Politics in Central Europe* (Budapest: Central European University Press, 1998).

3 Ferenc Fehér and Ágnes Heller, *The Postmodern Political Condition*.

4 For the importance of critical intellectuals' critique of populist authoritarianism and the continuous need to articulate the liberal alternative to such trends, see Timothy Garton Ash, "Surprise in Central Europe", *New York Review of Books* (March 1999); see also the special issue "Intellectuals and Social Change in East-Central Europe", *Partisan Review* (Fall 1992).

5 See Vladimir Tismaneanu, *Fantasies of Salvation: Democracy, Nationalism and Myth in Post-Communist Europe* (Princeton: Princeton University Press, 1998) as well as the thoughtful reviews of this book by Steven Fish, *East European Constitutional Review* (Winter 1999); and Arista Cirtautas, *American Political Science Review* 93:1 (March 1999).

6 See Olivier Mongin, *Face au scepticisme: Les mutations du paysage intellectuel ou l'invention de l'intellectuel démocratique* (Paris: Editions La Découverte, 1994).

7 See Milan Kundera, "Tragedy of Central Europe", *New York Review of Books* (26 April 1984): 33–38.

8 See György Konrád, "L'Europe du Milieu, patrie intérieure", *Cadmos* 39 (Fall 1987): 25–38; Radu Stern and Vladimir Tismaneanu, "L'Europe Centrale: Nostalgies culturelles et réalités politiques".

9 See Timothy Garton Ash, *The Magic Lantern: The Revolutions of '89 Witnessed in Warsaw, Budapest, Berlin and Prague* (New York: Vintage Books, 1993); Vladimir Tismaneanu, ed., *Revolutions of 1989* (London: Routledge, 1999), especially the essays by Chirot, Eisenstadt, Garton Ash, and Isaac.

10 See *Gazeta Wyborcza*, 28–29 January 1995, quoted by Michal Cichy, "Requiem for the Moderate Revolutionist", *East European Politics and Societies* 10:1 (Winter 1996): 145. For similar views on the rampant cynicism and moral squalor in post–1989 Romania, see H.R. Patapievici, *Politice* (Bucharest: Editura Humanitas, 1996); as well as Mircea Mihăieş and Vladimir Tismaneanu, *Neighbors of Franz Kafka* (Iasi, Romania: Editura Polirom, 1998).

11 Borusewicz, "Tygodnik Powzechny", in Cichy, "Requiem", 149.

12 See Slavenka Drakulic, *Café Europa: Life After Communism* (New York: Norton, 1997).

13 See Bernard Guetta, "Pologne: La normalisation démocratique", *Le Nouvel Observateur* (23–29 November 1995).

14 See Timothy Garton Ash, "Prague: Intellectuals and Politicians", *The New York Review of Books* (12 January 1995): 38.

15 It is noteworthy that Judt, known for his criticism of the dissidents' "naïve idealism", has significantly nuanced this approach in his recent book. See Tony Judt, *Burden of Responsibility: Blum, Camus, Aron and the French Twentieth Century* (Chicago: University of Chicago Press, 1998). Judt, Havel, and Camus share the same ethos of civic responsibility and commitment to the defense of individual rights.

16 See Tony Judt, "The End of Which European Era?" *Daedalus* 123:3 (Summer 1994): 1–19.

17 See Jirina Siklova, "Backlash", *Social Research* 60:4 (Winter 1993): 737–49.

18 Irena Grudzinska Gross (remarks made at a workshop on political psychology of postcommunism, Budapest, Collegium Budapest, 21 March 1996).

19 See Adam Michnik, *Letters from Freedom: Post-Cold War Realities and Perspectives* (Berkeley: University of California Press, 1998); Ralf Dahrendorf, *After 1989: Morals, Revolution and Civil Society* (New York: St. Martin's Press, 1997).

20 This point is discussed by Leszek Kołakowski, *Modernity on Endless Trial* (Chicago: University of Chicago Press, 1990), 175–91.

21 For the significance of Michnik's ideas, see Ken Jowitt, "In Praise of the 'Ordinary'", introduction to Michnik, *Letters from Freedom*; and Jacek Dalecki, "Political Evolution of Polish Dissident Adam Michnik" (Ph.D. diss., Indiana University, 1997). I want to thank Jeffrey C. Isaac for having brought to my attention and sharing with me Dalecki's excellent doctoral thesis.

22 See Tina Rosenberg, *The Haunted Land: Facing Europe's Ghosts After Communism* (New York: Random House, 1995), 116–17. The same could be said about Romania, where the obsession with the "Malta conspiracy" has imbued the political discourses of both neofascism and neocommunism.

23 See Jane Perlez, "The Fist in the Velvet Glove", *New York Magazine* (16 July 1995): 18.

24 See Václav Havel, *Summer Meditations* (New York: Vintage, 1993), especially the epilogue, 123–28; and Václav Havel, *Art of the Impossible: Politics as Morality in Practice* (New York: Knopf, 1997).

25 See György Konrád, *Melancholy of Rebirth: Essays from Post-Communist Central Europe* (San Diego, Calif.: Harcourt Brace/A Helen and Kurt Wolff Book, 1995), 82.

26 See Hannah Arendt, *On Revolution* (New York: Penguin Books, 1977); Jeffrey C. Isaac, *Democracy in Dark Times* (Ithaca: Cornell University Press, 1998).

27 See Wolf Lepenies, Inaugural Lecture at College de France, European Chair (21 February 1992). Romanian trans. in *Polis* 1 (1994): 5–17.

28 See Michael Ignatieff, "After the Revolution", *The New Republic* (19–26 August 1996): 42–45; Ernest Gellner, *Conditions of Liberty: Civil Society and Its Rivals*.

29 For the importance of freedom of the press in postcommunist societies, see G. M. Tamás, "Victory Defeated", *Journal of Democracy* (January 1999).

30 Quoted in Gale Stokes, *The Walls Came Tumbling Down: The Collapse of Communism in Eastern Europe* (New York: Oxford University Press, 1993), 157.

31 See Marshall Berman, "Modernism and Human Rights Near the Millenium", *Dissent* (Summer 1995): 333.

32 See "Rival Visions: Václav Havel and Václav Klaus, with a commentary by Petr Pithart," *Journal of Democracy* 7:1 (January 1996): 17.

33 See Andrew Wachtel, *Making a Nation, Breaking a Nation: Literature and Cultural Politics in Yugoslavia* (Stanford University Press, 1998).

34 Take, for instance, the cases of two brilliant intellectuals—Gabriel Liiceanu and Andrei Pleşu—in post–1989 Romania. The former chose to deal with politics as a committed spectator, whereas the latter has played an important political role, first as minister of culture in the early 1990s, then as minister of foreign affairs after 1997.

35 Konrád, *The Melancholy of Rebirth*, 87.

36 See Jerzy Szacki, "Polish Democracy: Dreams and Reality", *Social Research* 58:4 (Winter 1991): 712.

37 See Petr Pithart, "Intellectuals in Politics", *Social Research* 60:4 (Winter 1993): 751–61.

38 See Ira Katznelson, *Liberalism's Crooked Circle: Open Letters to Adam Michnik* (Princeton: Princeton University Press, 1996).

39 Havel's remarks quoted by Garton Ash, "Prague", 38; for an illuminating analysis of the "third way" illusions in Romania, see Adrian Marino, *Politica si cultura* (Iasi, Romania: Editura Polirom, 1996). A distinguished literary historian and theorist who spent more than ten years in communist jails, Marino has become, after 1989, a main proponent for an ideology of the democratic center and a strong advocate for the values of liberalism and Enlightenment. This is especially important in a country whose intellectuals (or many among them) have long been seduced by the ideas of philosopher Constantin Noica, a critic of western consumerism, positivism, materialism, and "democratic mediocrity". For Noica, see Katherine Verdery, *National Ideology under Socialism* (Berkeley: University of California Press, 1991); and Sorin Antohi, *Civitas Imaginalis: Istorie şi utopie în cultura română* (Bucharest: Editura Liters, 1994), 175–208.

40 See Aleksander Smolar, "Opposition to Atomization", *Journal of Democracy* 7:7 (January 1996): 37–38.

41 Jacek Kuroń (remarks at an international conference on Eastern Europe, University of Central Florida, Orlando, 5 January 1995).

42 See Philippe Schmitter, "More Liberal, Preliberal, or Postliberal", *Journal of Democracy* 6:1 (January 1995): 16.

43 See Konrád, *The Melancholy of Rebirth*, 18–19.

III Vulnerabilities of the New Democracies

10 Privatization as Transforming Persons

KATHERINE VERDERY

"Privatization is not simply a change in ownership;
it is a revolution in ways of thinking, acting, and governing."[1]

In his brilliant essay "The Leninist Extinction", Ken Jowitt defines 1989 as a "genesis" moment to be marked by creating, naming, and bounding in new ways.[2] As if to confirm his insight, many western policy-makers and academic advisors labeled this the moment of the "big bang", of original creation, before which all was chaos. They and their counterparts in the former Soviet bloc even produced a sacred trinity apt for the times: marketization, privatization, democratization. These were at once three aspects of the deity and three forms in whose likeness the new world of postsocialism would take shape. With central plans, collective property, and one-party rule reduced to dust, creative modeling would bring forth a new society in the divine image of the West. Although the creative process was understood to be a complex one, there seemed to be extensive agreement that something like this trinity was necessary for exiting socialism.

The present essay explores one element of this trinity—privatization—and asks what it would mean for privatization to "succeed"—a necessary step in assessing where a decade of privatizing has gotten us. I do not employ the sorts of measures used by economists but emphasize instead a broad understanding of what "property" is. Additionally, I spend more time thinking about what property was like under socialism than in asking what has happened to it lately, for I believe that this will help us to understand better the privatization process that is actually taking place. Although the result of my exploration is very inconclusive, I will be satisfied if I have impeded tendencies to assess privatization in a simple-minded way.

The Economists' Privatization

Those charged with effecting privatization began from the premise that socialist production was inefficient and wasteful due to the structure of ownership. They saw the transformation of ownership as essential to increasing productivity and the efficiency of factor allocation, enhancing motivation, and improving the quality of output. Privatization would create greater accountability by giving new owners stakes in outcomes; the result would be better performance. Benchmarks were developed for monitoring it, chief among them the percentage of the gross domestic product (GDP) that comes from activity in the private sector and the percentage of formerly state-owned enterprises (SOEs) or of total assets that have been privatized; the latter might be nuanced with indicators of enterprise restructuring.[3] While those who construct these indicators may express some doubt about the possibility of obtaining accurate figures on GDP, revenues from private-sector activity, or total value of state assets, their doubts do not prevent the offering of these figures, which then take on a spurious authority that leads us to think they tell us more than they do.

Among economists, disagreement has emerged as some take issue with the certainties of their colleagues. Josef Brada and Peter Murrell, to name only two, have concluded that the manner of implementing privatization shows less concern for actual improvement of the economy than for imposing a certain standard ownership form.[4] These scholars argue that there can be significant gains in the economic performance of SOEs through measures that fall considerably short of privatizing them—a conclusion supported by work in China.[5] Moreover, such observers argue that the customary measures of "success" in privatization do not necessarily reveal what they claim to—failing, for example, to show *how* corporate governance is operating and if new owners have achieved control that is *effective*.[6]

If privatization is nonetheless the policy of choice, then it must be because it serves goals other than improving economic performance through changing ownership. These include promoting "creative destruction",[7] increasing the legitimacy of new governments and encouraging a property-owning mentality,[8] bringing about ideological change,[9] and facilitating a shift to democratic politics by breaking up state monopolies.[10] I would add to this list a point to be explored further below: Privatization alters the very foundations of what "persons" are and how they are made. This partial listing of privatization's effects begins to suggest how complex a phenomenon property is. As Adams and Brock claim in the statement that I have used at the head of this essay, transforming it is a "revolution in ways of thinking, acting, and governing".

This being the case, how is it possible to draw up a "balance sheet" after ten years? Revolutions in thinking and governing are difficult to operationalize and quantify. If the kinds of data (percentages of GDP, voting and trade statistics, etc.) that seem to tell us the most about these processes mislead by their specificity, then how can we take the temperature of a dying communism? Further compromising the utility of those indicators is David Stark's argument that privatization indicators taking the *firm* as their unit are fundamentally misguided, for the essential unit of privatization is, instead, *networks* of firms.[11] In consequence, I believe that most such quantifying efforts to assess how far the "transition" has proceeded are mistaken. I prefer instead to meditate on the notion of property and to show in this way that one cannot usefully measure the success of privatization.

My argument runs as follows. Along with other anthropologists, I understand "property" as a construct that has something to do with "persons", and the forms taken by both of these notions as somehow connected to the kind of social order in which they are located. I label the three ideal-typical social orders I am concerned with here (fully cognizant that my procedure holds innumerable problems) "fordism", "socialism", and "flexible specialization". After briefly describing some person-property connections suited to the first and third of these, I discuss at greater length the status of property and person under socialism and then ask what it would mean to move from those arrangements to one of the other two—that is, what would "successful privatization" mean from this point of view. The argument is highly preliminary and schematic.

Property and Persons

A canonical text for thinking about the nature of property is the fifth chapter of Locke's *Second Treatise of Government*. Here he seeks to understand how individual appropriation can occur within a nature that God has provided for the use of all. Positing two forms, individual appropriation and collective ownership, he sees the latter as not *opposed* to the former but a *condition* of it. He goes on to argue that government originates in men's agreement to regulate property in the context of a developing money economy. Among the features of his discussion of property that I see as particularly significant are his relating property to

(1) a money economy; (2) forms of authority and government; (3) notions of "person"; and (4) ideas about morality. All these points have proved central to subsequent thinking about property.

Locke sees the connection between property and money as the reason why men had to form governments: before money, men merely appropriated what they could use, but with money, they could accumulate without respect to their immediate needs. This possibility requires regulation, introducing a second element of Lockean property thinking: a presumed relation to *authority*—a state that regulates, adjudicates, and sanctions. Locke's property world thus assumes a particular relation between state and citizens, a form of subjection to which property entitlements are central. In his work and that of subsequent political theorists, this becomes a connection between democracy and property: the property-owning citizen as the responsible subject of a democratic polity. (The ideological durability of this conception is evident in the language about privatization today.)

The kind of person this citizen will be emerges in part from Locke's relating property with personhood. In his famous formulation that "every Man has a Property in his own Person",[12] he establishes persons as autonomous, self-acting individuals whose ownership relation to themselves justifies appropriation through labor and ultimately sanctions accumulation beyond needs. Locke's free individual, owning property in his person as well as in whatever he mixed his labor with, was an effective agent whose liberty was inextricably tied with both his individuality and his (self-)ownership. One does not have to agree with all of C.B. Macpherson's argument about Locke and Hobbes to see in this formulation a blueprint for persons as "possessive individuals".[13] This kind of person had further moral qualities embedded in notions of "propriety"— a notion central to Locke's thinking about property; he often uses the two terms interchangeably. Placing property in a larger configuration of moral relations among men, between men and God, and between men and nature, Locke gives property relations an inevitable moral component: they are not just relations, but *proper* relations.

Property emerges from Locke's treatment, then, as a moral relation between people and things, mediated by people's relations with each other through government. It begins as collective entitlement that gives way to private accumulation by people conceived as possessive individuals. These possessive individuals are a specific kind of person, constituted in relation to property. A signal innovation of early modern times was to apply this notion of person not just to individuals but to corporations. They became jural persons, endowed with agency and will like free individual owners.

The connection between property and personhood is not limited to Locke's formulation but appears as well in the philosophies of Kant, Hegel, and Marx, among many others. Moreover, the same connection appears, if rather differently, in literature on property from anthropology. This literature problematizes a number of assumptions left unquestioned in most other work on the topic, in part by seeing property less as a political and economic relation than as a sociocultural one. To begin with, in anthropological data one often finds that the separation of humans from "things" is considerably murkier than most North Americans would have it. For instance, land may be seen as part of people: "Land is not so much owned as part of one's human substance";[14] indeed, land may even *own* people.[15] Living and dead can merge, as when ancestors are seen as both part of land and part of living communities.[16] Also part of their ancestors, in some sense, are other kinds of things people can own, such as magical spells or names.[17] Animals, people, and land may be understood as forming an organic whole of interconnected beings—not a great *chain* of being but something more like a giant stew.[18] The difference between a man and a deer may be of exactly the same order as the difference between a man and a woman,[19] complicating the assessment of which is the "person" and which the "thing" in the property relation. Likewise, material objects exchanged as gifts may be thought to carry traces of the people who gave them, as in Mauss's celebrated description of *hau*.[20] Some objects, indeed, so embody individual or group identities that to see them as "separate" seems erroneous.

For example, Fred Myers uses the word "property" in his fascinating discussion of Pintupi forms of property and identity,[21] yet the way property (especially land) works in this case scarcely resonates with property notions familiar to us. In Myers's analysis, property has to do, rather, with materializing the shared identity of groups and extending it through time.[22] "[P]eople's joint relationship through time to a named place represents an aspect of an identity they share".[23] Myers sees property here as a *sign*: establishing rights to "use" things is less important than is constituting ties through them with other people. Myers observes in closing, "[O]bjects, as property or not, have meanings for these people which cannot be limited to the analytic domains too often prescribed by our own Euroamerican cultures".[24] Here, one might argue that the "person" being constituted through property is a supraindividual one: the clan or lineage whose identity is materialized in named places on the land. Myers's views imply that just as there can be both individual and corporate "persons" in, say, the United States, "persons" can exist simultaneously at several levels of aggregation, including that of clan or lineage.

Further thought on the nature of persons and their connection with property comes from the ethnography of India and Melanesia, particularly work by Marilyn Strathern. In contrast with the autonomous possessive individuals characteristic of the modern West, Strathern finds in Melanesia what she calls (borrowing from Marriott's research in India) "dividuals", social beings defined in terms of their social interdependencies rather than their autonomy.[25] Here, "persons are frequently constructed as the plural and composite site of the relationships that produced them";[26] composed of diverse relations, they are not bounded and indivisible but multiple and partible. Whereas western persons tend to be defined as "owners"—owners of objects, their own person, their labor power, their culture, and so forth—persons in the New Guinea highlands are defined rather as microcosms of relations.[27] It follows that the place of objects differs considerably in the two instances: these Melanesians "do not have alienable items, that is, property, at their disposal; they can only dispose of items by enchaining themselves in relations with others".[28]

This kind of "enchaining"—the creation and reproduction of social interdependencies—relates to the idea of *social obligations*; it suggests modifying the heavy emphasis accorded the notion of rights as compared with obligations in thinking about property. A standard conception of property is to define it as a "bundle of rights". This definition does not wholly neglect obligation but merely relegates it to the background, as if they were simply two sides of the same coin (my right with respect to you is your obligation to me). The rights of property, however, do not necessarily point one in the same direction as its obligations. In Stark's words, "[A]ssets and liabilities have distinctive network properties".[29] The notion of rights focuses attention on a particular kind of person—the autonomous, rights-bearing individual of liberal theory—rather than on the entire field of relations in which "dividuals" are enmeshed. The notion of obligations brings that wider field into view.

From this kind of work on property, I formulate a broad conception of it, one that centers on its link with persons. I see property as one of a small set of cultural mechanisms (others might include kinship and religion) by which persons are made. Property makes persons by relating human beings to one another and to specific *values* (a word I use in preference to "things" so as to avoid all connotations of concreteness). These values may be concrete objects (houses, land, arrows, pigs), other beings (deer, spirits, ancestors), ideas or formulae (spells, recipes, novels, procedures), other kinds of abstractions of value (shares in a company), and so on. The kinds of relations set up with other people and with these values are not seen as just any old relations but *proper* relations: that is, property is heavily colored by normative ideas concerning morality.

Among the ways it makes persons are by positing a relation in which they are implied and/or by materializing identities that are then seen as "belonging" to persons.

An economistic version of this view might speak of property as a system according to which access to "resources" (values) is regulated by assigning persons rights in them relative to other persons. Such a version presupposes, however, that one has already passed through the process of defining (1) what count as "resources" and as the "persons" whose access to them will be regulated, and that resources already have object status separate from persons; (2) how those are bounded; (3) what morality underlies the relations between them; and (4) what power has established the rules of access and the prevailing notion of "rights". This kind of definition also presupposes that "property" is necessarily about *appropriation*, whereas that may not always be the case. I thus prefer my more confusing and cumbersome formulation, because it requires one to do some work that otherwise will be omitted—and such omission will hide precisely what is most complex about the change in property regimes that is the privatization process. One might be tempted, for instance, to assume that individual firms are the unit of property transformation, or that "ownership" is the property relation of choice, rather than closely inspecting other kinds of property-relevant actors and relations or the many forms of obligation in which they may be anchored.

In introducing this section I mentioned ideas concerning property and person in which persons are construed as "possessive individuals". I wish now to schematize the transformation of this set of notions as a preliminary to talking about property and persons in socialism. My schematization assumes that there is a dominant mode of personhood in specific times and places—an assumption I would not want to take very far but will adopt heuristically, for purposes of argument, and will modify below. If in the period of "fordist" capitalism a dominant model of person is the autonomous, self-acting individual (corporations count as individuals) defined by a private property relation that emphasizes *owning*, in the contemporary shift to "flexible specialization" that notion of person is supplemented by another, which I will call the "portfolio-managing individual". I derive this concept from the work of Emily Martin on mental illness and the immune system[30] and William Maurer on financial services.[31] I see the change in types of persons as linked to a shift in the "steering mechanism" of the global economy, from capital-in-production to finance capital.[32] The rise of flexible specialization and of financial capital accompanies myriad other changes—among them, in the meaning of "nation", the form of corporations, the nature of states, and the core elements of personality.

For some time now, what increasingly matters with corporate wealth is not simply ownership of shares but their control or management. Corporate profits no longer go mainly to the owners of property but to those who manage it.[33] (In this sense, socialist societies, with their collective ownership of means of production managed by the party-state, merely carried to an extreme certain tendencies of twentieth-century capitalism: the separation of management from ownership.) Landownership or the wealth derived from successful manufacturing contributes far less power than does one's relation to capital markets. Scholars such as Maurer see alongside this a thoroughgoing change in conceptions of property as it becomes less a matter of *rights* to be *claimed* and more a question of *risk profiles* to be *managed*. This implies a modification in the role of state authorities: formerly guarantors of property rights, they now become arbiters of risk and hedges against it. Their relation to citizens also changes as subjects cease to be *bearers of rights* and become instead *bearers of risk.*[34]

How "persons" are conceptualized might be expected to change accordingly. The Lockean person is very different from the kinds of individuals now emerging in advanced capitalist states: their status as "possessive individuals" matters less than their status as *holders of a "portfolio" of assets and liabilities*. (Thus, it seems that individual persons no longer serve as the model for corporate persons but corporations as the model for individuals.) Among the items in this portfolio are their health or personality traits or pension plans, which they must competently *manage* (for example, by proper diet, exercise, therapy, medication, financial advice, and other good habits like not smoking.)[35] Persons of this kind are still envisioned as effective actors, their efficacy residing in their managerial rather than in their possessive attributes. The measure of these managerial capacities is no longer bankruptcy, reflecting their ownership status, but insurability and/or ratings such as Moody's, reflecting their level of risk.[36] Such persons (including corporate ones) increasingly look to the state not to guarantee their property rights but to mediate their exposure to risk.[37]

The question to be posed, then, is this: if privatization is more than simply changing ownership but consists at its most fundamental level of remaking persons,[38] what relation of property and persons was characteristic of socialism and might now be subject to a process of change? Do privatization programs connect more with the "possessive individuals" of earlier capitalism or rather with the "portfolio-managing" persons of flexible specialization? To consider this question, I will now turn to the property regime of socialism, using the terms laid out above to guide my characterization. I emphasize, in particular, how fixed socialist property created supraindividual persons such as "the whole people" and "the collective", while exchanges of objects from socialism's circulating fund by managers participating in a far-flung system of obligations consolidated the reality of *networks* as actors and of persons as embedded rather than autonomous. For this latter point I build on the work of David Stark on networks in the postsocialist period.[39]

Property in Socialism[40]

A property regime is a cultural system, a system of social relations, and a system of power: it consists of a set of categories, the meanings of which are peculiar to that system and relate to the organization of both power and social relations within it. In thinking about property in socialism, I begin by asking: What were some of the categories of socialist property regimes?[41] The 1977 Soviet Constitution states: "Socialist ownership of the means of production...constitutes the foundation of the economic system of the USSR". This statement posits two things and intimates a third: an *object* of property (means of production), a property *relation* (ownership), and a potential *subject* (socialist owners in the USSR). Each implies a larger contrastive field. As possible objects of property, the category "means of production"—further subdivided into fixed and circulating funds—is contrasted with means of consumption.[42] These property objects entered into different sets of property relations (ownership, control, use, etc.), which pertained to alternative possible subjects: the state, socialist cooperatives, other (non-producing) socialist organizations, and individual persons as well as ministries and commissions, state-owned enterprises, and central, regional, and local administrations. For purposes of exercising property rights, most of these subject categories were considered jural persons; only the first four of them, however, were privileged to serve as *owners*, though they were not privileged to own the same kinds of things. The remaining types of property subjects were largely limited to relations of control and use, exercised specifically with respect to *state* property.

Let me dwell further upon these subjects of property. In discussing property in the previous section, I observed that as a person-forming mechanism property often creates social groups and actors by objectifying and hence unifying them in some specific relation to values. To put this in more economistic language, if property involves regulating access to valued resources, this entails specifying the kinds of actors for whom access is to be regulated. Does access go to individuals, households, corporations, clans, municipal governments, or actors of some other type? Naming actors helps to constitute them as real in the sense that because they are recognized in law and practice, both resources and legal mediation to uphold their claims become readily available to them.[43]

In naming its principal actors, socialist law specified these in clear relation to property—that is, one could say "property" was the basis for making those actors real. Socialism thus institutionalized the construct "ownership" at its very heart, in the form of four recognized property types relating to three principal property subjects defined as owners. The four property types were state property, cooperative property,[44] personal property, and private property, each having its own legal regime; the three owners were the state, cooperatives, and individuals. Technically speaking, it was not "the state" but another abstract entity, "the people as a whole" or "the whole people" who owned state property; the state (better said, the *party*-state) served merely as the embodiment[45] of that collective actor, managing state property in the people's interest. We see here the division between *ownership* and *management* so characteristic of socialist property regimes—a characteristic they share with corporations in advanced capitalism. In all Soviet-type socialist societies, the great bulk of valued resources was held in state property.

The categories of state and cooperative property together made up the larger category of socialist property. This included nearly all society's major means of production and was by far the most important property category; the party center intended over time that its two components be merged into the single category of state property. In "dialectical relation" with socialist property[46] was the category of personal property, consisting primarily of objects of consumption. Laws constrained their use to keep people from turning them into means of production—for instance, one could own one's car but was prohibited from using it as a taxi to generate income; one could own a house, but not a second house, for that would permit income from rental.

The fourth property type, private property, consisted of the means of production owned and used by petty-commodity producers such as un-collectivized peasants and tradespeople. Viewed as a residue of the bourgeois order, this type was of minimal importance in all but Poland and Yugoslavia, where agriculture was never collectivized and where private property-owning cultivators formed the large majority of the rural population. In all socialist systems, private property was slated for eventual elimination. Not included in that category were the misnamed "private plots" of collective farmers: they formed, rather, part of the socialist property of collective farms, which assigned their members use-rights to it.

This set of categories names for us three distinct types of actors, whom we can thus see as constituted by the property regime: "the state" (or "the whole people"), holder of state socialist property-rights; "cooperatives", holders of rights to cooperative property; and "individuals", holders of rights to personal and private property. It is important to note that these actors are *defined as jural subjects precisely by their property status*; that is, they were made "real" actors by being made subjects of property. As Butler puts it: "Juridical persons are those organizations which possess separate property, [and] may acquire property and personal non-property rights and bear duties in their own name..."[47] Thus, jural personhood is a function of property status. Defined as a jural person, an entity could allocate rights to specific, recognized subunits. For instance, "the state" could parcel out rights to use its property both to cooperatives and to other lower-level actors, such as "state firms", "socialist organizations" (such as the trade unions or the Councils of National Minorities), or lower-level territorial units such as "republics" (in the Soviet case) or "counties" and "municipal governments". One might contrast this set of recognized actors with others that could conceivably be recognized as property-holding entities but in these systems were not: households, lineages, clans, royalty, or corporations.[48]

It is one thing to "name" social actors as does socialist property law (and not it alone), but it is quite another to constitute them as *effective* actors in practice. While the categories of property law tell us something about how the party authorities hoped to populate the economic landscape of production and appropriation, we need the niceties of social process to appreciate how property in socialism worked. For example, in practice, state property did not make a unified, real actor from the abstract concept "the state" or "the whole people": rather, it underpinned the dominant position of the communist party. Simply *positing* the unitary character of the fund of socialist property as pertaining to "the whole people" could not give social reality to that construct, for no way was found to make either "the state" or "the whole people" an effective actor in practice. As Campeanu puts it: "For [public property] to become real in economic terms, the property owned had first to become manageable...[N]one of the presumptive natural agents of ownership, e.g., the social classes, were capable of assuming that role. As a consequence, a surrogate agent, the state, replaced them, yet it too was unable to exercise ownership...Thus the practical day-to-day routines called into question the capacity of a weak state to exercise a strong monopoly".[49]

How, then, did state ownership work? What sorts of entities were constituted in practice to manage the task of putting all those state-owned means of production *into* production? And what sorts of social relations facilitated their doing so? Answers to these questions come more readily if one stops asking about ownership per se—which is far from the only way of organizing property—and looks instead at the distribution of various kinds of rights and relations. In socialist property regimes, the most important relationship, after the prerogatives of the state as owner, was based in the *right of direct (or operational) administration* (I will refer to this as "administrative rights"). By means of granting administrative rights, the state retained its claim to supreme ownership but exercised that ownership by allocating use and administrative rights downward to smaller entities. It assigned parts of the property of "the whole people" to lower levels in the bureaucratic hierarchy. Recipients of these rights could further parcel them out to others still lower down the scale. Such allocations of administrative rights enabled managing and controlling the state property allocated to lower units by central plans. As Heller puts it: "Instead of assigning an owner to each object, socialist law created a complex hierarchy of divided and coordinated rights in the objects it defined...The law integrated ownership of physical assets within overlapping state structures, often linking upward from a state enterprise, to a group of similar enterprises, to the local and then central offices of a ministry responsible for that branch of industry".[50]

The system of multiple and overlapping administrative rights over the unitary fund of state property permitted myriad transactions to occur without the institutions and forms associated with changes in ownership, such as mortgages or sale contracts.[51] For instance, if one firm made a contract with another to deliver its product (say, a piece of machinery), the machinery was at all times state property. Its owner did not change; all that changed was who held the power of administrative rights over it. Thus, the director of the first firm held the power to dispose of the product to the second firm (a power common to ownership relations), but ownership did not change thereby. A major consequence of these practices was that the boundaries within the unitary fund of property became blurred, and objects might move among numerous persons exercising rights to them that were akin to ownership rights but were not consecrated as such.[52]

Because the units who received administrative rights thereby entered as jural persons into direct relation with the means of production, their managers could come dangerously close to infringing on the state's property rights. The legendary hoarding, dissimulation, plan-bargaining, and other manipulations of state property by these managers produced internal contradictions in the notion of "the state" as a unitary actor and "state property" as an object of coherent planning. Indeed, the inability of the political center to keep these actors in check and their gradually increased autonomy in consequence were critical elements in socialism's transformation.[53] For this reason, it would be inadvisable to see administrative rights as an insignificant form of property relation. Their exercise in practice constituted state firms as powerful actors—particularly the directors of these firms, organized into robust networks that themselves became real social actors, as the aftermath of 1989 has amply shown.

How did directors of state firms make use of the administrative rights they held to state property? How did behavior within socialist organizations alter the contours of legal provisions, giving socialist property flexibility and producing a *working* property regime, the consequences of which affect the process of exiting from that system? What was the relation between formal categories and categories of actual use? How did the processes of socialist property constitute persons? The framework necessary to answering these questions comes from Kornai's notion of the economy of shortage;[54] its characteristics included incessant demand for investment on the part of firms, efforts to bargain the plan with central authorities, and widespread hoarding and bartering of raw materials for production.

Plans, targets, hoarding, and bartering all contributed to a far-flung system of obligations through which production took place within the confines of socialist property. This system of obligations—rather than just the patterning of property (administrative) *rights*—formed the core of socialism's property regime. The obligations were of several kinds. First was what we might call "socialist tribute": obligatory deliveries of the goods that firms produced upward to state procurement centers in fulfillment of the plan. Second were the obligations entailed in barter: if I give up inputs you need today, you have an obligation to provide from your inputs what I may need tomorrow. Because managers who did not know how to manage this sort of reciprocity would soon find themselves unable to mobilize enough inputs for production, the obligations of barter within the formal economy were highly binding. Third were reciprocal obligations of a more general sort that helped to lubricate the social relations already described; they involved gifts to both superiors and status equals, and their benefits might include looser plan targets, special bonuses, access to raw materials otherwise hard to obtain, and generalized bureaucratic goodwill. Further reinforcing these social relations of production might be other kinds of ties (kinship, godparenthood, birthplace, university class, etc.).[55] In my opinion, the far-flung system of exchange involving gifts and favors justifies seeing socialism as a form of "gift economy".[56] What we see in the workings of socialist property was part of a much wider set of reciprocal and largely nonmonetized exchanges characteristic of these societies.

This observation is more significant than it might seem if we recall Strathern's characterization of the nature of "persons" in a gift economy as not autonomous possessive individuals but deeply embedded in inter-dependent relations. Strathern calls these persons "dividuals", but I find this term confusing and will speak instead of "network-embedded actors" (a term that can incorporate single and multiple human beings). In work on Poland, Elizabeth Dunn has explored the tension that privatization has introduced into concepts of personhood, as Poland's new entrepreneurs or western managers strive to free themselves of the toils of obligations and to treat their workers as autonomous individuals—an attitude the workers fiercely resist.[57] Although Dunn focuses on enterprise govern-ance rather than on property relations, her argument is very apt for thinking about personhood within socialist property, and I adopt it here in order to explore the nature of personhood for different groups of peo-ple in socialism, active in its different property forms.

The "persons" who participated in widespread exchanges—both in-dividuals and firms—constituted robust networks: that is, their person-hood rested on their embeddedness in social relations, not on their autonomy. Not just socialist production but all facets of daily life de-pended on one's ability to mobilize contacts. These realities implied a socialist "person" very different from the autonomous, self-actualizing, possessive individual characteristic of capitalism. Socialist persons were, rather, embedded; instead of being self-actualizing individuals, they were nodes in a system of dependencies—dependent upon one another and upon the paternalist state. The selfhood of these network-embedded ac-tors was realized not in accumulating things but in accumulating people with whom to exchange things and favors.[58] We might say their person-hood depended on their "network properties".

Although the workings of the socialist system make *everyone* into this kind of person, we might hypothesize that the various forms of property in socialism introduced some variety into personhood as well. Network-embedded actors were *par excellence* the person-form of activity within state property; they were both single human beings such as enterprise managers and entire networks of firms, all enmeshed in exchange rela-tions necessary to realizing production. The networks might be very ex-tensive and more or less unbounded. Social relations within cooperative property, by contrast, may have been smaller in scope and more closely bounded (being the sets of resources collectively donated, worked, and increased by their particular members rather than by "the whole peo-ple"). Even though the managers of cooperative property also operated within networks of obligation, its special nature perhaps individualized it more and constituted its personhood as more limited. In the remaining two categories—personal and private property—we find the possibility of persons more closely resembling the "possessive individuals" of capitalism. Here, ownership relations prevailed over those of administration and use; here, as well, popular resistance to socialism took the form of identity-creation through consumption of personal property, even as the objects necessary for this came from operating within networks of exchange.

I am suggesting, then, that socialism produced mixed forms of personhood, along a gradient that ran from primarily network-embedded actors within the state sector to primarily possessive individuals in the domain of personal and private property. This may offer a way of talking about two interlinked phenomena: the greater ease and seemingly better performance of small-firm privatization, as opposed to that of medium and large enterprises. Heller, for example, observes: "[T]he more protection property received under socialist law, the less successful its performance has been in a new market economy".[59] Concerned with how rights should be "bundled" in order to achieve a workable property regime, he offers the working hypothesis that "private property emerges more successfully in resources that begin transition with a single owner holding a near-standard bundle" of property rights.[60] This interpretation assumes a particular kind of already-constituted person—the possessive individual who knows how to "hold" a bundle of property rights—and posits the resource (or set of them, perhaps the firm) as the unit of analysis. If one took, rather, the *property form* and its associated "persons" as the unit of analysis, one might offer a different interpretation: the property forms that came closest to constituting possessive individuals are the ones easiest to transform now, and these are *not* the ones characteristic of state property, which constituted a *unitary fund*, not a collection of separately propertied entities. Collective farms and trade cooperatives, by contrast, were defined more fully as individual entities by the kind of property relation that constituted them; so also, *a forteriori*, were the holders of personal and private property. It thus makes sense that privatization involving state firms has proceeded more slowly than small privatization: the smaller entities were more likely to have been already constituted as possessive individuals, while the larger ones were mere nodes in far-flung networks of exchange. This does not mean, however, that the larger ones are inapt subjects of a new property-regime, as I will now propose.

Privatization Revisited

I have been arguing for a conception of property that emphasizes its per-son-making features and have identified in the workings of socialism's property forms a dominant person-making principle (network-embedded-ness) and a subordinate one (a kind of possessive individualism), as well as different kinds of actors constituted by the different property forms. In closing, I wish to explore the implications of network-embedded actors for privatization. I have argued above that owing to widespread ties of obligation and reciprocity, *networks themselves* were made into a kind of social actor—and that actor, rather than the SOE, was the true analogue of the corporation-as-person of capitalism. This, it seems to me, is the insight David Stark develops in his research on networks of cross-ownership in Hungary since the mid–1980s.[61] "[T]he collapse of the formal structures of the socialist regime does not result in an institutional vacuum. Instead, we find the persistence of routines and practices, organizational forms and social ties, that can become assets [and] resources…in the postsocialist period".[62] Analyzing what he calls "recombinant property" as an emergent property form in Hungary, Stark draws attention to the networks of firms that collaborate to reorganize their assets while finding ways of shaking off their liabilities onto the remnants of the state. In consequence, he concludes that property transformation should target not individual firms but *networks* of firms.

I note three implications of Stark's argument. First, it destroys at one stroke the validity of using percentages of SOEs that have become private firms as an indicator of privatization's success. This point is so obvious that it requires no further elaboration. Second, it provides a counterargument to Heller's views about postsocialism as a "tragedy of the anticommons". He seeks to explain the underuse of certain public goods, such as storefront properties in Moscow. Drawing an analogy with literature on the "tragedy of the commons", overused because no one has rights to exclude others, Heller identifies in postsocialism a "tragedy of the *anti*commons", resulting when multiple participants have multiple rights that lead to everyone's being able to exclude uses proposed by everyone else; in consequence, the resource is *under*used. His solution to this problem is to allocate bundled property rights to sole owners, who will be sure the resource is used.

But anticommons property of this kind has neither the same roots in socialist property law nor the same persons/actors as the "successfully" performing single-bundled cases just mentioned. Like the champions of privatization, Heller concentrates on the rights held by individuals; what is decomposing, however, is socialist property managed collectively within networks of managers and firms, some of which may hold a workable bundle of property rights *as a network*. We might then see the problem to be solved not as how to bundle rights and assign them to individuals but, rather, as how to corporatize and bound existing networks. This solution might, in fact, produce entities better able to compete with the principal actors in global capitalism, which do *not* appear to be individuals holding clear bundles of rights but the increasingly complex networks we know as "multinationals". Stark suggests a related possibility in arguing that the "recombinant property" formed by networks of firms is adaptive in the short to medium run, because it enables transferring *liabilities* to the declining state sector and keeping control of the network's *assets*.

I would further extend Stark's suggestion, then (and third), to argue that it was precisely these skills that socialism's managers developed before, in exercising their administrative rights. Managing property, the ownership rights of which lay elsewhere (theoretically dispersed across "the whole people"), those managers became expert at what Stark points to for present day Hungary: separating assets from liabilities and trying to shed the latter onto the state. Some were so successful that they eventually turned the use of socialist property to their own account through large-scale, network-based forms of underground factory production that let the state pay the costs while they lined their pockets. This same division between ownership (dispersed masses of shareholders) and (corporate) management also characterizes modern capitalist corporations; but what is being managed now is risk, on the argument summarized earlier in this paper. In managing risk, capitalist firms now look to states to mediate their exposure to risk rather than to guarantee ownership rights. One could say that this too was precisely what socialist managers were good at doing—and that it was their quality as network-embedded actors that facilitated their doing so.

Given the way that networks can help to spread and absorb risk, it is interesting that privatization aims precisely to *bound* the principal economic actors, peeling away the layers of social embeddedness and exposing them to the hazards of markets in which they will therefore be less able to compete. Moreover, just as capitalist states increasingly serve to underwrite risks (the bailout of the Long-Term Capital Management hedge fund is only the latest example), privatization programs insist on dismantling state property and eliminating state subsidies to failing SOEs. That is, they insist on making formerly socialist states incapable of mediating risk for firms.

Alongside this, and despite their relentless focus on ownership, some privatization programs have institutionalized in a different way the accomplishments of Stark's Hungarian directors, separating assets from liabilities by placing tremendous funds of resources in holding companies under the management of international accounting firms. The "owners" are socialism's former citizens holding vouchers that entitle them to lose their certificates' entire value, while the managers continue to collect salaries and commissions. Privatization has thus appropriated management and assets while socializing risk in the complete absence of insurance for those who own the managed assets. Yet the rhetoric is of "possession", ownership—of persons constituted by owning rather than by managing, of writing bankruptcy law rather than shoring up the ability of formerly socialist states to help firms hedge their risks.

I am suggesting a parallel with Burawoy's argument concerning the potential aptness of the forms developed under socialism for the new "brave new world" of market competition.[63] Burawoy showed that workers in socialism had to behave in exactly the fashion that western managers would later promote under flexible specialization's "total quality management": working in teams, rapidly readjusting to variations in the production process with minimal guidance from middle-level management. Following Burawoy, Dunn shows that the introduction of total quality management into the Polish firm she studied paradoxically brought with it efforts to break up these team-based production processes and individualize workers through complex processes of performance assessment.[64] Similarly, I am implying that socialism's property regime may have produced notions of person and forms of behavior well-adapted to competing in the world of flexible specialization; the emphasis of privatization programs on *ownership* questions and *breaking up* the networks of socialist management, however, threatens these very adaptive forms. Is privatization somehow striving to create in the former socialist world, then, the very kinds of property and persons that the first world is abandoning, while breaking down socialist forms that might serve better? Will today's creation of obsolescent "possessive individuals" be tomorrow's reason for explaining why the Second World did not, after all, make the transition to markets and prosperity? Is privatization producing, in other words, yet another round of uneven development in the form of these divergently propertied persons?

To ask this question is to show that measuring the "success" of privatization a decade after 1989 is an exceedingly complex proposition. Quite aside from the problems of what one is to measure and how, one might begin by wondering: Success from whose point of view?

Notes

1 Walter Adams and James W. Brock, *Adam Smith Goes to Moscow: A Dialogue on Radical Reform* (Princeton: Princeton University Press, 1993), 150.

2 Ken Jowitt, "The Leninist Extinction", in *New World,Disorder: The Leninist Extinction* (Berkeley and Los Angeles: University of California Press, 1992).

3 See, for example, European Bank for Reconstruction and Development, *Transition Report 1998* (London: European Bank for Reconstruction and Development, 1998), Table 2.1. Thanks to Jan Svejnar and Don Kachman of the Davidson Institute, University of Michigan, for providing me with these data.

4 Josef C. Brada, "Privatization is Transition—Or Is It?" *Journal of Economic Perspectives* 10 (1996); and Peter Murrell, "What Is Shock Therapy? What Did It Do in Poland and Russia?" *Post-Soviet Affairs* 9 (1993).

5 See, for example, Andrew Walder, "Corporate Organization and Local Government Property Rights in China", in *Changing Political Economies: Privatization in Post-Communist and Reforming Communist States*, ed. Vedat Milor (Boulder, Colo.: Lynne Rienner, 1994).

6 Brada, "Privatization", 81–4.

7 Roman Frydman, Kenneth Murphy, and Andrzej Rapaczynski, *Capitalism with a Comrade's Face* (Budapest: Central European University Press, 1998), 7.

8 Leslie Holmes, *Post-Communism: An Introduction* (Durham: Duke University Press, 1997), 211; David Stark, "Recombinant Property in East European Capitalism", *American Journal of Sociology* 101:4 (1996).

9 Hilary Appel, "Justice and the Reformation of Property Rights in the Czech Republic", *East European Politics and Society* 9:1 (1995); Verdery 1994.

10 Peter L. Berger, "The Uncertain Triumph of Democratic Capitalism", *Journal of Democracy* 3 (1992): 7–16; Ellen Comisso, "Property Rights, Liberalism, and the Transition from 'Actually Existing' Socialism", *East European Politics and Societies* 5:1 (1991): 162–88.

11 Stark, "Recombinant Property".

12 John Locke, *Two Treatises of Government* (Cambridge: Cambridge University Press, 1960), 287.

13 See C.B. Macpherson, *The Political Theory of Possessive Individualism* (Oxford: Clarendon Press, 1962). Macpherson's views have been subjected to criticism by such scholars as J.G.A. Pocock, *Virtue, Commerce, and History* (Cambridge: Cambridge University Press, 1985); Kirstie McClure, *Judging Rights: Lockean Politics and the Limits of Consent* (Ithaca: Cornell University Press, 1996); and James Tully, *An Approach to Political Philosophy: Locke in Contexts* (Cambridge: Cambridge University Press, 1993).

14 Margaret Jolly, "People and Their Products in South Pentecost", in *Vanuatu*, ed. M.R. Allen (Sydney: Academic Press, 1981), 269.

15 Daniel de Coppet, "...Land Owns People", in *Contexts and Levels: Anthropological Essays on Hierarchy*, eds. R.H. Barnes, Daniel de Coppet, and R.J. Parkin (Oxford: JASO, 1985), 78–90.

16 Denis Numa Fustel de Coulanges, *The Ancient City* (Baltimore: John Hopkins University Press, 1980); Nancy M. Williams, *The Yolungu and their Land: A System of*

Land Tenure and the Fight for its Recognition (Stanford: Stanford University Press, 1986); Fred Myers, "Burning the Truck and Holding the Country", in *We Are Here: Politics of Aboriginal Land Tenure*, ed. Edwin N. Wilmsen (Berkeley: University of California Press, 1989).

17 Robert Lowie, "Incorporeal Property in Primitive Society", *Yale Law Journal* 37 (1928): 551–638; Simon Harrison, *Stealing People's Names: History and Politics in a Sepik River Cosmology* (Cambridge: Cambridge University Press, 1990).

18 Compare Sharon Stephens, "Ideology and Everyday Life in Sami (Lapp) History", in *Discourse and the Social Life of Meaning*, ed. Phyllis Pease Chock and J. Wyman (Washington, D.C.: Smithsonian Institution Press, 1986).

19 Compare David G. Anderson, "Property as a Way of Knowing on Evenki Lands in Arctic Siberia", in *Property Relations*, ed. C.M. Hann (Cambridge: Cambridge University Press, 1998).

20 Marcel Mauss, *The Gift* (New York: W.W. Norton, 1990); Bronislaw Malinowski, *Argonauts of the Western Pacific* (London: Routledge, 1922).

21 Myers, "Burning the Truck", 1.

22 Myers, "Burning the Truck", 18.

23 Myers, "Burning the Truck", 34.

24 Myers, "Burning the Truck", 41.

25 Marilyn Strathern, "Subject or Object: Women and the Circulation of Valuables in Highlands in New Guinea", in *Women and Property, Women as Property*, ed. Renee Hirschon (New York: St. Martin's Press, 1988); compare Elizabeth Dunn, "Privatization and Personhood: Transforming Work in Postsocialist Poland" (Ph.D. diss., John Hopkins University, 1998).

26 Strathern, "Subject or Object", 13.

27 Strathern, "Subject or Object", 131.

28 Strathern, "Subject or Object", 161. In some of her writing Strathern resists the notion that one can apply the term "property" to what she finds in New Guinea, to the extent that "property" requires objectification (Strathern, "Subject or Object"). Others, however, would rather expand the property concept—diminishing the requirement of subject-object separation—so as to include more cases for comparative analysis (see, for example, A. Irving Hallowell, "The Nature and Function of Property as a Social Institution", in *Culture and Experience* (Philadelphia: University of Pennsylvania Press, 1955).

29 Stark, "Recombinant Property", 1009.

30 Emily Martin, *Flexible Bodies: Tracking Immunity in America from the Days of Polio to the Age of AIDS* (Boston: Beacon Press, 1995); Emily Martin, "Colonizing Minds: Managing the Mental in Late 20th Century U.S." (paper presented at CSST Seminar, University of Michigan, 1997); Emily Martin, *Flexible Minds* (Princeton: Princeton University Press, forthcoming).

31 William M. Maurer, "Forget Locke? Dematerializing Property in Financial Services" (n.p.: 1998).

32 David Harvey, *The Condition of Postmodernity* (Oxford: Blackwell, 1989).

33 Adolf A. Berle and Gardiner C. Means, *The Modern Corporation and Private Property* (Harcourt, Brace and World, 1932).

34 Maurer, "Forget Locke?" 2. Maurer adds that crucial to the new emphasis on risk is a heightened role for *insurance* against risk. I have found Maurer's ideas on the place of risk very helpful in thinking about new concepts of property and person.

35 See Martin, *Flexible Bodies*; "Colonizing Minds;" and *Flexible Minds*.

36 Maurer, "Forget Locke?"

37 We might recall here the U.S. government's interventions in business crises, such as its bailouts of Chrysler and the Savings and Loan Industry. Both these actions effectively made *the entire U.S. population* bear the risks these industries had not successfully negotiated.

38 Dunn, "Privatization and Personhood".

39 Stark, "Recombinant Property".

40 To speak of "property in socialism" obviously reifies and homogenizes a reality that was much more complex, with variations occurring in both space and time. Since this is not an essay about socialist property, however, I offer a schematic, condensed account, aimed at clarifying the problems of making "private property" from the property relations of socialism. My account is drawn from literature on the Soviet Union and Eastern Europe; I make no claims for its applicability to socialism in other parts of the world.

41 My sources for this discussion, in addition to interviews with lawyers, judges, and notaries in Romania, are George M. Armstrong, *The Soviet Law of Property: The Right to Control Property and the Construction of Communism* (The Hague: Martinus Nijhoff, 1983); Salvator Brădeanu, Petre Marcia, and Lucian Stângu, *Tratat de drept cooperatist-agricol*, 2 vols. (Bucureşti: Ed. Academiei Republicii Socialiste România, 1968); W.E. Butler, *Soviet Law* (London: Butterworths, 1998); Pavel Campeanu, *The Genesis of the Stalinist Social Order* (Armonk, N.J.: M.E. Sharpe, 1988); F.J.M. Feldbrugge, *Russian Law: The End of the Soviet System and the Role of Law* (Dordrecht: Martinus Nijhoff, 1993); Michael Heller, "The Tragedy of the Anticommons: Property in the Transition from Marx to Markets", *Harvard Law Review* 111:3 (1998): 621–88; Ernest Lupan and Ionel Reghini, *Drept civil: Drepturi reale principale* (Cluj: Universitatea Babeş-Bolyai, Facultatea de Drept., 1997); and Daniela Păunescu, *Drept cooperatist* (Bucharest: Universitatea din Bucureşti, Facultatea de Drept., 1974).

42 I might note that these subdivisions into subjects and objects of property are not simply my own analytic grouping but that of the legal texts I have consulted.

43 This is not to say that other kinds of actors do not exist, of course; in order to be socially effective, however, they have to work harder, struggling to fit themselves into the confines of the established categories. For instance, households were not jural persons in socialism, nor were they instituted in relation to property. A household could not go to court as such; it could go only in the person of one of its members. But to do so might entail disagreements among household members as to which of potentially conflicting interests within the household were to be represented.

44 I use the term "cooperative" in referring to the category that includes both agricultural and nonagricultural enterprises of nonstate-type together. When I wish to speak of nonstate agricultural enterprises, I use the term *collective*, as in "collective farm", rather than speaking of "cooperative farms". Even though the latter is the better

translation for those entities in at least some contexts (for instance, the Romanian "cooperativa agricolă de producţie", agricultural production cooperative), I believe the term "collective farm" is the more widely used in English and carries connotations more appropriate than does the word "cooperative". Other kinds of cooperative property were small trades and service establishments set up, for example, for carpentry, shoe-making, tailoring, or repairs.

45 This relationship is not one of simple representation—that is, the party-state represents the people. Rather, it embodies it. In Romanian, one word used to describe the relation of state to "the whole people" (*întregul popor*) is *întruchipare*, translated as "embodiment" or "personification". *Chip* means "image", "face", or "likeness", *întru* indicating movement into and *-are* referring to a process: thus, the process of moving into a likeness. This is the relation of state to whole people.

46 Lupan and Reghini, *Drept civil*, 119.

47 Butler, *Soviet Law*, 179.

48 These are the subjects of ownership in other systems, such as those described by Max Gluckman, *Essays on Lozi Land and Royal Property* (Rhodes-Livingstone Institute, 1943); Gluckman, *The Ideas in Barotse Jurisprudence* (New Haven: Yale University Press, 1965); Bronislaw Malinowski, *Coral Gardens and Their Magic* (London: Allen and Unwin, 1935); et cetera.

49 Campeanu, *Stalinist Social Order*, 41, 85.

50 Heller, "Anticommons", 629.

51 Feldbrugge, *Russian Law*, 231.

52 This fact vastly complicates the assignment of ownership rights during privatization. For example, a piece of land might be "donated" to a collective farm by its owner (even though prior decrees had nationalized it from that owner), then the administrative rights to it transferred to a state farm, which might assign it to a farm employee for a houseplot. Although each of these entities might treat the land as "its own"— especially the employee whose house stood on it—and dispose of it as such, none of them had been registered as owner because ownership had not in fact changed. With decollectivization, if the farm employee wants to sell his house, he has no title to the land under it—nor is it certain from whom he might obtain that title.

53 See, for example, Armstrong, *Soviet Law of Property*; Jadwiga Staniszkis, *The Dynamics of the Breakthrough in Eastern Europe* (Berkeley and Los Angeles: University of California Press, 1991).

54 János Kornai, *Economics of Shortage* (Amsterdam: North-Holland Publishers, 1980).

55 In addition, managers had an obligation to pay their workers, but this obligation was less significant for property relations than the others I have mentioned.

56 Compare C. A. Gregory, *Gifts and Commodities* (London: Academic Press, 1982); Marilyn Strathern, *The Gender of the Gift: Problems with Women and Problems with Society in Melanesia* (Berkeley and Los Angeles: University of California Press, 1988); Dunn, "Privatization and Personhood". I acknowledge a debt to Elizabeth Dunn, who continued to insist on the importance of gift exchange in socialist systems until I finally got the message.

57 Dunn, "Privatization and Personhood".

58 This statement should be modified with respect to the identity-creating aspects of consumption items. Partly in reaction to a system that gave consumers the lowest priority, daily life included much creativity devoted to procuring things with which one could signal one's individuality. We might see this as the complementary constitution of possessive individuals relative to socialist acknowledgment of *personal property*, howsoever transitory it was to be, in relation to which identities as *individuals* were created.

59 Heller, "Anticommons", 631.

60 Heller, "Anticommons", 631.

61 Stark, "Recombinant Property"; David Stark and László Bruszt, *Postsocialist Pathways: Transforming Politics and Property in East Central Europe* (Cambridge: Cambridge University Press, 1998).

62 Stark, "Recombinant Property", 995.

63 Michael Burawoy and János Lukács, *The Radiant Past: Ideology and Reality in Hungary's Road to Capitalism* (Chicago: University of Chicago Press, 1992).

64 Dunn, "Privatization and Personhood".

11 Gendering Postsocialism: Reproduction as Politics in East Central Europe

GAIL KLIGMAN and SUSAN GAL

It is striking that abortion was among the first issues raised by virtually all of the postsocialist governments of East Central Europe. In Romania, liberalization of abortion was the second decree issued by the provisional government upon the fall of the Ceauşescu regime. Reconciling abortion's legality in East Germany with its restriction in West Germany almost derailed German unification. In Poland the question was a permanent feature of the parliamentary agenda. But abortion was only one of a range of issues associated with sexuality and human reproduction that has taken center stage in public consciousness since 1989. In the former Yugoslavia, rape was a weapon of war. Because women who had been raped and the children who resulted from rape were ostracized and rejected by their own ethnic groups, rape was also and intentionally a tool of "ethnic cleansing" through its tragic reproductive consequences. Unwanted babies became a political issue in Romania and Germany as well, but in different ways. A private adoption market in babies, not all of whom were unwanted by their birth mothers, emerged in Romania. The rate of voluntary sterilization increased dramatically among East German women, which produced a political scandal when it was noticed and labeled a "birth strike" by the mass media.

Throughout the region, as democratic institutions were created, fiscal and constitutional crises threatened, and legislative politics were rethought in dramatic ways, the leaders (themselves mostly male) of the new East Central European states also heatedly debated questions of "proper" sex, birthrates, contraception, family, and child care. We wondered at this attention. We also questioned how gender relations and ideas about gender are shaping political and economic changes in the region and what forms of gender inequality are being created. In this article, we focus on one aspect of the gendering of postsocialism: namely, how political process is influenced by reproductive issues, or how public discussion about reproduction makes politics.[1]

We define gender as the socially and culturally produced ideas about male-female difference, power and inequality that structure the reproduction of these differences in the institutionalized practices of society.[2] What it means to be a "man" or "woman", to be "masculine" or "feminine", varies *historically*. Such cultural categories are formed through everyday interactions that are framed within larger discourses and within specific institutions. There are reciprocal influences here: not only do state policies constrain gender relations, but ideas about the differences between men and women shape the ways in which states are imagined, constituted and legitimized. Thus, states themselves can be imagined as male, even though both men and women are involved in their operation; social categories such as "worker" can be identified with a single gender as well, even if both men and women work. Such socially constructed ideas linking femininity and masculinity to other social categories are often embedded in state policies.

Ideas about gender difference are also implicitly engaged in the forms of market expansion in the region. For example, if we examine how women and men are differently located in the emerging national economies, then the pervasive yet relatively ignored feminization of small scale, service sector marketization comes to the fore. In shaping institutional change, ideas about gender difference interact systematically with other central cultural categories such as the nation, the family, and the public good. At the same time, the ideologies and policies that states promote, as well as the constraints and incentives of economies, circumscribe the range of possible relations between men and women.

According to liberal theory, as well as sociological common sense, human reproduction is associated with the private sphere of domesticity and family and not the public sphere of politics, civil society, and state-formation. Yet the politicians, publishers, and media consumers who constituted the first democratic parliaments and public spheres after 1989 heatedly raised such allegedly private issues.[3] For feminist scholars, who have argued that the distinction between private and public is less a straightforward description of social domains than an ideologized dichotomy that produces the appearance of separation between activities that are nonetheless closely linked, this heightened interest in reproductive issues is hardly surprising.[4] It represents yet more evidence of important relations between supposedly private activities such as childbirth and child-rearing and public activities such as political debate. It is an example of the politics of reproduction, a field that studies the "intersection of politics and the life cycle".[5] The politics of reproduction takes as its object of study the "seemingly distant power relations [that] shape local reproductive experiences"[6] and investigates how "state policy and ideological control are experienced in everyday life".[7] It shows as well how reproduction "provides a terrain for imagining new cultural futures".[8] Indeed, the laws, regulations and administrative apparatuses that the new states are installing will have long-range repercussions on the ways in which women in East Central Europe give birth and how people practice contraception, raise their children and imagine their own and their children's futures.

Yet the politics of reproduction encompases not only how distant power relations affect childbirth, but also how political process itself is shaped through the discussion and control of reproduction. Debates about reproduction thus additionally "reveal the ways in which politics is being reconstituted, contested, and newly legitimated".[9] Here, we suggest four interrelated ways in which reproductive issues and policies are key features of the changing political landscape of East Central Europe: public discussions about reproductive issues (1) contribute to recasting the relationship between the state and its citizens; (2) serve as coded discussions about political legitimacy and the morality of the state; (3) constitute women as political actors in particular ways; and (4) make and remake the nation and its boundaries.

Human reproduction is the means by which both individuals and collectivities assure their continuity. It is a ground for political battle in part because states, families, and other social actors all understand themselves as having much at stake in the control of child-bearing and child-rearing.[10] Historically constructed and variable, these diverse perspectives or "interests" in reproduction are often at odds. Turning first to the interests of states in reproduction, throughout much of history, the vigor of the individual body has long served as a sign of the health or infirmity of the body politic; moreover, the health of a state has been linked to the rapid reproduction of its inhabitants. Building on this tradition, early modern political-economic theorists argued that population must be a central concern of statecraft. By the seventeenth century, the basis of a state's wealth and power was understood to lie in the size and productivity of its population. A large population increased the strength of armies and made available increasing supplies of labor.[11]

By the eighteenth century, not only did a large population make a strong state, but the abundance of inhabitants testified to the state's morality: "Every wise, just and mild government…will always abound most in people…", noted David Hume.[12] This link between population and the state's morality was a continuing theme in European politics. But at the end of the century, Hume's optimistic conviction was shaken by Malthus's thesis outlining the inevitable, socially deleterious effects of unbridled population increase. Steadily increasing populations came to be seen by some as less a reward than a danger to the orderly state. Suffice it to note that, whether population increase or decrease was at issue, the control of population remained defined as a matter of state.

The political concern with numbers of inhabitants gave rise to a growing interest of administrators in the life-condition of a territory's inhabitants. With the help of emerging disciplines (such as statistics, geography, etc.), population could be shaped and controlled through "policing" or regulation. The pronatalist activities of liberal, fascist, and communist states in the twentieth century have a long pedigree, forming part of what Foucault has called "bio-politics". The tracks of state power are evident in the legal enforcement of normative (reproductive) hetero-sexuality, the surveillance of women's bodies, and attempts to control women's fertility.

Shifting now to the concerns of families in the regulation of child-birth, generations of social historians, anthropologists, and historical demographers have conceptualized shifting population pyramids in Europe as the result of diverse and changing family strategies meant to ensure the inheritance of land, name, and property; to cement social continuity; to provide objects of love and recipients for consumption; or to fill family needs for labor or income.[13] Furthermore, social historians and historical sociologists have also shown that within families there may be systematic struggles between men and women who are committed to different arrangements in the timing, gender, and number of their offspring.

Social movements such as feminism, republicanism, labor unionism, eugenics, and nationalism, as well as various religious movements, also have ideologies of reproduction.[14] Very often, these movements define themselves through some implicit or explicit utopias in which images of ideal forms of reproduction and continuity play a crucial role: they define who should reproduce and how much; who should be responsible for which aspects of reproduction for what kind of remuneration or return; and how reproduction is related to morality.

Rhetorical battles among these variously constructed perspectives can be mobilized at any time. But they are unavoidable at times of political rupture, such as the events of 1989, when new and old elites negotiate and struggle over state forms. At such junctures, not only are the political players reshuffled, but the rules of the political project are radically re-thought and reorganized. For the remainder of this paper, we will address the aforementioned ways in which reproductive issues and policies are key features of the changing political contexts of East Central Europe.

First, discourses about reproduction contribute to the reconstitution of the relationship between a state and its populace. State making is a process of establishing and maintaining centralized authority over a territory and its inhabitants. But authority can be imagined in many ways. Whether people are figured in state discourses as "subjects", "citizens", "workers", "brothers-in-nationhood", "children", or "family members" (which are not always mutually exclusive) is dramatically enacted and demonstrated in practice through the implementation and justification of strictures on reproduction and sexuality. Such strictures also define who is a proper member of the state's populace. Thus, "citizens" are in many cases implicitly recognized as deserving of that title and a set of attendant "rights" by their display of particular forms of legally acceptable, usually reproductive (or hetero-), sexuality. When co-nationhood is how the state defines its relation to a populace, the boundaries of the horizontal fraternity that is the nation are defined by the details of reproductive behavior. To determine if a person is a legitimate member of the nation one must ask: Whose children are they and on what territory were they born?[15] In short, a state's relation to a populace—as paternalist, contractual, spiritual—is in part represented and performed through the control of reproductive practice.

Thus, for instance, when Hungarian leaders discussed the abortion issue from 1990 to 1992, a major concern was whether the relevant legal code was a "regulation" or a "law". Some leaders argued that if the inhabitants of Hungary were to be treated as the citizens of a democracy, no longer the infantile children of a paternalistic communist state that issued dictates, then matters of importance such as reproduction should be legislated by properly elected parliamentary representatives. If under communism legalizing or delegalizing abortion was a feature of party policies, they said, then for that very reason it now had to be challenged and negotiated as law, even if its substance was not at issue. In Germany, the obligation of the state to its citizens, and vice versa, was also at issue but in a different way. West German opinion put the fetus first, starting deliberations from the perspective of protecting its rights. East German opinion charged that while unification promised democracy and liberal rights, the restriction of abortion laws constituted a loss of democracy and individual rights for women.[16] The debate on abortion in East Germany was very much about which classes of people would be favored for the supposedly universal category of "citizen".[17]

A second way in which reproduction and sexuality contribute to the reconstruction of states explores such debates as coded discussions about claims to political legitimacy. That is, the issue of reproduction offers a means by which the morality and desirability of political institutions may be imagined and claims for the "goodness" of state forms may be made. Reproduction as veiled, allegorical talk about the political future is by no means peculiar to postsocialist transformations, but the nature of the politicization, the details of the arguments, reveal much about the particular polity in which they occur.[18]

In many of the newly constituted democracies of East Central Europe, debating the legal control of reproduction or of proper sexuality has been part of ongoing struggles for legitimacy among competing elites. Socialist states were chronically weak. For their inheritors, state forms continue to be deeply contested.[19] A contrast between the morality of democracy and the immorality of communism was often highlighted in particular through debates about their contrasting approaches to abortion legislation. If, as many claim, communism went against nature in allowing women to circumvent motherhood (excepting Romania), postcommunist states promised to restore a natural gender order, hoping thereby to rectify the wrongs of this "illegitimate" past. Discussions about human reproduction and sexuality have enormous power to moralize politics because reproduction raises fundamental issues about life and death. By discussing politics through the allegory of reproduction, politicians effectively efface their own ambitions, appearing to favor political arrangements not because politicians themselves might benefit, but because they stand for an independent moral good: to protect the fetus, the mother, the nation, or domestic privacy.

Whatever the justification for particular positions, reproductive debate is one of the few ways in which it is possible to avoid the shadow of self-interest, even in the face of cynical audiences. Such avoidance was—and is—particularly important in East Central Europe where political activity itself has been deeply stigmatized as nothing but opportunism and corruption. Thus, political actors indirectly demonstrate their own moral credentials through their concern with the future or their version of morality (in implicit opposition to the lack of morality associated with the formerly godless communist states). They make claims for the rightness of the political structures and initiatives they favor not by talking about governance per se, but by stating their positions on questions such as abortion, sterilization, women's sexuality, the proper forms of family life. Indeed, the legislation of such morality for its citizens is one way in which a state or government can appear as a moral actor in social life.

For example, in Romania the immediate legalization of abortion upon the fall of the Ceauşescu regime was not only a response to overwhelm-

ing popular sentiment, but also a gesture giving the provisional government the moral high-ground against the inhuman policies of Ceauşescu's
regime. In Poland, by contrast, it was through the restriction of abortion
during the same period that politicians attempted to signal the new Soli-
darity-dominated government's morality, opposition to communism, and
alliance with the Catholic Church. The Catholic Church remains actively
engaged in the on-going abortion debate in Poland's parliament. Zielińska cites a recent example of the Church's attempts to define the morality of a democratic state: a prior of the Jasna Gora monastery condemned pro-abortion deputies for treason to the motherland, noting that
these deputies "had divested themselves of the moral right to represent
Poland". Similarly, a bishop expressed both admiration for the mothers
of those deputies who voted for liberalization because these women had
not aborted, and regret because Poland would have been better off had
these deputies not been born.[20] The case of the sterilization scandal in the
unified Germany was different from Romania and Poland. The apparent
refusal of some East German women to have more children emerged as a
media story in which the former West Germany and its political legitimacy were presented as more desirable because it was more modern,
more orderly, more humane, and more moral than the backward, chaotic,
and immoral eastern Germany.[21]

Examples of reproduction as allegory abound. During the Hungarian
abortion debate in the early 1990s, those who argued that personal morality in abortion decisions should not be legislated were liberals—in the
European sense—who also demanded a minimal state and limitations on
state intrusion into private life. In this way, the discourse on human reproduction became an integral part of the process by which new state
forms were constructed. Or, turning again to Poland, a politician's opinion on abortion continues to be, in everyday politics, a litmus test usually
revealing his opinion on many other issues, ranging from the relationship
between church and state to social welfare questions.[22] In the reunified
Germany, as alluded to above, representatives of the west German media
and government, concerned about declining birthrates (or the "unprecedented demographic collapse") and reports of women from the
eastern part of Germany having themselves sterilized, accused women of
going on a "birth strike". Yet interviews with women from the former
East Germany who had been sterilized demonstrate the gap between the
morality tales created by the mass media from the reproductive behavior
of women, and the actual experiences of women of different walks of
life. The women who had been sterilized noted having achieved their
desired family size, trying to reconcile fertility with falling incomes or
unemployment, and trying to secure a job. In both Hungary and Poland,

elites arguing about abortion have also attempted to constitute the political principles according to which they wished to be judged in routine politics. Should leaders be chosen according to their moral standards or their expertise? Populist or Catholic politicians, conservative physicians, and lawyers insisted that only they understood the full moral weight of questions about abortion and, by implication, only they were fit to govern.

There is a third way in which debates about reproduction make politics. Such public arguments constitute women as a political group, characterizing women as political actors of a particular kind. The way the political roles of women are constituted varies considerably across systems. Yet debates about reproduction repeatedly face a fundamental contradiction: whether to treat women as producers or reproducers. This contradiction has been a perennial dilemma, differently handled in different historical moments and political systems. In liberal polities, the notion of rights assumes that for political purposes men and women are alike. However, for reproduction this is not the case; men and women are corporeally different, underlining the inconsistency of the "equal treatment" legislation that is the hallmark of liberalism.[23] During the communist period, women, like others, were treated as a corporate category. Their difference was legally "recognized". All communist states were pronatalist to greater or lesser degrees. Motherhood—and the production of more workers—was one of women's duties; wage labor was always another.

Since 1989, nationalist politics have become more explicit in many countries. And within most nationalist discourses, women and men are assumed to have quite different roles and subjectivities. Women are understood to owe a special kind of patriotic duty to the nation. Women give birth, are identified with spiritual values, and safeguard what is seen as the archaic, morally laden tradition of the past. Motherhood becomes sacred and is viewed as the primary form of female political agency. Recall the accusation in the German case mentioned above: women had exercised their special, essentialized form of political will by engaging in a birth strike against the very survival of the nation.

Discussions of reproduction also have a more direct effect in defining women as potential actors in political arenas. Anti-abortion legislation in Poland after 1989 motivated women to organize into groups that actively opposed this legislation; the abortion law produced women's groups that would not otherwise have materialized. Yet politics in East Central Europe, as elsewhere, is not only about politics; it is also a career path and work possibility for some segment of the population. In a situation in which forty years of communist rule created women who are at least as well—if not better—educated than men and who actually have political experience (in most cases as a result of quota systems), new arguments are needed to justify the claim by men of privileged access to the political arena as a newly created and often lucrative occupation. The communist party may be out, but who should go into politics? In Poland, arguments about women's responsibilities as reproducers are often made by politicians who are redefining the work of politics as specially suited to men, that is, as requiring specifically male talents.[24] Similar discussions about the suitability of men and women for politics are also evident in Bulgaria and Romania.[25]

Finally, one of the most dramatic ways in which debates about reproduction, along with the practices they propose and justify, are crucial in state making is in the (re)constitution of the nation and its boundaries. "Nation" is a category of identity, a system of social classification, a means of constructing the relationship between a state and (at least part of) its populace. While nations represent horizontal solidarities, that is, "imagined communities", states are centralized organizational structures with claims to sovereignty over a territory. People living within a particular polity need not be members of the same nation, and vice versa. Indeed, national identities are classically formed through oppositions and exclusions. That is, national identity is most often created against other cohabitating nations, or against colonizers or "natives", and also by ignoring other categories of identity (class, race, or region, for instance). We take nationalism to be a social movement built around (contestable) claims to such identity, one that is sometimes directed towards the capture of a state apparatus by those claiming to be members of a particular nation. But, whether demanding the formation of a new state or more influence within an already constituted state, nationalist arguments are a way of mobilizing collective action and thus bringing into being the solidary collectivity—the nation—itself.

In the strategies of political actors, nation and state are often intertwined. Thus, many anticommunist arguments in the post–1989 years identified new leaders as more authentically linked to their populace—and thus more "representative" of them in this special, and nondemocratic sense—because they were conationals (Croats and Serbs, Hungarians, Romanians, etc). Fears about the "death of the nation", justified by reference to falling birth rates, are a recurrent theme all over Europe. They gain general political significance when the interests of states are assumed to be coterminous with an increase in population of a single or dominant national group inhabiting the state's territory. Such policies are not at all incompatible with policies that simultaneously discourage the increase of another group, deemed less worthy or less legitimately linked to the state.

Much has been written about this with respect to Nazi Germany. In Franjo Tudjman's Croatia, the demographic renewal project was aimed at increasing the number of ethnic Croats by increasing births, curtailing emigration, and resettling Croat populations on Croatia's territory.[26]

It hardly needs emphasizing that in most forms of nationalist thought, biological reproduction and biological continuity are the centerpieces of imagining community and solidarity. Although nations are often enlarged and diminished by migration and assimilation, nationalist ideology routinely ignores or eradicates these processes and instead highlights blood ties. And while individuals may have claims to several national identities, and boundaries between categories are often permeable or fuzzy, nationalist discourse erases such "messiness". For most forms of nationalism, making the members of the nation is not only a symbolic classifying process, but also very much a material, embodied one: links between generations must, perforce, be reproductive links, embodiments of membership that guarantee a relationship to the future and to the past. And some forms of reproduction (for example, both parents as members of the same national group, or the mother as a member, or birth occurring on national territory) are defined as the sole legitimate means of national reproduction.

Remarkably, modern theorists of nationalism—among them Anderson, Gellner, Hobsbawm, Horowitz and Smith—have had little to say about the role of gender and reproduction in nationalism. But feminist criticism of this omission has produced an important literature on gender and nation as linked cultural categories, and operative in political action.[27] Studies of gender and nationalism have, for example, analyzed nationalism's family imagery that usually casts the nation as female and the state as male, simultaneously eroticizing the relation between men and the nation and valorizing motherhood.

The focus on motherhood and women as "vessels of the nation" also carries an interesting contradiction. Because national movements are most often conceptualized as "deep horizontal (male) fraternities", they often implicitly adopt the logic of patrilineal systems, in which women are not only the indispensable locus of continuity and the bearers of tradition, but also the outsiders who must be controlled: through the potential of their unruly sexual behavior, they are seen to pose a threat to the group.[28] Thus, women are blamed for demographic decline, women are charged with engaging in "birth strikes", women are accused of siding with political systems such as communism which are considered to be unnatural, or of committing treason if they do not wish their sons to die in wars. Oddly, then, the common narrative of national "victimization" by outside forces, especially by other nearby nations, can also often include a narrative of the nation victimized by its own women, who are seen as internal enemies.[29] The control of women thus becomes a logical project of nationalism. A classic means of such control is the regulation of women's reproductive capacity by forcing unwanted births or restricting wanted ones.

It is in part this link between nationhood and reproduction that made the use of rape in the Yugoslav war such a powerful weapon. The irony of ethnic cleansing, based ostensibly on the idea of national difference, is that the various sides understood each other only too well. As others have pointed out, the tactic of mass rape was effective because of similarity: all sides were speaking in the idiom of biologized essences in which women were the bearers of group identity. This is what made rape and the threat of rape not a crime against particular women, but a threat to the purity, honor, and ultimately the survival and future of the group.[30]

Thus, within the context of nationalist discourse focused on biological reproduction, state policies that regulate reproductive practices gain importance for a variety of reasons. Indeed, we have come full circle, back to the interests of state agencies in the control of reproduction. But here we see such interests justified not as an expression of a state's relation to its "subjects" or "citizens", but rather a government justifying its acts as the protection of the "national essence". Comparing Ceauşescu's policies with those of Serbia after 1989 nicely highlights this distinction. In Ceauşescu's Romania, abortion was forbidden for everyone, regardless of nationality, education, or other characteristics. In Serbia, laws were framed as a matter of encouraging the disproportionate increase of some subsets of the population—those considered the authentic or "proper" citizens of the state. The two policies are equivalent in demanding a sacrifice from women for the "collectivity" which, however, was the socialist state in Romania and the Serb nation in the other. They differ in that nationalist policies create a social hierarchy ostensibly based on the inheritance of biological characteristics in the case of Serbia, which was not so in Ceauşescu's policy aimed at transforming all individuals of co-inhabitating nationalities into new citizens of the Socialist Republic of Romania. A demographic panic expressed in the motto "the nation is dying" often hides the fact that population decline is a problem because immigration is not seen as a legitimate way of increasing population. Only some inhabitants—not immigrants—count as genuine citizens.[31]

Many levels and aspects of state organization can be mobilized for the construction of biologized national selves. All involve reproduction in some way: legal strictures on who may marry whom; regulations on what constitutes "normal" sexuality; the proper work of men and women; assumptions (often written into tax codes) about acceptable family forms concerning who is expected to provide child care and other care-taking support; the timing, rate, and ease of marriage and divorce. Clearly, not only ideas about nationhood, but also about health, respectability, sexuality, and idealized gender are often involved. The social actors who espouse them may be politicians, bureaucrats, or administrators. The ideas, when legislated and enacted, create the embodied boundaries by which national selves, and ultimately national groups, are systematically produced.

In outlining these four ways in which discourses of reproduction make politics, we have been arguing that state policies concerning the linked issues of reproduction, contraception, and normative sexuality are importantly shaped by the ways in which discussions and struggles around reproduction are used in a broader political field. In this sense, reproductive discourses make politics regardless of the actual effects on reproductive behavior. Public debates have strong effects on the shaping of negotiations and strategies from which such laws emerge.[32]

In turn, the laws and regulations that result from a political process, while never entirely determining action, nevertheless impact upon the range of actual practices of reproduction that are possible for ordinary men and women. They define the boundaries of legality, as well as the official expectations and imagery against which people must struggle and which they may on occasion resist.[33] And so we have returned to the classic subject matter of the politics of reproduction: the effect of seemingly distant power relations on local reproductive experiences.

Furthermore, between the political arguments already discussed and the processes that frame a policy and put it into practice, there are inevitable compromises, lapses, gaps, and contradictions. In any polity, men and women also ignore, reinterpret, and deflect explicit state actions and maneuver around them, creating and engaging alternatives outside the purview of legal strictures and state structures. As a result, the routine forms of everyday reproductive practice that emerge depend not only on the framing of issues and the range of rhetorical patterns reviewed here, but also on the details of national and political contexts and on broadly economic—and sometimes international—processes that fall outside the domains of state agencies. In Poland, for instance, some doctors have set up private abortion clinics where they make healthy profits performing abortions that are apparently morally offensive to them when done in state-supported hospitals during customary working hours.[34] Reproductive questions intersect with market interests in other ways as well. Some east German women who have themselves sterilized are acting in part to improve their chances in a newly hypercompetitive job market that re-

wards women who can prove they will have no reproductive responsibilities that might interfere with their work.[35] Some scholars have argued
that the invocation of reproductive responsibility is being used as a way
to get women out of the labor market at a time of economic restructuring
that requires the streamlining of production and, relatedly, increasing
unemployment.

There are also important international dimensions to reproductive
policies and practices. States that legislate against abortion within their
boundaries often do not interfere with women travelling abroad for
"abortion tourism".[36] This has become a popular strategy for women who
have the money to do so, which produces an income stratification in
reproductive practices. The increased availability of contraceptives has
had a similar effect, since they are not available to everyone.[37] The influence of the Vatican on Polish parliamentary discussions of abortion has
already been mentioned, but the Vatican is only one of the many transnational organizations that pressure East Central European governments.
Romania has repeatedly resisted West European insistence that homo-
sexuality be decriminalized. Clearly, local discourses are powerful even
in the face of international pressure.

Such dynamics have repercussions not only on the domestic front but
also the international. How governments react to International Monetary
Fund and World Bank advice on social benefits or reproductive health
and family planning strategies, how reproductive policies are seen to
intersect with minority politics, how the criminalization of homosexual-
ity is seen to violate democratic rights: all contribute to the way the
states of East Central Europe are treated by supranational organizations
and in international fora. Accordingly, the governments of East Central
Europe are very sensitive to their images abroad. We have yet again
come full circle: representations about reproduction make politics, not
only at home, but on the international stage.

Notes

1 This article is excerpted from S. Gal and G. Kligman, *The Politics of Gender after
Socialism* (Princeton University Press, 2000), and reprinted with the permission of
Princeton University Press. It forms part of a broader synthetic analysis of the gendering of postsocialism that we have been developing which grew out of our own research on the politics of reproduction, and that of an international, comparative research project on postsocialist transformation analyzed from a gendered perspective
that we co-organized. The results of this comparative study are published in S. Gal

and G. Kligman, eds., *Reproducing Gender: Politics, Publics, and Everyday Life After Socialism* (Princeton University Press, 2000). Project funding was obtained from the Open Society Institute, the American Council of Learned Societies, and the Wenner-Gren Foundation for Anthropological Research.

2 This definition relies on the influential work of J. Scott, *Gender and the Politics of History* (New York: Columbia University Press, 1988).

3 See, for example, I. Dölling, D. Hahn, and S. Scholz, "Birth Strike in the New Federal States: Is Sterilization an Act of Resistance?" in *Reproducing Gender*, eds. Gal and Kligman; M. Ferree and E. Maleck-Levy, "Talking about Women and Wombs: The Discourse of Abortion and Reproductive Rights in the G.D.R. During and After the 'Wende,'" in *Reproducing Gender*, eds. Gal and Kligman; M. Fuszara, "Abortion and the Formation of the Public Sphere in Poland", in *Gender Politics and Post-Communism: Reflections from Eastern Europe and the former Soviet Union*, eds. N. Funk and M. Mueller (New York: Routledge, 1993), 241–52; S. Gal, "Gender in the Post-Socialist Transition: The Abortion Debate in Hungary", *East European Politics and Societies* 8:2 (1994): 256–287; G. Kligman, "The Social Legacy of Communism: Women, Children, and the Feminization of Poverty", in *The Social Legacy of Communism*, eds. J. Millar and S. Wolchik (Washington DC: Woodrow Wilson Center and Cambridge Presses, 1994), 252–70; E. Zielińska, "Between Ideology, Politics, and Common Sense: The Discourse of Reproductive Rights in Poland", in *Reproducing Gender*, eds. Gal and Kligman.

4 The feminist literature on the public and private spheres is voluminous, with M. Rosaldo, "Woman, Culture and Society: A Theoretical Overview", in *Woman, Culture and Society*, eds. M. Rosaldo and L. Lamphere (Stanford: Stanford University Press, 1974), 17–42 an influential piece as one of the earliest contributions. In anthropology, a thorough critique of cross-cultural, universalist approaches appeared in J. Collier and S. Yanagisako, *Gender and Kinship: Essays toward a Unified Analysis* (Stanford: Stanford University Press, 1987), with related arguments on the nature/culture dichotomy in C. MacCormack and M. Strathern, *Nature, Culture and Gender* (New York: Cambridge University Press, 1990). See M. di Leonardo, ed., introduction to *Gender at the Crossroads of Knowledge: Feminist Anthropology in the Postmodern Era* (Berkeley: University of California Press, 1991) for a critical review. In thinking about this dichotomy, we have also been stimulated by several traditions of feminist work about states, including Z. Eisenstein, *Feminism and Sexual Equality* (New York: Monthly Review Press, 1984); W. Brown, "Finding the Man in the State", *Feminist Studies* 18:1 (1992): 7–34; N. Hartsock, *Money, Sex, and Power: Toward a Feminist Historical Materialism* (Boston: Northeastern University Press, 1984); Carole Pateman, *Sexual Contract* (Stanford: Stanford University Press, 1988); L. Gordon, ed. *Women, the State, and Welfare* (Madison: University of Wisconsin Press, 1990); R.W. Connell, "The State, Gender and Sexual Politics", *Theory and Society* 19 (1990): 507–544; A. Phillips, *Engendering Democracy* (University Park: Pennsylvania State University Press, 1991); K.B. Jones and A.G. Jonasdottir, eds., *The Political Interests of Gender: Developing Theory and Research with a Feminist Face* (Newbury Park, Calif.: Sage Publications, 1988); A. Sassoon, ed., *Women and the State: The Shifting Boundaries between Public and Private* (London: Hutchinson,

1987); Birte Siim, "Towards a Feminist Rethinking of the Welfare State", in *The Political Interests of Gender*, eds. K. Jones and A. Jonasdottir (London: Sage, 1988), 160–186; and the closely related works on forms of patriarchy, such as S. Walby, *Theorizing Patriarchy* (Oxford, England: Blackwell, 1990). See also N. Fraser, *Unruly Practices* (Minneapolis: University of Minnesota Press, 1989); and Phillips, *Engendering Democracy*, for recent critical discussion of related European and American social theories.

5 G. Kligman, "The Politics of Reproduction in Ceauşescu's Romania", *East European Politics and Societies* 6:3 (1992): 364.

6 F. Ginsburg and R. Rapp, "The Politics of Reproduction", *Annual Review of Anthropology* 20 (1991): 313.

7 G. Kligman, *The Politics of Duplicity: Controlling Reproduction in Ceauşescu's Romania* (Berkeley: University of California Press, 1998), 3.

8 F. Ginsburg and R. Rapp, eds. *Conceiving the New World Order: The Global Politics of Reproduction* (Berkeley: University of California Press, 1995), 2.

9 Gal, "Gender in the Post-Socialist Transition", 258.

10 To study empirically the involvement of states in reproduction, it is necessary to reject any definition of states as reified or personified entities with set social functions and unified goals. "States are always given form through the actions of people" (Kligman, *The Politics of Duplicity*, 4). The objectification of the state as an entity unto itself masks the active participation of people in "making" the state.

11 Thus, Frederick the Great compared his own backward Prussia with fortunate Holland that, though vastly smaller in extent, had the dense settlement and industrious population that made it a greater European power. This example is from Foucault's discussion on "Governmentality" in *The Foucault Effect: Studies in Governmentality*, eds. G. Burchell, C. Gordon, and P. Miller (Chicago: Chicago University Press, 1991), 87–104. C. Gallagher, "The Body Versus the Social Body in the Works of Thomas Malthus and Henry Mayhew", in *The Making of the Modern Body: Sexuality and Society in the Nineteenth Century*, eds. C. Gallagher and T. Laqueur (Berkeley: University of California Press, 1987), 83–106; and L. Jordanova, "Interrogating the Concept of Reproduction in the 18th Century", in *Conceiving the New World Order: The Global Politics of Reproduction*, eds. F. Ginsburg and R. Rapp (Berkeley: University of California, 1995), 369–386 provide useful analyses of changing European ideas about population and reproduction into the nineteenth century.

12 Cited in Gallagher, "The Body vs. Social Body", 83.

13 An excellent overview of feminist historiography on family strategies and social reproduction in Europe is B. Laslett and J. Brenner, "Gender and Social Reproduction: Historical Perspectives", *Annual Review of Sociology* 15(1989): 381–404; S. Watson, *From Provinces into Nations: Demographic Integration in Western Europe 1870–1960* (Princeton: Princeton Press, 1991) is exemplary in exploring the relationship of family strategies about reproduction to increasing state and market integration in Western Europe over the last century and a half.

14 S. Michel and S. Koven, "Womanly Duties: Maternalist Politics and the Origins of the Welfare State in France, Germany, Great Britain and the USA 1880–1920", *American Historical Review* 95 (1990): 1076–1108 provides a useful synthesis of de-

velopments in the maternalist feminisms of Western Europe. For a variety of feminist ideologies of reproduction see also G. Bock and P. Thane, eds., *Maternity and Gender Policies: Women and the Rise of the European Welfare States, 1880s–1950s*, (New York: Routledge, 1991). R. Bridenthal, A. Grossman and M. Kaplan, eds., *When Biology Becomes Destiny: Women in Weimar and Nazi Germany* (New York: Monthly Review Press, 1989) discuss eugenics, sex reformers, and other social movements in twentieth-century Germany. It is important to note the many nineteenth- and twentieth-century feminist movements that made a much broader politics of morality around their concerns for protecting reproduction and children.

15 In 1997, a Czech couple brought home a Roma child from a children's institution; however, the child was of Slovak nationality. Although she had been born in the Czech Republic, her birth parents had not applied for permanent residence. The Czech couple, attempting to adopt the child, was soon denied childcare benefits. The social benefits law had changed, and because the child did not have Czech citizenship, this meant the family was ineligible. Moreover, because a foreigner had been incorporated into the family, they lost the benefits for which they had been eligible on behalf of their own biological child. See "Adopting a Child? Don't Want a Foreigner", *Mlada fronta dnes*, 23 October 1997.

16 M. Ferree and E. Maleck-Levy, "Talking about Women and Wombs".

17 For details on the Hungarian abortion debate, see Gal, "Gender in the Post-Socialist Transition". On the abortion debates in Germany, see also U. Nelles, "Abortion, the Special Case: A Constitutional Perspective", *German Politics and Society* 4–5 (Winter 1991–92): 111–121; M. Nimsch, "Abortion as Politics", *German Politics and Society* 4–5 (Winter 1991–92): 128–134; H. De Soto, "In the Name of the Folk: Women and Nation in the New Germany", *UCLA Women's Law Journal* 5:1 (1994): 83–101; E. Maleck-Levy, "Between Self-determination and State Supervision: Women and the Abortion Law in Post-unification Germany", *Social Politics* 2:1 (1995): 62–76; Ferree and Maleck-Levy, "Talking about Women and Wombs".

18 For instance, in contrast to Eastern and Western Europe, American battles about abortion have been posed as questions about the bounds of "privacy", women's self-determination, and images of the sort of female life worth living. See, for example, R. Petchesky, *Abortion and Woman's Choice: The State, Sexuality, and Reproductive Freedom* (Boston: Northeastern University Press, 1984); F. Ginsburg, *Contested Lives: The Abortion Debate in an American Community* (Berkeley: University of California Press, 1989); K. Luker, *Abortion and the Politics of Motherhood* (Berkeley: University of California Press, 1984). In Western Europe the terms of debate have formed around the responsibilities of the state to women [see M. Glendon, *Abortion and Divorce in Western Law* (New York: Cambridge University Press, 1987)] and in China around the meanings of modernity [see A. Anagnost, "A Surfeit of Bodies: Population and the Rationality of the State in Post-Mao China", in *Conceiving the New World Order: The Global Politics of Reproduction*, eds. F. Ginsburg and R. Rapp (Berkeley: University of California Press, 1995), 22–41)].

19 See, for example, J. Sztaniszkis, *The Dynamics of Breakthrough in Eastern Europe: The Polish Experience* (Berkeley: University of California, 1991); K. Verdery, *What was Socialism, and What Comes Next?* (Princeton: Princeton University Press, 1996).

The arguments in the preceding paragraphs are indirectly supported by the recent work of J. Linz and A. Stepan, *Problems of Democratic Transition and Consolidation: Southern Europe, South America, and Post-Communist Europe* (Baltimore: Johns Hopkins University Press, 1996), who make the point that "statehood" cannot be taken for granted, in fact must be constructed, in situations of "transition". There are bound to be arguments about who "belongs". Furthermore, creating an appearance of morality for the state gains importance in light of the empirical evidence that markets and economic arrangements themselves do not legitimate democratic systems; if anything the sequence appears to be the other way around.

20 Zielińska, "Between Ideology, Politics, and Common Sense".

21 Dölling, et. al, "Birth Strike".

22 Zielińska, "Between Ideology, Politics, and Common Sense".

23 Petchesky, *Abortion and Woman's Choice*, and Z. Eisenstein, *The Radical Future of Liberal Feminism* (Boston: Northeastern University Press, 1993), among others have discussed the contradictions of liberal states on the issue of reproductive rights.

24 M. Fuszara, "New Gender Relations in Poland in the 1990s", in *Reproducing Gender: Politics, Publics, and Everyday Life after Socialism*, eds. Gal and Kligman.

25 K. Daskalova, "Women's Problems, Women's Discourses in Bulgaria", in *Reproducing Gender*, eds. Gal and Kligman; D. Kostova, "Similar or Different? Women in Post-Communist Bulgaria", in *Women in the Politics of Post-Communist Eastern Europe*, ed. M. Rueschemeyer (Armonk, N.Y.: M.E. Sharpe, 1998), 249–66; L. Grunberg, "Women's NGOs in Romania", in *Reproducing Gender*, eds. Gal and Kligman; M.E. Fischer and D. Harsanyi, "From Tradition and Ideology to Elections and Competition: The Changing Status of Women in Romanian Politics", in *Women in the Politics of Post-Communist Eastern Europe*, ed. M. Rueschemeyer, 201–24; see also M. Rueschemeyer, ed., *Women in the Politics of Post-Communist Eastern Europe*.

26 Silva Mežnarić, "Populacionizam I Demokracija: Hrvatska Nakon Osamostaljenja", *Erasmus* 19 (1997): 58–63; Silva Mežnarić, "Populacija, nacija, broj: demografija i politika etnosa u modernoj Europi", *Revija za sociologiju* XXVIII:1–2 (1997): 1–18.

27 The feminist literature on nation and gender covers most contemporary nation-states. The collection by N. Yuval-Davis and F. Anthias, *Woman-Nation-State* (New York: St. Martin's Press, 1989), and their introduction to it were important early contributions; more recently, special issues of *Gender and History* [see C. Hall, J. Lewis, K. McClelland and J. Rendall, eds., "Gender, Nationalisms and National Identities", special issue of *Gender and History* 5:2 (1993)] and a special issue of *Feminist Review* [A. Whitehead, C. Connolly, E. Carter, and H. Crowley, eds., "Nationalism and National Identities", Special Issue of *Feminist Studies* 44 (1993): 1–111], have further explored these issues. Not all the contributors distinguish clearly between nation and state. Verdery, *What was Socialism*, discusses gender and nationalism in Eastern Europe, as do many of the articles in the collections by S. Rai, H. Pilkington, and A. Phizacklea, eds., *Women in the Face of Change: The Soviet Union, Eastern Europe, and China* (London: Routledge, 1992); Funk and Mueller, eds., *Gender Politics and Post-Communism*; T. Renne, ed., *Ana's Land: Sisterhood in Eastern Europe* (Boulder, Colo.: Westview Press, 1997). While most of these studies are about gender in general, G. Heng and J. Devan, "State Fatherhood: The Politics of Nationalism,

Sexuality and Race in Singapore", in *Nationalisms and Sexualities*, eds. A. Parker, M. Russo, D. Sommer, and P. Yaeger (New York: Routledge, 1992), 343–64, has particular relevance for our discussion of reproduction. Also see Kligman, "The Social Legacy of Communism".

28 See B. Denitch, "Sex and Power in the Balkans", in *Woman, Culture and Society*, eds. Rosaldo and Lamphere, 243–262.

29 In Croatia, five women who criticized Tudjman's policies were labeled "witches" (see, for example, V. Kesić, "Confessions of a 'Yugo-Nostalgic' Witch", in *Ana's Land*, ed. Renne, 195–200). In Belgrade, the Women in Black starkly and silently protested the war and Milošević's government.

30 G. Kligman, "Women and the Negotiation of Identity in Post-Communist Eastern Europe", in *Identities in Transition: Eastern Europe and Russia after the Collapse of Communism*, ed. V. Bonnell (Berkeley: International and Area Studies, 1996), 68–91; A. Stiglymayer, ed., *Mass Rape: The War Against Women in Bosnia-Hercegovina* (Lincoln: University of Nebraska Press, 1994); J. Mostov, "'Our Women/Their Women': Symbolic Boundaries, Territorial Markers, and Violence in the Balkans", in *Women in a Violent World: Feminist Analyses and Resistance Across Europe*, ed. C. Corrin (Edinburgh: Edinburgh University Press, 1996), 515–29.

31 This also hides a further embarrassment. Part of the reason for population decline in Croatia, Poland, Slovakia and other states is that members of those nations would rather migrate out, presumably for the sake of higher standards of living, than stay to "be" the nation. See Mežnarić, "Populacija, nacija, broj".

32 Zielińska, "Between Ideology, Politics, and Common Sense".

33 Kligman, *The Politics of Duplicity*.

34 Zielińska, "Between Ideology, Politics, and Common Sense".

35 Dölling, et al., "Birth Strike in the New Federal States".

36 Zielińska, "Between Ideology, Politics, and Common Sense"; Kligman, *The Politics of Duplicity*.

37 A. Baban, "Women's Sexuality and Reproductive Behavior in Post-Ceauşescu Romania: A Psychological Approach", in *Reproducing Gender*, eds. Gal and Kligman.

12 The Morals of Transition: Decline of Public Interest and Runaway Reforms in Eastern Europe

KAZIMIERZ Z. POZNANSKI

Introduction

While the moral aspect of the ongoing transition to capitalism in Eastern Europe is largely ignored, rapidly growing numbers of those who analyze institutions of modern capitalism remind us of the significance of morals in organizing economic life. George Soros's series of writings on the threats faced by contemporary advanced capitalism is one of the best examples of this line of thinking.[1] To him, modern capitalism, with the market as a core institution, is under threat from excessive individualism. Manifested in the unconstrained operation of the market, rampant individualism undermines morality, since morality means self-restraint out of concern for possible gain/harm to others, the public. The most destructive of these forces is at the global level, but they cannot ravage the worldwide capitalist system without first fracturing morals within national economies. However, the moral problems that Soros claims are faced by advanced capitalism pale by comparison with those experienced by transition economies that have embarked on the task of building genuine markets. Markets are emerging here under conditions of a severe decline of public virtues—perverse corruption of state officials and the indifference of private citizens. If Soros is correct that forces of demoralization can severely undermine the existing genuine state of developed capitalism, then it is very unlikely that such capitalism could emerge despite similar neglect of group (public) interests. This crisis of public virtues explains why reforms—while quite diverse in terms of speed and content—are failing badly, as manifested in the deep and yet unfinished regional recession. Even more, these reforms are failing to deliver a healthy economic system, for what has emerged in the midst of this economic distress is a system where ownership is mainly foreign. As a result, only a very weak—largely petty—domestic capitalist class is emerging. This means that the transition has basically failed to undo the major damage done by communism—the extinction of endogenous capitalist classes.

In this essay I search for the most defining characteristics of capitalism-building in East European economies (inclusive of the European parts of the former Soviet Union—the Baltic states, Belarus, Russia, and Ukraine). I first identify a certain common quality in the initial stage of transition, which I call "the origins". By this I mean the collapse of communism, the development that opened the door for subsequent capitalism-building efforts. The existence of some disparities between East European economies in terms of their endings to communism cannot be denied. For instance, Poland's uniquely powerful opposition movement led by outspoken intellectuals stands juxtaposed to the situation in countries like Bulgaria or Russia, where the communist party faced no serious external challenge of this kind. In spite of many differences, the communist declines throughout the region shared one important feature: the collapses all happened in a very peaceful—almost uneventful—manner.

Next, I turn to the second stage of the transition—the process of remaking the existing economic system itself. While recognizing numerous, even major, cross-country differences, I again find a critical commonality among transition countries. Poland and Bulgaria can again serve as examples of the differences. Poland has conducted a very bold and well-articulated reform program from the start, while Bulgaria has not, allowing instead for indecisiveness and the implementation of confused reform measures. Despite these discrepancies, the two economies in question—and, in fact, every country in the region—share the same fate. With the very launching of their respective systemic reforms, they have entered into an extensive, unprecedented recession, though admittedly quite uneven. Continuing with this pair of countries, it is quite apparent that economic adversities have been far less pronounced in Poland than in Bulgaria.

Finally, I look at the third stage, the destination of the transition—an emerging form of capitalism—and again notice some obvious cross-country differences. For instance, Russia has established an economic system with overpowering criminal elements that substitute for the system of state and the rule of law. Such criminal forces are, however, not as pronounced in countries such as Hungary and Slovenia. Nevertheless, there are other aspects of emerging capitalism that are found universally in the region. The most important is the general pattern of ownership relations, or property rights. All of these countries are rapidly heading for systems of capitalism in which the majority of capital assets, in industry and banking, belong to foreigners, largely as a result of privatization. This is already the case in Hungary, and it appears that Poland and a few others are following close behind. Indeed, there is further evidence that even the countries that are the least advanced in terms of privatization of capital seem to be heading in a similar direction.

After identifying these three special features of the transition from communist to capitalist systems, I attempt to provide a unified explanation for all these features. I do so by carefully examining a single variable—the status of morality in transition economies. I chose this approach because, as evolutionary economics informs us, a moral order is at the foundation of all institutions. Moral order is about self-restraint, specifically about a sense of respect by each individual player for the other actors involved. This moral outlook assures a cohesive operation of all members whose actions, when routine rather then deliberate, create a given institution. For this reason, no major institutional change can be understood without a reference to morals, those of both officials who form the state and citizens who constitute the society.

Taking the evolutionary position, I conclude that a decline of morals was most critical for the initial stage of transition—the demise of communism. Specifically, officials—particularly the party cadres—decided to abandon the public agenda for private, often illegal, gains. Some may reject this statement as implying that communism at some point relied on public virtues, but to retain order for an extended period it had to have this quality. Otherwise, for instance, coercion will not be correctly applied by the rulers and approved by the ruled at a cost that the rulers can afford. Officials underwent this change of mind after realizing that the system that provided them with positions of great power offered them only mediocre material rewards and little protection against possible job termination. While the party/state members played the key role, society—the citizens—knowingly went along with the corruption of the officials, which helps explain, in part, why this collapse was so docile.

This largely unnoticed and negative turn in public outlook at the conclusion of communism was difficult to reverse, since morals, given their inherent fragility, tend to further deteriorate once they are upset. This trend has not been reversed anywhere in the region. Instead, an antipublic spirit has been allowed to flourish. Unleashed under these conditions, reforms have been shaped by officials who above all have sought additional opportunities to attain personal gain through corruption. Given the insecurity of their positions—in part related to the prevalence of corrupt behavior itself—officials have preferred actions with immediate payoffs, even if such actions are clearly adverse to the public at large. This explains why the second stage of transition everywhere in the region assumed a radical and often misguided form. Radical reforms, in turn, mostly by means of creating financial adversities, have collectively forced the respective transition economies into recession.

The collapse of public virtues also explains the third stage of transition, since only under these conditions of broad-based corruption by officials and indifference of the citizenry would these countries have engaged in a wholesale, rather than only selective, transfer of assets to foreigners. The same financial adversities—due to a crippled banking system and minimal protection from imports—that caused recession have reduced domestic buyers' ability to make their acquisitions profitable. Unable to survive on their own, state-owned enterprises have been forced to seek foreign financing, which has been forthcoming almost exclusively in the form of payment for assets. This transfer typically has taken place under nontransparent procedures and without proper parliamentary oversight. Within this framework, state officials have been able to offer preferential access and discounted prices. In their search for illegitimate gain, they have favored foreigners, since most are more resourceful in providing payments and/or lucrative positions.

The final judgment of transition depends less on the fact of recession, for recessions come and go, and more on the type of ownership, which will determine economic performance for decades to come. In such terms, the only conclusion to be drawn is that the transition has been a serious failure. By analyzing the whole process more carefully, we see that the ownership—and market—structure in Eastern Europe is basically left unchanged. Under the communist system, public property dominated, and under the emerging system of—let's call it—"incomplete capitalism", private property rules. This represents a major change, though at the same time foreign capitalists are replacing the party/state as the principal agents holding decision-making powers and claims on income from capital. This represents, of course, an important continuity, since in both cases, as a consequence of nationalization under communism and as a result of privatization during postcommunism, the domestic capitalist class is largely missing from the social picture (with the market continuing to be dominated by highly concentrated entities that enjoy monopolistic positions).

Replacement of the internal agency by a foreign one is not without consequence for the economies of the region, and this consequence may ultimately be negative. When domestic agents—even those as inefficient as the communist party—are largely substituted by foreign agents, this provides an opportunity for an illegitimate and undeserved transfer abroad of income from capital. This particularly may become a reality if the states are too weak to resist undue influence from foreigners and/or are unable to enforce fair practices (for example, business accounting, profit transfers, product pricing). Given the enormous weakness of the East European states, related in part to the corruptibility of their officials, "incomplete capitalism" may indeed prove detrimental to regional wealth. In the extreme case, losses caused by the extraction of undeserved income—rents—for use abroad may exceed the efficiency gains from foreign ownership.

The Theory: Morals (Public Virtues) and Institutions

There are clearly certain economic issues that cannot be properly addressed without reference to morals, and most of these issues happen to be central rather than peripheral. Massive changes in institutions within which economic activity is conducted belong to this class of principal problems that call for bringing in morality. The transition to capitalism taking place in Eastern Europe is definitely such a case in point, but the current debate generally fails to focus on transition's moral dimension. Formal aspects of reforms—rules of the game—are stressed, but informal aspects such as attitudes (values) practiced by economic agents are not. Consequently, a greatly distorted picture of the transition is offered, which adds to confusion among reformers and the public. Some major failings of the transition are either unnoticed or incorrectly viewed as insignificant developments or, in a more extreme version, they are seen as successes.

While trying to introduce the moral dimension into the analysis of transition, it is important to note that the process of building capitalism in some form or another is not without precedent. History shows not only numerous successful attempts at establishing a genuine capitalist system but also numerous efforts that failed, leaving economies with inefficient institutions of a capitalist type. These diverse attempts have been carefully studied, particularly the positive experiences in building capitalism, such as the complex changes that led to the eighteenth century industrial breakthrough. Classical economists and other liberal thinkers (such as Hume, Locke, and Smith) have commented upon this historic period with particular insight. Therefore, it makes sense to borrow from their works in studying recent transitions to capitalism in Eastern Europe, or for that matter, elsewhere in the former communist economies.

The classical thinkers understood—even took for granted—that capitalism successfully emerged in the eighteenth century as a product of people with strong moral convictions, solidly grounded in religious beliefs (a view that was later developed by Weber into a complex theory in reference to Protestant ethics). A principal figure among classical economists, Smith certainly believed that both religion and morality were essential in bringing about capitalism as an organizing principle. He believed, however, that religion, and not morality, would eventually be replaced by legal rulings. Smith also argued, overly optimistically, that the major justification for the capitalist system is its moralizing influence on fallible people.[2] Markets discipline people into decent behavior and material prosperity—which markets ensure—and thus make them less tempted to break moral rules as well.

Classical thinkers accordingly assumed a central role for morals, which were defined as powerful but fragile guidelines for actions that can benefit others—that is, the public. Thus, they firmly believed that economics as a social discipline is a moral science where morals are a central category in explaining behavior.[3] The classical thinkers also placed great emphasis on the role of institutions in guiding economic activities, with institutions understood by them subjectively—that is, as being formed by agents' morally driven behavior. This was an individualistic, rather than collectivist, view of institutions, which are said to emerge when individual actions become both regular and routine in nature. In this way, the so-perceived institutions make up social systems, and when morals alter agents, they revise their mode of action. This revision, in turn, changes the whole social system.

Taking one extreme case of such change, when morals collapse across the board and agents turn sharply away from the public good, the unavoidable consequence is that the respective social system collapses as well. But this eventuality was of no concern to the classical students of capitalism, not only because of their unshaken optimism, but also because their era was one of strong morals. Paradoxically, later in the development of capitalism when these moral foundations had been periodically fractured, followers of the classical school were no longer well equipped to address this aspect. The original classical perspective concerning the nature of institutions has been largely discarded or forgotten by its modern followers—neoclassical economists. This is true insofar as they assume morals (and institutions) to be given. Alternatively, neoclassical economists do not directly address the moral (and institutional) dimensions in their models at all.

Interest in institutions, however, has not vanished from economics, as evidenced in the great currency recently earned by the so-called neoinstitutionalists, such as North and Williamson. They surely stand out in this respect, since they find institutions central to our understanding of economic processes. They also assume that institutions are external to agents, and as such, institutions impose norms on agents. In this collectivist approach, the genesis of norms in general and morals in particular is not explained. For this reason, norms are not afforded a truly independent status. With this approach, neoinstitutional theory is quite suitable for comparative-static analysis, including how economies operate under various forms of markets. It is not prepared, however, to engage in intertemporal—dynamic—analysis (for instance, one that tries to figure out how markets emerge and submerge).

Only the so-called evolutionary economists—following Hayek, Mises, and Schumpeter—continue the early tradition, in which values, both private and public, are an independent economic variable (paying less attention to Smith and more to Malthus, who preceded him). This attention to morality is especially clear in the work of Schumpeter, particularly in his examination of the origins and fate of the capitalist system.[4] He argues that the capitalist order was animated by rationally thinking and profit-seeking actors, but that this order could not have emerged if not for the moral tradition of feudalism. Capitalism needs feudal groups— aristocrats, clergy, and military—for their moral makeup, which is not a product of reason alone. These feudal values represent a protective shield against the self-destructive instincts of capitalist groups themselves. If the protective strata, as he calls the feudal groups, are undermined, the capitalist system will collapse, giving way to some form of socialism.

Hayek also argued forcefully that morals are critical for the working of economic institutions, though his most elaborate remarks on this point came late in his life. Hayek holds that there are certain principled rules of behavior that constitute a prerequisite for the survival of human beings. Most important among these rules are moral practices, and since institutions are formed to aid men in their struggle for survival, institutions have to conform.[5] There is only one general set of moral rules that assures a continuity of human life, which happens to be the one on which capitalism is based. Socialism, with its own rules of conduct, does not have this capability and for this reason is not feasible for any extended period. Most importantly, putting people under a collective—totalitarian—rule damages their ability to exchange information at an acceptable cost, and this in turn undermines economic calculus and leads to inefficient production.

This view of Hayek is contrary to the more affirmative position outlined by Schumpeter, who argues that as long as people believe in socialist ideals, socialism, as a complex system, may actually work. Being himself a strong advocate of capitalism, Schumpeter agonizes over what he perceives to be a rather inevitable drift towards various forms of socialism. These forms, in Schumpeter's view, include the labor-controlled system of Great Britain, the national socialism of Germany, and the state communism of Soviet Russia, all of which were contemporary to him. This possibility is particularly real for less extreme forms of socialism, such as the one in Great Britain. In such a system, ownership of assets remains private, but trade unions through the state control the appropriation of capital gains. According to Schumpeter, having an efficient state apparatus ready to execute any agenda, such as Great Britain had at the time, makes the working of socialism much more feasible.

The focus on morality was not shared by all of the early evolutionary scholars, including as critical a voice as that of Popper, who stayed away from moral issues his entire scholarly life. This fact has been recently highlighted by Soros in his effort to revive Popper's theory of social change and of capitalism in particular.[6] Soros correctly observes that Popper takes the sound morals on which capitalism must be founded as a given. For this reason, Popper—like Hayek—was of the view that capitalism, as an "open society", faces one threat—that of socialism. Socialism, as an irrational return to a "closed society", represents a threat because it is based on a collective principle, a group dictate, rather than on an individualist principle, which calls for freedom of choice. But, as Soros argues, capitalism may also be mortally threatened from within, when individual freedom is taken to an extreme and markets take over, causing the moral order to deteriorate.

An important addition by Soros, not just to Popper's theory but to evolutionary thinking, is his effort to demonstrate that the greatest risk to capitalism comes from global markets.[7] Global markets emerge when national markets are united. Such merger is possible only as a consequence of states giving up their prerogatives over national economies. This release would make no difference for the status of capitalism if nation-states were replaced with supranational agencies. Then such agencies could provide (political) restraint on markets that would assure those markets deliver outcomes that are morally acceptable. But it is much more difficult to design such controlling mechanisms at the global level than at domestic ones. Consequently, when capitalism becomes global as it has nowadays, the greatest internal threat to the system is expected to come from the operation of global markets (a point that echoes the arguments of Polányi[8]).

Soros further argues that, if left without political restraint grounded in sound moral practices, global forces cause an unequal distribution of welfare gains from cross-border exchange. Financial capital is best prepared to take advantage of liberalization, followed by industrial capital, while labor is likely to gain the least. This is due to different levels of flexibility enjoyed by all three of these productive forces in terms of reallocating their activities around the world in search of the best yields. The differences in factor flexibility in part are purely technical, for clearly it is easier to move money than fixed capital, and labor is physically the hardest to move. This allows the countries that enjoy advantages in financial services to raid economies with underdeveloped banking. Stronger economies can be predatory on weaker economies through unfair—monopolistic—practices and, if necessary, by means of instigating costly financial crises in the latter.

The Origins: Peaceful Collapse of Communism

Let me begin with a clarification of my evolutionary position by taking a closer look at the first stage of the transition, its initial conditions as determined by the collapse of communism. Given the general belief that the communist system was not only economically wasteful but also morally deplorable, its collapse should have resulted from forceful rejection, or revolution. That is what usually happens when morally inspired masses, their rage doubled by economic suffering, employ force to take power away from their rulers, seen as perpetrators of immoral acts. It is this highly morally charged atmosphere that leads disfranchised masses to suspend concern for the legality of their actions. By decisively ousting the rulers, the masses assume power, and in doing so, they infuse the state—in their view at least—with a sound moral understanding.

But there is no evidence to suggest that the cause of communism's downfall in Eastern Europe was revolutionary in nature, and nowhere did the masses overthrow the party or, more correctly, the party/state. This was most apparent in places like Russia or Romania.[9] In these countries there were no real opposition forces, but merely small groups of vocal dissident intellectuals who posed no threat to authorities well equipped with coercive means. Here the masses remained passive even during political change, while in other places where there was no real opposition, as in Czechoslovakia and East Germany, people took to the streets only when the authorities were ready to abdicate. In Poland a broadly based and organized opposition movement failed to mobilize the masses for the final showdown with the party in 1989 (for example, appeals for a general strike were largely ignored).

Not only were the masses universally passive at the time of power transfer, but there is no evidence that they succeeded in displacing the party cadres in the months following the collapse of the respective regimes. Retribution against former functionaries has been rather mild, even in east Germany, where massive legal campaigns to scrutinize former apparatchiks were launched. Elsewhere, sanctions simply did not materialize, even in Hungary, with its strong and painful memories of the brutally crushed 1956 uprising. In fact, many former cadres were allowed to engage in public activities, including political life, and nowhere, not even in east Germany, were the former parties prohibited from engaging in the new political process (not counting an episode in Russia in 1991, when the Communist Party was temporarily banned from politics but reinstituted after a successful legal challenge).

In light of these facts, there seems to be little choice but to admit that in all probability the collapse of the communist systems was engineered largely by party/state officials themselves. In the minority of cases, the party monopoly ended through a relatively orderly process of negotiation, dragging the opposition along almost against its will, as was the case in Hungary and Poland (where through most of 1989 representatives of the opposition repeatedly rejected initial invitations to join talks with the communist leadership on reforming the political system). In the majority of cases, political change was contrived through intraparty power-brokers, usually without resort to violence (except in Romania, where the ruling clique was ousted in a bloody putsch by a military faction, and in Russia, where the ruling group lost power as a result of its failed, rather grotesque, and—most importantly—almost completely bloodless putsch).

This explanation of the communist collapse would be incomplete if it didn't also offer a plausible indication of what might have motivated the members of the party/state to relinquish their monopoly on power. The answer I propose is that, somewhat paradoxically, they did so because of the very power monopoly afforded to the party. To persist, such a monopoly required a commitment that at a critical point proved inconvenient to the interests of the officials themselves, the party cadres and state operatives. Some have speculated along these lines that at this juncture the party members came to realize that the existence of the communist system put them in an unattainable position. Namely, that the system made them solely responsible for the general welfare of the people while concurrently offering the masses only weak incentives to create the material wealth needed to continuously feed overblown social programs.

In actuality, party/state officials found the communist regime inconvenient for another reason: namely, that at some point their perception of their own roles within the system dramatically changed. As long as the party cadres and state officials believed they were empowered to assure a better future for the people, they behaved as a more or less cohesive group to protect the powers of the party/state as an obvious precondition for meeting this objective. But this general attitude vanished when they individually chose to pursue the path of personal betterment, even through corrupt measures. In the new mode, they began to act as individuals indifferent to group power, and in so doing they began largely unintentionally, though systematically, the process of undermining the party/state.

This was a predictable change of attitude on the part of officials insofar as it grew out of the worst flaw of the communist system: namely, the extreme concentration of power in the hands of the rulers. This power monopoly enjoyed by the party/state at least potentially gave officials immunity from social recourse for any corrupt behavior on their part. In the initial period of communism, officials did not engage in corruption on any substantial scale because the system of internal control had party members routinely policing each other. However, when the officials' collective sense of public duty was replaced by the pursuit of private vices, the system of self-policing went with it. At the same time, the state and the party retained their immunity from society's revulsion over the state's neglect of public interest by officials.

The masses—those outside the party/state—could not be unaffected by the communist regime's principal design either, for in their case the political system rendered them powerless. As such, communism drove citizens toward a sense of irrelevance, and inevitably that caused them to endorse the extreme selfishness of authorities uninterested in the public good. While the officials gradually turned away from public responsibility to casual corruption, citizens abrogated their public concern for the pursuit of narrow gain (only in some places, like Poland, was this trend mitigated from within dissident forces by elements appealing to a higher morality by, for example, Kuroń and Michnik). Due to this inward turn toward individual consumption and a focus on private life, support for the party/state was undermined as well, which in turn accelerated its eventual political demise.[10]

But the party/state was not only eroded through a spontaneous withdrawal of officials and citizens from public obligation. The party/state and society also engaged in a more or less systematic dismantling of the regime, though mostly without declaring their goal to be the complete disposal of the planning machinery. Whatever the declared goal, these changes were largely undertaken to ease the pressure for the legality of actions and equality of outcomes, for which the party/state, however deplorable its basic design, initially seemed to stand. Through this device, both sides—officials and citizens—acted in unison, though without explicit coordination, to expand opportunities for the unrestrained quest for selfish gains. This is how the rationale for the incessant, almost endemic, communist reforms should be understood.

Ample evidence shows that at the end of communism, the party/state had become exceedingly corrupt, most visibly in the former Soviet Union (adequately captured by Jowitt).[11] Already under Brezhnev, officials started haphazardly engaging in taking bribes and misappropriating public funds while introducing the nomenklatura system that reduced the risk of punishment. This was largely unnoticed by most experts in western academia who were preprogrammed to seek evidence of a technocratic evolution in the Soviet polity (consistent with modernization theory). They also failed to acknowledge that further institutional reforms under Gorbachev were aimed at expanding profit-oriented activities (for example, the formation of cooperatives) and thus indirectly increased the room for corruption by officials.

This trend within party/state membership in Russia was paralleled elsewhere. This was quite certainly true in the familial, or kinship, version of communism found in Bulgaria and Romania as well as in embattled communist Poland. In Poland, major changes first took place under Gierek, when embezzlement became frequent, though less dramatic than in Russia. Instrumental was the introduction of open planning with flexible targets and limited supervision as well as the policy of concentrating production in the powerful middle-level industrial bureaucracies. This process largely accelerated after Gierek's forced departure, with various import concessions conferred on the nomenklatura, and subsequently, during Rakowski's brief rule, with the introduction of the largely unsupervised self-privatization of public assets by the nomenklatura.

Thus, even with all the allowable and undeniable cross-country differences, the communist system in Eastern Europe did not collapse under any kind of frontal anticommunist assault by the masses, but from an internal rot (without denying the corrosive role played by external pressures, particularly the very costly arms race with the capitalist world). The system tumbled from demoralization, or retreat from public virtues, by both the party/state and the masses, which were mutually reinforcing. The fact that officials and citizens shared concurrent motives also explains why this collapse was devoid of violence directed at the party/state as well as a lack of vengeance toward its former members. This confluence of opinion also reveals why in the final days of the communist collapse there was no direct clash of ideas, morally grounded or otherwise, between the party/state and the masses.

Those who hold a conventional view of communism may reject this analysis, since in their eyes it would imply that communism, at any point, relied on public virtues; hence, that it was grounded in some moral code. According to this view, communism was a system of arbitrary verdicts unconstrained by morality rendered by an overpowering party elite and by its leaders in particular. But any realistic student of societies will have to admit that to retain order for any extended period of time, communism as much as any other system had to have some type of moral authority. Specifically, moral restraint or guidance was necessary under communism to make sure that force, or coercion, was correctly applied by the rulers and approved by the ruled. The communist system can be questioned on moral grounds, but this does not preclude that for much of its existence, it was a moral order. And, as Gellner stresses, it was a moral order that had a remarkably powerful appeal.[12]

It appears that Soros is among the few students of communism who, like Gellner, recognize the fact that communism was a moral order and that its demise was not caused by the lack of such a complex order. According to Soros, it was an uncritical (excessive) application of its organizing principle—primacy of the collective—that forced the system into decline. This is true, as Soros argues, about any kind of organizing principle if it is left without critical reevaluation in an open space, including the moral base on which capitalism is founded. The threat to capitalism comes from a similar lack of criticism that makes it impossible for people to comprehend the limits of its organizing principle—the primacy of the individual. But, of course, threats to communism or capitalism come not only from within these systems. These systems represent a direct threat to each other, for their organizing principles are exclusive or incompatible.

However, while Soros's theory posits that pushing the individualist principle too far is a destructive force for capitalism, he does not find excessive individualism responsible for the communist collapse. Since perverse individualism is synonymous in this theory with demoralization, this means that moral decay so understood is not to be blamed for communism's demise. Excessive stress on the primacy of the collective was, as already stated, the underlying reason for the system's agony, but it is necessary to understand how this itself could take the system down. Such a dogmatic application of the collectivist principle could drag communism to its final demise only by destroying any sense of collective (or public) responsibility. In other words, excessive collectivism becomes destructive when it eventually causes the release of its opposite—an unrestrained individualism, or demoralization.

My alternative interpretation of the communist collapse leads to the view that among all the legacies of communism, or how communism has affected postcommunism, the most relevant is the condition of moral decay. This negative legacy posed a serious risk to subsequent systemic reforms—the process of transition—certainly sufficient to the point of distorting or even permanently derailing them. The risk was indeed very serious, since once the process of moral decline begins, it tends to worsen, and reversing this moral deterioration becomes increasingly difficult. Behavior once judged immoral is redefined as moral. To make matters worse, things once considered moral are redefined as questionable. Human vices intensify, and yet people feel neither apprehension nor the desire to fundamentally rethink their own moral positions.

This critical fact about the disintegration of public virtues in late communism, however, has been largely lost in the ongoing discourse. The romanticized version of events—the earlier identified claim that the collapse was brought about through a revolution—has won the day. This claim is certainly gratifying for those who see themselves responsible for overthrowing the communist system, mostly intellectual veterans of the old opposition. These individuals, in some confused way, ended their fight with the old regime by making the very same claim of revolutionary breakthrough as that manufactured by the communists when they originally instituted their authoritarian systems. However gratifying, this distorted and remarkably persistent view of the collapse of communist systems has greatly increased the risk of the postcommunist transition's derailment.

The Process: Unprecedented Economic Recession

Although the collapse of communism was uneventful, the same definitely cannot be said of that which followed. At the time when reforms were assumed to bring about capitalism, all reform economies saw their global production fall and unemployment rise in an invariably dramatic fashion. Collectively, the region saw its production decline by a weighted thirty percent at its nadir in 1994, and a one-fifth loss of jobs was not uncommon (with east Germany reporting an initial one-third loss and Poland a one-quarter loss). Many countries, including Russia and Ukraine, have not yet arrested their recessions, while some have moved strongly out of recession, as in the cases of Poland, Slovakia, and Slovenia. Other economies managed to reverse their decline only to enter a second, possibly briefer, recession, like Bulgaria in 1996–1997, the Czech Republic in 1998, and Romania in 1997–1998.

With this kind of performance, Eastern Europe as a whole will not return to its prerecession level of production until fifteen—or even twenty—years after the initiation of reforms (though in Poland, for example, this whole cycle lasted only seven years). This means nothing less than the permanent loss of fifteen years of economic development, since at the point of return to the prerecession level these economies will be traveling along a different—and lower—trajectory than the one they would have followed had the region been spared the downturn altogether. Economic assessments of the current recession often miss this point, and it is omitted in assessments of the only case of recession under communism—namely, that of Poland from 1979 to 1982 (with a drop in output by twenty-five percent, compensated for only in 1989 when the lower growth trajectory—in this case, the first—was resumed).

This recent recession in Eastern Europe is an incredible economic phenomenon, by all accounts the worst in modern history, even when compared to the Great Depression of the 1930s, which shaved ten percent off overall production but was over in about five years. During that period, no country saw its production fall by one-half, as happened recently in Russia and Ukraine, or by sixty percent, as in Lithuania's case. The worst losses of the 1930s were in Germany and the United States, where production fell by about one-fifth (close to the least-affected East European economies, like the above-mentioned Poland and the relatively successful Hungary). While such quantitative comparisons with the Great Depression are made on occasion, there is still a great reluctance to treat them as comparable cases, usually on the grounds that each was driven by completely different forces.

Since this economic downturn occurred everywhere in the region, it might really appear—and it does to quite a number of economists—as nothing but the legacy of communism. Such an explanation appears to many as a plausible answer due to the general perception that the communist systems were very inefficient, if not irrational. In fact, the systems allowed quite a bit of waste, even tolerating production that did not respond to real demand but was kept alive through unconditional state subsidies. Since elimination of these subsidies was a predominant component of post-1989 reforms, such misdirected—usually called "unwanted"—production had to be eradicated, implying the need to fire workers. For these reasons—absent during the Great Depression—the postcommunist recession must be viewed as inevitable, a view widely shared among economists, particularly those involved in the reforms.

If the recent recessions were caused only by this destruction of unwanted production, there would be no reason for concern, since eliminating production for which there is no effective demand cannot lead to welfare loss. Moreover, the release of misused capital and labor from unwanted production would instantly translate into a gain in resources for the creation of wanted production, thus leading inevitably to economic recovery. But the statistical data, admittedly subject to some imprecision, shows rather unequivocally that actual production losses in the region were much more dramatic than the removal of unwanted production would imply, with much the same losses registered in both the subsidized, or presumably unwanted, and profitable lines of production.

In Poland, production declined sharply in all three areas where households felt most deprived during the days of communism. Shortages of food were common, but agricultural production fell by at least fifteen percent from 1990 to 1992 and showed only a modest increase thereafter. Shortages were also prevalent in housing, but construction declined by seventy percent before 1993, falling back to the 1954 level and not yet rebounding. Automobiles were desperately sought during the communist years as well, but in 1990–1991 production of automobiles declined by one-third and, significantly, only started picking up when the domestic (internally designed) model was revived. This model, with only minor technological changes, represented the single best-selling car (mostly among farmers) until it was recently discontinued.

It is also a mistake to assume that subsidies are always attached to unwanted output. Housing and automobiles were not subsidized, while farming was. Here, subsidies have been sharply reduced since 1990, which proved a grave policy mistake rather than a correction of communist errors. These were not subsidies for unwanted production, and Poland's agricultural policy was not out of line with common practice among industrialized countries under communist rule. In both groups of countries, subsidies were at that time on average about fifty percent of production costs. Since 1990 East Europeans reduced such transfers to about ten percent on average, and in the Czech Republic and Hungary, both very strong food exporters, down to five percent. In most cases, subsidies have not increased since, and in a few countries transfers have been raised, though not to pre–1990 levels (for example, in Poland subsidies to farmers first went down to fifteen percent and then were raised to twenty-five percent in 1998).

While the removal of subsidies cannot be viewed as a completely harmless measure, this reform alone could not explain the uniform, dramatic production downturn. This economic catastrophe has to be explained by reference to forces more powerful—and lasting—than a removal of subsidies, however radical and misguided. To provoke a recession of this magnitude, the whole economic system would have had to collapse, unless there were some comparable external shocks, which did not exist in this case. At the outset of the transition, the economic system in Eastern Europe was almost completely state-based, the state being the exclusive owner and production manager. Thus, systemic crisis would have to be preceded somehow by state crisis. This is what happened in the region, mostly due to the reformers themselves. The reformers provoked the state crisis by reducing the state's capacity to govern beyond the levels required for other agents (producers and consumers) to act efficiently.

The effects of this state overwithdrawal can be seen in the financial sector, where after rushed commercialization (that is, the introduction of independence in decision-making but also an advent of self-financing) banks lost adequate state insurance and even prudent supervision. Consequently, they refused to extend credit to producers to assist in their times of need (and turned instead to money-seeking states as more secure borrowers). Furthermore, the quick removal of import controls cost producers profits, worsening their financial condition. This deprotection—or tariff reduction—also resulted in increased uncertainty. Uncertainty over financial outcomes was further aggravated by the announcement of rapid privatization lacking a clear-cut design and timetable. This process, often combined with the rupture of existing organizational ties, left producers unsure of their continued ability to support their production. Faced with these two adverse developments at the same time—a liquidity crisis and additional uncertainty—all producers responded rationally by reducing production efforts.

This argument suggests a direct link between the depth of the recession in Eastern Europe and the state's inability to manage economic affairs (that is, aid market development). Indeed, ample evidence supports this correlation. The most radical reform countries are also those in which recession was the worst. Of all cases, east Germany is among the most radical—if not *the* most radical—with an instant opening of trade and a two-year complete privatization program that no other country has matched so far. By the same measure, Russia, despite all the obvious differences in the particularities of respective reform packages, can also be viewed as a very extreme case. Both have suffered some of the worst declines, with east Germany losing a third of its production in just one year and Russia losing half of its output during the first eight years (and most likely awaiting another decline in 1999).

In this context and using the same indicators, Poland and Belarus have to be seen as less, but still quite, radical cases of transition. Contrary to common characterizations, Poland is not one of the most radical reformers, surely not in terms of privatization. Currently, Poland has divested less than half of its industry. After a quick restoration of relatively high selective trade barriers (for example, for cars and foodstuffs), Poland is one of the most protectionist economies in the region. Still,

Poland had suffered a lesser, though year longer, recession than did east Germany, and Poland's economic recovery has been far more impressive (with east German industry still one-fifth below its prerecession output). And, if one dares to be fair, Belarus, with even less-advanced systemic change than Poland's, looks at least on paper much better than superradical Russia (for example, the Belarusian economy lost not half, but about two-fifths of its national product).

After this thorough analysis of recession, one important question remains: Why would the East European countries, one by one, engage in such radical reforms that would have such excessively adverse repercussions for the institution of the state? This question can be answered in terms of an underlying change in ideology. Specifically, after dropping Marxism, a new, liberal ideology has been adopted with an openly antistate attitude, perceiving reforms as a simple substitution of the state by the market. This explanation is typically offered by critics of the radical approach to transition that, in accordance with the liberal interpretation, called for a swift downsizing of the state agency. Such criticism is coming as much from those who represent a prostate (statist) position on the transition as from those who take the individualistic stand that characterizes the evolutionary approach to postcommunist reforms.

At this ten-year point, it is quite clear that the ideological shift has undoubtedly been a factor in such countries as Hungary and Poland, where the transition approach has become an important issue for public debate. However, this is not the main factor responsible for the radical reform course taken, for surely some of this radicalism should be viewed as a consequence of insufficient experience by the reformers. Their knowledge of liberal theory was as insufficient as their preparedness to manage the economy indirectly, and they wrecked some of the vital elements of the inherited state-based system by mistake. Even more important, if not essential, for the initially excessive dismantling of the state has been the force of narrowly defined personal or political (party-related) interests of state officials themselves.

Accepting this latter, less benign explanation, the main reason for the attack on the state was the fact that the largely unnoticed negative turn in the public outlook at the conclusion of communism was not reversed, but was allowed to intensify with the introduction of transition. Unleashed under these conditions, reforms have been shaped by officials who mainly sought additional opportunities to achieve personal gain through corruption. Given the insecurity of their positions—in part related to the prevalence of corrupt behavior itself—officials have preferred actions with immediate payoffs, even if clearly adverse to the public at large. This best explains why reforms—the second stage of the transition—assumed a radical and often misguided form everywhere in the region, negatively affecting the state's capacity to assist emerging markets.

For instance, rapid bank commercialization has disabled the state, making it unable to allocate money to needy companies. This step provided officials with some of the most lucrative jobs, where salaries are at their discretion and money is spent without close scrutiny (for example, on advertising campaigns for hefty kickbacks). Similarly, the removal of import tariffs, while depriving the state of income from duties, has enabled selected officials to benefit—for gratification—as importers or move themselves into jobs in the import sector. A perfect example is the abolition of alcohol tariffs and of the state monopoly for alcohol to enrich a few, while leaving the state, as in the cases of Poland and Russia, with a big hole in its budget (so much more damaging because of the serious inefficiency of tax systems).

This is also true for privatization, which probably provided the greatest opportunities for the attainment of illegal proceeds, given both the enormous—accumulated over decades—volume of assets involved and the quick and relatively unsupervised, at least from the public point of view, manner of asset disposal. The fast pace of the divestment process has made it difficult to monitor if the state is actually getting fair prices for its assets. Under a short timetable, careful valuations of assets held by privatized companies are essentially impossible. However, these rapid sales provided officials with the tempting prize of becoming owners by taking over capital for nothing or at large discounts. Alternatively, officials assumed unrestricted control of remaining state property in order to plunder without regard for the value of capital. In other cases, divestment provided officials with the opportunity to become brokers, guiding public capital at favorable prices to others in exchange for kickbacks (that is, lucrative and secure jobs and/or monetary gratification).

The Destiny: Foreign Owned Capitalism

Since so many countries are coming out of the recession, the negative impact of reforms on the economic system might be seen as subsiding and capitalism assuming a normal form. This should be particularly true in the economies that have been the quickest to establish the capitalist institutions needed for recovery: for example, in Hungary and Poland, where the share of private ownership is almost as high as in Western Europe. The sense of normalcy in Eastern Europe is very strong among economists, with some even extending this characterization to recession-ridden Russia, where private ownership also dominates. But the process of switching to private property in these countries, particularly those with the best economic performance, has created an abnormal form of capitalism where most private assets belong to foreigners and labor remains local.

The major vehicle for the rapid expansion of foreign holdings in Eastern Europe has been privatization and not the establishment of new (green-field or joint-venture) entities, the process of which already has been completed in east Germany. In this undeniably special case, the west German state agency sold almost all capital directly to outsiders—west German investors—in the remarkably short timeframe of two years. A similar process has taken longer in Hungary, with most of the direct sales concentrated during the 1996–1998 campaign to rapidly dispose of public capital. While privatization has not yet come to a close, nonetheless, foreigners already control seventy percent of Hungary's industry and banking (with the balance of assets left with mostly loss-making entities that are kept alive by the state through steady bailouts).

As for the Czech Republic and Poland, the respective proportions are thirty and thirty-five percent for industry and twenty-five and fifty percent for banking, and these numbers are steadily increasing in both cases (with Poland ready to sell its last major viable bank to a foreign strategic investor in 1999 and with Czech leaders on the verge of doing the same with their few remaining major banks). In the Czech case privatization has been much faster than in Poland, for the former resorted to a voucher, free-of-charge distribution of assets to citizens while the latter resisted such a method. Poland has relied mostly on leveraged buyouts for smaller units and sales for larger ones, but Czech reformers also allowed sales to take place. It is acutely through direct sales that they transferred some of the most valuable assets to foreigners even before voucher privatization started.

Presently, foreign ownership in other East European economies is not as widespread; though indications are that these states are also on their way to establishing foreign majority-owned capitalism. This is certainly true of Russia, where after fast privatization (comparable with that of the Czech Republic) the state holds only small equity in some key sectors. The situation in Russia is very nontransparent due to the fact that many legal titles remain unclear. There is even evidence of such titles not always being available, making it is quite difficult to gauge the extent of foreign involvement. However, there is enough evidence to suggest that foreign holdings in industry, particularly in the extraction of natural resources (for example, many oil companies have large foreign stakes), are sizable and expanding. Another such case is banking, where reportedly as much as twelve percent of assets are in foreign hands (with banks largely engaged in asset acquisitions).

Where privatization has been delayed, foreign penetration has been even slower, with Bulgaria and Romania being good examples. Both countries tried to engage in divestment, contemplating Czech-style distribution as well as Polish-style fast paced sales, but with limited results. However, the newly elected governments have quickly made clear that they are ready to engage in massive divestment to close the lag. The new coalition government in Romania has already sold many assets, often in some of the most critical sectors (which typically are to be considered for privatization at a later date). Romania began its spurt with one such sector: telecommunications, with a big chunk of the state phone monopoly going to a foreign buyer. The automobile industry is another case in point, with the only passenger car plant—one of the flagship industrial companies—sold to a single foreign investor. And most recently, the only major bank—accounting for one-quarter of the domestic market—has been designated for sale to a foreign strategic investor.

Furthermore, it will be hard for any country to escape the trend, since no variant of privatization attempted thus far has produced different results. The best evidence comes from Poland where, unlike in most other places, all major methods have been tried, including the sale of assets either directly or through subscription. This method undoubtedly gave officials leeway in determining which domestic and foreign buyers would get the assets, but invariably, and from the very beginning, it was the foreigners who clearly had the upper hand. This bias in favor of foreign investors did not meet with much contempt from the workers, who were coopted by officials through attractive equity packages (initially contributing up to ten percent of the initial offering at a discounted price and more recently up to fifteen percent for no payment).

The Polish experience also demonstrates that investment funds created in connection with voucher privatization programs (also called "democratic capitalism") have turned into another vehicle for transferring assets to foreigners. Intended to block foreigners, Poland's own limited approach to the Czech style of free distribution did little to thwart foreign acquisitions. Unlike in the Czech case, the Polish program required that vouchers be deposited with the state-appointed fixed pool of funds. These funds were directed to find new owners for the assigned pool of about five hundred companies. By now it is clear that, at least among the viable units, a majority has been handed over to foreign buyers, though usually after complicated negotiations. These extended talks were needed to ensure that shares, which were initially dispersed among funds, are consolidated into packets sizable enough for foreign buyers to accept them.

Nor is there evidence thus far to suggest that the political orientation of respective reformers has mattered much for access to assets by foreign owners. Apparently, even major shifts on the political scene do not affect decisively the pattern of privatization in the respective countries described here. True, there is considerable evidence that reformers linked to the former communist—now mostly renamed and turned socialist— parties tended to be less willing to turn assets over to foreigners. But there is at least one striking exception: Hungary, where privatization started slowly under the anticommunist (conservative) opposition government, but was greatly accelerated under the 1994 coalition government built around the former communist party. During this latter stage, the value of privatized assets doubled in just a few years, and at the same time the majority of state capital—particularly in the financial sector— was turned over to foreigners.

In the Polish case, the post-1989 coalitions linked with the anticommunist opposition, with Balcerowicz as their main champion, have presided over the most aggressive period of selling assets to foreigners. In contrast, while positively predisposed to divestment, the forces rooted in the old-time parties were rather reluctant to pursue sales that benefited mostly foreigners. When these parties were elected in 1993, the pace of privatization was slowed and efforts were made to favor domestic buyers, allowing for the solidification of domestic capital groups (also called holdings) within industry. Preparations were also made to consolidate banks that were still owned by the state to make them less vulnerable to foreign takeover and to further fortify them by merging them with domestic capital groups. With all these efforts, the majority of privatized capital was still being sold to foreign buyers (for example, cement, tobacco, and household chemicals).

This trend has not reversed since 1997, when the former communists (and their Peasant Party allies of the old days) lost a very close parliamentary election. The election was won by a coalition of forces led by a union-based cluster of parties allied with the smaller party of Balcerowicz that represented the core of the first postcommunist government. The union-based forces were widely expected to take an even harder position on foreign takeovers, but nothing of this kind has happened. In fact, the pace of privatization has greatly accelerated, and no serious effort has been made to fulfill the election promise to begin a large scale, Czech-style distribution of state assets. The coalition, with Balcerowicz again as the main reform architect, has been pursuing a radical program expected eventually to quadruple state revenues from sales by the end of 1999. At the same time, most assets have been targeted to foreign buyers, including assets in the most capital-intensive sectors (for example, telecommunications, steel, energy).

If all countries, despite the various privatization methods adopted, seem to be converging on the same end point, some common underlying forces must be at work. This common factor is that the initial reforms have seriously undermined the financial health of most domestic companies, leaving many of them with no profit and burdened by heavy debts. New domestic investors seeking to turn these companies around would require a massive infusion of money that, with the damage done to banking systems and endemic problems with state budgets, has not been forthcoming. This liquidity crisis has extended beyond the early stage of the transition, even in the economies that are recovering. Here as well, banks have remained reluctant to issue credit to private parties, and states have not assumed more active financial policies.

Many states could administer some form of import protection to help domestically owned companies to start generating healthy profits. Instead, most states early in the transition implemented an open trade policy through official tariff reductions, driving down tariffs to levels hardly known among most other countries at a similar level of development. Alternatively, massive smuggling, often assisted by the state (as in Russia and Bulgaria) has opened respective transition economies to severe import competition. This has only added to the financial difficulties faced by domestic investors. It is important to note that this situation has not been reversed; strong import exposure has continued and often has even been intensified. This is particularly the case in the Czech Republic, Hungary, and Poland, the three countries that have aggressively pressed for entry to the European Union.

With internal systemic conditions largely unchanged, regardless of the privatization technique selected, domestically owned companies, public or private, have come to realize that they have no better choice than to seek foreign money. Companies that were still state-owned usually pressured privatization officials to allow for the transfer of assets in hope that new owners would bring fresh financing. However, privately owned ones typically sought buyers for their equity as a source of recapitalization, too (as in the case of the short-lived Polish-owned holdings, mostly led by the former state trading companies). With both state and privately owned companies, the preference has been to find strategic investors willing to buy a majority share of equity, for only then will a proper financial commitment result.

This sense of desperation has provided foreign buyers with a very favorable bargaining position, making it easier for them to demand controlling or exclusive equity positions and to drive down the price of assets. This has been well documented in Hungary, where about one third of the companies taken over by foreigners are under nearly one hundred percent foreign ownership. Pricing is not as well documented, but there can be no doubt that asset prices were low, with foreigners paying about $7–8 billion for all assets acquired through 1998. This represents fifteen percent of the estimated book value of all assets in industry and banking as reported at the outset of the privatization program, or twenty percent of the portion of the book value that was actually dispersed through sales.

If this way of estimating the extent of underpricing is not convincing, one can try another approximation: comparing the revenues from foreign sales with the value of capital derived from capital/output ratios. If we assume that both industry and banking account for thirty-five percent of Hungarian national income, which is approximately $50 billion, then these two sectors produce $17.5 billion in revenue. If we further assume that the capital ratio for industry and banking is three to one, then the value of their capital stock should equal $52.5 billion. Since foreigners control seventy percent of it and own, say, sixty percent, it means that they paid $7–8 billion for a stock of capital whose estimated value is about $30 billion—or about one-quarter of the value.

These payments are indeed a strikingly low figure for an economy whose annual savings rate is twenty percent and annual (mostly personal) savings represent at least $10 billion. This would simply imply that, theoretically speaking, Hungarians save enough to be able, in a course of one year, to purchase at their actual prices all privatized assets—those already sold and those that are left for sale. It is highly ironic that at the outset of privatization, Hungarian economists claimed that the value of assets for divestment was so high and personal savings so low that it would take about three decades to sell all the capital at market prices. These estimates were very instrumental in shifting public sentiment to support a radical approach to privatization.

In fact, asset pricing may be even lower than just indicated, since the above estimates are based only on revenues from privatization and ignore related state expenses. Additionally, Hungarian sources provide information on expenditures its privatization agency has incurred in connection with asset sales, such as subsidized credits, presale recapitalization, tax privileges, etc. A significant case is that of banking, which prior to privatization brought about $2 billion in sales, and for which two waves of recapitalization were required to rescue the system at a total cost to the state budget of approximately $2 billion. Total expenditure on privatization of industry and banking was reportedly close to the total revenue incurred from privatization by 1997,[13] which would imply that assets were essentially transferred free of charge (following the earlier completed east German privatization, which generated a $60 billion deficit for the privatization agency).

The pressure to attract foreign owners has come not only from companies, managers, and workers, but from state officials, and not simply— or even mainly—out of concern for bolstering faltering economies. Seeking personal gain, officials have found foreign buyers more suitable than domestic buyers. One quite perverse reason for this preference is the public's suspicion of domestic transactions. One of the major fears has been the concern that assets will be handed over to the former nomenklatura, including managers of major state-owned companies. Such individuals are typically despised by the public for their political past. This feeling has been particularly strong in countries where the dissident movement during the communist period was relatively strong, Poland being a good example (the first postcommunist Polish government even passed a law to curtail this form of privatization).

However, concern for public image has not been the most critical variable in shaping preferences among officials. More significant has been the fact that officials have looked for private gain under either the pressure of severe time limits on action or the threat of being phased out of their positions of influence. Transfers of assets have thus provided officials with opportunities to collect kickbacks. These transfers required a timely mobilization of large sums, something foreigners have been better able to produce. At the same time, foreigners have been no less prepared than domestic buyers to gratify officials either with cash payments or lucrative jobs. Moreover, foreigners correctly have been seen by officials as more "reliable" than domestic buyers both in terms of keeping their questionable dealings discrete and holding up their end of the bargain.

There cannot be a greater contrast between the pattern of divestment described above and the manner in which West European countries have conducted their own privatization, for among the latter, divestment invariably favored mostly domestic buyers. In Austria, for instance, privatization did not lead to the takeover of any major state companies by foreigners. Likewise, the more recent privatization in Great Britain also focused on putting assets into domestic hands, with cheap credit extended to those willing to purchase assets. To take an even more recent case of a less developed country, state-owned capital in Turkey (like the East European countries, an applicant to the European Union) has gone mainly to domestic buyers, especially large family-owned conglomerates.

Although there has been some significant foreign penetration in West European industry, nowhere have the levels reached the emerging East

European standards. An extreme case is Ireland, where fifty percent of industry but only ten percent of banking is in foreign hands. In Austria, where thirty percent of industry is foreign owned (since 1975), banking is almost exclusively in domestic hands, largely for reasons mentioned above. In most West European cases, foreign ownership of industry is under twenty percent (for example, in Germany it remains around ten percent), and in banking the average share for the whole European Union is close to ten percent (including the two nations most comparable to Eastern Europe: Portugal and Spain).

Does the fact that Eastern Europe is building, in an unusual manner, an unusual type of capitalism in itself have to mean that something is wrong with the direction that the transition has assumed? Unfortunately, it does. It could be argued that the rapid shift of most capital resources to foreigners, while unusual, might have been rational because foreign owners, with undeniably greater experience, increase capital efficiency. With the likely divergence of interests, however, these gains may prove to be much smaller than what might be generated were decisions made by well-established local capitalists. This lack of representation for domestic capital interest makes the emerging system of foreign owned majority capitalism a potentially disturbing proposition.

It would be biased to evaluate the effects of a strong foreign presence only in terms of efficiency gains, since there is also an important distributive aspect related to the allocation of income from capital. This latter aspect should be of no concern for the host economy as long as the system under which foreigners operate is perfect. In such cases, foreigners pay not only the full price for the assets but also earn legitimate, deserved profits, leaving the local wage-earners with a fair, market-driven share of whatever efficiency gains foreigners can produce. These conditions, however, never apply in real life; as a result, the host economy faces a real risk of losing a portion of its wealth to foreign owners due to various rents. At present in Eastern Europe, the conditions required for a fair and legitimate distribution of efficiency gains are critically violated on more than one account.

In order to examine the distributive consequences of foreign takeovers for East European welfare, it would be useful first to consider conditions under which assets are acquired. There can be no doubt that these conditions are not particularly suitable for careful asset valuations, which create opportunity for rent collection either by domestic or foreign buyers. Among the complicating factors is the lack of developed capital markets, including the backwardness of investment banking and the nascent nature of emerging stock markets. Other negative factors include obscure accounting methods, general liquidity shortages (hampering restructuring), and very limited supervision of valuation procedures and, in fact, the entire privatization process.

Opportunities for rent collecting go beyond asset acquisitions mainly because foreign investors are by and large able to establish oligopolistic positions or, more accurately, to extend them. As a rule, sales of assets involve basically unbroken monopolies that were formed by communist planners before 1989. The fast paced sales have not permitted any major reorganizations, and states have not been prepared to execute such changes. Foreign investors have not been interested in the partial acquisition of existing state-owned companies, and importantly, they have been able as a rule to secure dominant equity positions (for example, one-third of the foreign controlled companies in Hungary are, as said before, one hundred percent in foreign hands, and in all companies sold to foreigners by Poland through public offerings, foreigners secured at least small majority stakes).

Such large holdings of capital provide a basis for the transfer of income abroad unless such transactions are restricted or prohibited by the host-economy state. Currently, most East European states allow for the uninhibited transfer of income, Hungary being a good case in point. But even if such restrictions were put in place, it would be difficult for well-intended and resolved states to enforce some sort of effective control over capital-income outflows. Various types of financial operations that are currently allowed, including foreign exchange operations, facilitate escape from such controls and allow for tax evasion. Transfer pricing is another way of avoiding controls, for trade is being turned over mainly to foreign controlled companies (for example, eighty percent of manufacturing exports in Hungary and sixty percent in the Czech case).

It is difficult to estimate the amount of such undeserved income, but until now the potential for draining undeserved income has been largely ignored, in part because most profits in foreign owned companies were reinvested or even augmented by money from abroad. But this clearly cannot go on forever, since all investors spend money to eventually collect income. Hungary offers the first such evidence. Starting in 1997, when most assets were already sold, large transfers of income from capital apparently began, reaching the official figure of $1.5 billion in 1998. These overt outflows, mostly through profit remittance and consulting fees, were large enough to neutralize the net inflow of direct investment in 1998 (and made the government officially complain to a group of major foreign companies that their behavior damaged the country's balance of payment).

Concluding Remarks: Three Stages of Crisis

Within the evolutionary position, given its individualist and subjective outlook, focus is placed on morality as the guiding force that organizes human actions. No society can survive without solid morals that make individuals respect the needs of a collective—family, community, or nation. Everything of real importance in societal life is, basically speaking, an affirmation of such public morals. Consequently, it is assumed that moral practice forms the basis on which institutions rest. In other words, institutions are manifestations of routine actions by morally driven individuals. These are not perfectly fixed rules; there is some margin to allow morals to be tested for their enduring value. Since institutions have to be rooted in morals, once individuals—largely unintentionally—develop them, they are as stable and helpful in assisting people as morals are.

The above methodological approach to institutions derives from an evolutionary position, itself stemming from a broad range of scholarship including the work of two major Viennese thinkers—the philosopher Popper and, even more so, the economist Hayek. These ideas have been employed by a small group of economists working on the postcommunist transition mostly to give a critical assessment of the actual process of change. This line of thinking has gained another major voice with the recent statements on the transition by Popper's intellectual follower Soros, who offers a rather critical account of the state of emerging capitalism in Eastern Europe (particularly addressing the case of Russia, about which he has very good direct knowledge). But Soros's remarks on advanced capitalism are most relevant to the study of postcommunist transition as well, as far as the underlying methodology applied in this analysis is concerned.[14]

Taking this position, where morality becomes the central explanatory variable, makes sense, of course, mainly in the context of an analysis that deals with some major (secular) shifts in institutions that structure social life. Such an approach is suitable for the study of transition, but only if one has the courage to take a serious, impassionate look at this process.[15] Within this perspective, there is no choice but to argue that the former communist countries entered transition in the midst of an institutional collapse—that of communism. This important phase of the transition is best understood as a consequence of a major deterioration in morals, the pervasive corruption of state officials, and civic indifference. In fact, this was only the first stage of a lengthy demoralization process, one in which negative social forces had just begun to come into the open.

My account may appear inconsistent with Soros's explanation of how the communist system collapsed, for in his direct statements on the subject, Soros adopts a conventional line of thinking. In his view, communism collapsed from excessive collectivism, which like excessive individualism comes from dogmatic thinking (which he calls "closure"). While excessive collectivism is not sustainable, so that a system based on such a principle eventually has to crack, such fracturing manifests itself in excessive individualism. Under late communism it was not that collectivism was cut to some workable size, but that it degenerated into a system in which rampant individualism began to rule. Excessive individualism may not just be a threat to capitalism, as in Soros's theory, but also to communism, for—as Soros will certainly agree—the collapse of morals may damage any type of social system.

Since the collapse of public virtues is exactly the force that destroyed the communist system, it is under the conditions of this moral crisis that the postcommunist transition had to be initiated. When these reforms began, this crisis of public values was not confronted, and rather than be reversed, the crisis entered into an even more intense second phase. One of the unfortunate consequences of this negative turn is that East European states lost much of their capacity to aid emerging markets through proper regulations, law enforcement, and necessary assistance. This observation is consistent with Soros's understanding of how demoralization manifests itself. As he argues, demoralization involves an excessive shift from collectivist states to individualist markets with adverse consequences for those in need of state protection. In the context of the transition, the most devastating effect of such state corrosion is the unprecedented post-1989 recession that has benefited a few but hurt the majority.

Introduced under conditions of low concern for public good, reforms have not only resulted in an economic recession, but also, more importantly, allowed the majority of capital to be transferred to foreign owners. Even if large-scale entry of foreign investors had proven positive in reducing economic adversities—and there is no reason to doubt this— such a divestment strategy is not without economic cost. Such unusual ownership structures, particularly when combined with such high concentrations, may permit the collection of undeserved income from monopolistic rents that may be transferred abroad. Foreigners, in fact, have been gaining considerable market power, since private owners typically recreate communist era monopolies (even strengthen them, adding new layers of influence, for example, through integration of production with sales and/or through advertising).

Importantly, such a property system seriously thwarts the emergence of a local capitalist class, which may actually prevent a full articulation of domestic economic interest. It would be very naïve to think that domestic and foreign interests have to coincide, particularly when the parties involved represent economies that are at vastly different levels of development. Besides, without a strong domestic capitalist class it is hardly possible for transition economies to recover from the crisis of public virtues. It is not necessarily the case that its substitute, foreign owners, will be more vigorous in fighting corruption of the state and in energizing citizens for civil action. Instead, these economies may easily slip into a third stage of the crisis where strong public disinterest exists in a reduced but chronic, firmly institutionalized form.

Given the potentially negative economic consequences of turning over the majority of capital to foreign hands, it is necessary to reconsider the commonly held perception of the relative success of the transition economies. Hungary, Poland, and (until recently) the Czech Republic are heralded as the most successful not only because they have managed to privatize more of their assets, but also because they have enforced property rights relatively well. It is said also that their success is evidenced in the fact that they have received the most foreign investment, which in turn raises their productivity growth above rates found in most other countries. The flip side of the coin is, however, that these economies are also leaders in terms of building this quite awkward version of capitalism, in which a majority of capital is foreign owned. By the same token, where ownership reforms are less advanced, as in Russia, there is also less foreign investment, and some room still exists for the possible retention of large units of capital in domestic hands.

Notes

1 George Soros, "The Capitalist Threat", *The Atlantic Monthly* (February 1997); and George Soros, *The Crisis of Global Capitalism: Open Society Endangered* (New York: Public Affairs, 1999).

2 See Albert Hirschman, *The Passions and the Interests: Political Arguments for Capitalism Before Its Triumphs* (Princeton: Princeton University Press, 1977).

3 See Peter Berkowitz, *Virtue and the Making of Modern Liberalism* (Princeton: Princeton University Press, 1998).

4 Joseph Schumpeter, *Capitalism, Socialism and Democracy* (New York: Harper and Row, 1942).

5 Friedrich Hayek, *The Fatal Conceit: The Errors of Socialism* (Chicago: University of Chicago Press, 1988), 6.

6 Karl Popper, *The Open Society and Its Enemies* (London: Routledge and Kegan Paul, 1945).

7 Soros, *Global Capitalism.*

8 Karl Polanyi, *The Origins of Our Time: The Great Transformation* (London: V. Gollancz Ltd., 1945).

9 Kazimierz Z. Poznanski, "An Interpretation of Communist Decay: The Role of Evolutionary Mechanisms", *Communist and Post-Communist Studies* 26:1 (March 1993).

10 Kazimierz Z. Poznanski, *Poland's Protracted Transition: Economic Growth and Institutional Change in 1970–1994* (Cambridge: Cambridge University Press, 1996).

11 Ken Jowitt, "Soviet Neotraditionalism: The Political Corruption of the Leninist Regime", *Soviet Studies* 35:3 (July 1983).

12 Ernest Gellner, "Homeland of the Unrevolution", *Daedalus* 122:3 (Summer 1993).

13 Béla Greskovits, "Progress in Hungarian Transition" (conference paper, Warsaw, 1998).

14 My full-length examination of Soros's interpretation of the open society concept by Popper as well as of Soros's own contribution to the analysis of modern capitalism is contained in a separate essay (Kazimierz Z. Poznanski, *Openness and Wealth: Revisiting the "Capitalist Threat" Argument* (Seattle: University of Washington, 1999). More on my effort to extend Soros's method to the study of postcommunist transition can be found in my essay review of his recent book *The Crisis of Global Capitalism* (Kazimierz Z. Poznanski, "The Crisis of Modern Capitalism in Post-Communist Eastern Europe", *East European Politics and Societies* (forthcoming 1999).

15 See Timothy McDaniels, *The Agony of the Russian Idea* (Princeton: Princeton University Press, 1997).

13 *Counterrevolution*

ISTVÁN RÉV

A legal case that had been under consideration for seventy-three years was closed on 28 November 1994 in an open session of the Supreme Court of the Hungarian Republic. The Supreme Court upheld the death sentence brought against Mihály Francia Kiss in 1957 for war crimes and other criminal acts by the Council of the People's Tribunal of the Supreme Court of the Hungarian People's Republic. The Supreme Court reexamined the case on the appeal of Francia Kiss's bereaved daughter. Since according to the criminal code a claimant may make such an appeal only once, and since there may be no appeal to a decision made by the Supreme Court in such criminal cases, this legal procedure, which was initiated in the summer of 1921 and which continued with interruptions until the end of 1994, was finally closed.[1]

In August 1921 Albert Vári, assistant royal prosecutor, and Péter Kovács, prosecutor, were directed by the minister of justice to undertake an investigation of murders and other atrocities committed in the region between the Danube and the Tisza rivers in 1919 and 1920. The investigation, however, was interrupted when Governor Horthy—who came to power after the defeat of the 1919 first Hungarian Soviet Republic—granted a general amnesty to those who had committed crimes out of "patriotic fervor" between 1919 and 1921. This clemency was granted primarily to paramilitary detachments and was especially directed to the countless murders committed by Iván Héjjas's so-called "supplementary gendarmerie" after the summer of 1919. During the prosecution's investigation in 1921, only one charge was brought against Mihály Francia Kiss (despite the fact that his name arose in connection with a number of crimes) in the case of the murder of a trader from Pusztamérges, Vilmos Kalmár, in the woods at Orgovány on 6 June 1920. The victim's relatives brought the charges against the defendant. Mihály Francia Kiss never denied committing the crime, but, though the evidence indicated murder and robbery rather than "patriotic fervor", the government's amnesty brought an end to the prosecution.[2] (Afterwards, a remarkable instance occurred in which the judge said "God bless you, Mihály!" to the departing defendant, who then threatened to kill his accusers.)[3]

On 13 May 1947 after the end of World War II, Budapest's People's Tribunal delivered a murder conviction in the case of Iván Héjjas and company (in fact, due to Iván Héjjas's absence, Zoltán Babiczki and company were convicted). Mihály Francia Kiss, defendant No. LXII in the case, was sentenced in absentia to death by hanging.[4]

The lawyer of eight of the defendants on trial submitted a petition debating the political nature of the crimes. According to the lawyer, "if forces arising are under such great stress that they believe they can achieve their goals only through the introduction of violence, terror, and struggle, a revolution is born. Acts, especially violent acts, carried out in the interest of achieving such a revolution may be considered to be of a political nature..."[5] Thus, according to the defense lawyer, only revolutionary acts are political in nature. "The Dictatorship of the Proletariat, which achieved power through the use of violence and was only able to keep power through violence and terror, had already fallen on 1 August 1919. By autumn 1919, and in 1920, there was no longer any need for acts of a political nature to overturn the existing state, social, and economic order. By that time the counterrevolution had succeeded, and the regime served by those accused in the Orgovány case was already in power. The motives and reasons for the actions carried out in Orgovány were not the desire or attempt to achieve political goals, but rather revenge!"[6]

Governor Horthy's amnesty of November 1921 was for those who committed acts of "patriotic fervor"—in other words, acts with political motivation and (at least on paper) not common crimes. However, Dr. Nagy, the defense lawyer—keeping in mind the fact that the statute of limitations was invalid in the case of crimes with clear political motivation or crimes against humanity—attempted to show that the acts committed by the accused "were common crimes, as is proven by the methods with which they were carried out...and also proven...by the fact that they were accompanied by theft, robbery, and other means of extorting money".[7]

In its accusation, the People's Tribunal had originally referred to Act VII of 1945, according to which "crimes are to be punished and are declared not to have reached the statute of limitations, in which human lives were taken in 1919 and the times following, and which were left unpunished over the twenty-five years following the counterrevolution due to Amnesty Decree No. 59 391/1921.I.M., passed on 3 November 1921, and due to the sympathy shown by the authorities responsible for punishing these criminal acts, sympathy which went beyond even the bounds of Amnesty".[8] (The legal reasoning cited here is identical to the logic of the so-called Zétényi-Takács legal draft of the Hungarian Parliament, which recommended in 1991 that the statute of limitations had not been reached for certain types of crimes not punished for political reasons during the decades of communist rule in Hungary, as the statute should be counted from a point in time following the fall of the communist system—in fact, from the time when the first democratically elected postcommunist government came into office in May 1990.)

The appeal in the case of Héjjas's detachments came before the appellate court, the National Council of People's Tribunals (NCPT), which brought a sentence on 25 November 1948. The NCPT for its part decided that the incidents under question in the case could be considered war crimes under different paragraphs—under Pt. 11 & 5 and Pt. 13 & 2—and this is why the statute of limitations did not apply to them. The National Council stated that the decree, which brought the People's Tribunal into existence and which later became law, had been formulated "so that as soon as possible, punishment would be meted out to all those who were the cause of, or participated in, the historic catastrophe which struck the Hungarian People".[9]

This passage in the law quoted by the People's Tribunals refers to World War II as the historic catastrophe and specifically to the fascist Arrow-Cross rule of 1944. The reasoning of the National Council, therefore, created an immediate connection between the acts carried out by detachments some twenty-five years before in 1919 and the reign of Szálasi's Arrow-Cross forces:

"It is a commonly known historical fact that following the fall of the Dictatorship of the Proletariat of 1919…which made a heroic, revolutionary attempt to liberate Hungary's repressed working classes and other social strata and to establish a socialist economic and political system, our homeland fell into a dark age of counterrevolution and white terror, followed by the Horthy-type reactionary system of consolidation, that logically—that is, with unavoidable consistency and as if by law—led to the servile affiliation with Italian-German policies, which eventually led to the evil and insane intervention in World War II, and finally, in 1944 poured the filthy, murderous flood of Arrow-Cross rule onto our people and our nation, a rule whose terrible acts and destruction of human lives and material goods were in proportion, scale, and methods beyond human comprehension…It is, therefore, an unquestionable historical fact that the multiple and typical crimes discussed in this case, whether committed directly by Héjjas's detachments or under their direction or inspiration, were spawned in the filthy, deadly swamp of the counterrevolution, from whence they drew their bestial power and outrageous nature."[10]

In its charges in 1947 the public prosecutor had already established that the crimes of the accused had arisen from the "national-Christian theory" of the 1919 provisional counterrevolutionary government in the provincial city of Szeged. "It was this Idea from Szeged which Miklós Kállay [then prime-minister] referred to in 1943 in his unfortunate speech as a theory predating the idea of National Socialism by more than a decade, and yet being essentially identical to it and having a major influence on it. This Idea from Szeged was one which even Adolf Hitler had to admit was his inspiration. This Idea from Szeged was the first sprout of the enormous tree of Fascism".[11] The reasoning behind the accusation treats Hitler and Szálasi as if there had been no other historical alternative to fascism after 1919; events that followed the logic of history had to lead to 1944, then to 1947, and finally to the courtroom where these events and their consequences were being discussed. Thus the executioner, Mihály Francia Kiss, was in fact already a member of the Arrow-Cross in 1919, long before the party was set up, and perhaps even then knew of Hitler—in contrast to those who in 1889 failed to notice that an infant called Hitler had been born. In fact, in its view of history and its style, the logic of the court is not at all far from the views of George S. Berkeley, who, in discussing the suicide of crown Prince Rudolf and his lover, Marie Vetsera, in his book *Vienna and its Jews*, notes that: "The other event of special significance to the Vienna Jews that occurred in 1889 passed unremarked by almost everyone, Jews and Gentiles alike. Three months after Rudolph's death, in the border village of Braunau, a son was born to Alois and Klara Hitler".[12]

In addition to the link between Szálasi and Iván Héjjas (and the crimes committed by Francia Kiss in 1919), the prosecution found other direct links to fascism. According to the prosecution's reasoning, the crimes committed by the detachments not only preceded but also served as a model for Hitler and the national socialists. The prosecutor also found proof of the detachment's historical roots and their defining role in the development of European fascism in his introductory remarks, in which he discussed the biography of the former prime minister, Gyula Gömbös: "The organizer of the Horthyist National Army was in fact Staff Captain Gyula Gömbös who had served for some time in Croatia and who was well acquainted with the secret South Slav military organization called the 'Black Hand,' as well as its cover organization 'Narodna Obrana.' He established his own secret society, called the Etelköz Association (EKA), on this model…This association attempted to realize the holy trinity of the Szeged Idea. EKA, under the leadership of its founder, who later became Prime Minister, was secretly in complete control of the whole country during the quarter of a century of Horthyist rule. Ministries, the Parliament, social, political, and economic organizations were all merely puppets on EKA's stage..."[13]

Thus, according to the public prosecutor, the crimes committed by the detachments were not merely a preview of what Hitler's theories and Szálasi's rule of terror were to bring, but in fact from 1919 on the members of the detachment—Héjjas, Mihály Francia Kiss, Gömbös, and the secret fascists of the Etelköz Association—were in control of the country, "for only people who were, or who became members of EKA were allowed to play a serious role in politics in Hungary".[14] From the very minute of the defeat of the dictatorship of the proletariat onward Hungary was in fact controlled by fascists, who moved political players like puppets. By starting the story in 1919 with the defeat of the first Hungarian Soviet Republic, the court succeeded in presenting fascists as primarily anticommunists, as if fascism had come into existence in the first place in order to challenge communism. Without emphasizing 1919, it would have been difficult to push the other targets, other victims, other adversaries of fascism into the background.

In the reasons for its judgment in the appeal, the National Council of People's Tribunals also highlighted the fact that "[t]he 'Orgovány methods'—the binding with barbed wire, the gouging out of eyes, scalping, burying alive, and all the rest of the bestiality which is incomprehensible for a European—were, if not in extent, then at least in content, a true forerunner of concentration camps and gas-chambers. The inhumane irresponsibility of the leaders of the detachments can only be compared with the leaders of S.S. bands and Fascist party units...[A]fter the course of twenty-five years Hejjas's detachment made it possible for Sztójay's and Szálasi's regimes in 1944 to afford this country the dubious honor of calling the counterrevolution Europe's first Fascist system, and thus Hungary was brought to the judgment of the world after World War II with an even greater burden of sin and guilt".[15]

This is apocalyptic history, and an indictment is an appropriate genre for such a depiction of events. Methodologically, if not stylistically, the court's text is closely related to the flashback as used in film and fiction. The U.S. literary historian, Michael Andre Bernstein, calls this technique "foreshadowing"—"a technique whose logic must always value the present, not for itself, but as a harbinger of an already determined future...At its extreme, foreshadowing implies a closed universe in which all choices have already been made, in which human free will can exist only in the paradoxical sense of choosing to accept or willfully—and vainly—rebelling against what is inevitable".[16]

It is as if the prophecies of the Old Testament had referred to events in the New Testament, as if the former were merely prefigurations of the latter, as if at a higher level the New Testament, in its completeness, were to perfectly fulfill the promise of *praeparatio evangelica*.[17]

At the beginning of 1957 the police in Dunavecse village gained information that (as was included in the text of the judgment of the Budapest capital court) "during the counterrevolution [of 1956] Mihály Francia Kiss appeared in the region of Szabadszállás in a Soviet-made *Pobeda* automobile and there met the president of the local counterrevolutionary National Committee. The investigation that followed showed that it was most likely that the person who called himself József Kovács of Bodakút and Mihály Francia Kiss were one and the same person".[18] On 8 March 1957 Mihály Francia Kiss was arrested and imprisoned. On 22 March 1957 in the Interior Ministry's Csongrád county police headquarters, Mrs. Jenő Rácz appeared and accused Mihály Francia Kiss of the kidnapping and murder of her brother, Vilmos Kalmár, in Pusztamérges in the summer of 1920. The mutilated upper body of the kidnapped trader had been found in the woods at Orgovány with other extremely mutilated and beheaded corpses. A suit had been brought against Mihály Francia Kiss in this case at the start of the 1920s, but the case was then dismissed due to the general amnesty granted by Admiral Horthy.

Budapest's capital court initiated a new suit in Mihály Francia Kiss's case. In contrast to the judgment of 1947, the capital court did not restrict its charge to "the crime of the illegal torture and murder of humans", but also found Francia Kiss guilty of "the production of one counterfeit identity card, the crime of the registration of false personal data in his identity papers, the attempt to commit a crime by using one counterfeit identity card, and the crime of concealing one weapon and bullet". The court condemned him to death for all of these crimes.[19] In the course of the trial the court found that the accused had taken part in the kidnapping, torture, and murder of sixty-six victims in twelve separate incidents.

The court also found that the procurement of a counterfeit personal identity card and the hiding of a pistol after World War II was proof that the defendant had not abandoned his criminal ways and that there was continuity in his constant criminal activities between 1919 and 1956: "In addition to the crimes committed by Mihály Franica Kiss in 1919 and 1920, he also committed crimes following the liberation of Hungary in 1945…there can be no doubt that Mihály Francia Kiss was, and remains to this day, an individual with undeniable Fascist sympathies".[20]

This judgment placed an even greater emphasis on the continuity of fascism in Hungary and on the vital role played by the white terror of 1919 in the development of fascism worldwide. "[Francia Kiss was one of those] who represent the catastrophic political tendency which led to true Fascism, Nazism, World War II, the terrible and horrifying acts of the Arrow-Cross Party, and the deaths of hundreds of thousands of working people".[21]

The Council of the People's Tribunal of the Supreme Court (which acted as the appellate court in the Francia Kiss case and which confirmed the death sentence reached by the first court) reversed the chronology of history in its judgment on 9 August 1957 by declaring that in 1919, the detachment already

"rightly claimed that it was the predecessor and harbinger of Hitler's Fascism and Szálasi's reign of terror...[T]hese Fascist-style acts of terror and the driving of the country into the reign of terror of open Fascism and World War II are links in a chain which are joined one to the other, just as the acts of terror and the heinous acts of the Arrow-Cross hordes are not merely related to the vandalism of October 1956 [the 1956 revolution] in form, but are a part of the bitter struggle of the former ruling classes...The crimes committed by Mihály Francia Kiss, therefore, are to be considered war crimes, but not because the country could not be regarded as being in a state of peace when they were committed, as the court first suggested, but rather because they are part and parcel of the causes of the historic catastrophe which bestruck the Hungarian nation at the fall of the glorious Hungarian Soviet Republic [in 1919], with the twenty-five years of Horthy's Fascism, and directly led to and peaked with our role in World War II and to Szálasi's reign of terror".[22]

Such turns of phrase as "rightly claimed that it was the predecessor and harbinger of Hitler's Fascism and Szálasi's reign of terror" sound as a German burger might have sounded running through town shouting: "the Thirty-Year War has just begun!"[23]

In 1957, however, the court felt it was its duty to find and prove the connection between the white terror of 1919 and the so-called "second coming of white terror", the counterrevolution of 1956. The elderly white terrorist murderer served as a link between 1919, 1944, and 1956, and this link became one of the most important elements of the explanations of the outbreak of the counterrevolution in 1956:

"[The] Fascist-type acts of terror initiated by Iván Hejjas and Mihály Francia Kiss, which grew in size and scope over time, became a seed for the worldwide movement which is known everywhere as 'Fascism' and which initially oppressed and destroyed millions of people and finally drove the whole world into the World War II Catastrophe [sic]. The Hungarian counterrevolution became a cradle for Fascism, and through the mutilation of human souls led in a straight line to the events which exploded in Hungary on 23 October 1956...The detailed and well-established facts of the case are entirely recognizable in the acts of terror and mass murders committed by the Arrow-Cross in 1944 and are also clearly visible in the movements which were committed against the faithful sons of the Hungarian People's Republic during the counterrevolution after 23 October 1956. The sadistic murders, skinning of humans alive, cutting out of sexual organs, and similar acts committed in Orgovány, Izsák, and the region of Kecskemét in 1919 were not unknown to those who carried out similar murders in the Arrow-Cross's Party Headquarters in Budapest. The murderers of our executed and mutilated martyrs on Republic Square [in front of the Budapest headquarters of the communist party where the only truly bloody anticommunist atrocity of the revolution occurred on 30 October 1956] and those who committed murders in front of the police department in Miskolc [another site of bloodshed during the revolution] used the same methods and carried out their acts with the same sadistic cruelty as Mihály Francia Kiss and his terrorist companions did in 1919. All of this makes it clear that the crimes committed by Mihály Francia Kiss and Iván Héjjas some thirty-eight years ago are closely connected to the latest round of vandalistic Fascist attacks which are to be found right through Hungarian history."[24]

"Mihály Francia Kiss was one of the cruelest counterrevolutionaries of all time", indicated the court in its judgment of his guilt and the effects of his acts. "His crimes point the way down a lasting trail leading to the next horrors and were a cradle to the deformity which was later called Fascism. His behavior laid its stamp on the quarter of a century of rule by Horthy Fascism; it was to be found throughout the underground organization of the counterrevolutionary movement, throughout the period of the building of Socialism; and this same spirit eventually exploded with elementary power in the horrible days of the rebirth of the counterrevolution on 23 October 1956. The seeds Mihály Francia Kiss and company sowed in 1919 grew into a terrible harvest in the days of the counterrevolution of 1956. The orgy of murder and blood roared identically in both periods, and the connection between the two is to be found in Mihály Francia Kiss and his spirit".[25]

Even without a deeper analysis of the text, it is clear that the evoking of white terror in 1956 was not merely a stylistic formula. Historical continuity was presented both on the positive as well as on the negative side in the court's judgment, for as the capital court had established in 1957, history was continuous on the other side as well: "In October 1918 a proletarian revolution broke out in Hungary. The imperialist formation of Austro-Hungary collapsed, fell to pieces, and this initiated the process which finally, after decades and decades of hard fighting, led to the liberation of nations and eventually to the development of People's Democracies. This journey, however, was not an easy one..."[26]

According to the account of history given in the accusation, the advance of history was first interrupted by the white terror of 1919 that drove the forces of progress underground. After the victory of the Soviet Union and the working classes in 1945, however, the forces of fascism hid underground and continued their work illegally (as had the Croatian "Black Hand" in its time), waiting for the moment when they could again break to the surface. October 1956 brought the moment for which they had waited. "The true character of 23 October was expressed on 30 October [the date of the siege of communist party headquarters on Republic Square in Budapest]. What was still hidden on 23 October came out into the light of day on 30 October. On 30 October the hour struck for the beginning of the black carnival. We were witnesses when the counter-revolution removed its mask", wrote Ervin Hollós and Vera Lajtai, apologists of the post–1956 communist restoration in *Republican Square 1956.*[27]

The communist historical thriller *Spearmen* by András Berkesi and György Kardos was created to illustrate and popularize the court's—and official communist—theories. The book, which was reprinted nine times (it retained its popularity even after 1990) and was finally turned into a film, follows the story of one Major Ákos Rajnay (whose real name is István Korponay) from the time of his involvement in the white terror through the hibernation of the "Spearmen" in 1944 until their reawakening and reactivation in 1956. The Spearmen were a paramilitary organization that the authors based on the communist interpretation of the Etelköz Association. Iván Héjjas clearly serves in part as a model for Ákos Rajnay. The two authors present the counterrevolution as the outcome of the joint conspiracy of international imperialist intervention—this provided the justification for Soviet military intervention to help the Hungarian communists—and the underground forces of the white terror. (According to the book, the Spearmen were left behind as saboteurs-in-hibernation by the German and Hungarian fascists, who ordered them to hide themselves as ordinary and loyal citizens until the time arrived for an armed counterrevolutionary uprising.) The novel could not have been written without the active cooperation of the Interior Ministry, the Secret Service, and the Communist Party's Department of Propaganda and Agitation, for its authors clearly used classified documents about the Spearmen from the Interior Ministry's secret archives.[28] This was all the easier to assume, as the coauthors both served in the Ministry's Military-Political Counterintelligence Department before they began their writing careers.[29]

According to the restored post–1956 communist regime, the counter-revolution of 1956 was a continuation, or rather the second edition, of the counterrevolution of 1919. The white terror of 1919—as depicted in the accusation of the People's Tribunal, and in the judgment by the People's Court of 1947—was a precursor to fascism, or rather was fascism in its first form. The counterrevolution of 1956 was closely connected to and rooted in fascism. By using this historical theory, an immediate link was found between 1919, 1944, and 1956. Mihály Francia Kiss symbolized the logic of historic continuity in person. However, even though some alleged witnesses saw the former white terrorist driving the Pobeda automobile to a meeting with the president of the local National Council, the old mass murderer who hid in a field watchman's shack on the great Hungarian plain from 1945 until his arrest in 1957 could not have convincingly claimed to have taken an active part in the terrible crimes of the counterrevolution. A stronger, more direct link was needed.

On 14 March 1957, eight days after Mihály Franica Kiss's arrest and two days after the publication of news of his detention, the official daily of the communist party *Népszabadság* printed a story under a headline typed in bold: "Mihály Francia Kiss's Offspring Arrested". The story gave an account of how Béla Francia, the "offspring" of the infamous white terrorist (the exact relationship between the two was obscured with this imprecise noun), was arrested for his role in breaking into a grocery store with other common criminals during the days of the counterrevolution. Béla Francia was to be sentenced to four years in prison. (After 1963 he was rehabilitated, for he had ironclad proof that he could not have been on the scene when the store was broken into. It was also proven that he was in no way related to Mihály Francia Kiss. He was not even an "offspring" of the man's family. He merely—to his very bad luck—bore the same family name.) Béla Francia's arrest, the report about it, his trial, and his condemnation provided the missing link to the tale that began in 1919. If the white terrorist himself was humanly incapable of carrying out the long list of horrible deeds, his offspring was not: blood is thicker than water (even blood on a murderer's hands).

In the course of the trials Francia Kiss became the archetype of the fascist: the fascist who had been there at the beginning of all things, who had hidden and survived underground (as the Black Hand had under the name Narodna Obrana). In all that time he had not changed one whit. He was just biding his time and waiting to do what he had done from the start—to show the world the true face of fascism. The crimes committed by Mihály Francia Kiss only gain their true meaning in the context of later horrible events, especially following 1956. According to the court's judgment, the anticommunist had to be, by definition, a fascist.

Fascists, before all things, were—in this reading— anticommunists. The history following World War I was a history of constant, ongoing struggle between the forces of communism and of fascism—as the 1919 white terror clearly revealed. Fascism's true enemies were always communists, even if its victims may have appeared to be others. The only true goal of fascism was the destruction of communism. Communism, for it's part, was the only active, uncompromising, and organized arm against fascism, the only guarantee against the dark forces.

"Miklós Horthy and the officers who massed around him proclaimed far and wide that the causes of the ruin of Hungary, of the 1919 revolution, and of the country's mutilation after World War I were the Marxist socialists, or in other words, the Bolsheviks and Jews, whom they believed to be one and the same. Horthy himself, his friend, the German General Ludendorff, and his protégée [sic] Adolf Hitler, all fully believed the anti-Semitic and antisocialist book of trash, 'The Protocols of the Elders of Zion,' which was edited by the Russian teacher Nilush at the behest of the chief of the Tsar's secret police, the Okhrana, in 1903. After the Russian Revolution the book was widely disseminated throughout Europe by none other than Russian counterrevolutionary officers. One could say that it became a sort of bible for Horthy and the coattail politicians and officers who massed around him. In this spirit Gyula Gömbös, István Zadravetz, and their counter-revolutionary company in Szeged initiated the most unbridled propaganda and hate campaign against anything that could be called left-wing or—what was to them one and the same—Jewish".[30] The public prosecutor found it important to mention the fact that the anti-Semitism of the counterrevolutionary forces in Hungary was rooted in the work of the Bolsheviks' sworn enemy, the Okhrana, the Tsar's secret police, which was then disseminated throughout Europe by counterrevolutionary officers who worked against the Bolshevik revolution. Horthy's friend's protégée, Adolf Hitler, also borrowed from this source, even if later than the leaders of the Hungarian counterrevolutionaries. (Thus Hitler himself becomes Horthy's protégée.)

In its opinion in 1957, Budapest's capital court defined the essence of fascism's anti-Semitism in an even clearer and more direct way:

"The imperialist forces in every country recognized the danger posed to capitalism and the furthering of imperialism by the strengthening of the dictatorship of the proletariat, and this is why they felt that no means are too low to be used in the suppression of movements working toward the democratic transformation of the masses and to uphold the power of the upper classes. In working toward this goal, especially under the conditions that prevailed in Hungary at the time, they found that the most successful strategy would be to misdirect the class struggle into a religious conflict. Due to Austrian policies at that time, beside the conflict between nationalities that became sharper and sharper on the territories of the Austro-Hungarian Empire, it was especially the so-called Jewish question, which was constantly and carefully kept on the platter at all times by the governments of the Monarchy. This religious contradiction was the one that was most useful over the course of time in suppressing every sort of democratic movement among the working class, because the loss of the War and the following events were ascribed to Hungary's Jews, and the attacks directed against leftists were also used to feed and fuel the hatred directed against the Jews".[31]

In this system of argumentation it was not the Jews who were the real victims. Quite the opposite: the insults they suffered served to "misdirect the class struggle into a religious conflict", to fool the "masses"—"...the dubious characters who gathered in Szeged...openly propagated the claim that the Communists caused Hungary to lose the War and to fall apart, and that it was the Jews who invented Communism, and thus the entire policy of the counterrevolution was the uprooting by root and shoot of the power of the proletariat".[32] The counterrevolution—that is, fascism, in the narratives of the court and communist historians— associated Jews with Bolshevism in order to hide its true nature and work, which was—according to the communist court—nothing other than anticommunism and the struggle against the only protectors of the working masses. In other words, the Jews were useful for the fascists only in order to disorient the workers, to fool them in order to suppress them by leading them in a false direction.[33] "Anti-Semitism, which cannot in theory be reconciled with Christian ideology, budded to such a degree in the practice of the Héjjas detachment and in its pre-Fascist cruelty, that it showed it was a worthy partner of the vandalism carried out by Fascism in the 1940s. Because of the association of the terms 'Jew' and 'Bolshevik' in their propaganda, every Jew was an enemy and, thus, to be destroyed".[34]

In Western Europe following World War II it was only a short time before a new history of the war, the myth of wholesale national resistance, was established.[35] In Europe's Soviet half, however, the communist movement retroactively took complete control of resistance to fascism. In the West—allegedly—only certain well-defined and marginalized figures and groups collaborated with the Nazis—that is, with the Germans—who, in this tale born not long after 1945, were primarily and almost solely responsible for the horrible crimes committed in World War II.[36] Germans stood accused by the court at the Nuremberg Trials, and the prosecution proved German responsibility. Thus, the outcome supported this view of history. ("The aim of the Nuremberg Military Tribunal was to try 'the highest level' German war criminals".[37]) The Germans started World War II, and they robbed and murdered throughout Europe. The guilty were to be found among the citizens of Germany—a slowly disappearing country that effectively no longer existed, that was merely a group of zones of occupation, and that soon became two separate entities, attached to two separate worlds.

The communist parties of Western Europe also played their own, not so insignificant, role in the creation of the retrospective fiction of wholesale national resistance. Communist antifascists could thus become members of the national majority, and even its avant-garde in France and Italy. It is no coincidence, then, that the first draft of the Italian amnesty bill was prepared by the secretary general of the Italian Communist Party, Palmiro Togliatti, in 1946. Right until the end of the 1970s, and in some countries even up to the crumbling and collapse of the communist systems at the end of the 1980s, there was hardly any attempt to carry out critical or self-critical analyses of the history of national resistance in the western part of the European continent.[38]

In Europe's eastern half only communists were allowed to be antifascists in histories that could only be written by communists, for fascism—in communist historiography—came into being in opposition to communism, and the placement of someone other than communists in the role of the victim was only a dirty trick on the part of the fascists—a transparent attempt to fool the people, "nothing but a weapon of the ruling class for the enslavement of the German working class", as East German history books taught.[39] Fascists tried to destroy communists, who were the only real adversaries of fascism. (The explanation for the Molotov–Ribbentrop Pact was confusing and opaque in history books printed after 1945. It was described as a sign and consequence of the Soviets' naïve trust and their peace-loving character. The secret clause was never even mentioned, as it was impossible both historically and by definition for communism and fascism to be allies.) This is one of the reasons why Jews had to disappear from the list of the true victims of fascism, and is the explanation for the triangle inscribed in stone on a memorial at Birkenau to differentiate among the political inmates there, and is why during the reign of the Polish communist regime the text on gravestones at Auschwitz emphasized the murder of a highly-inflated number of political inmates.[40] This is why in its issue on the twenty-fifth anniversary of the liberation of Auschwitz the Hungarian Jewish newspaper *Új Élet* (New Life) reported: "The delegation waited by the gates to Auschwitz for Jozef Czyrankievicz, [Polish] Prime Minister, to whose coat his former fellow political deportees pinned the symbol of political prisoners, the triangle with a red letter P".[41] This is also why the National Executive Committee of Hungarian Israelites was forced to make the following statement in 1951: "There is not a single person of Jewish faith among the ranks of those who are being forced to leave the cities and resettle in the countryside at this moment, not a single person who is being deported because of membership to our denomination. In contrast to rumors, those being deported were all filthy rich traders, factory owners, and landlords, and enjoyers of Horthy's fascist system—a system which is known throughout the world for its persecution of the Jews, and a system to which those being deported now gave their material and moral support before the catastrophe of World War II".[42]

The Tel Aviv correspondent of Radio Free Europe noted during the Eichmann trial that: "The governments of Eastern Europe are ready to help the Israeli government in preparing for the Eichmann trial, in case the trial aims to be more than merely an investigation of the crimes the one-time Nazis committed against the Jews". An East European diplomat who gave an interview to the Radio Free Europe reporter emphasized that "the people's democracies wish the Eichmann trial will shed light on all acts committed by all Fascists, including those of the neo-Nazis of present day West Germany".[43] In communist historiography, the twentieth-century history of fascism was continuous not only from the beginning of the century up to World War II but even from the end of the war until the arrival of the final victory of world communism. In a six-part article printed in a series in the Hungarian party's daily during the trial in Jerusalem, two mercenary pen-pushers, László Szabó and István Pintér, uncovered how Eichmann's Hungarian assistants allegedly became agents of West German intelligence and the U.S. Central Intelligence Agency, and thus were the direct link between the *Endlösung* and the anticommunist manipulations of the West after the war.[44]

The officers of Hungarian antifascist military units that were not under communist control during World War II were not allowed to be members of the Partisan Union until the late 1980s. They were not awarded the Freedom Medal, granted to other members of the resistance. The activities of the Görgey Battalion, KISKA, and the Buda Voluntary Regiment (noncommunist, antifascist, armed resistance battalions) were scarcely, if ever, mentioned. Hungary's communist historiography of communist antifascist struggle was not an exception in Eastern Europe. In Tito's Yugoslavia, "textbooks stuck to a dogmatically simplified dichotomy of 'revolutionaries' (i.e. the partisans) and 'counterrevolutionaries' (ranging from Croat ustashe and Serbian chetniks to native 'quislings' and 'bourgeois' governments in exile) reserving, of course, not just political legitimacy, but also the 'good' virtues and morals only for the first ones". Another typical tendency of the textbooks was "to 'de-ethnicize' World War II on Yugoslav soil, describing the events predominantly from a 'class-perspective' as a war between Communist partisans and all kinds of 'bourgeoisies,' thus ignoring the war's ethnic dimension and its character as a civil war...According to the 'class-approach' it was the 'bourgeoisie' on all sides—the Serbian, Croatian, Slovenian—which was held responsible for the ethnic violence and the war crimes..."[45] In the German Democratic Republic, the Socialist United Party tied its legitimacy to the long fight between anticommunist fascism ("the highest stage of imperialism") and antifascist German communism. The Holocaust became "de-Judaized" in the G.D.R.[46] It was as if only Ernst Thälmann, the secretary of the German communist party, had been killed in Buchenwald, as if the victims of fascism—in the memory of the G.D.R.—were first and foremost communists. The postwar exhibition in the Buchenwald concentration camp focused almost exclusively on political inmates, leaving the Jewish victims in the shadows, and not mentioning Roma, homosexuals and others persecuted in the camp. Postwar individual guilt and responsibility for the past was absolved through this collective antifascist communist sacrifice. The G.D.R. presented the confrontation between the communist German Democratic Republic and the bourgeois German Federal Republic as a continuation of the war between communists and (the "offspring" of) fascism. In Bulgaria, in the war crimes trials initiated by the Fatherland Front, no distinction was made between those who actively collaborated with the Germans, the so-called "friends of the West", and anticommunist democrats.[47]

After the end of World War II both the perpetrators and the victims wanted to forget—to leave the terrible memories of their past behind. The communist party—which in the interest of enlarging its own antifascist role, had retroactively driven Jews out of the camps anyway—offered Jews a chance to abandon their Jewish identities while remaining antifascists. The great majority of the Central European Jewry was thoroughly assimilated before the outbreak of the war. (According to the last census before World War I, for example, about seventy-five percent of Hungarian Jews considered themselves to be Hungarian.) Most Jews were confronted with their Jewish identity only at the moment they were forced to wear the yellow Star of David in the ghettos or in concentration camps. Jewishness for them did not mean much more than victimization, starvation, suffering, the loss of relatives, the gas chambers, and other unimaginable horrors. Most of them were unable to do anything with their lately discovered Jewishness, but naturally wanted to stand firmly opposed to fascism.[48]

On the other hand, the majority of the witnesses and perpetrators of genocide hoped that as long as they maintained the appearance of loyalty to the communist system, they would be able to avoid being held responsible for their actions. The stigma of being "Hitler's last ally" and a "fascist people" (depending on political needs, these titles could be applied either strictly to the members of the former ruling classes or to all members of Hungarian society) was constantly harped on in the rhetoric of the leaders of the Hungarian communist party. This served as a reminder and warning that if the need ever arose to punish people for their pasts there was something to remember. The opponents of Stalinism, the defendants in the show trials of the 1940s and 1950s, were almost always accused of having been fascists or collaborators among other things either before 1945 or after. During the course of the criminal prosecution of the 1946 pogrom in Kunmadaras (in which Jews, who had just survived the concentration camp, were killed), the prosecutor and the court transformed the case, which was a twentieth-century mutation of the medieval blood libel, into an antidemocratic and—naturally—anticommunist fascist conspiracy.[49]

For tribunals, especially for people's tribunals sitting in judgment over war criminals, *in extremis veritas*. The ghastly crimes committed by the mass murderer Mihály Francia Kiss—the torture and murder of at least sixty people—therefore understandably compelled the court to make use of historical statements, which suggested that something had happened even before it could have happened and that everything that happened later was already part of the past.[50] The need to construct and prove historic continuity in such a view of history—and the grave dangers inherent in this—were obvious in the first judgment of Mihály Francia Kiss's case, or rather in the opinion of the court. An ambition to introduce continuity to the case compelled the court to develop an official reading of history which was fraught with dangers, especially for the restored communist order after 1956, but which were not foreseen at the time.

It can probably be proven that the construct of 1956 as a counterrevolution is the key to the understanding of the history of the Kádár era. Through the optics of the counterrevolution, the period before and after 1956 can be seen in a unique perspective, and this view would even surprise the official history writers of the period. The construct of the counterrevolution—in an unintended way—created continuity between the Stalinist era and the period following 1956. The problem that arose and that the leadership of the party had to deal with was similar to the one that early Christian apologists faced when they argued the uniqueness of the New Testament and it's special status, while simultaneously trying to prove to heretics the continuity between the two Testaments, for both were given by the same pastor.

One of the officially produced reasons for the outbreak of the counterrevolution was found in the pre–1956 Stalinist system—the showtrials, which demonstrated the unlawfulness of the period; but an equally defining role was given to the permanently present, underground fascist counterrevolution which continuously operated in secret from the white terror of 1919. In this narrative, the post–1956 Kádár regime continued the anti-imperialist, antifascist struggle of the pre–1956 period: it protected the same values against the same enemy that had now committed crimes against humanity in its attacks against communism on three occasions—in 1919, 1944, and 1956.

For 1956 to feature as a replay of the white terror of 1919 and the continuation of fascism, the first Hungarian Soviet Republic had to be rehabilitated. Before 1956 the Hungarian Soviet Republic could only be mentioned in a vague and confusing way or was barely mentioned at all in textbooks, as it was too difficult to remind the public that most of the leaders of the first Hungarian Bolshevik experiment did not die in the prisons of the protofascist Hungarian counterrevolutionary regime, but rather in exile in Moscow as defendants in the show trials, as victims of the great terror in Stalin's prisons, or in Soviet gulags. Stalin's death and the disappearance of the Hungarian hard line leadership after 1956 (most of them once more went into exile in the Soviet Union) provided the chance to resurrect the almost forgotten Soviet Republic. This resurrection was the precondition for substantiating the counterrevolutionary interpretation of 1956, for the references to the first white terror of 1919, and also for presenting the counterrevolution as just another appearance of the ever present fascist danger. It was no accident that the reorganized communist youth organization took the name "Alliance of the Communist Youth", the name of the youth organization at the time of the first Hungarian Soviet Republic. On the banner of the Alliance there were two dates: 1919 and 1957 (the years when the Alliance was established and then reorganized).

Paradoxically, continuity with the pre–1956 regime provided legitimacy for the restoration of the communist system after the Soviet troops defeated the 1956 revolution. The populace, especially after the 1963 amnesty when most of those who survived the postrevolutionary terror were released from prison, found that although those in power were mostly the same and although the system did not deny its close connection to the period before 1956, still, life was easier to live, was less unpredictable and frightening than it had been before; it was different, and yet the same. In comparison with itself, the Kádár regime seemed better than itself; it was less frightening than it might have been, and people felt that they had to fear the regime less than they should have had to. Had the basis of comparison been another country—such as neighboring Austria—or another political system and not a previous incarnation of the regime itself, it would have been much more difficult for the communist restaurateurs to legitimize their unconstitutional and arbitrary rule. Kádár blamed his predecessor for all the political mistakes that led to the outbreak of the uprising in 1956, and he distanced himself from this Stalinist predecessor, but at the same time he emphasized continuity. This delicate balance between continuity and discontinuity, in which the counterrevolution played the key role, proved to be a stabilizing factor, even if, perhaps, stability was not the initial historic and ideological intention.

This history of continuity, however, gave populist reformers in 1988–1989 a chance to say, like Imre Pozsgay at the occasion of the opening of the reconstructed Széchenyi Palace which had been turned into a luxury hotel, that "the long decades of demolition and destruction have finally come to an end". With the help of one single sentence, any distinction between the pre–1956 and the post–1956 periods was demolished—the two eras simply collapsed into one undifferentiated continuous history. This enabled and encouraged people to talk about the "Bolshevik rule of bloody terror" when referring even to the events of the late 1980s, a time when in reality there were no political prisoners in Hungary and the majority of the population spent most of its time making money by whatever means possible in the second economy, which was informally tolerated by the regime. When the final days of communism arrived, nobody was ready to remember any differences between Kádár and anybody or anything that had preceded him. The history of continuity that originally ensured the legitimacy of the Kádár regime after 1956 proved to be one of the most important elements of its delegitimization in 1989. Communism in part fell victim to its own historical construction.

One of the important goals of the East European war crime tribunals was to prove that, as a rule, anticommunists became fascists, that anyone who was an anticommunist was a fascist. But these trials and communist history-writing had another aim as well—to prove the truth of historical trivialism: that all fascists were anticommunists. These two statements combined have had a significant impact on the formation of views about communism after 1989. I believe that the history of the twentieth century, written by communists—with the fight between communism and anticommunist fascism as its focus—has proven to be a serious obstacle to the development of an intelligent, honest, critical, and self-critical debate about communism after its fall in 1989.

"Representing Mihály Francia Kiss's daughter, Mrs. Gyula Mészár, 'The National Union of Former Political Prisoners' appeals against the judgment of the Budapest Capital Court [of 1957], because the appellant believes that during Mihály Francia Kiss's prosecution the torture and murder of humans was not verified". The legal counsel of the National

Union of Former Political Prisoners appealed to the Supreme Court arguing that Mihály Francia Kiss had been condemned to death by hanging in the course of a typical show trial and was accused of war crimes and executed by the communist court after the 1956 revolution merely because he was an anticommunist. His crime was that he fought against communism as early as 1919 and then throughout the whole of his life, just as the Hungarian Army had when it attempted to stop Bolshevism during World War II at the Don River. The leaders—who were some of the generals of that army, which fought as allies of the Nazis and who were then condemned for war crimes and crimes against humanity—had been rehabilitated by the Supreme Court of the Hungarian Republic after 1990.

In the formerly communist part of the world, the rehabilitation of war criminals after 1989 is not exceptional to Hungary. Among others who gained acquittal, or for whom serious attempts have been made to gain such acquittal, are the Croatian leader Ante Pavelic, the Serb Draza Mihajlovic, Bishop Stepanic of Zagreb, and the one-time leader of the Romanian Iron Guard, Antonescu. Similarly Miklós Horthy was given a (partially) official reburial with the participation of the members of the first postcommunist, right-wing government. So there is nothing surprising or exceptional in the fact that the Union of Former Political Prisoners tried to gain rehabilitation for the mass murderer Mihály Francia Kiss. According to those who worked for the rehabilitation of such people, their common crime, the reason why they fell victim to the communist system, was that they were all anticommunists, just as the courts and historians after 1945 had indicated. The communist judges deemed anticommunists as fascist in order to sentence them as war criminals. Those who tried to rehabilitate fascists and war criminals after 1989, after the disappearance of communism, did nothing more than take the logic of the communists seriously in order to use it as a reason for acquittal.

"[T]he genocide of the Jews was the only mass atrocity in history which was followed and concluded by an explicit, formal, judicial, and practical precedent-setting act of international judgment…Furthermore, the legitimacy of the postwar liberal democratic order of the 'West' was explicitly tied to this judgment. Auschwitz was then, on the level of juridical clarification, not only 'settled' through the clear identification of perpetrators and victims. But in addition, it was transformed into the ground for a reorganized international order based on the principle of 'freedom,' allowing that order to appear 'transpolitical' (especially in its constitution as 'natural' opposition to 'totalitarianism')".[51] For the West after 1958–1959 and especially following the Eichmann trial, fascism meant and became equal with the Holocaust and Auschwitz. This was the crime and the name that had to be remembered and recalled so that it would never be repeated: for as long as the memory of this horror lasts (goes the assumption) it can be controlled, and we might be able to defend ourselves from ourselves. Memory—in this historiographic and political practice—is the force whereby distance can be created from crimes against humanity. The West committed itself to intervention in Bosnia only when the western press began to write about the "Holocaust" and "genocide in Bosnia", when the unique crime was evoked whereby, in a paradoxical way, the unbearable situation suffered by the Muslims was posed as a denial of the uniqueness and singularity of the Holocaust. This historiographic and logical paradox was repeated in Rwanda, and this is why the successors to Nuremberg, the International War Crimes Tribunals, were established to bring judgment to these crimes. The memory of Auschwitz and Nuremberg has become an important part of the self-definition of western democracies and one of the most important sources of internationally accepted human rights.

The strange silence surrounding the history of communism after 1989, however, seems to suggest the belief that, unlike fascism, communism has finally and truly come to an end, and that there is neither the need nor the time to remember it, to face it, or to talk about it. "Communism never conceived of any tribunal other than history's, and it has now been condemned by history to disappear, lock, stock, and barrel. Its defeat, therefore, is beyond appeal."[52] A thing has come to an end that we, in any case, did not make, a thing for which we are not responsible. Just as was the case with the Germans, those nonexistent citizens of a nonexistent country, communism was made by the Soviets, the already nonexistent subjects of the nonexistent Soviet Union. While before 1989, when talking about the occupying army, Hungarians referred to the Russian troops, now only Bolsheviks and Soviets are mentioned and remembered—people who cannot be found anywhere anymore.

In the East the Jews, the Holocaust, Auschwitz, and even Nuremberg have fallen victim to the historiographic and ideological battle between communists and anticommunist fascists. The system after 1945 was not legitimized by resistance to Auschwitz, the absolute crime, but by the mythologized rhetoric of the continuous struggle against anticommunist fascists. Before 1989, Nuremberg and the judicial prosecution of crimes against humanity and war crimes could only be a footnote in the history of post-World War II events. After 1989 in the former communist world Nuremberg is presented as the justice of the victors. The Soviet prosecutor of the Stalinist show trials; the memory of Katyn, for which the Soviet prosecutor Pokrovskii tried to blame the Germans; the argument of *tu quoque*, that the Soviets committed even more and even greater crimes than the Germans did—all these have been used to delegitimize Nuremberg.[53] After the fall of communism the Nuremberg trials, the source and basis of international human rights, have become just as suspect in post-communist countries as everything else that was once associated with the Soviets or communism.

The other element of communist historiography and legal argumentation also makes a fair assessment of communism difficult. The reasoning, namely, did not just state that all anticommunists were fascists, but also the reverse: that every fascist is an anticommunist. Following the fall of communism, religious, national, and ethnic incitement is less complicated and holds fewer political risks than does a judgment of the history and legacy of communism based on careful analysis. Anyone who doesn't want to be called fascist might insist that the former members of the communist party were just good, patriotic, true born Hungarians (Slovaks, Romanians, Russians, etc.) who did not take communism seriously for a minute—which is why they were able to join the party so lightheartedly. Such a person would also argue that by using methods borrowed from the old (Jewish) Bolshevik tradition (signing petitions, publishing *samizdat* journals and publications, organizing demonstrations, etc.), members of the former democratic opposition who seemingly opposed communism in fact legitimized the communist system.

In the West, a wall built upon the ruins of Auschwitz grows ever more massive and protects humanity from itself: the international system of human rights desperately tries to keep catastrophe at bay (even in Kosovo). In the East, however, the soft, crumbling construction of communism promised false protection—before falling utterly to ruin—against the simplified danger of fascism fashioned as anticommunism. In the communist reading of recent history, anti-Semitism and race-hatred were just a mask on the face of fascism that had nothing to do with its true nature. Race-hatred and national and religious persecution in this interpretation are not defining characteristics of fascism, which is why it is so easy to incite hatred in the eastern half of Europe today. Extreme nationalists, anti-Semites, and racists are not necessarily seen as fascists—for this is what the East European history books taught. "An anticommunist is fascist", said the communists; for anyone who does not want to be stigmatized as fascist nowadays in the former communist world, it is hard to face communism. It is easier to be a racist.

As the postmortem consequence of communist agitation, propaganda, its representation of history, any condemnation of communism coming from any direction, for any reason or out of any conviction, appears to be fascist, whatever the motivation of this criticism may be. Even in death, the suspicion to which communism gave birth—and this is becoming less and less obvious and more and more difficult to recognize—makes it difficult for anyone to analyze the history of the past half century and to utter words that mean what they mean and not what justices meant by them in their judgment in the Francia Kiss case.

On 4 June 1996 at 4:20 p.m. during parliamentary debate over the bill that proposed to enshrine in law "the memory of Imre Nagy, martyred prime minister of Hungary", Ottó Sándorffy, representative of the right-wing Smallholders' Party, took the floor: "It's not likely that the Prime Minister, who struggled against the cult of personality in all of its forms, would have liked to have been raised above his fellow martyrs, and isolate himself from other victims. (Applause from the ranks of the Smallholders' Party). All other executed victims suffered the same injustice. This is why it is right and just to read their names, one after the other, together with the name of the martyred Prime Minister aloud to this House. The names of the 278 heroes and victims executed by the Communist dictatorship in retaliation following the 1956 Revolution and Freedom Fight: Géza Adamszky (Members of Parliament rise.)...Tibor Földesi, Mihály Francia Kiss, Ferenc Franyó..."[54]

Notes

1 Naturally, the white terrorist's was not the longest legal procedure ever. According to the records: "When the State of Israel was established and the Supreme Court inaugurated in Jerusalem, dozens of Christian clerics implored President Smoira to allow the Supreme Court, as the successor of the Great Sanhedrin (the Supreme Jewish Court during the time of Roman rule), to retry Jesus Christ and thereby rectify the injustice caused to him". See Asher Maoz, *Historical Adjudication: The Kastner Trial and the Commission of Inquiry into the Murder of Arlosoroff* (1998), 1. The president of the Supreme Court sent the request to the state attorney, who in turn started extensive research, the result of which was published in the book *The Trial and Death of Jesus* (New York: 1967).

2 Archive of the City of Budapest (BFL) B. XI. 1798/1957–9 (BFL-VII. 5.e/20630/III/49), 17.

3 Office of the Attorney of the City of Budapest. BÜL 638/1957 (BFL 1798/57/I).

4 Besides Francia Kiss, Iván Héjjas, the chief of the supplementary gendarmerie was sentenced to death in absentia.

5 Nb. IV. 131/1947 (BFL-VII. 5e?20630/I/49), 6.

6 Nb. IV. 131/1947 (BFL-VII. 5e?20630/I/49), 6–7.

7 Nb. IV. 131/1947 (BFL-VII. 5e?20630/I/49), 7.

8 NÜ/13672/5. Sz. 1946 (BFL-VII. 5e/20630/III/49), 1.

9 NOT. II. 727/1`947/9 (BFL-VII 5e/20630/I/49), 4.

10 NOT. II. 727/1`947/9 (BFL-VII 5e/20630/I/49), 4.

11 NÜ 13672/5sz/1947 (BFL-VII. 5e/20630/49), 1.

12 George S. Berkeley, *Vienna and its Jews: The Tragedy of Success* (Cambridge, Mass.: Madison Books, 1987), 87. Quoted in Michael Andre Bernstein, *Foregone Conclusions: Against Apocalyptic History* (Berkeley: University of California Press, 1994), 18. In opposition to such apocalyptic reasoning, Arthur Danto remarked that "no one came to Mme. Diderot and said: 'Unto you an encyclopaedist is born.'" Arthur C. Danto, *Analytical Philosophy of History* (Cambridge: Cambridge University Press, 1965), 12. Quoted by Bernstein, *Foregone Conclusions*.

13 NÜ. 13672/5sz.1947 (BFL-VII. 5e/20630/49), 2.

14 NÜ. 13672/5sz.1947 (BFL-VII. 5e/20630/49), 2.

15 NOT. II. 727/1947/9 (BFL-VII. 5e/20630/I/49), 6–7.

16 Bernstein, *Foregone Conclusions*, 2.

17 See Amos Funkenstein, "Collective Memory and Historical Consciousness", *History and Memory* 1:1 (1989): 14.

18 B. XI. 1789/1957–9 (BFL-VII. 5e/20630/III/49), 19.

19 B. XI. 1789/1957–9 (BFL-VII. 5e/20630/III/49), 1.

20 B. XI. 1789/1957–9 (BFL-VII. 5e/20630/III/49), 18–19.

21 B. XI. 1789/1957–9 (BFL-VII. 5e/20630/III/49), 5.

22 Nbf. II. 5123/1957/14 (BFL-VII. 5e/20630/49), 2 and 8–9.

23 Bernstein, *Foregone Conclusions*, 26. See also how Habermas formulated the same idea: "The sentence, 'the Thirty Years War began in 1618,' presupposes that at least those events have elapsed which are relevant for the history of the war up to the Peace of Westphalia, events that could not have been narrated by any observer at the outbreak of the war". Jurgen Habermas, "A Review of Gadamer's Truth and Method", in *Understanding and Social Inquiry*, eds. Fred R. Dallymayr and Thomas A. McCarthy (Notre Dame: University of Notre Dame Press, 1977), 346.

24 B. XI. 1798/1957–9 (BFL-VII. 5e/20630/49), 8.

25 B. XI. 1798/1957–9 (BFL-VII. 5e/20630/49), 32.

26 B. XI. 1798/1957–9 (BFL-VII. 5e/20630/49), 3.

27 Kossuth Publishing House, (Budapest, 1974), 318 and 197 respectively.

28 In the fall 1997 all copies of the book were checked out from the Budapest Central Public Library.

29 According to the information General Béla Király was kind enough to pass to me, at the end of 1944, when the Soviet Army was already in the country, he was approached by some of Szálasi's military leaders, who offered him the post of the chief of staff of the secret "Spearmen" organization. According to General Király—who had served in the Hungarian army from the 1930s and who in 1956 became the leading general of the revolutionary armed forces—the "Spearmen" was most probably an existing secret organization that came into being at the beginning of the 1920s and was active mostly in Transylvania, where it was engaged in intelligence operations and sabotage activities. The Fascist leadership hoped that the "Spearmen" would be able to perform the same functions in the rear of the Soviet Army. General Király—who became a member of the Hungarian Parliament after 1990—found the situation absolutely hopeless in 1944 and declined the offer.

30 NÜ. 1372/5.sz./1946 (BFL-VII. 5e/20630/III/49), 2.

31 B. XI. 1798/1957–9 (BFL-VII. 5e/20630?III/49), 4.

32 B. XI. 1798/1957–9 (BFL-VII. 5e/20630?III/49), 5.

33 "Those who spread anti-Semitism today, do this in order to misdirect the attention from the sabotage of the supporters of the pseudo-feudal order, the big capitalist and the reaction that is the cause of all our troubles today", argued Erik Molnár, the would-be director of the Historical Institute of the Hungarian Academy of Sciences, the would-be minister of foreign affairs and minister of justice in the 1950s, at one of the rare public debates still held right after the war. Erik Molnár, *A zsidókérdés Magyarországon* (The Jewish Question in Hungary) (Budapest: Szikra, 1946), 16.

34 NÜ. 13672/5. sz./1946 (BFL-VII 5e/20630/III/49), 6.

35 "When the postwar quest for truth began, forms of resistance were in place of honor, forms of collaboration were being concealed..." Natalie Zemon Davis, "Censorship, Silence And Resistance: The Annales During The German Occupation Of France", *Litteraria Pragensia* 1:1 (1991), 21.

36 On the myth of nationwide antifascist resistance in the West, see Tony Judt, "The Past is Another Country: Myth, Memory in Postwar Europe", *Daedalus* (Fall 1992): 83–118; especially 90–108.

37 M. Cherif Bassiuni, *Crimes Against Humanity in International Law* (Dordrecht: Martin Nijhof Publishers, 1992), 245.

38 "A silence of the Occupation days that persisted after the Liberation was silence about the Jews. It was not until the last number of the *Annales* of 1947 that two books on Jewish history were finally reviewed, and there was little more till two essays in 1957. The lack here was not so much practical as conceptual. In 1945, when Febvre proposed to Gallimard a grandiose seventy-seven volume inquiry on the state of France, 'Sémitisme et l'antisémitisme' were included under the rubric, 'Quelques virus,' but under the rubric 'Quelques forces', where he had envisaged books on 'nourritures chrétiennes' and on 'le protestant français'. There were no books on Jews. Only around 1953 did he conceive of a 'bel ensemble' of three books: 'un protestant français, un catholique français, un Israélite français'. What seems likely is that the category 'Jew' had been so powerfully filled with negative and exclusionary association during the Occupation that it took time, outside of the active world of Jewish scholarship, to establish it as a meaningful historical subject—even around the elevated and assimilating term 'Israélite'". Davis, *Censorship*, 22.

39 See Angelika Timm, *Jewish Claims against East Germany: Moral Obligations and Pragmatic Policy* (Budapest: Central European University Press, 1997), 39.

40 See James E. Young, *The Texture of Memory: Holocaust Memorials and Meaning* (New Haven: Yale University Press, 1993), 141.

41 *Új Élet*, 1 February 1960, 1.

42 *Magyar Nemzet*, 17 July 1951, 2.

43 Open Society Archives (OSA) 300/40/12371.

44 "Dr. Höttl, The Champion of Survival", *Népszabadság*, 25 June 1961.

45 Wolfgang Höpken, "War, Memory, and Education in a Fragmented Society: The Case of Yugoslavia" (paper for the conference on "Remembering, Adapting, Overcoming: The Legacy of World War Two in Europe", New York University, 24–27 April 1997), 14.

46 See Timm, *Jewish Claims*, 40.

47 See Tony Judt, "Myth, Memory in Postwar Europe", 91.

48 "What should we think of those so-called socialist Zionists, who would like to furnish the most developed form of society, the Socialist society, according to the laws of a semi-nomadic shepherd people?...The progressive way of solving 'the Jewish question' in Hungary cannot be anything else but the total assimilation of the Jews. This road is the only one that leads to democratic development and to the elimination of those facts [sic] on which anti-Semitic propaganda subsists". Molnár, *A zsidókérdés Magyarországon*, 17.

49 See Peter Apor, "The Lost Deportations: Kunmadaras, 1946" (master's thesis, History Department of the Central European University, 1996).

50 "Supersessionist theology necessarily reduces the predecessor text to an 'Old Testament', whose independent significance is fundamentally annulled once it is construed as only the first stage of a process culminating in the annunciation of a 'new and more complete truth'". Bernstein, *Foregone Conclusions*, 3.

51 Adam Katz, "The Closure of Auschwitz but not its End", *History and Memory* 10:1 (Spring 1998): 62.

52 François Furet, "Democracy and Utopia", *Journal of Democracy* 9 : 1 (January 1998): 79.

53 On the connection between Nuremberg and Katyn, see Telford Taylor, *The Anatomy of the Nuremberg Trials* (New York: Knopf, 1992), especially 466–472.

54 http://www.mkogy.hu/naplo/183/18300046.htm.

14 The Handshake Tradition: A Decade of Consensus Politics Bears Liberal Fruit in Hungary—But What Next?

MIKLÓS HARASZTI

These days, I am often asked: Does Hungarian democracy resemble the system I imagined ten years ago? And then comes the logical second question: Do I like what it turned out to be?

My answer is a quite resolute, double yes—as far as the ten years up to now are concerned. Hungary's democracy certainly resembles the desired boredom of normalcy I had predicted in my more optimistic moods. And I have liked, throughout this decade's mess and confusion, one consistent quality in our public life: the flavor of a consensus-seeking democracy—the first, by the way, in Hungarian history.

I call this system of consensus-based democracy the "handshake tradition". It stemmed from the actual handshake, the contractual democratization of 1989 and 1990, but it was strengthened throughout the decade by its institutionalization. I believe that our transformation has been a success thanks to this enduring self-limitation of the country's political forces.

Unfortunately, however, I feel that this success, and the handshake tradition as a whole, is now endangered. I will here describe both the success of the "handshake" process over the past decade as well as my reasons for concern as I look ahead.

The Hungarian system over the last decade came as close as possible to the Lijphartian ideal of a consensus-seeking, pluralistic democracy. In reality, of course, it was a mixed system just a bit richer in pluralistic features than average alongside the majoritarian ones. It is sufficient to remove one or two basic antimajoritarian institutions of the system in order to retransform any advanced Central European liberal democracy into an ordinary jacobinist-to-mafioso East European nightmare.

Ten years after 1989, Hungary's third freely elected government obviously nurtures a vision of a "Westminsterian", majoritist polity and quite systematically seeks to eliminate obstacles to what its leaders call "a more resolute enforcement of the majority principle". Is this sudden change simply politics as usual, within the limits of the infinite transformability typical of democracy, or is it something intrinsic to postcommunism's problem of quality?

I tend to believe it is precisely here that lies the point of no return toward illiberal, purely technical, authoritarian democracy. My final thesis will be that in postcommunism, only consensus-based—as opposed to majoritarian—politics can produce a western quality, liberal democracy.

A Contract of Self-Limitation

Self-limitation has not always been a virtue, of course. At first it was constructed as such by the outer limitations of cruel history, starting with Hungary's 1956 classic but failed revolution. The events of 1956 proved that the communist party could not be defeated; the fate of Prague Spring in 1968 showed it could not be reformed. Thus the solution offered by Adam Michnik and our Polish friends in 1976—a self-defending civil evolutionism circumventing the party—developed into the concept of a self-limiting civic revolution.

By the time—in the late eighties—our generation of dissidents moved to establish parties and was driven into normal politics, we all had become perfect self-limiters. (That's how I voluntarily lost my personal freedom of expression by switching genres from essays to slogans, such as "Kádár must go!") Along with our Polish and Czechoslovak friends, our movement aimed at a nonrevolutionary revolution, the radicality of which expressed itself only as a consistent constitutional legalism.

We worked for a contractual transition, a shaking of hands rather than a coming to blows, in bittersweet anticipation of what Herbert Marcuse in the sixties pessimistically called a "one-dimensional society" and what Francis Fukuyama decades later rejoicingly called the "end of history".

Our revolution reminded me of a classic joke told all over the former Soviet bloc: "What's the dictatorship of the proletariat?" The answer: "It's self-control of the working classes". Jokes aside, the self-limiting, anti-evolutionary character of our revolution evolved into a democratic quality that this region never before had experienced.

Both the favorable and the damnable qualities of our "handshake tradition" were obvious in advance. A negotiated, peaceful democratization is clearly the best start for truly liberal change that seeks to avoid the predictable wave of revenge in the aftermath of its victory. It is also the worst start for revolutionary change that aims to eliminate former elites.

Following the handshake, ninety-five percent of the electorate—representing all parties except for the hard-line former communists—supported change in our March 1990 parliamentary elections, the first truly free postcommunist vote after the semi-free but path-breaking Polish one. Obviously, even the old guard decided it was time to embark on something new. In the nick of time, they became as sincerely devoted to civic rights as were the veterans of democracy. On the other hand, within the chrysalis of its own defeat, the communist nomenklatura prepared for the happiest period of its life: its re-emergence as the new bourgeoisie.

It has to be noted that in Hungary the contractual way of democratization consisted of two steps. Half of the job was done in 1989 at the round table between the communists and the united opposition. The other half came in 1990 with the results of the first elections, involving the victorious conservatives and the opposition liberals. The final product of these two compromises—the first, between old and new, and the second, across the democratic spectrum—was a fully reconstructed constitution, enacted in 1990 and brought to compliance with the strictest requirements of western polity, including separation of branches of power, checks and balances.

In prescribing numerous two-thirds laws, the amended constitution ruled that mutual understanding should exist between the majority and the opposition when important decisions are made. At the same time, it carefully arranged the governability of the country.

Neither the nomenklatura nor any party could have accomplished on their own what these agreements concerning free elections and constitutional reform have achieved. In retrospect, the blessings of the "handshake transition" still dominate our democracy. The postcommunist decade has been more successful in every respect than it should have been purely on the basis of its prehistory, players, old and new institutions, and economic constraints.

Hungary Ahead of Itself

Thanks to its contractual origins, Hungary's postcommunist democracy is quite ahead of our own postcommunist society.

Most remarkably, ours is a firmly liberal system. Freedoms are more functionally anchored in the founding handshakes and in the established legal system than in the active concerns of our citizens. The press in Hungary is freer now than the journalists are; capitalism is deeper than its popular legitimacy; rights are more elaborate than tolerance of them.

The system continued to develop in a liberal direction under two consecutive partisan administrations. Each, however, accused the other of restricting democratic rights, a reproach that distinguishes postcommunist democracies from more established ones. Nevertheless, under both the conservative coalition of József Antall and the socialist-liberal coalition of Gyula Horn, rights and freedoms have further solidified and grown.

Just as in the case of the U.S. Constitution, many important features have been built into the system, relying on the design of the founders. A replica of the U.S. First Amendment, declaring that freedom of expression is more important than other liberties, was the result of the famous media war of the early 1990s, a feud over the public broadcasting system. Hungary now has patients' rights, partnership rights for homosexuals, laws against marital violence, government obligations for the disabled, and laws protecting privacy and providing access to public information.

Many of these tasks have been accomplished by Hungary's Constitutional Court. The court is a typical product of the handshake, originally empowered to assure the communists that no retroactive legislation would follow after they succumbed to elections. And there have been some useful fears on the other side, too, concerning how strong the democratic sentiments of the former communists would be in case of electoral victory. The court also has become the guarantor of the survival of the handshake due to its membership selection rule, which ensures a near-total consensus among the parties represented in Parliament in the choice of new justices.

As a bridge between the fictitious constitutionalism of the communist regime and the democratic rule of law, the court has taken Hungary quite far into the future. It is more "activist" in its scope of intervention than any similar western model. It relies on an "invisible constitution" along with the written one, embodied in its own rulings. That invisible law is unmistakably the liberal spirit of the handshake.

The Constitutional Court has protected former secret police agents from public identification, as well as the rights of their victims to look into their own files. It has helped to guard the sanctity of private property, and, by the same token, it has saved the nomenklatura-bourgeoisie from the confiscation of what it acquired during history's most uncontrolled management buyout in the late 1980s. It has given the green light to market capitalism and protected social rights during Hungary's belated shock therapy in the mid-1990s.

The Place Where World Wars Started

There are two miraculous achievements of which Hungary obviously would not have been capable without consensus politics. One is the stabilization of the economy, the other its foreign policies.

For a long time, western observers discussed whether postcommunist economies needed shock therapy or gradual transformation. But the successful reform countries decided that dispute for them. For years they went against political logic, and with heavy restrictions and a severe decline in the incomes of the larger part of their electorates, they transformed their command systems into privatized, demonopolized, globalized economies. The speediness of stabilization—that is, its "cruelty"—turned out to be a socially responsible answer. If it had not happened relatively quickly, the state would have become empty handed anyway, and chaos would have taken over.

But Hungary's example proves that taking swift action is not the only precondition of success. After all, quite a few countries experimented with shock therapy and failed. Equally important, success depends upon the compromises of the political class, its factions mutually depriving themselves of their favorite trump cards: the living standards card; the unemployment card; the nomenklatura-turned-comprador, bourgeois-selling-out-the-country card. Can the political class become almost antipolitical? Only through consensus politics can this come to pass.

Another miracle of the spirit of 1989 is that the Hungarian political elite voluntarily disposed of its traditional weapon of ethnopatriotic agitation. Hungary offered "land for ethnic rights" treaties to its neighbors where ethnic Hungarians live on former Hungarian territories: Romania, Slovakia, and Ukraine. Times of austerity are not typical ones for cutting reconciliation deals in Europe. Yet the Hungarian liberal polity was strong enough to do so and provided replicas of earlier French-German and Austrian-Italian reconciliation treaties. Germany agonized for thirty years after World War II to reach a similar agreement with Poland over the Oder-Neisse border. Hungary accomplished this in the first five years of its democracy, notwithstanding the uproar of shock therapy at home.

In the region where both world wars started, how could all this have happened without the handshake that committed all parties to western integration of the country and of the region? What nobody believed in 1989 has been proven: that the "masses" can understand and support rational policies, provided the political elites do the same.

Also worth consideration is that this tenth year of democracy is the first year in which the country has experienced modestly rising living standards after fifteen consecutive years of falling real incomes. Without the liberal and somewhat elitist design of the handshake tradition, it would have been impossible to maneuver any democracy through a total reorganization of life—one that is actually ending up in dramatically growing class differences. With few exceptions, it is the poor of communism who have become even poorer and the powerful of the *ancien régime* that have become the new upper class. Capitalism thus far has not delivered much on its promises of a market-based social counterbalance and of the rise of a self-made middle class. Add to this injustice the future shock of one-tenth of society's newly unemployed.

For this kind of miraculous social peace to come about you would need either—as in the case of West and East Germany—a powerful and democratic "Western Hungary" or "Western Poland", ready to offer a Wessie constitutional dictatorship over the Ossie part of the reuniting country. Or you need the handshake. Without one or the other you only can have combinations of prefascist, Weimarian, precommunist, Lublin features of weakness: competing and conspiring brown and red majoritarian claims and a self-annihilating democracy.

Whose endurance should be praised more during this decade of the handshake? That of the people of Hungary, who in spite of evident social injustice have renewed at every vote their confidence in the system's declared direction—the western shore? Or the commitment of the political class to the original liberal design? I personally cannot imagine any western democracy where fifteen consecutive years of falling living standards would not have prompted a mutiny of populist sentiments or the rise of extremist political adventurers—or both. There has been nothing like that in Hungary, where the political class enjoys a surprising lack of competition from outside the original handshake club.

An End to Consensus?

At the same time, the basic tensions of this liberal Hungarian transition also have derived from the handshake. Suddenly, for the first time during this transition, it is the third government, that of Viktor Orbán, which has decided to ride class sentiments, play majoritarian rather than consensus-based governance, and build a political constituency based upon a "them or us" theme.

Naturally Orbán, himself a long-time beneficiary of the healthy constraints of our historic handshake, would not even be able to experiment with ignoring them without the success of the economic and legal transformation, nor, of course, without the inequities and injustices preserved rather than created by the transition. Those, too, have been part of this peaceful, contractual shift from oppression to freedom.

It remains to be seen whether Orbán has purely political reasons in doing so—namely, to unite a broad right wing party in the hope of forging a two-party system—or if this is simply the style of a strong political personality who thrives on conflict. The broader question with which we are presented is whether or not postcommunist democracies can remain liberal ones without cultivating their consensus elements.

An empirical answer is provided by Hungary's new administration. Since the summer of 1998, when it officially opted for a majoritarian model, hardly any of the liberal features of our system have remained untouched.

Executive power and even the volume of actual state property started to grow. A more or less open war has been declared against any and all autonomous or self-governing social services and public and civil institutions, whether created by the spirit of consensus or antimajoritarian by the book: the controlling function of Parliament, the prosecution system, social security, the judiciary, trade unions, trade chambers, endowments of artists, the press—be it publicly or privately owned—and even soccer alliances. "Opposition" municipalities feel punished by resource-allocation mechanisms. Rights of the individual are reported by ombudspeople, victimized by the authorities' majoritarian moves. These include the illegitimate joining of databanks, condemnation of nontraditional churches, and a mad aggravation of the penal code—all features which were previously thought to be "eastern" in our liberal democracy.

Typically, it is the two-thirds laws that are at stake. Most features of the handshake have been secured by them. Neophyte majoritarianism consists of getting around them by applying fifty-one percent laws by fifty-one percent decisions and then heaping up the inertia of the system caused by an inevitably delayed correction of other branches of power.

Here is one example of how this works. The house rules prescribe a weekly session, since in Hungary a continuously sitting parliament has become one of the symbols of the revolution of 1989. During the communist decades, there were only four parliamentary sessions per year, each lasting only a couple of days—not more than a week's work altogether, in that gigantic building on the Danube, the biggest parliament in Europe after Westminster. In 1988, demonstrations forced the communist parliament to convene weekly and to televise its sessions. Recently, Prime Minister Orbán decided that it is sufficient to let the opposition show off only once every three weeks. But to change the house rules, he needed the support of two thirds of Parliament; that is, the consensus of the opposition. He changed the rule nevertheless by deciding in a simple majority, linguistic vote that the word "weekly" in the house rules is not a normative on the frequency of sessions; it simply describes the duties of the House during the actual weeks it convenes.

Can all this just be political style, and thus a viable alternative? I think not. Even a majoritarian-type western polity is based on the centuries-old skills of unwritten consensus. But postcommunist majoritarianism is not contented with a rearrangement of power in conformity with the rules of the game; it seeks to change the rules of the game as it goes. That could fill any country's political life with poisonous disputes about the abuse of power, as, for example, in Slovakia under the regime of Vladimir Mečiar.

But shouldn't it be Slovakia's experience precisely that fills us with optimism? Doesn't Slovakia's case prove that the liberal qualities of democratic foundations cannot be lost? The answer is dependent on how we assess the spectacular liberal breakthrough of the past decade.

One possibility is that the "contractual state" has been Hungary's very own way to liberal democracy. Although the founding fathers used western patterns, they did so by popular demand. The success of consensus politics—the handshake tradition—means that Eastern Europe is not only capable of liberal democracy but actually will recreate it despite any loss. Illiberal majoritism will prove to be a short interlude.

The other, less optimistic scenario is that liberal democracy was a mirage of 1989, the illusion of the generation of founding fathers. Consensus was rather dictated by the mutual weaknesses of the parties involved. Constitutional self-restraint is a laboratory experiment, not viable in the longer run. In this case, it is Eastern European social reality itself that pulls Central European polity back after the decade of the handshake. Following this scenario, we will sink into the ocean of illiberal democracies east of Eden.

Each should decide for oneself. We certainly are at the crossroads.

One thing is sure: If the handshake tradition is lost, "Central" Europe loses its tiny edge over "Eastern" Europe. Claiming "a more resolute enforcement of the majority principle" is a bad pretext. This is not England; people still understand Russian here and know that "Bolshevik" meant an originally credible devotion to the majority principle. In 1933 and in 1948, this region "democratically" liquidated democracy. In several countries of the postcommunist region, it is a majoritarian, brownish, or reddish system that silences the press and the opposition.

Therefore my conclusion: Under postcommunist circumstances, unlike in the more established western democracies, there is no "free choice" between consensus politics and its technically equivalent alternatives that theoretically also could be conducive to a liberal system. Here, democracy cannot be of a "western quality"—that is, liberal— without a rigorously fostered tradition of consensus.

15 *Politics and Freedom*

IVAN VEJVODA

"Our people are not politically educated, which is no reason for surprise; since political education is arrived at through the prolonged use of social and political rights and freedoms, and is fostered by schools and books. Only it is terrible to even contemplate for how long the Serbian people have been alienated from not only political but also human rights and liberties, how many obstacles the people have had to confront on the political terrain in these parts of the world when they have more or less recovered their long lost liberty, and how few good schools, honest teachers and good books they have had in the past. Until social and political education reaches the majority of the people, until then they will not be free and autonomous, and their inner liberty will be constantly exposed and a permanent prey to power mongers and to state cunning and art. Until this is achieved there shall be no spirit of freedom, without which there can be no true social and political freedom."

These few succinct thoughts, written by Nastas Petrović and published in Belgrade in 1872 in a short preface to his translation of Alexis de Tocqueville's "Democracy in America",[1] do not solely depict the problem of modern day freedom and modern politics in the country where they were published. In spite of individual efforts (such as those of Petrović) and collective desires for freedom, peace, and stability, historical ebbs and flows have given precedence to wars, invasions, and occupations, to the absence of possibilities for rational and efficient economic development, for the creation of a stable state with consolidated democratic institutions, rules, and procedures. Thus, in these societies, such a state of affairs has been created whereby civic and political rights and freedoms, a free and open public sphere in which there are competing social, economic, and political visions, programs, and projects, seem to be a more or less distant prospect.

Nonetheless, for a long time in this geographic area there has also been awareness that without civic and political liberties, there can be no spirit of freedom to foster the appearance of a democratic political culture and, linked to it, social and other improvements. It seems, though, that we are in many ways as distant from those goals as we were in the latter part of the nineteenth century, at the time of Nastas Petrović.

The historical experience of the twentieth century has been one of two attempts to return to undifferentiated communities and to recreate homogeneous collectivist societies. Beyond their mutual lesser or greater differences, Nazism and communism were both regimes in which the key dividing line for modern democratic politics between state and civil society was obliterated and its appearance impeded. This antimodern or conservative tendency created (in the case of communism) a regime based on the idea that there existed a true theory of history, that in secular matters one could rationally orient social life, and that leadership in political, social, and economic affairs should be delegated to the experts of that theory, technicians of that particular rationality—that is, to the communist party, and within the party to (in Stalin's words) the "coryphaeae of Marxism-Leninism". Such a worldview led to an extreme and all-encompassing retrograde development of society.

The decade-long establishment of democratic institutions, rules, and procedures in the countries of Central and Eastern Europe has not been able to change overnight what communist rule and its totalitarian logic (C. Lefort) had accomplished in transforming the political, social, and civil behavior of individuals during its many decades of existence.

In a polemic conducted between Joseph Brodsky and Václav Havel under the revealing title "Post-Communist Nightmare" the debate centered on the heritage of communism and the participation of large strata of society in the support and legitimization of the *ancien régime*. While Havel stressed the fact that communism had been imported, imposed on the people, and thus was foreign to these societies, Brodsky retorted: "True our particular [commun]-ism wasn't conceived on the banks of the Volga or the Vltava, and the fact that it blossomed there with a unique vigor doesn't bespeak our soil's exceptional fertility, for it blossomed in different latitudes and extremely diverse cultural zones with equal intensity. This suggests not so much an imposition of something, but our -ism's rather organic, not to say universal, origins". And, pleading for an understanding of the roots of people's acceptance of communism in these societies, Brodsky underscored: "And if self-examination is unlikely (why should what's been avoided under duress be done at leisure?), then at least the myth of imposition should be dispelled...Why don't we simply start admitting that an extraordinary anthropological backslide has taken place in our world in this century, regardless of who or what triggered it? That it involved masses acting in their self-interest and, in the process of doing so, reducing their common denominator to the moral minimum? And that the masses' self-interest—stability of life and its standards, similarly reduced—has been attained at the expense of other masses, albeit numerically inferior? Hence the number of dead?"[2]

To contemplate the possibility of democracy in postcommunist societies means foremost to confront the problem of understanding why and how the longevity of such a regime was at all possible. Without studying the macro- and micro-physics (M. Foucault) of communist power, the unrelentless instrumentalization and manipulation of politics, the manner in which a legitimation basis for the regime was assured, the sense of social security the regime created by anaesthetizing the need for what had been known since the ancients as *vita activa*—that is, for an active participation in public life for the common good and general interest—there is no understanding of the difficulties and pitfalls confronting the democratic invention. This is a process that, along with the creation of institutions, should enable the "reanimation" of a society whose social fabric, social bonds had decomposed and been rendered impotent.

The indifference expressed by large parts of the populations in the Central and East European countries during the final years of the communist regime's existence consciously or unconsciously sustained self-exclusion from public affairs coupled with the ban placed by the regimes on any "real" political activity—that is, on participation in decision-making processes dealing with crucial questions pertaining to the nature and type of regime in which individuals would like to live. On the other hand, in certain countries existing political energies were oriented toward new/old orthodoxies of a nationalist kind and thus again were diverted from questions of individual and societal freedom, of political liberty, civic rights, and democracy.

Hence, to a greater or lesser extent, societies exiting communism are disabled societies. The capacities of individuals, groups, and associations of society as a whole vis-à-vis the state and all its forms of rule and power and politics are still weak at many levels. This general remark should be tempered by stating that the experiences of, for example, Albania, Azerbaijan, or Georgia are not those of the Czech Republic, Hungary, or Poland. The object of this paper is not to dwell on this otherwise necessary analytical approach to differences appearing among each of the individual countries in Central and Eastern Europe and the former Soviet Union in the past ten years since 1989.

We are witnessing in the former Yugoslavia and in some of the successor states renewed attempts at realizing homogeneous, undifferentiated communities based on ethnic criteria. The reappearance of the need for transcendental determinations of power testifies to the reappearance of the need for new certainties—this time not divine or communist-teleological, but ethnic; certainties seen as the safe haven away from the cold winds, high seas, and uncertainties brought forth by a nascent democracy and a mixed/market economy as an open, unlimited field for the actions of individuals, the expression of their aspirations, and a "well-understood interest" (Tocqueville).

What we have today in the case of ethnically or nationally driven politics is that rulers, this time legitimately elected in more or less free elections (an important issue that cannot be dealt with here), are again concentrating all political and state prerogatives into their own hands and are making decisions concerning the destinies of whole societies while marginalizing parliaments, public opinion, and other key intermediary institutions. They present this as being in the utmost national interest. Society has weak forces to resist; it has little capacity to articulate the evident but unexpressed demand for a return to something one could conditionally and rather simply name a return to normal life. The degree of uncertainty that reigns everyday life, the fear that exists because of the possible worsening of circumstances and of institutions of power (a fear inherited from the *ancien régime*), the insecurity that arises from this situation at the individual, group, and collective level incapacitate the appearance and germination of forms and dynamics of a new noninstrumental pattern of political action.

The result of these processes is a combination of the consequences of modernization at the level of the individual combined with the negative political legacy of the *ancien régime*. In the communist regime of the former Yugoslavia a respectable level of modernization of social and economic life was achieved, albeit under a soft version of totalitarianism. A level of inclusion in international economic and cultural currents was attained, but without the essence of modernity—that is, democracy, democratic institutions, rules and procedures, and an amnesia of the otherwise meager democratic traditions of the past. What remained was an awareness of the existing "liberty of the moderns" (B. Constant). Modern liberty entailed that the individual could pursue one's self-interest without coercion to engage in public (political) affairs. Ancient democracy fostered active public engagement as the utmost virtue. After the modern democratic revolutions, the forging of a democratic political culture and democratic institutions along with the progressive development of forms of representative democracy, individuals were freed of the need to constantly be active and vigilant concerning public affairs. This enabled them to concentrate their energies on other nonpolitical spheres of activity. What occurred was the differentiation and relative autonomization of social spheres of activity. In communist regimes, though, there was no such parallel development. On the contrary, the sphere of the political remained outside the reach of the common mortal, who was nonetheless able to pursue self-interest (depending on the country) to variously limited degrees.

This situation and experience of politics—in which the individual was forcefully "politicized" through the party and its transmissions and harnessed to the project of creating a "new community", a new homogenized collectivity on the basis of the creation of a "new man"—substantively determined the relationship of individuals to politics and the political. The devastating influence of these processes and of that experience can be seen today when a renewed pattern of *vita activa* and *vivere civile* is indispensable to the opening and "rehabilitation" of society, in view of a dynamic that will create spaces for political and public liberty for the benefit of the common good.

We are witnesses to a state of pervasive anomie, apathy and "minding one's own business"—all with the aim of preserving oneself from the destructive forces of the present. It is the "liberty of the moderns" that is being practiced without the existence of the other half of modernity, without the *Sittlichkeit* (Hegel) of democracy. There are no stable guarantees for that "modern liberty" in a situation where under a type of authoritarianism certain spaces of liberty are allowed, but where the need for enlarging spaces of political and public freedom is not recognized or tolerated. On the contrary, the degree of attained freedom is being curtailed. Many individuals tend to protect themselves by concentrating on (retreating into?) their professions, attempting in an oblique manner to contribute to the emergence of autonomous spaces or spheres of activity in which the manipulative aspect of politics cannot penetrate and from which at some hypothetical point there could occur feedback—in an as yet unclear way—into processes for the forging of new, more rational forms of politics.

There is a sense of fear and apprehension concerning involvement in politics because it is thought that not only will there be a "dirtying of hands", but that any such direct present engagement might impede the emergence of political rationality through its tainting by political instrumentalization. It is in this way that the urgent endeavors of the present are being delayed and the furthering of political modernity is being retarded.

In 1819 Benjamin Constant noted: "Individual liberty ...is the true modern liberty. Political liberty is its guarantee, consequently political liberty is indispensable". But a little further he admonishes:

> "The danger of modern liberty is that, absorbed in the enjoyment of our private independence, and in the pursuit of our particular interests, we should surrender

our right to share in political power too easily. The holders of authority are only too anxious to encourage us to do so. They are so ready to spare us all sorts of troubles, except those of obeying and paying! They will say to us: what, in the end, is the aim of your efforts, the motive of your labors, the object of all your hopes? Is it not happiness? Well, leave this happiness to us and we shall give it to you. No, Sirs, we must not leave it to them. No matter how touching such a tender commitment may be, let us ask the authorities to keep within their limits. Let them confine themselves to being just. We shall assume the responsibility of being happy for ourselves. Could we be made happy by diversions, if these diversions were without guarantees? And where should we find guarantees, without political liberty? To renounce it...would be a folly like that of a man who, because he only lives on the first floor, does not care if the house itself is built on sand."[3]

Disregarding the other differences existing between Constant's frame of reference and that of postcommunism, on which we are focusing here, clearly there can be no liberty for the individual, no lasting freedom to meaningfully engage in one's own life and professional activity without guaranteed political liberty that presupposes a free public sphere. It is illusory to believe that only by engaging in the "liberty of the moderns", without the underpinnings of a meaningful politics, there can be any substantive improvement at the individual or more general societal level. Similar warnings were being voiced in Constant's time by Tocqueville in his considerations on the role of individualism in modern society.[4]

It is evident to anyone who does not view social processes in postcommunism in a simplified or schematic way that the renewal (forging) of politics, the "ennobling of democracy",[5] the redignifying of politics, requires vigorous efforts, a prolonged period of state and societal stability, and a certain level of economic prosperity and certainty.

The legacy of communism[6] is present in a capillary form in many social domains, but the changes brought about by 1989, the new spaces of freedom with its difficulties and challenges, have given postcommunist societies a chance to engage in the process of uncovering and inventing solutions for their present and near future on the basis of existing democratic models and prior historical experiences.

The velvet revolutions and velvet divorce (Czechoslovakia), the period of velvet restorations,[7] and all subsequent alternations in power are a testimony to the great changes and to the difficult rooting of a modern political dynamic over the past decade. In several postcommunist countries, parties that were communist before 1989 came back to power and were then defeated. The difference is that they ruled without having reinstated a communist regime after their return and by adapting to the new pluralist order within which they had competed for power in elections

and won. Adam Michnik warned that "although restorations do not rein-
state the old order, they may provoke gangrenes within democracy".[8]
Gangrenes are of course possible, especially if "power mongers and state
cunning" (Petrović)[9] take over the whole space of political activity and
monopolize key segments of the public sphere such as the media. Society
and the individuals that constitute it, even in the darkest of times, endeavor to live their "independent" lives as best they can, but if there is
not even minimal awareness or energy to engage publicly and voice
grievances and demands for greater freedoms and rights, for the respect
of the common and individual good, then social and political dynamics
are stifled and new openings are put off for an undefined future.

In her book on people in dark times, Hannah Arendt wrote: "History
knows many periods of dark times in which the public realm has been
obscured and the world becomes so dubious that people have ceased to
ask any more of politics than that it show due consideration for their vital
interests and personal liberty".[10] The situation today is in some ways
similar. The spirit of freedom, which is the framework for a stable peace
and for the possibility of furthering individual and social existence, can
exist if the bases of political rights and freedom and a democratic political culture can start putting down roots. Without it there is no prolonged
freedom for the (modern) individual. War and violence (whether of state
or social origin) are in every sense destructive elements for any normali-
zation of political processes and a renewal of politics. Arendt in the same
text stresses that those who have lived in such dark times are inclined to
despise the public realm "in order to arrive at mutual understandings
with their fellow men without regard for the world that lies between
them" and concludes, "in such times, if things turn out well, a special
kind of humanity develops".[11]

Maybe dark times, experiences of extreme suffering, bring forth an
understanding that through friendship and survival a path leads to a renewed *vivere civile*, to civility and democracy. There is no straight road,
but a constant reinvention of the least damaging route towards a tolerant
and decent society.

Notes

1 A. Tokvilj, *O demokratiji u Americi, Drzavna stamparija* (Belgrade, 1872), II-III.
2 Václav Havel, "The Post-Communist Nightmare", *New York Review of Books* (27
   May 1993); Joseph Brodsky and Václav Havel, "The Post-Communist Nightmare—
   An Exchange", *New York Review of Books* (17 February 1994): 29.

3 B. Constant, "The Liberty of the Ancients Compared with that of the Moderns", in *Political Writings*, ed. B. Constant (Cambridge: Cambridge University Press, 1988), 323, 326.

4 A. de Tocqueville, *De la democratie en Amerique* Volume II (Vrin, 1990), 93–117, 263–70.

5 T. Pangle, *The Ennobling of Democracy—The Challenge of the Post-Modern Age* (Baltimore and London: Johns Hopkins University Press, 1992).

6 Particular emphasis has recently been put on research into this issue. See, for example, J. R. Millar and Sharon L. Wolchik, eds., *The Social Legacy of Communism* (Cambridge: Cambridge University Press, 1994).

7 Adam Michnik, "The Velvet Restoration", *The East and Central Europe Program Bulletin* 5:16 (October 1994): 1–4, 6–7.

8 Michnik, "The Velvet Restoration", 7.

9 Tokvilj, *O demokratiji u Americi, Drzavna stamparija*, II-III.

10 Hannah Arendt, *Men in Dark Times* (London: Jonathan Cape, 1970), 11.

11 Arendt, *Men in Dark Times*, 11–12.

IV The New Europe: Prospects for Cooperation and Conflict

16 Electocracies and the Hobbesian Fishbowl of Postcommunist Politics

KAREN DAWISHA

All but two postcommunist countries (Tajikistan and Turkmenistan) have held at least one election that international observers have deemed to be largely free and fair. Fully sixteen of the twenty-seven postcommunist states have held multiple, free and fair elections. Yet at the same time, less than half a dozen countries have made sufficient overall progress toward a full and self-sustaining democratic transition to justify inclusion in the first rounds of planned North Atlantic Treaty Organization (NATO) and European Union (EU) expansions. And beyond that, in many states (Bulgaria, Croatia, Georgia, Moldova, Romania, Russia, and Ukraine) democracy has been so fragile at one point or another in the last ten years that we can speak of a total breakdown of the transition. Indeed, in some of these states, violence has not decreased, trust has not increased, and elections are treated by the population as an insufficient instrument for achieving the dramatic break with the past they feel is required.

This sketch rather begs the questions: What did we expect elections to deliver, and what have they delivered? In general, what does democratic theory tell us about the carrying capacity of regular elections in entrenching the habits, rhythms, and norms of democracy even when other features of developed democracies—like civil society, the rule of law, and a stable market-oriented economy—may be either absent or only emerging? By relying largely on minimalist or procedural definitions of democracy (as a polity in which the formal and actual leaders are chosen through regular elections based on multiple candidacies and secret balloting with the right of all adult citizens to vote), did we overemphasize and oversell their capability to build democracy?

One could argue that the procedural or minimalist definition works as shorthand, not because any or many democratic theorists believe that free and fair elections will in and of themselves both produce a transition to democracy and sustain it over time, but simply because such elections are unlikely to take place (and historically have not taken place) unless a large number of prior conditions are met, including the rule of law, the existence of civil society, and a democratic political culture. Yet in none of the postcommunist countries are all conditions fully present, and in some countries they are largely absent. We expected—or perhaps more honestly, we wanted to believe—that these other conditions would operate not as preconditions but as coconditions and that progress could be made simultaneously in a number of sectors, each mutually supporting the other in the so-called triple transition. In no other democratic country has transition taken place so quickly and along so many fronts simultaneously. We hoped that, given their unified desire to rid themselves of communist oppression, the postcommunist publics would unite like spokes in a wheel with an equally single-minded international community to move democracy forward.

At the hub of the wheel we placed free and fair elections, monitored by the international community, with electoral systems heavily shaped by consultants and advisors from Europe and the United States. But my argument is that in placing them at the center of the wheel, we hoped they would achieve more in the East than they had in the West: that they should not only reflect the general will, but shape it; that they could not only cement the social contract, but write it; that they might not only mediate states' interactions with civil society, but substitute for it.

Where elections served only as the hub holding multifaceted spokes together, as has occurred in Central Europe, where the triple transition has been largely successful, they have helped to promote, deepen, and regulate democratic patterns. But in many other countries, including those of the former Soviet Union, in which elections have taken place against a bleaker and starker backdrop, elections have not been able to substitute for, or stimulate the production of, conditions that are otherwise absent. Indeed, and most worrying, there is concern that good elections in bad conditions could even hinder the transition to democracy. As will be discussed below, do free and fair elections that elect gangsters, anti-Semites, and antidemocratic communists and fascists really help democracy? Can such elections equally institutionalize both democracy and its opposite?

Elections and Suffrage in Early American and Western Democracies

The difficulties and failures of some postcommunist countries are easier to understand when one stops to consider the monumental burden placed on these modern elections as compared with the development of suffrage and the electoral system in the United States and elsewhere in the West. In America, democracy was developed by a narrow elite that established the rules of the game by which an equally narrow electorate would choose its representatives. The elite was generally divided along a single socioeconomic axis, and the electorate, too, was highly unrepresentative of the general population. A stable two-party system emerged, fully capable of orchestrating the genteel minuet that was called American democracy at the beginning of the nineteenth century. Thus, in the 1824 presidential election, the first for which the popular vote was even officially recorded, John Quincy Adams won with a total vote of a mere 114,023—and this in a country that, by the time of the 1830 census, would have a total population of 12.3 million. The franchise was regulated state by state, but certain similarities existed among them. Lacking the franchise were all women (as a footnote, women had the vote in New Jersey up until 1807, but were subsequently denied it), all slaves, all Native Americans, all citizens under the age of twenty-one, most freed blacks, most non-property owning white males, most non-income tax paying white males, indentured servants, recent immigrants (including all Asian, nonwhite, and non-English speaking immigrants), felons, illiterates, and those unable or unwilling to pay a poll tax where levied.

The actual—rather than the purported or subsequently mythologized—principle behind the franchise until the end of the century appears to have been the minimization, and not the maximization, of participation in suffrage. Not until the twentieth century was there success in realizing the communitarian aims set out in the Declaration of Independence: direct election to the Senate was introduced (unlike direct elections for the president and the House of Representatives, senators were chosen indirectly by state legislators until 1913, when the Seventeenth Amendment to the Constitution introduced direct popular election), women were given suffrage in 1920, and the rights of blacks to vote without encumbrance (through the 1965 Civil Rights Voting Act) were given full recognition. This is to suggest that the interests of the founding fathers in establishing strong governance were at odds with the principle of universal suffrage. Yet it was the commitment to governance more than the principle of universal suffrage that explains the ability of

U.S. democracy to emerge as a rule-governed, stable, and strongly institutionalized system. One naturally wonders how the institutions of U.S. democracy would have emerged if all those groups denied suffrage until the twentieth century had the vote from the beginning. And it is also probably the case that U.S. attitudes toward the problems of transition in postcommunist countries would be more forgiving if we were more mindful of the tortuous path that this country itself traveled.

The wisdom exported to and received by the East from both the United States and the West generally has been that shock therapy could deliver the same big bang for democratic transition as it was designed to deliver for economic transition. But this notion is based on a revision of the rich and, frankly, anguished history of democratic development throughout the West. Writ large, that history has been reduced to the simplistic notion that democratic development was an unbroken chain of accomplishment in which a country's founding fathers reflected the general will of the entire population and established the rules of the game by which the electorate would choose them. Yet this history of "for the people, by the people" overlooks the fact that throughout Europe and the United States until well into the second half of the twentieth century, both the electorate and the elite overwhelmingly were white, Christian, affluent males. Divisions within the elite along a single socioeconomic axis produced a narrow, but stable, two-party system over time. However, even these systems did not emerge in exactly the way that current policy-makers mythologize. The gloss of uninterrupted and steady development forgets the U.S. Civil War, the glorious revolution in England, five republics with monarchist restorations in France, the collapse of the Weimar Republic in Germany, and the fact that democracy did not even begin to emerge on the Iberian peninsula until the 1970s. Historical amnesia may have served well the cause of the legitimization of democratic regimes in the West over time, but it is not necessarily the case that this amnesia is helpful as a guide to avoiding pitfalls in the same process for postcommunist states.

The narrow basis of both the elite and the electorate in most western democracies did allow, however, the conflict between the needs of governance and the desire for representation to be kept in balance by the mutual observance of rules, including the rules and rhythms of elections. The desire for expanded representation certainly produced protests and demonstrations, but not of an antiregime or revolutionary nature. When it did finally occur, the expansion both of suffrage and of representation of nontraditional elites and interests at the top did not destabilize any of these systems because of the mediating influence of electoral rules that by and large were regarded as neutral and nonpartisan. The systems were seen as functioning to provide proportional representation of societal groups within the elite and to aggregate rather than suppress the upward flow of demands. The fact that no western democracy operated an electoral system of pure proportionality means that the regimes were able to legitimize themselves even without pure proportional representation as long as the society trusted the state to operate on the dual principles of the rule of the majority and the noncoercion of minorities.

Democratic Development in Countries with Full Suffrage: The Hobbesian Moment

At the moment of transition in postcommunist states, they shared other interesting features besides emerging from authoritarian pasts. Full suffrage had been a feature of communist regimes since their founding, and the expectation that citizens would vote as a duty was deeply ingrained. Furthermore, the regimes' so-called "nationality policy"—most prevalent in the Soviet Union but adopted in different guises in Eastern Europe—had allowed ethnic groups to maintain their cultural and (occasionally) linguistic autonomy. Newspapers and books were published in multiple languages, "houses of culture" for ethnic groups flourished (albeit under strict political guidelines), and national leaderships and elites arose, many of whom gained surreptitious popularity for their ability to achieve symbolic victories in promoting ethnic rights while sailing close to the political wind. The suppression of economic distinctions in the name of egalitarian principles meant that when communist rule ended, classes expressing different economic objectives did not emerge. Rather, a jumble of ill-formed socioeconomic aspirations rubbed up against often more robust conflicts concerning national rebirth and primordial identity. Consequently, rather than a party system emerging along a single axis characterized primarily by socioeconomic splits, as largely occurred in the West, a cacophony of parties erupted in postcommunist countries with each party staking out a corner of a multidimensional, fragmented, factionalized, and inchoate party system. Moreover, unlike in the West where elites were fundamentally homogenous and cooperative as to interest, background, and basic orientation, elites in most postcommunist states were diverse and competitive—the case of Poland being more the exception that proves the rule. And whereas the West had the "luxury" of establishing core institutions before universal suffrage, mass political participation, universal education, and minority-oriented media outlets emerged, in postcommunist states independence took place against the backdrop of extensive popular mobilization that preceded the collapse of communism. Ethnic and minority groups were fully mobilized, widely divergent interests had full access to newspapers and media outlets, and the population at large was infinitely more aware of the plethora of choices available to them once communism collapsed. In general, they looked to the electoral system first and foremost as the place where their democratic aspirations for "full" and "true" representation would be fulfilled.

Popular and elite interests converged at the moment of transition; populations were ill-inclined to trust elites to represent their interests indirectly, and elites for their part were united only on the basis of two negative values: wanting to rid the system of the worst excesses of the authoritarian past and wanting to create systems that would be open to manipulation in the future. This consensus, based on negative values of high mobilization and low trust, led to the introduction of electoral systems that in general emphasized representation over governance. The absence of trust produced electoral systems that shared some basic features: for parliamentary elections, voting based on total or partial proportional representation rather than majoritarian formulae was favored in eighteen of the twenty-seven states, low or no (zero to four percent) thresholds were required for parties to gain seats in parliaments in eleven of the states, and the balance of power between parliaments and presidents kept the presidents weak vis-à-vis parliaments, with seven of the twenty-seven opting for parliamentary systems and thirteen of the twenty-seven giving parliaments complete immunity from dismissal by the executive. And of course, in the former Yugoslavia and Chechnya, where even these measures failed to attract the support of minorities bent on self-determination and titular nationalities bent on oppression, conflict soon broke out, serving as a vivid harbinger of the Hobbesian view that life without order can be "nasty, brutish, and short". The first impulse of postcommunist societies, therefore, was centrifugal: to construct systems that provided high degrees of representation, even if at the expense of strong government. Indeed, the very idea of strong government, associated as it was in the minds of the population with authoritarianism, was eschewed. Only in those countries where the communist party managed to maintain a strong institutional presence were single member districts and majoritarian formulae retained (Albania, Belarus, Kazakhstan, Kyrgyzstan, Macedonia, Tajikistan, Turkmenistan, Ukraine, and Uzbekistan).

Burke to the Rescue: The Emergence of Governing Institutions

Under the cumulative impact of multiple social and economic crises throughout postcommunist states, demands for strong government grew and popular support declined for highly fractionalized party systems that either produced unlimited numbers of small "sofa" parties that never got elected or put parties in parliament that would not cooperate in finding a way out of these various crises. Electorates wanted electoral systems to work to limit and aggregate the upward flow of demands; they did not want to see the Hobbesian fishbowl of their own societies reflected at the elite level. Public opinion in most states (the Czech Republic and Hungary being among the exceptions) increasingly showed a desire for stronger government, still elected democratically but capable of solving outstanding and critical issues. At the same time, elites who won majorities in the first postcommunist governments began to think of political reform that would extend and deepen their own grip on power. Once again, a convergence of interests set the backdrop for the next, Burkian, phase in which the principles of gradualism, governance, and delegative democracy would take precedence.

A number of reforms were introduced, all of which were designed to increase governability, while moving the transition from communism forward. The results these reforms actually achieved have not, however, always been in line with their intentions. Looking first at thresholds, in eight countries thresholds were increased with an eye to decreasing the impact of minority and extremist parties, magnifying the influence of centrist groups, and reducing the number of parties actually represented in parliament. Democratic theory generally favors the view that the fewer the number of parties (above two), the more stable the system will be over time, since splinter or "sofa" parties are less responsive to voter preferences (they have little chance of being elected and thereby influencing policy) in any but the most divided parliamentary systems. So an increase in the percentage of votes a party requires in order to have any representation in parliament (a threshold) was favored and supported by Western specialists in many postcommunist countries as a way of moving the polity toward a more stable, centrist competition among a small number of parties, any of which might over time form a government and all of which have an imbedded interest in playing by the rules. Between the first and second parliamentary elections, the average for thresholds increased from 3.9 percent to 4.6 percent, with higher thresholds for coalitions of parties also being increasingly employed (in Hungary, for example, a threshold of fifteen percent for coalitions was introduced).

A second aspect of the reform process was the introduction of electoral formulae that rewarded winning parties by giving them a higher proportion of seats in parliament than the proportion of the vote they received. For example, pure proportionality would require that a party winning twenty-five percent of the vote receive twenty-five percent of the seats. But formulae exist and are widely used throughout democratic countries that favor winning parties by giving them a higher proportion of the seats than they "deserve"; once again, by favoring winning parties, democratic theory presupposes that parties, seeking the advantage of getting extra seats if they win the most votes, will move their message to where the votes mainly reside—in the center. Therefore, it is surmised that these formulae will both create stronger governments in the short-run and make them more centrist in the long-term. Thus, among the seventeen states utilizing proportional representation to elect some or all representatives to parliament, in the first postcommunist elections, nine used formulae that were more proportional, while eight from the beginning put in place systems that would give a disproportional number of seats to the winning parties. By the second round, only five states allocated seats using proportional formulae (St. Lague, Droop, and Hare); twelve used formulae that would favor winning parties (notably Hagen-Bischoff and d'Hondt).

A third aspect of the political reforms undertaken was the introduction of mixed electoral systems in which only a part of the seats would be chosen by proportional representation (PR), while another part would be chosen by first-past-the-post (FPTP) elections. The introduction of systems in which a percentage of the seats would be chosen through FPTP elections was also designed to increase the power of parties with a strong field of locally well-known candidates who could command majorities in their districts. Smaller ethnic groups would be disenfranchised unless they held a majority in geographically concentrated districts, as would minority political interests, both of which could still find a voice via the seats chosen through PR, but here parties that could field a list of nationally known candidates also could do well under PR. Clearly the dilution of PR was designed to decrease the influence of minority political and ethnic opinion and further stabilize the center.

Finally, in the balance between the executive branch and legislature, popular interest in decreasing the ability of "debating society" parliaments to forestall swift action by executives to ameliorate the collapse of people's standards of living led to the introduction of reforms to strengthen presidential authority vis-à-vis the legislature in some countries, giving presidents the right to rule by decree, call referenda, and otherwise circumvent divided and divisive legislatures under certain circumstances. Particularly in the post-Soviet states, the extent of popular dissatisfaction with parliaments' inability to agree on appropriate measures to resolve crises set the backdrop for popular support of increased executive authority, most notably in Russia in 1993, but also in Belarus, Kazakhstan, Kyrgyzstan, and Uzbekistan, where parliaments lost ground to strong presidents. Indeed in several of these republics presidents actually manipulated this resentment to roll back democratic gains.

Good Ideas Go Astray

If these were the intended results, what actually happened? To be sure, the introduction of thresholds decreased the number of parties represented in parliaments. The introduction of electoral formulae to strengthen winning parties in parliament did work to provide more seats to those parties. The use of mixed systems has indeed rewarded various kinds of parties, ensuring a diversity of representation.

But if one of the clearest intentions of these reforms was to diminish and eventually eliminate the organized and institutional power of "red" postcommunist parties on the one hand and their opposite "brown" parties of power on the other, then this clearly has not occurred. Early optimistic forecasts opined that communists' strength was actuarially limited and would "naturally" decline as young noncommunist voters became more numerous and voted for centrist and liberal parties. But then postcommunists came to power in Poland in 1993, and analysts had to reevaluate their forecasts. The glib view that this most anti-Russian of countries would never elect "real" communists (only the Russians were somehow seen as still capable of having an authoritarian communist party) was really only part of the picture. Did voters go to the booth and decide that they wanted to vote for the noncommunist communists? And if that was their preference, why not vote for any one of the centrist or social democratic alternatives? The answer is simpler: The electoral system had been reformed by the 1991 government with support of western policy makers to strengthen governance and ensure the emergence of strong centrist parties, but instead, the communists were the unintended victors. This occurred not because voter preferences changed that much; what did change were the rules that raised thresholds (ensuring that fewer parties gained seats in parliament), gave more seats to the winning parties (the postcommunists and their agrarian partners), and introduced a mixed system, which favored parties that had both a strong central organization and regional clout (the postcommunists).

To be sure, other elites and parties subsequently learned the lesson. The postcommunists lost the next election in Poland under the same rules and gave up power, but the point here is that these and similar electoral reforms throughout the area have had the unintended consequence of stabilizing and institutionalizing postcommunist parties. Electoral competition has indeed pulled them away from the extreme left but also into the ideational space where new independent and liberal-minded social democratic parties might otherwise have arisen. The result therefore is both that postcommunist parties are not disappearing from the scene and that they are preventing the emergence of a genuine social democratic alternative in most postcommunist countries. Additionally, the failure of postcommunist parties to disappear from the political scene (and even their resurgence in some—especially post-Soviet—states) has had the dialectic effect of keeping parties of the right on the map longer than expected. And these "parties of power" have also benefited from the adoption of reforms that favor strong presidencies, including in countries like Armenia, Azerbaijan, Croatia, and Georgia. And finally, because postcommunist parties are not declining in power, other parties— including both ethnic and right wing parties that are ideologically arrayed against them—are also not disappearing, even though their vote percentages might not be increasing.

The institutionalization of postcommunist parties, while not foreordaining the failure of democracy, nevertheless does little to strengthen the prospect of its success, if only because fear of communist revanche creates a point of poisonous distrust at the core of the system. Rival parties calculate that if communist elites could succeed in destroying the brick-like wall of interlocking structures that made up communist rule through their sustained abuses, they could certainly undermine what is widely seen as a more benign and straw-like set of democratic electoral rules. And in addition, few elites believe that under all circumstances communists (and, for that matter, parties of the right) would necessarily give up power if parties of the opposite ideological persuasion won an election.

This perception prevents, or at least impedes, the buildup of social capital—trust in the neutrality and power of the system to maintain itself over time. The multidimensionality of the challenge that the postcommunists present (socioeconomic, secular versus religious, nonethnic versus ethnic, illiberal versus liberal, anti-West versus pro-West, pro-Russian versus anti-Russian) also ensures that there is no single, stable,

or even coherent outcome of the challenge that can satisfactorily be predicted in the longer term in many of these states. Yet the legacy of oppression by the communists ensures that as long as they exist, no amount
of theorizing by western political scientists will produce the desired tendency toward a reduction in the number of political parties. Indeed, contrary to predictions based on democratic development in the West, in
some of the postcommunist states the number of registered parties has
actually increased and not decreased between elections; in the Czech
Republic, for example, the number of parties increased from seventeen to
twenty, in Georgia from forty-seven to fifty-four, in Lithuania from seventeen to twenty-four, and in Hungary the number of registered political
parties has remained very high at nineteen.

The Descent into Hell: The Divine Comedy of Electocracies in Postcommunist States—of Dead Souls and Wasted Votes

In states in which at least a portion of legislative seats is chosen by proportional representation and a threshold is employed, a certain percentage of voters will vote for parties that do not receive a single seat in the
legislature because they fail to win a minimum threshold number of
votes. In Western Europe, the mean of wasted votes for all proportional
representation elections in the postwar era is six percent—that is, slightly
more than one vote in twenty will be cast for a party that doesn't gain
any representation in parliament. However, in postcommunist elections
the average to date has been almost seventeen percent; in other words,
when citizens cast ballots in elections using proportional representation,
there is an almost one in five chance that they will vote for a party that
does not gain a single seat in parliament. The figure is alarming because
there is obvious concern that voters may not be willing to change their
preference by voting for parties that have a better chance of winning
(like the postcommunists); rather, they will either continue to vote for
splinter parties that fare poorly in elections or lose faith over time in the
power of the process altogether (while the average turnout for elections
has declined slightly over time, it is still well above western averages).
The seventeen percent of wasted votes, moreover, applies only to PR
elections, or that portion of the legislature chosen by PR in mixed systems. In FPTP elections, many more votes are cast for candidates who
are not elected, but voters regard the system as legitimate since, while

any given *candidate* may not be elected, *parties* in most western democracies do normally gain some representation. But in postcommunist states, where large numbers of parties also contend for seats in FPTP elections, many parties end up without a single seat in these elections as well. Consequently, the total percentage of votes wasted is far in excess of seventeen percent.

This trend toward wasted votes may be increasing and not decreasing. The more the electoral systems are changed to achieve "governance" at the expense of "representation", the more votes will be wasted. Two examples suffice to illustrate the point. In 1991 in Poland, elections were held using no thresholds; thus no votes were wasted. The electoral formula used—the St. Lague—did not give more seats to winning parties (sixty-nine were registered), so that when the Democratic Union won the most votes with twelve percent of the vote, it received only thirteen percent of the seats. By 1993, however, the electoral laws changed: a five percent threshold was in place (eight percent for coalitions) that led fully thirty-five percent of the votes cast to be wasted. And the electoral formula had been changed from St. Lague to d'Hondt, favoring winning parties, so that when the Democratic Left Alliance (or DLA—the postcommunists) won twenty percent of the vote they received thirty-seven percent of the seats. The Peasant Party received sixteen percent of the vote and twenty-nine percent of the seats, ensuring that with the DLA they were able to form a government even though they received fewer votes between them than the total votes that were wasted.

A second example comes from Russia in 1995, where of the forty-three parties on the ballot only four received more than the five percent threshold, producing a result in which a staggering forty-nine percent of the total vote was wasted—the highest number of wasted votes ever recorded in European postwar elections. The Communist Party of the Russian Federation (CPRF) received only twenty-two percent of the total vote, but thirty-five percent of the seats were distributed through proportional representation. When added to the seats the CPRF gained by FPTP balloting (including a large number of local bosses who ran as independents and only when elected declared their affiliation with the CPRF), it held a clear majority in Parliament.

Electoral theory assumes voters and candidates will behave rationally: voters will have a preference for voting for candidates that have a chance of winning, and candidates will adopt policy positions close to those of the median voter in order to maximize their chances of being elected. Over time, therefore, rational choice theory suggests that voters will stop voting for parties with little chance of winning, and parties at the margins will increasingly decrease their share of the votes as candidates vie for votes at the center. In a two-party system, any voter knows that a third party is an irrational vote, even though it may be undertaken for perfectly good reasons (protest, etc.). But in a thirty-four or forty-three party system, what is an irrational vote? How can voters know in advance how to structure their preferences? If they cannot know, given the number of votes that will be wasted, at what point does it become truly irrational even to vote at all? And if the median voter is a communist voter, or a Serbian or Croatian nationalist voter, is a rational candidate well-advised to move toward that median in order to capture votes? Does western policy favor reducing the number of parties to stabilize the system even if by doing so postcommunist parties and parties of power will further increase their share of the vote? Or is it not more likely that postcommunist politics in some countries may proceed not toward the center but away from the center, and candidates and voters group not around a unidimensional axis but around rather stable, yet multiple, groupings involving admixtures of ideology, regional identities, ethnicity, and religious affiliations—affiliations that are deeply rooted in the animosities and illiberal oppressions of the communist and precommunist eras and therefore are less negotiable than the socioeconomic status and associational identities more common in current western liberal democracies, but which emerged very slowly and with greater difficulty than is sometimes accepted even there.

Such centrifugal forces might be contained without overwhelming a democracy if centripetal forces are greater—including civil society; unifying norms, values, and institutions; a growing economy; and the rule of law. But even in western democracies, elections are not sufficient for resolving the most intractable centrifugal issues like those raised, for example, by the "troubles" between Catholics and Protestants in Northern Ireland, Basque separatism, devolution in the United Kingdom, the antigovernment orientation of the Montana militia, or by the demands for recognition by minorities and "first nations". Such issues have to be dealt with by multiple means at both the elite and societal levels over long periods. In many postcommunist states, and particularly in the post-Soviet states, populations still hungry for revenge, lacking in basic tolerance and trust, and unable to make the economic transition to a market-based economy combine with elites to undermine democracy. Under such circumstances, the demands placed on the electoral system are excessive. The carrying capacity of elections is not sufficient; they can assist in building democracy, but not substitute for it. The prospects are truly frightening; if communist elites could organize elections without any pretense of building democracy in the Soviet era, so can postcommunists and other parties of power if they choose. Does the international community assist in building democracy in, for example, Armenia, Croatia, or Kazakhstan by sanctifying an electoral process whose result is foreordained? Or is it not more likely that setting the bar so low on our definition of a free and fair election in fact gives dictators a smooth ride to an electocratic authoritarianism? Could electoral fraud of the kind seen in St. Petersburg's local elections be repeated in the forthcoming parliamentary and presidential elections? Will the cause of democracy in Russia be aided if the international community turns a blind eye in the interest of not wanting to be "discouraging"? Perhaps the question, therefore, is not whether or not elections will succeed in building democracy if other aspects of the transition fail, but why did we ever believe they could?

References

Bawn, Kathleen. 1993. "The Logic of Institutional Preferences: German Electoral Law as a Social Choice Outcome." *American Journal of Political Science* 37:965–989.

Brady, David and Jongryn Mo. 1992. "Electoral Systems and Institutional Choice: A Case Study of the 1988 Korean Elections". *Comparative Political Studies* 24:405–429.

Cohen, Lenard. 1995. *Broken Bonds: Yugoslavia's Disintegration and Balkan Politics in Transition.* Boulder, Colo.: Westview.

Dawisha, Karen and Bruce Parrott. 1994. *Russia and the New States of Eurasia: The Politics of Upheaval.* Cambridge University Press.

Dawisha, Karen and Bruce Parrott, 1997. *Conflict, Cleavage and Change in Central Asia and the Caucasus.* Cambridge University Press.

Dawisha, Karen and Bruce Parrott. 1997. *The Consolidation of Democracy in East-Central Europe.* Cambridge University Press.

Dawisha, Karen and Bruce Parrott. 1997. *Democratic Changes and Authoritarian Reactions in Russia, Ukraine, Belarus and Moldova.* Cambridge University Press.

Dawisha, Karen and Bruce Parrott. 1997. *Politics, Power and the Struggle for Democracy in South-East Europe.* Cambridge University Press.

Dawisha, Karen. 1997. *Post-communism's Troubled Steps toward Democracy: an Aggregate Analysis of Progress in the 27 New States.* University of Maryland: Center for the Study of Postcommunist Societies Occasional Paper.

Duverger, Maurice. 1954. *Political Parties: Their Organization and Activity in the Modern State.* New York: Wiley.

Elster, Jon, Claus Offe, and Ulrich Preuss. 1998. *Institutional Design in Post-Communist Societies: Rebuilding the Ship at Sea.* Cambridge: Cambridge University Press.

Gunther, Richard. 1989. "Electoral Laws, Party Systems, and Elites: The Case of Spain". *American Political Science Review* 83:835–858.

Huntington, Samuel. 1991. *The Third Wave: Democratization in the Late Twentieth Century.* Norman: University of Oklahoma Press.

Kettner, James H. 1978. *The Development of American Citizenship 1608–1870.* Chapel Hill: University of North Carolina Press.

Lijphart, Arend. 1994. *Electoral Systems and Party Systems: A Study of Twenty-Seven Democracies, 1945–1990.* Oxford: Oxford University Press.

Linz, Juan and Alfred Stepan. 1996. *Problems of Democratic Transition and Consolidation: Southern Europe, South America, and Post-Communist Europe.* Baltimore: The Johns Hopkins University Press.

Lipset, Seymour and Stein Rokkan. 1967. *Party Systems and Voter Alignments: Cross-National Perspectives.* New York: Free Press.

O'Donnell, Guillermo. 1994. "Delegative Democracy". *Journal of Democracy* 5 (January): 55–69.

Rae, Douglas. 1967. *The Political Consequences of Electoral Laws.* New Haven: Yale University Press.

Remington, Thomas and Steven Smith. 1996. "Political Goals, Institutional Context, and the Choice of an Electoral System: The Russian Parliamentary Election Law". *American Journal of Political Science* 40: 1253–1279.

Rokkan, Stein. 1970. *Citizens, Elections, Parties: Approaches to the Comparative Study of Development.* Oslo: Universitetsforlaget.

Rose, Richard and Christian Haerpfer. 1992. *New Democracies Between State and Market: A Baseline Report of Public Opinion.* Studies in Public Policy No. 204. Glasgow: University of Strathclyde.

Rose, Richard and Christian Haerpfer. 1993. *Adapting to Transformation in Eastern Europe: New Democracies Barometer II.* Studies in Public Policy No. 212. Glasgow: University of Strathclyde.

Rueschemeyer, Dietrich, Evelyne Huber Stephens and John D. Stephens 1992. *Capitalist Development and Democracy.* Chicago: Chicago University Press.

Sartori, Giovanni. 1986. "The Influence of Electoral Systems: Faulty Laws or Faulty Method?" In *Electoral Laws and their Political Consequences*, ed. Bernard Grofman and Arend Lijphart. New York: Agathon Press, Inc.

Shugart, Matthew Soberg. 1996. "Executive-Legislative Relations in Post-Communist Europe", *Transition* 2 (13 December 1996):6–12.

Taagepera, Rein and Matthew Shugart. 1989. *Seats and Votes: The Effects and Determinants of Electoral Systems.* New Haven: Yale University Press.

Wiarda, Howard. 1993. *Politics in Iberia: The Political Systems of Spain and Portugal.* New York: Longman.

Wilentz, Sean. 1990. "Property and Power: Suffrage Reform in the United States, 1787–1860", In *Voting and the Spirit of American Democracy,* ed. Donald W. Rogers, Urbana: University of Illinois Press.

Woodward, Susan. 1995. *Balkan Tragedy: Chaos and Destruction after the Cold War.* Washington, D.C.: The Brookings Institution.

17 *The Europe Agreements and Transition: Unique Returns from Integrating into the European Union*[1]

BARTLOMIEJ KAMINSKI

Introduction

No other institution seems to evoke so much controversy as the European Union (EU). Its administrative arm, the European Commission (EC) has been accused of excessive bureaucratization. Complaints about faceless, under-worked, and overpaid EC functionaries abound. The term "democracy deficit" seems to have become synonymous with the workings of the EC. Predictions about inevitable failure accompanied each turn of the EU's history including, most recently, the launching of the Euro on 1 January 1999.

Yet the EU has remained the most successful experiment in regional integration. The movement toward deeper integration has been slow but persistent. It has helped lay to rest the Franco-German conflict and has thus established foundations for European stability and economic prosperity. It has outlived other European attempts at integration, such as the European Free Trade Association (EFTA) and the Council for Mutual Economic Assistance (CMEA). Defections to the EU—first by Denmark, Ireland, and the United Kingdom in 1973, followed by Portugal in 1986, and then by Austria, Finland, and Sweden in 1995—have characterized the history of the EFTA. If anything, it has shown that the seven original EFTA founders opted for the wrong path to European integration. The six founders of the European Economic Community chose the right one.

Unlike EFTA members, CMEA members did not have the option of exit (at least until 1989). The CMEA produced neither stability nor prosperity; on the contrary, it only magnified the distortions inherent to central planning. Its collapse under the weight of accumulated economic inefficiencies in 1991 was welcomed with a sigh of relief. Despite fears to the contrary, its dissolution did not trigger economic catastrophe, proving its complete irrelevance to the economies of its member countries in post-cold war circumstances.

Due to its mere size and geographical proximity, if not because of its policies, the EU has quickly emerged as a major economic partner of the former CMEA countries. For most of them, the EU has always had the potential to be both their largest trading partner and their most important source of capital and technology. However, as long as politics determined their external relations, this potential could not be explored. With the collapse of central planning—that is, once external commerce was finally subordinated to economic considerations—the EU has provided their major market.

The initial stages of the transition from central planning underscored the importance of the EU to Central and East European countries (CEECs).[2] With the collapse of domestic demand, which followed the shift from a supply- to a demand-constrained economic regime, booming exports to the EU were the only bright spot for rapid reformers. The quickly expanding demand in the EU for CEEC products moderated the decline in economic activity and facilitated combat against inflation. Exports to the EU initially drove economic recovery. Improvements in market access granted by the EU helped CEEC exporters to compete with suppliers from nonpreferential countries.

Yet there was perceptible dissatisfaction with the policies of the EU vis-à-vis CEECs, despite the European Association Agreements. For instance, looking at developments in trade balances between CEECs and the EU, some argued that "the Community appears to have received the better part of the bargain."[3] *The Washington Post* warned about another (iron) curtain descending in Europe.[4] Václav Klaus, then prime minister of the Czech Republic, complained that the absence of "symmetrical relations based on the principles of equality...[resulted]...in discriminatory and protectionist measures that have greeted any success of our exports in Western markets."[5] Nothing short of a miracle could produce greater symmetry in EU-CEEC relations. Furthermore, neither has the curtain fallen nor have the CEECs acquired such a bad bargain after all.

These comments seem to have missed the real meaning of the European Association Agreements (EAs). The EAs had all the necessary ingredients to launch deeper integration. Modeled after similar agreements signed among founding members of the European Community, they in fact held the possibility for future membership. The process of policy-induced integration into the EU, which began with the signing of the first European Association Agreements by the then-Visegrád troika, demonstrated a unique feature when compared to other regional integration arrangements. First, it involved countries at widely divergent levels of economic development, thus representing the case for "north-south" integration. Except for the North American Free Trade Agreement and EU Southern Enlargement, there are no other cases of such attempts at integration. Second, it has created both the challenge and opportunity to increase the wellbeing of their respective societies, modernize their economies and legal systems, and accelerate restructuring.

But politics is about perception. By falling short of articulating the conditions for accession, the European Commission failed to provide adequate encouragement for postcommunist leaders to take the bold measures necessary to shift to new political and economic regimes during the first stages of transition.

On the other hand, it is not clear if a more activist EU policy would have changed the course of developments in CEECs. One doubts it, as reforms tend to be driven by domestic politics. Those who embarked on the path of reform easily obtained external assistance elsewhere. But proponents of rapid reform have enormously benefited from the European Association Agreements. Preferential access to EU markets was only one of these benefits; there were other, even more important gains related to the introduction of new economic institutions and policies. European Agreements have obligated CEECs to "modernize" many policy areas, including antitrust legislation and institutions, customs, foreign trade, services, the right of establishment, etc. They have also given reformers a convenient domestic political shield to pursue these policies. The business climate in those countries that introduced such policies has significantly improved, resulting in a surge of foreign capital inflows. Hence, analysts coined the term "the EU factor" to describe the special attraction of foreign investors to Europe Agreement signatories.

The EAs have triggered measures to liberalize restrictions on capital movement, opening so-called strategic sectors to foreign investment, and introduced other institutional measures toward meeting the requirements of the *acquis communautaire*. The overall impact of these measures has been the reduction of legal, policy, and regulatory uncertainty. This in turn has attracted new flows of investment, accelerated growth, and helped improve economic efficiency. The benefits of the sound economic policies that resulted from compliance with EAs have improved the CEECs' chances for formal membership in the EU.

The Returns of Integration into the EU for Economies in Transition

Politics has been at the core of European integration. Note first that the EFTA was merely a response to a much more ambitious project embodied in the Treaty of Rome. This project was based on the use of economics to pursue political objectives. Robert Schuman and Jean Monnet, the founding fathers of the European Economic Community, saw it as an arrangement that would make a Franco-German war not only "unthinkable, but materially impossible".[6] The solution of this problem could be achieved in the framework of broader European cooperation. The loss of some sovereignty over the national economy that is implicit in regional arrangements has since been regarded as a price worth paying for improved international security.

Furchart convincingly shows that neofunctionalist attempts to explain European integration driven by internal economic logic have failed miserably.[7] European integration did not develop through a process of economic spillover; that is, the integration of one sector generating through the demonstration effect the integration of other economic sectors.

While Northern Enlargement in 1973 and the EFTA's enlargement in 1993 admittedly were driven mainly by economics, political considerations were responsible for the Southern Enlargement of the EU. Preoccupation with the consolidation of democracy was at the core of the accession of Greece in 1981, and that of Portugal and Spain in 1986.[8] These three countries would not have met the economic criteria for accession had they been the only considerations. Their gross domestic product (GDP) per capita was well below the average of the EU, and it was clear that they would not be net contributors to the EU budget; on the contrary, they were net recipients of EU funds. It appears that the increase in spending from the EU budget was deemed a small price to pay for stability in these countries. Similar considerations appear to have influenced the EU's decision to initiate the accession process vis-à-vis CEECs.

Returns of "policy-driven" integration with a highly developed partner such as the EU are huge for the CEECs. But such returns do not come by default. Only a combination of liberal economic policies and the absorption of the best practices and standards used by EU members yield significant benefits to a CEEC. Although some of these benefits could be accrued as a result of commitment to unilateral liberalization, integrationist arrangements with the EU magnify them. Regional accords, even those limited to trade, enhance southern credibility in terms of commitment to economy-opening reforms and facilitate access to technology, know-how, and capital.

The accords do not have to have special clauses on treatment of foreign investment to serve as a credibility-enhancing mechanism: a domestic liberal regime lends additional credibility when a developing country becomes party to the agreement. By reducing the risks that foreign investors face and improving a country's business climate, they increase the flow of direct and portfolio investment, often diverting them from other regions. By the same token, these arrangements have a positive impact on the macroeconomic situation, thanks to the enhanced growth potential of a country—that is, higher growth of real GDP triggered by the larger inflow of foreign direct investment (FDI).

But the returns go beyond economics. Preferential arrangements provide an anchor to domestic politics by putting a heavy price on attempts to move away from democracy.[9] Both the EA and implicitly spelt-out criteria of EU accession contain political conditions. Moreover, with the adoption of the Amsterdam Treaty in May 1999, these no longer apply to acceding countries. The present Article "O" of the EU "constitution" will contain a new statement recognizing that the EU "is founded on the principles of liberty, democracy, respect for human rights and fundamental freedoms and the rule of law".[10]

The EU's Response to the Collapse of Communism

Notwithstanding its policies, the EU was deemed as the most important external factor for CEEC reform. For all of them the EU had potential as their largest trading partner and the most important source of capital and technology. However, this potential could not be explored as long as CEECs remained bound by membership in the CMEA and trade-averse economic regimes. With the collapse of both—that is, once external commerce finally was subordinated to economic considerations—the EU quickly emerged as their largest trading partner. This outcome was bound to occur with or without a network of special preferential arrangements.

The response of the EU to the collapse of communism contained two ingredients: assistance programs and preferential arrangements. An analysis of EU assistance programs would go beyond the format of this paper, but the package initially offered by the EU has been the subject of many analyses.[11] The general conclusion of these critical comments is that the big bang in Central Europe produced merely a whimper in the European Union.[12]

Indeed, the EU's first response to the demise of communism in Central Europe did not live up to the historical significance of this event. By granting General System of Preferences (GSP) treatment to their exports, the EU merely "upgraded" the status of some postcommunist countries to that of developing countries. Not all CEECs obtained this status during their first year of transition. Bulgaria and the former Czechoslovakia had to wait a year, whereas the Baltic states obtained it almost immediately after independence.

The turning point for progress toward preferential status was the EA (European Association Agreement), which went beyond a traditional preferential trading arrangement. Its preamble contained a clause recognizing that an ultimate goal for the CEECs is full membership in the EU. More significantly, however, it contained provisions committing CEECs to deeper integration. The following section begins with the discussion of the EA's contribution to the credibility of commitment. Then I turn to an assessment of the other benefits attributed to north-south integration that have transpired.

Institutional Change and Credibility of Commitment: The Europe Agreements and Beyond

The most important benefit related uniquely to "policy-induced" integration of a "poor" country into highly developed economies is that the former can become like the latter in terms of economic institutions and policies.[13] The effectiveness of an agreement to lock a country in a virtuous circle of economic reform hinges critically on its scope and depth, as well as on punishment mechanisms for exits.

The "Europe" Agreements—as they came to be called to emphasize differences with the agreements on association signed earlier by the EU with other countries—went well beyond narrowly conceived issues of market access.[14] They had several unique features, which have been crucial to the process of integration. For one, the Agreements have set up entirely new frameworks for economic and political relationships between the EU and its "European associates". They have also launched the accession process. Their preamble recognized that the ultimate goal of the CEECs is full membership in the EU. Moreover, the EAs were modeled after agreements among founding members of the European Community—a point somehow ignored in subsequent discussions of their significance—during their initial stages of integration from 1958 to 1961.[15] As such, they contained provisions for gradual yet full integration into the economic, if not explicitly the political, structures of the EU. By including provisions concerning convergence of the CEECs' economic legislation with EU standards, the "Europe" Agreements were more comprehensive than free trade arrangements. Although they initially fell short of granting EU membership (though the EU officially recognized this as a goal for the CEECs at the Copenhagen Summit), they placed the CEECs close to the top of the preferential pyramid of EU external relations.

Kramer argues that the provisions of the Europe Agreements, which are compatible with the 1987 Single European Act, do not set the path for CEECs to adapt to extensive integration along the political and economic dimensions foreseen in the Maastricht Treaty.[16] Under these circumstances, the issue of membership either has to be addressed outside the framework set in the Europe Agreements or its provisions have to be renegotiated. As a result, an extra barrier to the aspirations of CEECs is in place. Subsequent developments in EU-CEEC accession negotiations do not seem to corroborate Kramer's assessment.

The CEECs were expected to align the legal infrastructure of their new economic systems with the EU archetype. These institutional measures included, among others, laws on competition—company law, company accounts and tax regulations, banking law, laws on mergers and state aid, intellectual property law, rules of indirect taxation, and transport and environmental laws.[17] In this respect, the main advantage of the Agreements was that they might provide guidance to CEEC institutional transformation and incentives to implement regulatory infrastructures enhancing economic efficiency and growth. Due to their significant dependence on trade with the EU, the Agreements played the useful function of shielding some important institutional issues or policies from possible vicissitudes in the domestic politics of these countries.

This potentially positive impact, however, has been considerably weakened by the absence of a timetable and criteria for full membership, easy-to-use safeguards, and weak punishment measures for exit. Despite pressures from Central European governments, the Copenhagen Summit fell short of making a firm commitment. As a result, the Agreements set the framework for the new European order without, however, determining its future shape. This clearly contributed to CEEC uncertainty and reduced incentives to accelerate the transition process.

The EAs envisaged deep integration spread over a transitional period during which the CEECs would bring economic legislation to EU standards. The EA called for the establishment of institutions supporting competitive markets; hence, CEECs were obligated by the EA to implement legislation on unfair competition and antimonopolistic regulations that are currently in force in EU countries. The introduction of such measures had a three-year grace period. Legislation regulating state assistance and subsidies was to be brought in line with Articles 85, 86, and 92 of the EU Treaty. The requirement concerning its implementation, however, was even weaker than in the case of antitrust legislation. The EA allowed such reforms to be deferred by five years with the possibility of an additional five-year extension. In the meantime, the General Agreement on Tariffs and Trade (GATT) subsidy code would be used to assess distortions in market competition caused by monopolistic practices and state subsidies. The problem with this arrangement was (and still is) that GATT disciplines are weak, and the absence of these regulations has made CEECs' exporters more vulnerable to various EU nontariff actions.

Although the use of safeguard clauses concerning foreign trade policy was less restrained under the EA than under GATT rules, which link safeguards to ongoing liberalization, the EA has not deprived the EU of the ability to resort to its favored import restricting tools: "voluntary" quotas in the name of safeguards and tariffs against dumping. As Messerlin notes: "the safeguards provisions are powerful enough to reverse the trade liberalization aspect of the Agreements".[18] Many analysts predicted that this indeed would happen.[19] Hindley argues that the danger of reversal is there, especially if the CEECs sustain their export expansion.[20] But most CEECs sustained their impressive export growth performance, and except for some products, the EU has not "abused" exporters from these countries. Rather, it appears that the ramparts of "fortress Europe" have turned out to be quite porous, even for sensitive products.

Although first-wave accession negotiators—Hungary and Poland in particular—often resorted to various measures restraining imports from the EU and other partners, there was no massive reversal of trade-liberalizing measures. In hindsight, the value of the EA was that it assured a pretty credible commitment to trade liberalization, at least among first-wave entrants. Even when safeguards were used, these measures were applied on a nondiscriminatory basis. Overall, the EA and the power of the EU derived from the sale of around two-thirds of CEEC exports have restrained protectionist temptations in these countries.[21] On the other hand, the EA has failed miserably to discipline trade policies of such countries as Bulgaria and Romania.

Following the EU Council Summit in Copenhagen (21–22 June 1993), the scope of the EA was expanded significantly by including conditions for membership. These boiled down to one message: Those who want to be considered for membership must meet the "four freedoms" of the 1986 Single Market and establish functioning democracies.

Beyond the harmonization of legislation, adopting the *acquis communautaire* includes providing for the implementation and enforcement of legislative and regulatory systems, standards, and certification methods compatible with those of the EU. Hence, in addition to the adoption of some components of the *acquis*,[22] acceding CEECs would have to satisfy special economic and political conditions. Due to these political conditions, the Copenhagen criteria are substantially different from the general requirements for countries that previously sought EU membership. These criteria include: 1) stability of institutions guaranteeing democracy, the rule of law, human rights, and respect for and protection of minorities; 2) the existence of a functioning market economy; 3) the capacity to cope with competitive pressures and market forces within the single market; and 4) adherence to the aims of political, economic, and monetary union.

Explicitly linking membership to the consolidation of democracy and competitive markets was clearly a step forward. It had, however, two deficiencies. First, no timetable was set for a country to meet these conditions. Applicant CEECs simply had to provide evidence of their democratic institutions, market orientation, competitiveness, and commitment to other EU political and economic goals. Second, the Copenhagen declaration did not indicate which components of the *acquis* a country had to adopt, and when, to be eligible for accession. It took the commission another two years to address these issues. The 1995 White Paper finally identified the items in the *acquis* that had to be met by an acceding country. Its focus was clearly on components that would enable the internal market to function.[23] There is no premise, however, that all aspects of the *acquis* must be implemented prior to admission.

With the progress made in preparations for membership, the effectiveness of EU-controlled arrangements, in terms of their influence on the shape of economic institutions and policies, has significantly expanded. In contrast to earlier stages, the process has become bureaucratically structured and thus more predictable. It has also become more intrusive, forcing governments to actively look into the compatibility of institutional arrangements with the *acquis*. It also provides an opportunity for the extra push on reforms that would accelerate much needed adjustment and modernization of institutions and policies; consider, for instance, that responding to the *acquis* involves a painstakingly detailed examination of a country's regulations and administrative arrangements. It thus offered a unique opportunity to assess strengths and weaknesses. Screening, selection, and subsequent accession negotiations exert enormous pressure on a government to stay on course of reform. The requirements of accession—that is, adoption of the *acquis communautaire* and meeting the Copenhagen criteria—give a government extra legitimacy to introduce sound policies, provided it is committed to do so.

Has the accession, broadly conceived here as the process initiated by the EA, conferred stronger credibility on reform programs and facilitated their implementation? In general, for governments committed to the transition to competitive markets, the "EU factor" has offered an extra weapon to demonstrate their credibility of persistence in moving to a market-based democracy. The greatest threat to such persistence comes from changes in government policies in response to domestic pressures. If strong support for accession to the EU exists among the populace, the risk of jeopardizing it may offer the reformers an extra tool to stay on the course of reform.

The EU integration process has also facilitated transition in another way. Seliger notes that seeking accession to the EU narrows institutional development to simply emulating EU solutions,[24] but this is not entirely so. The EU does expect applicants to solve problems by institutional imitation to a degree, but only insofar as they involve issues embraced by the *acquis*. While this provides guidance to reforms, the danger is that, in areas not covered by the *acquis*, the wrong institutions and practices may be copied. There is significant institutional diversity within the EU, which embraces countries as different as Austria and Ireland or the United Kingdom and Greece. Thus, an applicant country faces a choice in its path of development. The bottom line is simply that the path chosen should not obstruct integration.

Some interest groups within applicant countries support accession because they see it as providing them with arguments in favor of copying not market-based policies, but its bureaucratic components. The latter include agricultural policies and social regulation. For instance, the Common Agricultural Policy attracts Polish farmers. Import-competing industries would like their governments to adopt EU-contingent protectionism. The problem is that bad practices are usually politically more rewarding. Their adoption in a country with a low GDP per capita may undercut its growth potential, as the case of Greece amply illustrates. Hence, although aspiration to EU membership narrows institutional choice, it does not wipe it out entirely.

The Trade Component: On the Path to
a Single European Trading Bloc

Until 1988 there were no significant differences in the access of European CMEA countries to EU markets.[25] The differentiation in treatment began when the EU established diplomatic relations with Hungary and Poland and signed nonpreferential Trade and Cooperation Agreements with them. The agreements set a 1994–95 deadline for the elimination of specific quantitative restrictions. But in response to the collapse of communism in Central Europe in 1989, the European Commission overturned these agreements.

The measures designed to support transition were initially limited to market access and were geared toward countries that moved fastest in dismantling communism. The major stipulation was the granting of GSP status, first to Hungary and Poland, and later to other CEECs. The demise of the east-west division in Europe initially led to a mere "upgrade" in the status of CEECs to that of least developed countries. No other attempt was made to help CEECs during their first year of transition. Czechoslovakia and Bulgaria obtained such status in the second year after the collapse of their communist regimes.

Access to EU markets by CEEC exporters was significantly improved by GSP status, especially for industrial products. GSP preferential rates embraced sixty-three percent of all Combined Nomenclature (CN) tariff lines in EU imports, and most of them (ninety-four percent of GSP items) were subject to zero rates.[26] This share was higher for industrial products and amounted to seventy-four percent—all GSP preferential rates for these products were zero. As a result, the share of exports with duty-free access almost doubled from approximately eighteen percent to about thirty-five percent.[27] Other measures included: the removal of specific quantitative restrictions and the suspension of nonspecific restrictions (excluding imports of agricultural products, textiles, and steel) in 1990 and 1991; the elimination of quantitative restrictions (excluding exports to the Benelux countries, Germany, and Italy) on steel and iron imports; and increases in textile and clothing quotas.

Thanks to these measures, in 1990–91 CEEC suppliers had obtained considerable EU tariff preferences over exporters from non-European OECD countries, and in many markets they had similar access to importers from Lomé Convention countries. However, GSP status had three shortcomings that rather substantially reduced its significance. First, tariff concessions did not extend to many products in which these countries seemed to have comparative advantage, including agricultural and chemical exports. Second, although GSP preferential rates embraced sixty-three percent of all EU tariff lines, many of these imports were subject to GSP preferential rates within limits, and above them to "normal" most favored nation (MFN) rates. Last but not least, the GSP status was subject to annual review, introducing uncertainty as to whether or not it would be maintained.

Even when assessed narrowly in terms of changes in market access, the EA was clearly a step toward increasing preferential treatment of CEEC exporters. Although in some instances its trade provisions narrowed the preferences enjoyed in access to EU markets,[28] it overshadowed GSP arrangements by retaining most preferential tariffs and making them permanent rather than subject to annual reviews to maintain GSP status.

The EU offered CEECs an attractive market for many of their labor-intensive products, but it is difficult to estimate the overall impact of the European Association Agreements. European transition economies inherited large distortions in their trade patterns, as they had significantly undertraded with the EU, and changes in their trade performance during the first stages of transition can be to some extent attributed to this. But, like the South European countries earlier,[29] they recorded market gains in footwear, textiles, and apparel. Interestingly, a majority of them initially gained most in products not subject to extensive liberalization measures.[30]

The EA had provisions that offered CEECs unrestrained access to EU markets for industrial products for a five-year period. In the wake of the conclusion of the Uruguay Round of multilateral trade negotiations and in response to pressures from CEECs, these transition periods were subsequently shortened. Consequently, exports of industrial products from CEECs already by 1996–97 did not face tariff barriers to EU markets. In contrast to earlier EFTA-EU free trade agreements, the EA provided enhanced access to agricultural markets similar to those granted to developing countries by the Lomé Convention and the Mediterranean Agreements.

But the importance of the trade component of the EAs—as well as the process they have activated—goes beyond the issue of access to EU markets. First and foremost, the Agreement has committed "European Associates" to open their markets as well, though gradually and over a period of ten years. Since hardly any political constituency has been in favor of free trade, this has been an important factor contributing to the liberalization of market access for the bulk of their imports.[31] This has benefited producers and consumers alike by increasing competitive pressures in domestic markets. Interestingly, this gain is rarely mentioned.

Second, because the European Economic Area established a common market for EU and EFTA countries, the latter had little choice but to negotiate free trade agreements with CEECs modeled after the European Agreements. Their economic objective was to avoid less favorable treatment in CEEC markets than that bestowed upon EU exporters. Similar considerations drove CEEC decisions to enter in agreements with EFTA partners.

Third, flaws that emerged in the trading system triggered a policy response facilitating further integration through trade. The emergence of such bilateral trade agreements created a very fragmented system of independent free-trade zones. The system facilitated commercial relations between a CEEC and the EU or EFTA, but it had two major shortcomings. First, it spurred the proliferation of a hub-spoke pattern putting spoke (CEEC) firms at a disadvantage vis-à-vis their hub (EU or EFTA) firms. Second, it added a new disincentive to trade among CEECs: although each had a preferential agreement with the EU and EFTA, intermediate inputs that one CEEC produced to be exported by another CEEC to the EU or EFTA did not qualify as local content. Nell notes that the system had become so messy that West European industry supported measures that would eliminate obstacles to trading across preferential zones.[32]

Over time, attempts to address these deficiencies led to the replacement of several independent preferential trade zones by a single pan-European trade zone. The EU Council adopted the so-called European Cumulation in July 1996, which set the stage for the formation of a single European trading bloc. Several steps preceded it. With the establishment of the Central European Free Trade Agreement (CEFTA) by the three Visegrád countries, a single trading zone replaced three separate zones, each with the EU. Next the EC recommended that other CEECs join CEFTA or sign free trade agreements with one another. Both the trade components of the EAs and the new agreements standardized the removal of tariffs and nontariff barriers, to be achieved by the end of 2001. Then a single pan-European trading zone will become a free trade zone.

Thus, the interim trade component of the EA turned out to be more important than anybody could have anticipated when it went into effect in March 1992. It was the starting point in a process that actually improved market access not only for the (then) twelve EU members, but ultimately for all other EU and EFTA countries and CEECs. This strikes as a huge return from integration.

Foreign Investment

Although the original Agreements had some shortcomings, their overall impact on foreign investment is quite significant. Some original drawbacks were eliminated over the accession process. Others lost their relevance once accession negotiations were launched. It would be difficult to estimate the portion of FDI inflows for which the EAs bear direct responsibility, yet their implementation has amounted to the promise of a country becoming part of a larger market, as well as providing assistance in the establishment of market-supporting institutions.

Yet the EAs were partially deficient in terms of creating an environment that provides satisfactory incentive for inflows of capital and know-how to CEECs, which are crucial to the restructuring of their industrial bases, for three reasons. First, with their rich collection of instruments of managed trade, the Agreements have offered back-door entry for those demanding higher levels of government intervention in the economy and encouraging a shift to managed trade.[33] During the initial stages of the transition, CEECs significantly liberalized their foreign trade regimes. Various provisions related to safeguard clauses, trade in automobiles and apparel (especially outward processing traffic rules), are a potentially major factor in the erosion of the initial commitment of many CEECs to free trade. Empirical evidence suggests that liberalization of foreign trade is an important factor in attracting FDI. The lack of stronger commitments to liberalization might have weakened the interest of foreign investors.

Second, the Agreements allow the EU to resort to protectionist measures, which in turn may seriously deter investment in the CEECs.[34] As for foreign direct investment, this contingent protectionism affects not only non-EU firms, but also those from non-EU countries. Although "there is no direct evidence that protection by OECD will in fact be a major problem for CEEC exports",[35] its possibility—sanctioned by the Agreements—influences investment, growth, and trade specialization.

Third, the rules of origin that determined the goods and services entitled to preferential treatment were rather restrictive, requiring at least sixty percent local or EU content. The rules of origin could easily be used as protectionist tools, influencing sourcing decisions by firms in both the EU and CEECs.[36] On a positive note, they provided incentives to EC firms to invest in production in CEECs, thus setting the groundwork for the development of intra-industry trade. Yet, since the initial stages of production often required the massive use of imported intermediate products and components, the rules of origin "effectively preclude many non-EU firms from establishing viable plants in the Central and Eastern European countries".[37] As a result, many potential investment opportunities were lost—a point of considerable consequence given the relatively large involvement of non-EU firms in investment in CEECs. Clearly simplifying and decreasing "local" content requirements would have had a positive impact on industrial restructuring in the CEECs.

Another weakness of the EA, also related to the rules of origin, was that imports from other CEECs used in exports to the EU did not qualify as local content (the so-called bilateral cumulation), thus discouraging CEECs' mutual trade. However, the Commission addressed this issue by first replacing bilateral cumulation with diagonal cumulation, extending local content to the founding members of CEFTA (the Czech Republic, Hungary, Poland, and the Slovak Republic). In 1997 a new system of rules of origin extended the common local content rule (the so-called European cumulation of the rules of origin) to ten CEECs. Consequently, intermediate inputs from EU, EFTA, and CEEC suppliers are accounted at domestic origin.

Despite these initial weaknesses, the EA-triggered accession process offered a number of advantages with potential for attracting foreign investors. Leaving aside higher investment attracted by economies of scale associated with access to EU markets, other provisions aligning economic regimes with those in the EU were even more significant inasmuch as they improved the business climate. The right of establishment of foreign firms as well as commitments to liberalize access to services, along with other provisions envisaging an orderly process of interaction between the EU and its associate members, serve as a credibility-enhancing mechanism.

Another concession—permission for CEECs to use a duty drawback—was a mixed blessing. Generally, free trade agreements do not allow each signatory to use a drawback rule—that is, refunding exporters for duties paid on imported inputs. Since tariffs may vary across participating countries, this might give an extra advantage to an exporter shipping its products to another country. The EU wanted to strengthen CEEC competitiveness by reducing the negative impact of CEEC tariffs and providing them with an extra tool to lure foreign investors.[38] Indeed, this provided extra incentive to investors from non-EU member countries to invest in CEECs rather than in the EU. An outside investor targeting EU markets and investing in a CEEC could save on import duties, since a similar investment in the EU would be subject to duties on the import of inputs. With some modifications, this provision remained in place until the end of 1998. In 1999, CEECs can no longer reimburse exporters for duties paid on imports, as the Pan-European Cumulation is based on a no-drawback principle.

Although the duty drawback mechanism in the EA has been described as an important concession of the EU, it removed the incentive for governments to lower their tariff rates to those in the EU. With the exception of the Czech Republic (the rates of which were close to EU levels) and Estonia (which had zero tariff rates for almost all products), CEEC tariff rates are significantly higher than those of the EU. As tariff rates on EU imports have been lowered by CEECs in accordance with provisions of the EA, the extent of reverse discrimination against nonpreferential suppliers (for example, the United States and Japan) has been on the increase. So has the potential for trade diversion, often to more expensive suppliers in the EU. They seem to have been the main beneficiaries of this provision, as high tariff rates kept competitors from non-EU countries at a disadvantage. Had there not been the no-drawback provision, protectionist CEECs would have reconsidered the option of lowering their MFN protection to EU levels instead of giving rents (gifts) to EU suppliers.

Impact on Economic Performance

The main returns from integration with a "northern" partner include institutional convergence, the enhancement of economic reform credibility, and improvement of business climate. These benefits appear to occur when a developing country that is already committed to a liberal regime becomes a party of the agreement. They increase the flow of direct and portfolio investment by reducing the risk that foreign investors face and improve a country's business climate. The enhanced growth potential of a country results in higher growth of real GDP triggered by the increased inflow of FDI. By the same token, these arrangements have a potentially positive impact on the macroeconomic situation.

How has the integration process affected the CEECs? In order to address this question, one may start by asking if the European Commission has picked up the most institutionally advanced negotiation countries for accession. These countries are in bold text in Table 17.1. Columns 7 and 8 contain scores prepared by a panel of experts to describe a country's attractiveness to business and the rule of law.[39] They can be used as a proxy for institutional advancement. Not surprisingly, the two are strongly correlated. Five first-wave negotiators are at the top in terms of both these variables, with Hungary and Poland leading the pack. While

Latvia is close to Estonia in terms of the rule of law, it falls well behind in terms of attractiveness. Hence, countries most advanced in establishing market-supporting institutions are also most advanced in the accession process.

Table 17.1 Performance of Central and East European Countries: Selected Characteristics

Country	GDP growth, 1998 (1)	Output recovery, year and growth rate (3)	Growth reversals, year (fall in %) (4)	Peak inflation in %, year (5)	Inflation rate, end of 1997 (6)	Attractiveness to business, scale 0 to 10 */ (7)	The rule of law, scale 0 to 10 */ (8)	FDI per capita, total for 1990–97 (in $) (9)
Albania	8.0	1993 (10%)	1997 (–7)	1992 (337)	42	2.8	1.9	106
Bulgaria	5.0	1994 (2%)	1996 (–10), 1997 (–7)	1997 (2,040)	579	4.7	5.5	130
Croatia	2.5	1994 (6%)	No	1993 (1,945)	3.8	6.6	6.9	245
Czech Republic	**–1.7**	**1993 (0.7%)**	**1998 (–1.7)**	**1991 (68)**	**10**	**7.2**	**8.7**	**761**
Estonia	**5.1**	**1995 (4%)**	**No**	**1992 (67)**	**13**	**7.2**	**7.8**	**693**
FYR Macedonia	5.0	1996 (0.8%)	No	1992 (2,100)	2.7	5.3	5.8	29
Hungary	**5.3**	**1994 (2.9%)**	**No**	**1995 (31)**	**18**	**8.0**	**9.3**	**1,489**
Latvia	5.5	1994 (2.1%)	1995 (–0.8)	1992 (1,445)	7.0	6.3	7.7	589
Lithuania	5.3	1995 (3.3%)	No	1992 (1,413)	8.5	6.2	6.0	202
Poland	**5.6**	**1992 (3%)**	**No**	**1990 (173)**	**13**	**7.8**	**9.0**	**405**
Romania	–5.5	1993 (1.5%)	1997 (–6.6)	1993 (317)	152	5.7	6.4	113
Slovakia	4.0	1994 (4.9)	No	1991 (74)	6.4	5.8	6.2	213
Slovenia	**3.9**	**1993 (3%)**	**No**	**1992 (88)**	**9.4**	**7.7**	**8.6**	**478**
Correlation between FDI per capita					–0.27	0.67	0.68	

Source: Derived from Havrylyshyn and Wolf, *Global Development Finance* (Washington D.C.: The World Bank, 1998); *Economic Survey of Europe 1998, No. 1*, (New York and Geneva: UN Economic Commission for Europe, 1998); and *Central European Economic Review*, Dow Jones, June 1998.

Total capital inflows to transition economies during the 1990s were quite large in comparison to other developing countries.[40] They were also highly concentrated, with CEECs accounting for more than eighty percent of total inflows since 1992 and the balance going to other former

Soviet republics.[41] FDI inflows show similar distribution. From 1990 to 1997 all transition economies attracted around $64 billion in FDI, of which $15 billion went to the former Soviet republics (excluding the Baltic states); $41 billion, or sixty-three percent of the total, went to first-wave accession negotiators; with other European transition economies absorbing $8 billion.

While all first-wave countries attracted more FDI than others (with the exception of Latvia, which had higher inflows per capita than Slovenia and Poland), Bulgaria and Romania obtained less FDI than Croatia. Hungary was clearly at the top. Considering Slovenia's high GDP per capita and superior geographic location, the FDI was surprisingly low.

What factors are responsible for this variation? Regional arrangements do not provide a full explanation. Such associates as Bulgaria, Lithuania, Romania, and Slovakia attracted fifty percent less than Poland, which is at the bottom of first-wave countries in terms of FDI per capita. On the other hand, associates are clearly at the top. Thus, the accession process is a necessary though not sufficient condition.

Institutional environment, the mode of privatization, and the record of servicing sovereign debt seem to be among the most important factors explaining the variation. Institutional environment especially appears to stand out. Using a vigorous econometric analysis, Garibaldi shows that the legal and political climate rather than macroeconomic fundamentals have shaped FDI flows to transition economies.[42] It appears that macroeconomic stability without a business-friendly environment is not enough to attract foreign investment. Claessens, Oks, and Palastri arrive at a similar conclusion, linking progress in economic reforms with FDI.[43] These conclusions find support in simple calculations of correlation coefficients between total FDI per capita from 1990 to 1997 (column 9 in Table 17.1), the rule of law (column 8), attractiveness to business (column 7), and inflation in 1997 (column 6). There appears to be a strong positive correlation between FDI and institutional parameters (0.67 and 0.68), and a very weak negative correlation (–0.27) with the rate of inflation in 1997.

The choice of the mode and scope of privatization as well as debt-servicing record have favored Hungary.[44] Hungary opted for privatization to an outside investor and opened the so-called strategic sectors (telecommunications, utilities, and financial services) to foreign investors. Furthermore, the decision to avoid foreign debt default put to rest the debate about the "dangers" of foreign capital. Privatization-related FDI flows to Hungary accounted for around forty percent of total inflows. Long negotiations on Poland's private debt under the aegis of the London Club kept investors away until 1993–94, despite the selection of a similar mode of privatization—albeit much less extensive in scope initially than in Hungary.

The EU integration project seems to offer an explanation why CEECs have obtained so much more foreign capital than the economies of former Soviet countries, as it has provided special opportunities in terms of exploiting economies of scale associated with access to a large market. But it does not explain the variation among CEECs, since neither market access nor provisions concerning the right of establishment discriminate across EA signatories; these are roughly the same. Such observations seem to suggest that EU integration is at most a necessary, but not sufficient, condition. It serves as a credibility-enhancing mechanism insofar as the government is committed to liberalization of the economic regime. And it also provides insurance against government policies that are potentially hostile to foreign investors.

No firm links about the benefits of integration can be established concerning macroeconomic performance. All first-wave negotiators adopted a radical approach (often misleadingly referred to as "shock therapy") to economic reform, with some caveats. The Czech Republic implemented a radical macroeconomic stabilization program but did not extend it to microeconomic restructuring. So did Slovenia. On the other hand, Hungary followed gradualism in macroeconomic stabilization but adopted a radical approach to microeconomic restructuring. Estonia and Poland followed relatively radical paths in both policy areas. The EU did not seem to weigh in these strategic decisions.

While inflation has been on the decline in all countries (as demonstrated in Table 17.1), Bulgaria and Romania, the only two countries that have yet to achieve a modicum of macroeconomic stability, still face triple digit inflation rates. Not all CEECs have been consistent growth performers (see columns 3 and 4 in Table 17.1). Even among the radical reformers, the Czech Republic, having recovered from the "transformational recession" in 1993, recorded a contraction in GDP in 1998. This appears to be the price for delays in microeconomic adjustment. Other first-wave entrants have been consistent growth performers and significant recipients of FDI.

Thanks to their growth performance, all first-wave entrants should be able to meet the Copenhagen criterion of adherence to the aims of the European Monetary Union. While not a single applicant would be able to meet the Maastricht "convergence criteria" in the near future, they all seem to have the macroeconomic underpinnings that assure price stability on a long-term basis.[45] These underpinnings include control of public expenditure as well as sufficient budget flexibility to deal with real shocks in a countercyclical fashion. In 1997 all first-wave negotiators would have met the public debt/GDP criterion, Hungary would have flanked on the fiscal balance/GDP criterion, and none of them would have met the inflation or long-term interest rate criterion. Both inflation rates and long-term interest rates remained stubbornly high.

Although it would be impossible to assess the value of preferential market access in terms of contribution to the expansion of exports from CEECs, it seems that the impact has been significant. Since CEECs undertraded with the West before 1989, a sizable reorientation would have occurred with or without preferential agreements. This alone, however, probably does not explain the magnitude of the increase. Consider, for instance, that between 1989 and 1993 the value of aggregate exports of the Czech Republic, Hungary, and Poland doubled. Between 1993 and 1997 the value of exports of first-wave negotiators roughly doubled again from $25 billion to $50 billion (Table 17.2). As a result, the share of the EU in their total trade turnover (on average around two-thirds) is now larger than that of many EU members themselves. Last but not least, exports of machinery and capital equipment have driven their export expansion to the EU.

Table 17.2 Exports of First-Wave Negotiators to the EU, Shares in Total (%), 1992–97

	1992	1993	1994	1995	1996	1997
Czech Republic	22	25	26	27	26	26
Estonia	1	1	2	3	3	4
Hungary	26	22	22	23	24	27
Poland	41	38	36	35	34	32
Slovenia	10	14	14	13	12	11
Total ($ billion)	25.1	26.1	33.0	43.8	46.2	49.8

Source: Derived from EU trade statistics in UN COMTRADE database.

Duty-free access gives an extra edge over competitors equal to the MFN tariff rate for a given item. Admittedly, the EU has an extensive web of preferential arrangements with many of its trading partners. Consequently, a number of preferred partners compete in EU markets on the same footing with products originating in CEECs. These agreements, however, do not cover such formidable exporters as East Asian countries (including China), Canada, the United States, and exporters with the potential to compete in many similar products, such as states that emerged from the dissolution of the Soviet Union. Exporters from these countries are subject to MFN treatment.

Conclusions

In one stroke the end of the cold war transformed the geographical location of CEECs from a liability into an asset. The dismantling of central planning has activated their reintegration into world markets driven not exclusively by politics but mainly by economics. The policy-induced process of "deeper integration" into the EU has provided them with the unique opportunity to shift to modern market-based democracies and simultaneously participate in European political and economic structures. Its notability stems from the full overlap of the economic interests of deeper integration into the EU with political and national security considerations.[46] This is a "win-win" situation for CEECs, but they have yet to capitalize on opportunities offered by EU integration.

In contrast to regional integration among countries at a similar level of development, which often entails economic cost to the participants though deemed desirable on political grounds,[47] the potential returns to integration into the EU combine both political and economic gains. The size of these gains does not depend on the EU's "generosity". It critically hinges on how a country approaches the integration process. When the process moves to a higher stage, the pressure on acceding countries to harmonize their regulatory frameworks not only accelerates, but becomes more structured.

The discussion in this paper gives empirical support to the findings of research on north-south integration. The conclusions are presented along the dimensions of potential returns to a developing country entering into policy-induced integration with a "rich" country or a regional bloc composed of highly developed economies.

Liberal Reforms and Credibility of Commitment

Policy-induced integration into the EU does not seem to have had a significant impact on reforms in CEECs. First, the EAs, establishing the process of deeper integration, were signed after CEECs launched their stabilization-cum-transformation programs. Second, the Association Agreements were devoid of incentives to reward CEECs for moving quickly in their transitions to market-based democracies. Rather, they offered easy exits and lacked a well-defined promise of membership. Finally, one finds both laggards and quick reformers among countries that have signed the EA.

For slow and vacillating reformers, the "EU factor" has amounted to geographical proximity and market access provisions. For instance, such countries as Bulgaria and Romania have failed to take advantage of the opportunities offered by the EA. They not only moved slowly toward implementing the requirements of the *acquis* driven by the EA, but also failed miserably in achieving macroeconomic stability and micro-economic restructuring. If anything, this shows the congruence of transition and EA requirements.

These observations seem to corroborate two findings of integration theory. First, in order to obtain high returns thanks to the enhanced credibility of reforms, a government has to be strongly committed to a liberal economic regime from the start. Second, the agreement has to be deep and extensive and contain transparent punishment mechanisms. Third, its initial impact works mainly through the "regional" liberalization of foreign trade.

Reduction of Risk and Foreign Investment

Combined with the additional incentives of improved market access, the EAs have probably stimulated foreign investment inflows. There has been considerable variation among CEECs in terms of attracting FDI. Market access provisions and those related to the right of establishment for foreign firms have provided an incentive to FDI. But the EA was only a necessary condition. Microeconomic environment friendly to private business, the mode of privatization, and improvements in the rule of law seem to explain the variation in FDI flows to CEECs.

Impact on Foreign Trade

Due to its size and geographical proximity, if not its policies, the EU was destined to influence developments in the European, formerly communist countries. For all of them the EU was a potential trading partner and source of capital and technology. However, this potential was not explored, and the members of the Council for Mutual Economic Assistance were their primary partners. With the collapse of central planning, the EU quickly emerged as their largest trading partner. This outcome was bound to occur with or without a network of special preferential arrangements.

Yet policy-driven integration has helped CEECs shift their trade to EU markets, despite the rather timid initial response of the EU to the collapse of communism. It offered exporters preferential status vis-à-vis MFN suppliers. Expanding exports eased the pain of transformation, led to economic recovery in CEECs, and generated resources to buy imports.

Improved Macroeconomic Performance

It seems that the EAs have had a positive impact on the macroeconomic situation, albeit only in countries which followed the path of radical reforms. Radical reformers experienced the fastest reorientation of foreign trade towards the EU and recovery of economic growth. Larger exports to the EU and larger inflow of FDI have contributed to higher growth of GDP.

Notes

1 The author gratefully acknowledges very helpful comments from Maurice Schiff.
2 CEECs here denote Central European countries, which formally applied for membership in the EU. These are Bulgaria, the Czech Republic, Estonia, Hungary, Latvia, Lithuania, Poland, Romania, Slovakia, and Slovenia.
3 D. Marsh and L Barber, "Morsels from a Groaning Table", *The Financial Times*, 7 June 1993.
4 J. Pomfret, "Is Another Curtain Descending on Europe", *The Washington Post*, 27 April 1993.
5 Václav Klaus, "The Ten Commandments of Systemic Reform" (occasional paper 43, Washington, D.C., Group of Thirty, 1993), 7.
6 Quoted in Maurice Schiff and L. Alan Winters, "Dynamic Politics in Regional Integration Arrangements: An Introduction", *The World Bank Economic Review* 12:2 (May 1998): 275.
7 Vincent Furchart, "An Analysis of the Logic of European Enlargements" (Paper presented at a conference, Bloomington, Indiana University, 14 April 1998).
8 Christopher Preston, *Enlargement and Integration in the European Union* (London and New York: University Association for Contemporary European Studies, 1997).
9 This does not apply only to North-South integration, as a failed coup in Paraguay illustrates. Presidents of Mercosur-member countries, acting upon a clause of the Treaty of Asuncion stipulating that democracy is a necessary condition of membership, threatened to oust Paraguay from Mercosur (*The Economist*, 12 October 1996).
10 Composite paper reports on progress towards accession by each candidate country (Brussels: European Commission, 1999), 3.
11 See, for example, Patrick A. Messerlin, "The Association Agreements between the EU and Central Europe: Trade Liberalization vs. Constitutional Failure", in *Trade, Payments and Adjustment in Central and Eastern Europe*, eds. J. Fleming and J.M.C. Rollo (London: Royal Institute of International Affairs and European Bank of Reconstruction and Development, 1992) and Patrick A. Messerlin, "The EU and Central Europe: The Missed Rendez-Vous of 1992?", *Economics of Transition* 1:1 (1993); L. Alan Winters, "Should Eastern Europe Feel Privileged with Its Limited Market Access to the European Community?", *Transition, The World Bank* 4:8 (1993); and L.

Alan Winters, "Expanding EC Membership and Association Accords: Recent Experience and Future Prospects", in *Regional Integration and the Global Trading System*, eds. K. Anderson and R. Blackhurst (New York: Harvester Wheatsheaf, 1993).

12 Winters, "Limited Market Access".

13 This should not imply transplanting all institutions, but only those that would enhance potential for economic development.

14 With the benefit of hindsight, it is rather ironic that mass media and many politicians in both East and West examined the EA solely in terms of market access, thus ignoring its larger significance. See, for instance, Klaus, "Ten Commandments".

15 Gerhard Pohl and Pirita Sorsa, "European Integration and Trade with the Developing World", *Policy and Research Series No. 21* (Washington, D.C.: The World Bank, 1992), 56.

16 H. Kramer, "The European Community's Response to the 'New Eastern Europe,'" *Journal of Common Market Studies* 31:2 (1993).

17 These institutional and regulatory requirements are similar to the treaty between the EU and EFTA, establishing in 1992 the European Economic Area. In a marked contrast, however, the Europe Agreements proscribe the free movement of labor during the first five years and, after that time, promise only an examination of the situation.

18 Messerlin, "The EU and Central Europe", 98.

19 According to this view, the EA has granted the EU almost unlimited opportunities to use nontariff barriers. See for instance Sylvia Ostry, *The Threat of Managed Trade to Transforming Economics* (Washington, D.C.: Group of Thirty, 1993); Sandor Richter, "East-West Trade Under Growing Western Protectionism", *WIIW Forschungsberichte No. 198* (Vienna: The Vienna Institute for Comparative Economic Studies, 1993); Jim Rollo and Alasdaire Smith, "The Political Economy of East European Trade with the European Community: Why so Sensitive?", *Economic Policy* (April 1993).

20 Brian Hindley, "Exports from Eastern Europe and Contingent Protection", in *Trade, Payments and Adjustment in Central and Eastern Europe*, eds. J. Fleming and J.M.C. Rollo (London: Royal Institute of International Affairs and European Bank of Reconstruction and Development, 1992).

21 For an extensive discussion of the impact of the EA on foreign trade policies of first-wave entrants, see Bartlomiej Kaminski, *Trade Policies in Central European Countries: Protectionist Temptation and the EU Facto* (Geneva: World Trade Organization, 1999).

22 Note that even today many members are not in compliance with all provisions of the 1986 Single Market Program. The Maastricht criteria are not part of the Copenhagen criteria, although the adherence to its objectives is. Nor has the EC indicated that these would become part of them.

23 The essential internal market legislation of the White Paper is divided into twenty-three areas. These cover the free movement of capital, the free movement and safety of industrial products, competition, social policy excluding the social chapter of the Maastricht Treaty, agriculture, transportation, audio-visual, environment (with certain exceptions), telecommunications, direct taxation, the free movement of persons, public procurement, financial services, personal data, company law, accountancy, civil

law, mutual recognition of professional qualifications, intellectual property, energy, customs and excise, indirect taxation, and consumer protection.

24 Bernhard Seliger, "Integration of the Baltic States in the European Union in the Light of the Theory of Institutional Competition", *Communist Economies and Economic Transformation* 10:1 (1998): 95–109.

25 The exceptions were Romania, which enjoyed lower tariffs thanks to its GSP status, and the former Soviet Union, whose exports were subject to more restrictive controls (Kaminski and Yeats, 1993). GATT membership did not make a difference because the EU conferred MFN status on all countries. CEEC exports were subject to the same tariffs as EU imports from non-European industrial economies, which, in turn, were considerably higher than those applied on imports from developing countries, or European OECD economies. Moreover, their exports were subject to restrictions imposed only on centrally planned economies. Because of the state monopoly of foreign trade, CMEA countries—including those which were GATT members—were defined as "state trading countries" exempt from GATT's Article 13 abolishing quantitative restrictions. See Andreas Tovias and Sam Laird, "Whither Hungary and the European Communities?", *Policy, Research and External Affairs Working Papers* (Washington, D.C.: International Trade, WPS 584, The World Bank, 1991), 15.

26 An important caveat is that many of these imports are subject to GSP preferential rates within limits and above them to MFN rates. As a result, their significance may be overstated.

27 Kaminski, "The Significance of Europe Agreements for Central European Industrial Exports", *Russian and East European Finance and Trade* 31:1 (1995): 9–48.

28 Inotai, 1993

29 Winters, "Expanding EC Membership".

30 Elzbieta Kawecka-Wyrzykowska, "Poland", in *From Association to Accession: The Impact of the Association Agreements on Central Europe's Trade and Integration with the European Union*, eds. K. Mizsei and A. Rudka (New York: Institute for East-West Studies, 1995).

31 There were some notable exceptions. Poland suspended tariffs on all imports for almost a year in 1990. Estonia eliminated them entirely, while the Czech-Slovak Customs Union inherited relatively low tariff rates courtesy of the concessions made by the Czechoslovak communist governments in multilateral trade negotiations of the GATT (Kaminski, *Trade Policies*).

32 Philippe G. Nell, "Extension of the European Union/EFTA Regional Trading Bloc to Central and Eastern Europe", *World Competition* 3 (1997): 131–49.

33 For the latter point, see Messerlin, "Association Agreements".

34 Rollo and Smith, "Political Economy".

35 Hindley, "Exports from Eastern Europe", 145.

36 The impact of the rules of origin on trade between the CEECs and the EU is difficult to assess. They provide an extra incentive to trade within the Europe Agreements "preferential area". The extent of trade diversion depends on differences in external barriers (Ann O. Krueger, "Free Trade Agreements as Projectionist Devices: Rules of Origin", *NBER working paper No. 4352* (Cambridge, Mass.: 1993). Since the CEEC

economies probably have a higher effective rate of protection, one may expect CEECs' importers to shift more to EU suppliers than vice versa.

37 Winters (1993), 13.

38 Nell, "Extension of the European Union", 142.

39 A panel of experts for The Wall Street Journal Europe prepared these. See "Central European Economic Review", *The Wall Street Journal Europe* (July/August 1998).

40 Pietro Garibaldi, et al., "What Moves Capital to Transition Economies?", (paper presented at the IMF conference, "A Decade of Transition: Achievements and Challenges", Washington, D.C., 1 February 1999).

41 It is interesting to note that Russia has been the only net exporter of capital among transition economies over the whole period from 1992 to 1997 (Garibaldi, et al., "What Moves Capital".

42 Garibaldi, et al., "What Moves Capital".

43 Stijn Claessens, Daniel Oks, and Rossana Palastri, "Capital Flows to Central and Eastern Europe and Former Soviet Union" (Washington, D.C.: *The World Bank* (1998).

44 Bartlomiej Kaminski, "Foreign Trade and FDI in Hungary and Slovenia: Different Path-Different Outcomes", *Transition* 6 (1998): 22–26.

45 The Maastricht criteria include inflation, interest rates, budget deficit, government debt, and exchange rates. Consumer Price Index inflation should not exceed the three best performing countries in the EU (3–3.5 percent in 1996) by more than 1.5 percentage points. The interest rates on long-term government securities should not exceed the average of the foregoing economies by more than 2 percentage points. The general government deficit should not exceed 3 percent of GDP; gross debt of the general government should not exceed 60 percent of GDP; and the exchange rate (ER) must be held within the normal fluctuation range of the European Exchange Rate Mechanism (ERM) for two years without a realignment.

46 It may be tempting to argue that NATO addresses the national security issue. NATO deals with binary situations: war and peace. Membership in the EU—an economic superpower, after all—provides both a powerful shield against the use of economic statecraft by another country and tools of influencing developments outside the EU.

47 Schiff and Winters, "Dynamics and Politics".

18 *Nationalism in Postcommunist Russia: From Resignation to Anger*

ILYA PRIZEL

"Besides ours, no other nation in Europe has such a peculiar understanding of its own past and present. No other nation's consciousness is torn into two halves, completely foreign to one another and utterly disconnected. Like us, all the European nations have experienced abrupt turning points in their histories, sometimes more than once....But neither pre-revolutionary France nor pre-revolutionary Germany is separated, in the eyes of Frenchmen and Germans, from their reality by a wall as impassable as that separating ancient Russia, according to our perception, from modern Petrine Russia....To this day we Russians are deprived of a unified national consciousness. Theoretically, abstractly, we understand that...Peter and his reforms were prepared...but all this somehow seems dry to us, bookish and dead; it comes into our heads somehow without emotion, like the result of a mathematical calculation. In our immediate living consciousness we continue to be split in two, and this half-heartedness lies like a heavy stone on our whole being and on all our endeavors."—K.D. Kavelin 1856[1]

Nationalism: The Ubiquitous Factor

The defeat of Nazism in 1945 divided the international community into two hostile ideological blocs and also provided perhaps the sole point of convergence between western liberalism and Soviet-style Marxism—the rejection of nationalism as a historic force in favor of a universalist ideology. In the eastern bloc nationalism was supposed to give way to class solidarity; in the capitalist West the spread of individualistic liberalism was allegedly to lead to the inevitable "end of history".[2]

The universalist notion of an institution-based liberal polity was enormously reinforced by the rise of the United States to economic, political, and cultural hegemony after World War II.[3] Although there was a plethora of evidence that the teleological "universalist utopian" approach to history had no basis in reality, a powerful intellectual orthodoxy constrained debate that might question the inevitable rise of what Jürgen Habermas called *Verfassungspatriotismus*, or civic polities devoid of distinct nationalism. The apparent success of the United States and other English-speaking countries convinced an array of thinkers ranging from Hannah Arendt to Charles Taylor that the acceptance of a common political formula can create a successfully functioning polity with no reference to either ethnic or cultural nationalism.

The notion of a polity based on a political formula devoid of nationalist tendencies was further reinforced by the ability of political elites, enjoying twenty-five years (1948–73) of uninterrupted growth, to portray themselves also as agents of *equitable* growth, reconstructing the image of the nation as an agent of social justice. Thus, the new political coin of economic and social justice enabled Konrad Adenauer to legitimize the Bonn Republic on the basis of the "German economic miracle" and "social market;" Harold Macmillan to legitimize Britain's withdrawal from the empire following the Suez debacle with the motto "you never had it so good"; and Jawharlal Nehru to forge an Indian state on the basis of the "Indian socialism" of the Congress Party. Explaining the sources of strength of a denationalized civic society, Michael Ignatieff noted: "A strong 'civic' culture depends on public investment and public services: schools, hospitals, roads, street lighting, police, libraries, swimming pools, parks. These are the sinews of a strong [civic] national identity. If these services deteriorate, three things happen: the wealthy secede from the public realm and purchase these amenities on the private market; they cease to be willing to pay extra taxes to renew a public realm from which they decided to secede; those who are left both abandoned and dependent on failing services are tempted to withdraw from the national project".[4]

The world economic crisis that followed the 1973 oil embargo triggered[5] a postindustrial age dominated by the globalization of services and a databased global economy. It also eroded the ability of political elites to claim political legitimacy on the basis of social justice, leading to a resurgence of ethnonationalism.[6] All industrial countries saw a surge of unemployment and a growing economic gap between those who could participate in the global economy and those who could not. High levels of unemployment had a minor impact on those adapted to the global economy, but fundamentally fragmented the "civic" based polities that grounded their legitimacy in social justice.

Political elites on both sides of the Iron Curtain, unable to cope with the postindustrial economic reality, resorted to harnessing nationalism as a source of legitimacy and social cohesion. In the Soviet bloc, leaders such as Brezhnev and Ceauşescu abandoned their internationalist ideology in favor of nationalist legitimacy.[7] Similarly, in the West the advent of the "global village" and individualism not only did not lead to the decline of nationalism, but also led to the strengthening of the reliance on nationalism as a source of identity and belonging due to the deepening atomization and anomie of the postmodern world.[8] Ignatieff, analyzing the political success of Thatcherism, noted that, "the more anomic her [Margaret Thatcher's] vision of 'society', the more important it became to her to emphasize the stabilizing virtues of national belonging".[9] The negation of nationalism as the central force in politics was a short interlude that lasted less than an intellectual generation.

Not only have most postcolonial states that appeared in Asia and Africa succumbed to nationalism as their main legitimating force, but even the institutionalized liberal polities of Europe and the English-speaking world have increasingly relied on nationalism as the underpinning of their respective political legitimacy and cohesion. For example, in Belgium the national pension fund was divided along ethnic lines among the French-speaking Walloons and the Dutch-speaking Flems. In West Germany, *Verfassungspatriotismus* notwithstanding, there was a willingness to admit millions of immigrants from the former Soviet Union on the basis of ethnic solidarity, although the Volga Germans had emigrated to Russia in the eighteenth century. The willingness of West Germans to spend trillions of deutschmarks on the rehabilitation of East Germany and the mammoth reconstruction of Berlin are testaments to the enduring power of nationalism.

Even the English-speaking countries, the foremost proponents of civic as opposed to ethnocultural nationalism, did not manage to avoid the ubiquitous power of nationalism. The centrifugal ethnonational forces challenging the integrity of Canada and the United Kingdom are driven by powerful nationalisms, despite their centuries-old traditions of universal political institutions. Similarly, the rejection of the "melting pot" mythology in Australia and the United States in favor of "multiculturalism" is evident in response to the "One Nation" movement in Australia and to growing anti-immigrant sentiment in the United States. Despite powerful and well-established political institutions, polities cannot rely exclusively on inclusive political institutions as a substitute for a nationalist basis for legitimacy and coherence. Multiculturalism, which supposedly can thrive in institutional civic polities, is increasingly perceived by broad segments of the western body politic as a mere apology for relativism.[10] The historic reality is that nationalism, a force that has been present on the European scene at least since the Reformation, continues to be the dominant political force that endows polities with the essential consensus and sense of cohesion without which they cannot function.[11] Every polity relies on a mythical national ideal that determines the contours of its political life and institutions.

All national identities are continuous "works in progress" subject to endless debate, change, and revision. However, overwhelming empirical evidence suggests that no society can effectively react to the challenges of the day without a broadly accepted mythic "national ideal" legitimizing the existing order. The source of virtually all-legitimating ideology is an irrational and incoherent mélange of religion and nationalism that is the keystone to any nation-building endeavor. It is the manipulation of the irrational forces of nationalism that affects the political direction of polities. Historically, the more fugitive and incoherent the sense of self in a polity, the less stable it tends to be.

Russia's Embryonic National Identity

It should be noted that in all empires, the people who form the "core" of the empire tend to have a weaker extraimperial identity than do the "subject" people. Therefore, the English have a weaker identity than the peoples of the "Celtic fringe"; the Austrians in the Habsburg empire had a weaker identity than either the Hungarians or the Slavs; Turks were less conscious of their distinct culture than either the peoples of the Balkans or the sultan's Arab subjects. Thus, it is not surprising that the Russians have long had a far weaker sense of national consciousness than the subject peoples of the western borderlands or the Transcaucasus. It is therefore axiomatic that the postimperial adaptation of the "core" peoples is far more traumatic and complex than that of the "subject" peoples.

In the case of Russia, however, the weakness of the identity of the core population may well be more extreme than in any other case. There, the boundary between the nation and the empire was thoroughly blurred. As Geoffrey Hoskings noted: "Britain had an empire, Russia was an empire". Despite Russia's cultural wealth, Russian political nationalism is in its embryonic stages and, as with all young nationalisms, is subject to very rapid and radical redefinitions. Currently, the unstable nature of Russia's self-definition is a significant factor in the country's extreme political volatility. And Russia's underdeveloped national identity lies in the country's peculiar history. Russia is unique in that the birth of the Russian empire preceded the birth of a distinct national polity. As a result of this reversed sequence of national development, from the sixteenth century to the present, the concept of Russianness became blurred with that of empire.

Long before Russia could develop its distinct national institutions, those institutions were converted into imperial institutions, with no clear interest in distinctly Russian issues.[12] Since Russian leaders derived their legitimacy from a messianic-universalist ideology, notions of a distinct Russian identity were discouraged and at times even suppressed during both the Tsarist and Soviet periods. Although Russia did experience an intellectual reawakening after the Crimean War (1854–55), it was unlike what occurred in East-Central Europe, where the reawakening spurred the development of nationalism and a distinct national agenda. Russia's restless intelligentsia, whether westernizing or Slavophile, continued with a messianic agenda, all but ignoring Russia's distinct needs. As Russia's first prime minister, Count Sergei Witte noted: " [We] still have not realized that ever since the times of Peter the Great and Catherine the Great there has not been such a thing as Russia, only the Russian Empire".[13]

While there were times, in both the Tsarist and Soviet periods, when weakened regimes turned to Russian nationalism as a source of legitimacy, these intervals did little to create a sense of national community. During these times of state-promoted nationalism, such as the reign of Alexander III, late Stalinism, and late Brezhnevism, the thrust of "official" Russian nationalism was directed at the glorification of Russia's leading role within the empire; any discussion of Russia's distinct interests or agenda was suppressed. Consequently, neither the Tsarist nor the Soviet regime's use of nationalism managed to narrow the gap between the state and society.[14]

The collapse of the Soviet empire failed to generate the political experience that would help shape a clear Russian national identity. In a similar situation, the birth of the Turkish national state was ushered in by the Ottoman empire's defeat in World War I and by the massive population shifts caused by the Greco-Turkish War and the consolidation of a distinct Turkish nationalism. In the case of Russia, however, the demise of the Soviet Union occurred primarily because of the atrophy of a cohesive elite, rather than a popular challenge to the system. When the Soviet Union was dissolved in December 1991, most Russians, including the political elite, were not certain whether the Belovezhsk agreement (Minsk) signaled a new form of federalism or some other new arrangement. It was this uncertainty among the Russian elite that explains Russia's prolonged failure to establish either its own defense ministry or central bank. Therefore, the collapse of the Soviet Union cannot be equated with the birth of Russia. In fact, initially, the breakup of the Soviet Union was perceived by many Russians as a power-sharing deal between various elements of the Soviet nomenklatura, which had little relevance to their lives.

It is symptomatic of the psychological disorientation befalling Russia that eight years after the breakup of the Soviet Union, Russians have yet to agree on the proper name for the country, much less its borders, flag, seal, or national anthem. Russia at the end of the twentieth century has yet to find its "usable past"—its historic heroes and villains or, for that matter, a universal definition of what a Russian is. Sigmund Freud once observed that humanity always lives in the past and (guided by the past) is constantly thinking about the future; humanity never lives in the present. Contemporary Russia has not yet arrived at a consensus about its past, and thus is forced to contend with conflicting and contradictory visions of its future.

Russian Statehood: The Rise and Fall of Westernization

Russia's emergence as an independent state was not a "rebirth". Unlike the Baltic states or the republics of the Transcaucasus, there was no passionate national identity to invigorate the polity as a result of the Soviet collapse. Unlike Ukrainians, Russians could neither marvel at their newly won sovereignty nor anticipate a rapid improvement in their living standards as most Ukrainians did. To most Russians, the demise of the Soviet Union engineered by the intelligentsia and nomenklatura represented a rollback of Russia's frontiers to their pre-Petrine configuration, resulting in the loss of many "ancestral Russian lands", the creation of a massive diaspora of Russians in the "near abroad", and a profound sense of humiliation and defeat. Furthermore, the borders of the Russian Federation, its federalist structure, and the existence within it of quasi-sovereign republics dominated by their titular nationalities made the new state appear much more like an ersatz, truncated Soviet Union rather than a Russian state. Under these circumstances it was all but impossible to devise a postimperial myth as a compass for the new state.

While it is beyond the scope of this paper to retrace the dynamics that led to the dismantling of the Soviet Union, it is essential to note that the intellectual force behind Mikhail Gorbachev's perestroika—and later the supporters of Boris Yeltsin's reforms—were primarily the Moscow-

based westernized intelligentsia. Like other groups, the westernized intelligentsia was a complex body with a variety of subgroups, though
several common beliefs applied to most of its members. Their basic
dogma consisted of the following assumptions:

1. The source of all the evils that befell the Soviet Union was Russia's "falling out" of its natural western cultural orbit.
2. Nationality problems were a direct outgrowth of Bolshevik totalitarianism; thus, once the Soviet Union adopted "(western) common values", the nationality problem would resolve itself.
3. The Soviet Union's (and later Russia's) daunting economic problems could be easily overcome, given the country's human and mineral
wealth. With a rapid integration into western structures, Russia would
relive the post-World War II experience of Germany or Japan and rapidly become a pillar of the "civilized North", escaping the intelligentsia's
nightmare of *Aziatshchina*.
4. The integration into the West or the "civilized North" would be
facilitated by the West's appreciation of Russia's unilateral ending of the
cold war and by the gratitude of the East Europeans and the citizens of
the former Soviet republics for making their independence possible.

Both the Russian westernizers and their western counterparts agreed
that macroeconomic reform and stabilization through a spillover effect
would bring about democratization and the rule of law.[15]

Like Russia's westernizers in the nineteenth century, the new Moscow
intelligentsia adopted the prevailing western model of neoliberalism fashionable in the Thatcher-Reagan years, with little criticism of or allowance
for the Soviet Union's distinct features. For example, they paid no heed to
the fact that the keystone of the liberal economic model, a Lockian-type
civil society where a strong, largely self-regulating society "tolerates" a
weak and constrained state, was a phenomenon distinctive to a small group
of predominantly Anglo-Saxon states. They ignored also Russia's Hegelian legacy of the primacy of the state as the "rational extension of the
individual" and the fact that the post-Stalinist Soviet Union had attained
something of a Montesqueian version of civil society where the citizenry
organized into smaller subgroups which institutionally acted as intermedi-
aries between the individual and the state.[16] Thus, the westernized elite
proceeded to dismantle all intermediate institutions with an almost religious zeal, in the belief that these Bolshevik leftovers stymied the emergence of both a self-sufficient Russian citizen and the "free" market. Unlike their democratic counterparts in East-Central Europe, where the
agenda to destroy Bolshevik autocracy did not automatically coincide with

the establishment of neoliberalism and where former dissidents formed either social democratic or Christian democratic parties, the Russian intelligentsia proceeded to "build capitalism" with the same disregard for the predicament of the hinterland (*glubinka*) as their Marxist predecessors.[17] Egor Gaidar, the father of Russia's "shock therapy", declared the need for the destruction of Russia's "pathological backwardness" if Russia were ever going to join the civilized world.[18] Russian westernizers and their western counterparts adopted a neoliberal dogma with the same zeal as their western predecessors, who a generation earlier were enthralled by "development theories".[19]

The dismantling of the many institutions in Russia that mediated between the state and the individual did not result in the birth of a more individualistic citizen but rather led to the complete atomization of the individual. The result was that the individual's sole point of reference and sole means of interacting with the state was lost. Another result was the metamorphosis of many of these subgroups into criminal formations. In the end, the deliberate and often mechanical dismemberment of old state institutions created a polity which has neither public power nor individual rights, making it an incoherent political society tenuously linked to an ever more deeply atomized and alienated individual.[20]

Without a doubt, the massive criminalization and collapse of the economy deprived the Russian government of the ability to use economic wellbeing as an underpinning of legitimacy that was afforded to other postimperial polities after World War II. In addition to that, however, the collapse of the Soviet Union, the sudden willful denunciation of the last seventy years of Russian history, and the debasement of what were heretofore national icons triggered a bitter response across wide segments of Russian society, especially outside the two capital cities. This is a process that Oswald Spengler calls "psuedomorphosis", in which the borrowed culture overwhelms the receiving culture, leading to a profound disorientation on the part of the populace and creating a growing gap between an elite that assimilate the new culture and the masses that only superficially assimilate it. Societies experiencing psuedomorphosis usually follow two paths: either despotism by the assimilated elite or complete political paralysis.[21] Thus, even if the agenda of the westernizing elite had been successfully implemented, the cultural break (*perelom*) would have made the restoration of coherence to the new Russian state a daunting task.[22] Long before the economic collapse of August 1998, Genadii Zyuganov captured popular feeling when he referred to westernized Moscow as a "wart on the nose of Russia".

The utopian dream of the westernizers, in any case, failed to materialize. The newly independent states of the former Soviet Union not only did not express any gratitude to Russia for their painless liberation, but instead, in their attempt to fortify their own identity, turned Russia into the evil "other" responsible for all the calamities that had befallen them, including Stalinism. The Russian population and Russophone diaspora residing in these newly independent states suddenly became unloved leftovers of imperialism who perceived the growth of discrimination and outright persecution against them. In a similar fashion, within the Russian Federation itself, republics dominated by titular nationalities such as Chechnya, Tatarstan, and Bashkortistan asserted their "native rights", creating a large Russian population believing itself to be the subject of discrimination and even oppression. The westernizers' belief that the Soviet Union's and then Russia's nationality problems would be easily solved with the advent of democracy turned out to be a bitter disappointment.

Another westernizing notion to meet its Waterloo soon after the collapse of the Soviet Union was the belief that the nations of East-Central Europe would appreciate the Russian role in their liberation and would thus act as a bridge facilitating Russia's "return to Europe". As with the former Soviet republics, much of the pent-up hostility toward the Soviet Union was transferred to Russia. Across the region Soviet World War II cemeteries and monuments were vandalized, at times with the apparent blessing of the authorities, thereby attacking perhaps Russia's sole remaining national icon. Demands by Poland that democratic Russia assume moral responsibility for Stalinist travesties shook the underlying assumption of the westernizers that the peoples of the former Soviet Union and the Soviet bloc would realize that it was the Russians who were the prime victims of Stalinism. The countries of East-Central Europe not only failed to become facilitators for Russia but instead spearheaded the attempt to exclude Russia from Europe, a process that culminated in the applications of the Czech Republic, Hungary, and Poland to enter the North Atlantic Treaty Organization (NATO). The symbolic value alone of the decision to expand NATO severely discredited the notion of westernization in the Russian body politic. The liberal publicist Kara Muzra eloquently captured the desperation of the Russian westernizers: "We consider ourselves as a part of Europe in the cultural sense. But Europe does not consider Russia to be European. That's the problem. They fear us. We [are treated as] a guest of Europe. There is a saying: 'The uninvited guest has already been here for generations' (making everybody, especially the guest, uncomfortable, it would seem). [Ivan] Silaev [ambassador to the European Union] was right when he said to NATO that you are only stimulating Ziuganov".[23]

Perhaps the greatest disappointment to the Russian westernized intelligentsia was in Russia's relationship with the developed West in general and the United States in particular. By 1995 there was a growing consensus that the attempted return to the "common European home" was an economic, political, and security calamity for Russia. In economic terms the expectation that Russia would soon be integrated into the "civilized North" turned out to be an illusion. Western aid, never reaching the levels that some westernizers such as Yavlinskii anticipated, was either spent on western consultants or simply stolen by a parasitic rent-seeking elite.[24] Within a very short period, Russian society fragmented to produce a small, criminalized economic elite that, with the West's blessing, continued to loot the country. The perception of continued western support for Yeltsin regardless of how corrupt and arbitrary he proved to be was engrained in the Russian consciousness, especially following the events of 1993 when Yeltsin used tanks to subdue a duly elected parliament—again, with the approval of the West.

Similarly, the westernizers' belief that Russia, with its human and mineral resources along with a population used to low wages, would be able to repeat the experience of Southeast Asia, where export promotion became a locomotive of sustained growth, were dashed, in large part due to the "antidumping" policies of both the United States and the European Union (EU). The requirement that the "nonmarket" economies of the Commonwealth of Independent States illustrate *a priori* that their manufactured goods were not being dumped on western markets stymied any hope of an export-driven recovery. Thanks to tight monetary policies stemming from the Russian westernizers' heeding of International Monetary Fund advice, the "demonetized" Russian economy drove much of Russia's manufacturing sector to rely on barter as the main means of trade. The reliance on barter resulted in the inability of most Russian manufacturers to demonstrate costs and thus avoid countervailing measures designed to thwart dumping. Furthermore, the tight monetary policy foisted on Russia by the West led to an appreciation of Russian currency, creating an import-driven boom in Moscow, where eighty-five percent of foreign capital in Russia was placed, while further constraining the ability of industry to compete, leading to massive impoverishment outside the two major cities.

The hopes of Russia's westernizers for an export-driven recovery were crushed. Post-Soviet Russia, shorn of its empire and unable to sell its manufactured goods to its former clients and satellites, was quickly reduced to a mineral and semiprocessed commodities exporter, leading to the collapse of its manufacturing sector and to mass unemployment among the country's "technical intelligentsia", which, ironically, many early westernizers saw as the basis of a putative middle class. In what may well turn out to be the ultimate irony of Russia's experiment with westernization, Russia's westernizers fell victim to the neoliberal dogma gripping the West between 1979 and 1997. They both ignored Karl Polanyi's seminal work, *The Great Transformation* (1944), which so clearly demonstrated how the gold standard and tight monetary policy delegitimized the Weimar Republic,[25] and forgot that both the New Deal and the Marshall Plan included healthy doses of monetary injections into the economy. Western advisors and their Russian counterparts proceeded with their neoliberal prescriptions, ignoring all evidence that, in Russia's case at least, tight money did not result in greater savings and investments, but actually drove the economy toward barter and subsistence production. By 1998 the Russian Federation had fragmented into dozens of pseudoclosed economies while the country's gross domestic product was hovering at fifty percent of its 1988 level. In economic terms the Russian state ceased to be a coherent unit.

Finally, the westernizers' assumption that the collapse of the Soviet bloc and the devolution of the Soviet Union would lead to a partnership with the United States and an end to the cold war has failed to materialize in Russian eyes. The decision to expand NATO eastward was perceived across the spectrum of Russia's political classes at best as a violation of the Zheleznovotsk agreements, and a provocative step to isolate Russia within the international system at worst. This sense of defeat and betrayal was reinforced by the decision of the United States to hold naval exercises off the Crimean peninsula and later by the strong support of the Clinton administration for the Baku-Ceyhan oil pipeline, despite repeated statements by the oil industry that the project had no economic grounding. To most Russian observers, in security terms westernization did not return Russia to the "civilized West" but moved the line of containment from the heart of Germany to the Polish-Ukrainian border and from the Persian Gulf to the Transcaucasus.

The Yeltsin years may well be remembered as years of lost opportunities for both Russia and the West. In economic terms the Russian economy shriveled to less than half of its Soviet-era peak. In political terms the collapse of communism failed to create a modern citizenry and instead degraded the population to an amorphous mass, oscillating between atomization and anomie on the one hand, and criminalization on the other. Yet perhaps the most grievous loss inflicted on Russia was in psychological terms. Russia's westernized elite, ensconced in Moscow, perceived approval by the West as the highest form of legitimacy, giving the increasingly radical opposition almost a monopoly in shaping and defining Russia and its national myth. To many Russians, the warm relationship between Moscow-based westernizers occurring in the background of an ever deepening poverty and corruption appeared to be proof of the elite's duplicity and the West's perfidiousness. This was a reminder to them of Alexander Radishchev's observation in his *Journey from Petersburg to Moscow* (1790) that, while the French philosophers marveled at the liberalism and enlightenment of Catherine the Great, both the Russian empress and her western interlocutors conveniently forgot that she ruled a realm of enslaved serfs.

Similarly, at a time when millions went unpaid and a new form of serfdom[26] was introduced, the heroic treatment accorded to Yeltsin, Chernomyrdin, Chubais, and some of the new Russian tycoons discredited both the merit of westernization and the West.[27] The collapse of the Russian ruble in August 1998 and Russia's subsequent default on its foreign debt, followed by a banking crisis that decimated the proto-middle class and was felt even in Moscow and St. Petersburg, dealt a severe blow to the "imagined community" of the Russian intelligentsia.

While we may be historically too close to analyze thoroughly all the complex reasons behind the collapse of Russia's liberal westernization, an important general observation can be made. The failure of both the late nineteenth- and late twentieth-century liberalization movements continues to reflect the profound schism in Russian society. The contemporary Russian historian Aleksandr Akhiezer drew a striking analogy: "Every word of the 1861 reform harbored a schism, an abyss of a mutual lack of understanding. Liberal reformers, guided by the values of a developed utilitarianism as ways to become aware of the link between personal efforts and personal benefits, pursued liberal notions of growth and the importance of the individual in society. The peasants, by contrast, strove to close themselves off in their own local worlds; they were oriented toward the dominance of barter relations. Two sets of values, two types of civilization, two kinds of sociocultural reproductions were in conflict".[28]

Russia's lumpen urbanization and industrialization did not alter many features of Russian society. The end of central planning and the disintegration of the centralized state resulted in the reversion to economic fragmentation that enabled local power-brokers to close themselves in their own local worlds and revert to barter relationships. Thus, liberalization of prices in Russia did not lead to an explosion in production, rational prices, or an individual-based society.

By 1995, fully 64.5 percent of Russian adults were "ashamed of their country", 55 percent were certain that "[Russia] cannot go on living this way", and 82 percent longed to see Russia as a "great power".[29] In a symbolic coincidence, when in December 1998 one of the "poet laureates" of Gorbachev's glasnost, Anatolii Rybakov, died in his New York home, much of the Russian press virtually ignored the event. Russia's bout of political and economic liberalism was over.

Russia at a Crossroads: Ethnonationalism or Pan-Slavism

The new Russian national idea cannot be other than a continuation and a development of previous national ideas formed over the course of centuries and the embodiment of the integral experience of the nation and the principles of its existence.[30]

It may well be that the greatest strength of Russia's pseudodemocracy is the absence of programmatic political parties and the very deep atomization of society, both of which act as obstacles to the formation of authoritarianism.[31] However, this apparent apathy should not be confused with the profound rejection of the current Russian reality. In the popular arts, themes of Stalinist brutality, communist oppression, and Brezhnevite banality have all but disappeared. Russian music of today, especially among the heavy metal bands popular with the young, dwells on people's feelings of anger and humiliation, with xenophobic and antiwestern overtones. Among the middle-aged, there is a powerful return to Soviet era *estrada* and a mix of war songs from both World War II and the Civil War.[32] In the case of Civil War songs, however, it is the songs of the whites fighting for "holy Russia", rather than the reds fighting for a "new world", that are most popular. Betrayal and abandonment by the West are a recurrent theme.

Beyond popular art, which is one measure of public sentiment, public opinion polls indicate profound nostalgia for the Soviet past. Though as noted above nearly two-thirds of Russians are "ashamed" of their country, at the same time eighty-four percent regret the breakup of the Soviet Union.[33] The failure of the westernizing paradigm has left a huge psychological void in Russia, a void that is being filled with mythologies relying on nationalism as the basis of legitimacy. As was the case with German and Hungarian nationalism during the interwar period, there are two major variants of the nationalist paradigm competing within Russia's body politic: a nativist group that focuses on Russia in its current "narrow definition" of ethnic Russians within the Russian Federation, and a group with a "pan-Slavic" vision which extends the definition of Russians across the Slavic-Orthodox lands of the former Soviet Union. Both of the above currents in Russian politics are poorly formed and fluid in structure, with many individuals defying a strict characterization; however, while the process of formation might not be complete, several general observations can be made.

Nativist "Moderate" Nationalism

Nativist "moderate" nationalism emerged fairly soon after the collapse of the Soviet Union and, indeed, found some resonance across wide segments of Russian society. Among the prominent political actors that may fit in this nationalist paradigm, albeit imperfectly, would be all three major presidential contenders—Lebed, Luzhkov, and Primakov—along with Lukin and Solzhenitsyn. While the above-mentioned nationalists do not have identical views, there are several key characteristics common to all of them.

1. In terms of a usable past, they all refuse to categorize either the Soviet era or the Tsarist period in any unidimensional manner. While freely admitting the shortcomings of the previous eras, they invariably stress the accomplishments of Russia and its people under both the Soviet and Tsarist regimes.

2. They perceive Russia as a distinct culture and, while avoiding Messianism or anti-*status quo* policies, they nevertheless support a vigorous defense of the country's distinct culture and an assertive foreign policy defending Russia's national interests. This includes a sphere of influence across the formerly Soviet territory.

Their definition of Russianness tends to be relatively broad, with language and culture as the main markers of national identity.[34] However, unlike the westernizing liberals who insist that decentralization and federalism are essential pillars of Russia's democracy, moderate nationalists fear that uncontrolled decentralization will lead to the fragmentation of the Russian Federation and a repeat of the experience of the Soviet Union. Vladimir Lukin has noted that, given the regional and "civilizational" centrifugal forces across the unwieldy federation, Russia's sole priority over the next two decades is simply to "survive".[35] Solzhenitsyn has noted that federalism was a "Leninist invention" meant to culturally dilute and denude Russia.[36] The solution for preventing the disintegration of Russia is to create a unitary ethnonational state. Some of the more radical among the "narrow nationalists" (such as Vladimir Kabuzan, Ksenia Mialo, and Aleksandr Solzhenitsyn), while supporting independence for the Chechens, included in their agenda the recovery of "Russian lands" such as the Crimea, Donbass, the Narvan region, and Northern Kazakhstan.[37] Interestingly, while Ksenia Mialo narrowly focuses on Russia as a distinct entity (she traces the origin of the Russian state to Novgorod), others among the nativists link the birth of the Russian nation to the formation of a strong Muscovite state, abandoning the myth of Kievan Rus' as the birthplace of Russia as the Slavophiles tend to do.[38]

Strong centralized statehood is a key to Russian identity according to this group.

Their attitude toward the West is very ambiguous, often indicating suppressed hostility. They firmly believe that the West—and particularly the United States—is not "anticommunist" but rather "Russophobic". Thus, the liberals' dream of partnership with the United States never had grounding in reality. The United States, according to the "narrow" nationalists, have humiliated Russia and exploited Russia's weakness in order to undermine the Russian state.[39] However, while perceiving the United States as a rival, the narrow nationalists recognize that given Russia's economic weakness, Russia must avoid tension with the West until such time that its economy, particularly its industrial base, has recovered. While most "narrow" nationalists blame the West for the economic misfortunes that have befallen Russia, they remain very cognizant of Russia's dependence on western credits and hence are careful not to provoke a confrontation on truly substantive issues. Thus, at the current stage, Russia's policy should be limited to sustaining the integrity of Russia, for only upon regaining its strength can Russia asserts itself across "Russian lands".

Although the narrow nativist nationalist school may well contain some of the most respected names in Russian politics, and indeed dominated the political arena in the first five years of Russia's independence, their ideological paradigm suffered a severe setback with the outbreak of war with Chechnya and the subsequent Russian defeat. While the narrow Russian nationalists long rejected an intimate relationship with the West because it was seen as degrading to Russia's culture and status, many of these same nationalists adopted the view of the émigré "Eurasians" of the 1920s who perceived the non-Slavic peoples of Russia to be symbiotic friends of Russia in confrontations with the West.[40] The war in Chechnya followed by the rise of fundamentalist Islam (Wahabism) there as well as in Daghastan and in other parts of the Russian Federation, coupled with the quagmire in Tajikistan and the ascent of the Taliban in Afghanistan, shattered all notions of "Eurasianism" or of an "Orthodox-Muslim axis" against the West. Aleksandr Prokhanov, the editor of the ultra-nationalist publication *Zavtra* and a strong proponent of "Eurasianism", wrote in late 1996 that it will be China and the Muslim world that will benefit most from the dissolution of Russia.[41]

The defeat in Chechnya has become a turning point in post-Soviet Russian history. On the one hand that war exposed the decay in Yeltsin's Russia; at the same time, it delegitimized the Russian state that had emerged in 1991. Observing the status of the Russian state in 1998, the nationalist journal *Moskva* noted that "federalism destroyed Russia within the frontiers of the Soviet Union and will destroy the Russian Federation unless [federalism] ceases to be the state dogma".[42] He cites the writing of the Dagastani nationalist Mohamed Tagaev, who has claimed that the stated aim of the Islamic population in the Russian Federation is to reduce Russia to the medieval "Moscovy, Tver, and Novgorod principalities".[43] This initiated yet another shift in the center of gravity of Russian nationalism away from Eurasian nativism toward pan-Slavic imperialism, a process that would accelerate greatly after the economic crisis of summer 1998.

Pan-Slavists and Empire-Builders

There have always been segments within the Russian body politic that have never accepted the demise of the Soviet Union. However, after the defeat of the communist coup attempt in August 1991, the massive vote in Ukraine to secede from the Soviet Union, and the willingness of vast parts of the Soviet Armed Forces to "betray" the Soviet Union and declare loyalty to Ukraine and other newly emerged states reduced those whose sought the restoration of the Soviet Union to fringe groups consisting mainly of communists and other disaffected types. In the months following the demise of the Soviet Union, peripheral groups, such as the National Salvation Front led by Ilya Konstantinov, called for the restoration of the Soviet Union in the context of a "multi-ethnic nation" (*mnogonarodnaia natsiia*). The communists, both in Russia and Ukraine, from the very start did not accept the demise of the Soviet Union. As Roman Szporluk observed, "Independent Russia and independent Ukraine in their own ways define themselves through the negation of the Soviet Union",[44] a definition that from the start was rejected by hard-core communists. The regrouped Communist Party called for the revival of the Soviet Union on the basis "one Soviet people" (*edinnyi sovietskii narod*).

By 1993 the view of those wishing to restore the empire significantly changed. The growing crime wave in Russian cities coupled with the prevailing perception that immigrants from Central Asia and the Transcaucasus represented a "criminal element" cooled the internationalist ardor of many communists. The popularity of the expulsion of "Asians" from Moscow by Mayor Luzhkov in October 1993 followed by the outbreak of war in Chechnya led the communists to shift from calling for the restoration of the Soviet Union to an embrace of a pan-Slavic paradigm. The waves of Slavic immigrants from Central Asia and the perception of the oppression of Russians in the Baltic states and the titular republics of the Russian Federation rekindled an imperial version of pan-Slavism. Instead of stressing internationalism, the leader of the Russian communists, Zyuganov, declared that since only a nation can generate human values, "Slavic values" are superior to abstract "human values". Vladimir Govorukhin, a former advocate of Soviet restoration, declared his preference for a unitary Slavic state.[45] By 1997, Zyuganov asserted a distinctly pan-Slavic vision: "Our task is the reunification of Ukraine and Belarus with Russia".[46]

As the economic situation in Russia declined, an ever growing segment of the Russian population perceived the Russian polity as an illegitimate criminal entity. The illegitimacy of the Russian state was further accelerated by mass disenchantment in both Belarus and Ukraine with their respective independence. Interestingly, the term "the Soviet Union" was relegated to disuse, while the Russian political lexicon became increasingly dominated by terms such as "Slavic brotherhood" (*Slavianskoe bratstvo*) and the "triune Orthodox Russian nation" (*triedinaya pravoslavniia russkaya narodnost'*) consisting of Russians, Ukrainians, and Belorusians.[47]

Other important political actors joined this shift toward a pan-Slavic orientation in Russia, including the Russian Orthodox Church, large segments of the officer corps, and most recently, members of the middle class ruined by the collapse of 1998. The Russian Orthodox Church, historically an organ of empire, reacted to the demise of the Soviet Union with dismay. The breakup of the Soviet Union meant the rise of autocephalous churches in Estonia, Moldova, and Ukraine, de facto dethroning the patriarch of "Moscow and all Russias". Thus, from the very beginning the Orthodox Church launched a campaign against its twin enemies: "ecumenism", as represented by the westernizing liberals, and "renovationism", manifested in the rise of national Orthodox churches in the newly independent states.[48] Appealing to Russian nationalism, Orthodox Church leaders equated ecumenism with the creeping "Catholicization" of Russia, recalling the resistance of Aleksandr Nevskii to the Teutonic Knights.[49]

An even more extreme nationalist position was advocated by the late metropolitan of St. Petersburg, Ioann, who praised Stalin as the gatherer of the "lands of Rus'" and called for a crusade against the genocidal "Russophobes"—including Gorbachev, Yeltsin, Jews, and American capitalists—all conspiring to break up the "greatest empire in the world".[50] In Belarus, Metropolitan Filaret of Minsk routinely referred to "our homeland between the Baltic and the Pacific". While not all clerics embraced Ioann's sense of paranoia, Alexii II, patriarch of Moscow and all Russias, declined to take issue with the ultra-nationalist sentiments emanating from his church. Significantly, when presidents Aleksandr Lukashenko of Belarus and Boris Yeltsin of Russia launched the process of integration between the two countries, Alexii II presided over the ceremony, referring to it as a sacred task (*sviatoe delo*).

The call for a synthesis of Orthodox Christianity and a pan-Slavic ideology was enthusiastically endorsed by the publication *Literaturnaia Rossia* of the Union of Russian Writers.

Another advocate of pan-Slavic integration was the Russian Armed Forces. While the Armed Forces was once the embodiment of the Soviet Union as superpower, it is now reduced to humiliating poverty. The Russian Armed Forces—both institutionally and as individual officers—increasingly sees the current situation as untenable. In a text published by the Russian ministry of defense, both alarm about the current situation and a blueprint for the future was laid out: "Today (at the end of the twentieth century) Russia has no national idea, no national consciousness. We are about to resemble a modern day Atlantis indifferently plunging into the ocean".[51]

The authors, commissioned by the Russian defense ministry, argue that if Russia is not to disintegrate or become a band of mercenaries, a Russian state organically linked to the Russian Orthodox Church and to the legacy of Kievan Rus' must supplant the current incoherence.[52]

The Union of Slavic Officers, representing military officers from three Slavic states, has been active since 1993, organizing congresses and calling for a "Slavic rebirth". Many officers, especially on duty within the ministry of the interior, developed overt links with the fascist Russian National Union (RNU), a relationship that allowed members of the RNU to acquire weapons.[53] A recurrent theme among nationalist military officers is that only a "united Slavdom" can confront the tidal wave of Islam from the South as well as that of the latter day Teutonic Knights, by which he meant NATO.[54] In a bulletin published by the Union of Slavic Officers, there was a call for the defense of the "all-Russian" Slavic *ethnos* against a crusade to destroy Russia, a defense which is attainable only in the context of a "unified all-Russian state". Yeltsin, cognizant of the growing pan-Slavic sentiment in the Russian Armed Forces, stated in an official address to military officers: "It is impossible to tear Ukraine from our hearts. The Ukrainians are our own people. That is our destiny—our common destiny".[55] A few days after Orthodox Christmas, Primakov attended a gathering organized by Alexii, bringing churchmen, officers, and intellectuals together.

Another important indication of the shift of the Russian body politic from liberal to pan-Slavic orientation is the change in the elites' perceptions of the Commonwealth of Independent States (CIS). To the westernizers the CIS was a vital tool in dismantling the Soviet Union. Although the initial hope of the liberals that the CIS would resemble a "new and improved federalism" was dashed, the liberals found the CIS useful for several reasons. As Paul Goble aptly noted, they used the CIS as a "fig leaf" to deny the breakup of the Soviet Union—a reality that no Russian politician wanted to face. Trade relationships that developed between the banking oligarchs and the new elites in the newly independent states were favored as a means of participating in the "privatizations" of CIS countries and as a conduit to export commodities out of Russia. Boris Berezovskii and Gazprom were among the most vocal champions of the CIS.

The economic collapse of 1998, the demise of the banking oligarchs, and the ensuing shift of elites toward pan-Slavism changed the political attitude toward the CIS. Whereas in the past only nationalists and communists depicted the CIS as Yeltsin's fig leaf and fraudulent façade, in post-August 1998 even mainstream Russian media[56] started to depict the CIS as a Potemkin village, allowing Yeltsin the role of a Mongol khan, holding court for minor vassals.

Increasingly the CIS was perceived as a charade sustained with essentially free Russian natural gas, loans, trade concessions, and peacekeeping, robbing Russia of twenty-one percent of its national income.[57] The reelection of Nazarbaev (one of the most vocal supporters of the CIS) as president of Kazakhstan drew derision from Russian nationalist politicians. Several upheld Nazarbaev as a prototypical leader using the CIS to take advantage of Russia.[58] The calls for Russian withdrawal from the CIS were accompanied by ever louder calls for bilateral relationships. In fact, increasingly the term bilateralism has acquired a dual meaning. When dealing with Belarus, Ukraine and, at times, Kazakhstan, it implies degrees of integration, while when dealing with other states of the Transcaucasus and Central Asia the same term means cold, pragmatic relations without any Russian concessions. Reflecting the mindset of postliberal Russia, while most Russians claim to perceive the CIS as irrelevant, eighty percent welcomed the new plan to integrate with Belarus.

Conclusion: The Radicalization of Russian Politics, Prospects for the Future

All three Slavic countries were overcome with a tidal wave of nostalgia for the Soviet Union and a deepening perception that the only way for these Slavic peoples to survive the machinations of the "perfidious West", the "Zionist conspiracy", and "Wahabist adversity" was to join together. Within a very short time, a profound radicalization of Russian nationalism has occurred, fundamentally shifting the parameters of debate in Russia and launching to center stage what was in years past a fringe view. Xenophobic and nationalist rhetoric once considered unacceptable arrived with a vengeance and, indeed, gained respectability inconceivable only a year ago.[59] Nationalism and pan-Slavic or all-Russian (*obsherusskogo*) unification have become tools of rhetoric across the political continuum. The current Russian state has no legitimacy, and public imagination is increasingly dominated by a blend of nostalgia and paranoia, perceiving the West and its "agents" as the culprits responsible for calamities ranging from betrayal to "ethnogenocide". Russian nationalists increasingly wallow in self-pity, depicting Russia as an innocent entity driven by perfidious forces toward extinction.[60]

The mutation from Marxism to fascism is both possible and has its historic precedents.[61] A drift in Russia toward greater corporatism and state intervention is likely if not inevitable. The use of nationalist rhetoric, laced with doses of antiwestern verbiage will most likely dominate the political discourse in Russia as the Yeltsin era comes to an end. The mythology of a "distinct civilization" and some sort of restoration will continue to dominate the agenda of all political actors to varying degrees. Some remilitarization of the polity is bound to take place. The muted reaction even by liberals to the decision of the army to spend scarce resources on the Topol-M program is indicative of the current mindset of the Russian body politic.

However, the currently fashionable talk of "Weimar Russia" or "fascist Russia" is premature and potentially dangerous, as it could become a self-fulfilling prophecy. Despite the obvious similarities between interwar Germany and contemporary Russia, two key differences should not be overlooked. Unlike Germany with its hyper-politicized population and tight network of political organizations, Russian society is extremely atomized, with most of its population struggling to survive rather than eager to participate in politics of any variety. Additionally, Germany during the interwar period had a young population convinced of its superiority over its neighbors; Russia's population is aging and declining. Having lived through the political violence of both Stalin and Hitler, the Russian people make poor material for the anti-*status quo* politics of fascists.

The main danger that the West faces from Russia is not aggression but rather disintegration. This will potentially be accompanied by uncontrolled refugee flows, export of nuclear technology, and dissipation of its human capital to rogue states. The West cannot, nor should it try to, promote the "westernization" of Russia as it did in the 1990s. Russia simply lacks the infrastructure for a modern civil society, and the imposition of westernization from above (and from the outside) merely distances the elites from the country at large, adding to the country's political instability. All functioning polities retain their stability and viability through a strange mix of practical results and legitimizing mythology. Contemporary Russia has neither of these preconditions. The West, through an enlightened aid policy that actually reaches the people in need and a clairvoyant trade policy that bolsters and ultimately expands the tiny middle class, can introduce a degree of legitimacy to the current Russian state. It is noteworthy that what keeps the countries of East-Central Europe on the path toward modern democratic politics is the belief that they will be rewarded by the West, whether through membership in the EU, NATO, or the World Trade Organization. Although neoliberalism drew both Poland and Russia toward subsistence economies, the outcome was different. The Poles were able to capitalize on the shuttle trade that actually integrated individual Poles into the world economy and provided a locomotive for future growth. Russia's subsistence economy deepened the isolation of individual Russians, driving them to anomie and xenophobia. The Russians have nothing to hope for in this regard. Greater sensitivity to Russian national sensibilities on symbolic issues may help to prevent symbolic and psychological issues from boiling over into a real crisis.

The latest war in the Balkans and NATO unilateral action against Serbia appear to have drastically shifted the mindset of the Russian nationalists from the nativism focused on Russian spiritual and cultural values and an inward looking preoccupation with Russian internal woes. The perception of danger and the sense of humiliation of NATO's action pushed Russian nationalism toward the strand associated with statism and a powerful Russian state.

Nationalism, at times bombastic, will remain the coin in Russian politics for a long time to come. However, Russia's integration into the world may well lead to the emergence of a kind of Russian DeGaullism, in reference to a situation in which nationalism was used as an anaesthetic during a painful period of adjustment and modernization and, in the end, helped to create a new polity. At the current juncture of history, even ardent liberals such as Aleksandr Livshits concede that Russia's experiment with liberalism has failed and must be deferred until at least 2004, if not longer.[62] However, although Russia is bound for an authoritarian or chaotic period, it would be a mistake on the part of the West to write off Russia. We must be mindful that until the outbreak of the Korean War the United States tried to recast both Germany and Japan in its own image with very mixed results. It was only following the outbreak of the Korean War that the United States shifted its policy toward the integration of Germany and Japan into the world economy, despite obvious dumping by both countries and despite the odious pedigree of many members of the German and Japanese industrial elite. In the case of Latin America where dictatorships arose, again, since 1970 the policy of the United States was not to overthrow "disagreeable" regimes but instead to bolster the economic and political power of the middle class. The West must rise above the narrow interests of domestic lobbies and commence a profound integration of the Russian economy into the world economy and nourishment of its middle class. The West must also abandon its missionary effort to "enlighten" the Russians. In the next generation Russia is unlikely to become the democratic state we all seek; in the absence of a middle class, it cannot be.[63] The successful economic integration of Russia may lead to a repeat of the process of democratization through international economic integration as was seen in the cases of Northern Mexico, Spain, Taiwan, and other countries, where a shift from nationalism and a move to seek legitimacy through the provision of social justice led to gradual democratization.

Failure to integrate Russia may lead that country to echo its nineteenth-century cycle so aptly described by the historian Yanov, where a failed liberalization, mutated to inward-looking parochialism, resulted in an autocracy made possible by isolation.[64] An isolated Russia will repeat its historic cycle. It will experience a prolonged period of disintegration, chaos, and misery, a new "Time of Trouble" (*smutnoe vremya*) which will be followed by the consolidation of a new autocracy. The West may not be able to choose the future of this vast and enigmatic land; however, it can influence the choice the Russian people make, and indeed, it must.

354   *Ilya Prizel*

Notes

1 Quoted in Igor N. Ionov, "The Crisis of Historical Consciousness in Russia and the Ways to Overcome It", *Obshchestvennye nauka i sovremennost'* 6 (1994).
2 Francis Fukuyama, "The End of History?", *National Interest* 16 (Summer 1988).
3 America's inability to come to terms with the potent force of nationalism can be demonstrated by Washington's stubborn refusal to consider the partition of Bosnia-Herzegovina or Kosovo along ethnic lines, despite the clear indication that this was the will of the native population.
4 Michael Ignatieff, "Identity Parades", *Prospect* (April 1998).
5 Whereas prior to 1973, for each one-percent growth of gross domestic product, a two-percent increase in the consumption of energy was demanded. Following the increase in the prices of imports, the greatest value-added product became intellectual property, accelerating the process toward postindustrialism.
6 See David Brown, "Why is the Nation-State So Vulnerable to Ethnic Nationalism?", *Nations and Nationalism* 4:1 (1998).
7 Yitzhak Brudny, *Re-Inventing History: Russian Nationalism and the Soviet State, 1953–91* (Cambridge: Harvard University Press, 1998); Katherine Verdery, *National Ideology Under Socialism: Identity and Cultural Politics in Ceausescu's Romania* (Berkeley: University of California Press, 1995).
8 The Iranian Revolution of 1979–80 should have raised the question of whether modern liberal polities are a historical inevitability.
9 Ignatieff, "Belonging in the Past".
10 On the contradiction between civil society and multiculturalism, see Eamonn Callan, *Creating Citizens: Political Education and Liberal Democracy* (Oxford: Clarendon Press, 1997).
11 See Margaret Canovan, *Nationhood and Political Theory* (Cheltenham, England: Edward Elgar, 1996).
12 The only other analogous situation where the empire preceded the formation of a nation is the Ottoman empire.
13 Sergei Witte, *Vospominania* Vol. 3 (Moscow: 1900), 273.
14 Ilya Prizel, *National Identity and Foreign Policy* (Cambridge: Cambridge University Press, 1998), chapters 5–6.
15 See Robert Sharlet, "Legal Transplants and Political Mutations: The Reception of Constitutional Law in Russia and the Newly Independent States", *East European Constitutional Review* 7:4:62.
16 See Oleg Khakhordin, "Civil Society and Orthodox Christianity", *Europe-Asia* 50:6 (1998).
17 Boris Kagarlitsky, *Restoration in Russia: Why Capitalism Failed* (London: Verso Press, 1995).
18 See Michael Urban, "Remythologising the Russian State", *Europe-Asia Studies* 50:6 (September 1998): 975.
19 See Colin Leys, *The Rise and Fall of Development Theory* (Bloomington: Indiana University Press, 1996).

20 See Stephen Holmes, "What Russia Teaches Us Now: How Weak States Threaten Freedom", *The American Prospect* 33 (July-August 1997).

21 See Oswald Spengler, *The Decline of the West* (New York: 1926), 189–95.

22 See Ernest Gellner, "The Rest of History", *Prospect* (May 1996).

23 Urban, "Remythologising the Russian State", 986.

24 Janine R. Wedel, *Collision and Collusion: The Strange Case of Western Aid to Eastern Europe, 1989–1998* (New York: St. Martin's Press, 1998).

25 Karl Polanyi, *The Great Transformation: The Political and Economic Origins of Our Time* (Boston: Beacon Press, 1944).

26 The universal feature of serfdom is the serf's inability to leave his place of employment at will. Millions of Russian workers, who are not paid by their employers in legal tender but rather either in parallel currency or kind, have become *de facto* serfs, as they cannot leave their employer at will.

27 Vladimir Shlapentokh, "Early Feudalism: The Best Parallel for Contemporary Russia", *Europe-Asia Studies* 48:3 (May 1995).

28 Aleksandr Akhiezer, "Rossiskii liberalism pered litsom krizisa", *Obshchestvennye Nauki i Sovremmenost'* 1 (1993). Reprinted in *Russian Social Review*.

29 Nataliia Tikhonova, "Mirovozzrecheskie tsennosti i politicheskii protsess v Rossii", *Obshchestvennye Nauki i Sovremmenost'* 4 (1996): 15–27. Reprinted in *Russian Social Review* 38:5 (1997).

30 Eduard Batalov, "Kuda put' derzhim? O natsional'noi idee i gosudarstvennoi ideologii", *Rossiiskaia Federatsiia* 15 (1996).

31 See Stephen E. Hanson and Jeffrey S. Kopstein, "The Weimar/ Russia Comparison", *Post Soviet Affairs* 13:3 (1997): 252–83.

32 Missing reference.

33 *Interfax* 22 (January 1997).

34 I. Klymakin and V. Lapkin, "Russkii vopros v Rossii", *Polis* 5:29: 87.

35 Igor Zevelev, "The Russian Quest for New Identity: Implications for Security in Eurasia", in *Global Security Beyond the Millennium: American and Russian Perspectives*, eds. Sharyl Cross, Igor Zevelev, Victor Kremenyuk, and Vagan Gevorgian (London: Macmillan, 1998), 111.

36 "'Nashe interv'iu' Solzhenitsyn o Chechne", *Argumentyi i Fakty* 1–2 (January 1995): 1.

37 See Vera Tolz, "Conflicting 'Homeland Myths' and Nation-State Building in Postcommunist Russia," *Slavic Review* (Summer 1998): 282.

38 See Vera Tolz, "Forging the Nation: National Identity and Nation-Building in Post Communist Russia", *Europe-Asia Studies* 50:6 (September 1998): 1001.

39 Sergei Kortunov, "Kaitsa Rossii ne v chem", *Nezavisimaia Gazeta* (26 September 1996).

40 See Dmitry Shlapentokh, "A Problem in Self Identity: Russian Intellectual Thought in the Context of the French Revolution", *Journal of European Studies* 26:1 (March 1998).

41 See Vladimir Shlapentokh, "How Russians Will See the Status of Their Country by the End of the Century", *Journal of Communist Studies and Transition Politics* 13:3 (1997): 12.

42 Mikhail Smolin, "'Mein Kampf' po-Dagastanskii ili protokoly gorskogo mudretsa", *Moskva* 11 (1998): 147.

43 Smolin, "Mein Kampf", 147.

44 Roman Szporluk, "Nationalism After Communism: Reflections on Russia, Ukraine, Belarus, and Poland", *Nations and Nationalism* 4:3 (1998): 317.

45 Vera Tolz, "Conflicting 'Homeland Myths,'" 288.

46 Gennadi Zyuganov, *Geografiia Pobedy: Osnovy Rossisskoi Geopolitiki* (Moscow: 1997), 249.

47 Zyuganov, *Geografiia Pobedy*, 249.

48 Konstantin Dushenov, "By Silence God is Betrayed", *Moskva* 2 (1997).

49 Dushenov, "By Silence God is Betrayed".

50 See Ioann, "Russkii uzel", *Rus' Pravoslavnaia* 2; *Sovetskaia Rossia* 83 (15 July 1993): 3.

51 V.E. Gidirinskii, *Russkaia idea i armiia* (Moscow: Voennyi Universitet, 1997), 283.

52 Gidirinskii, *Russkaia idea i armiia*, 286–89.

53 Interpress Service (1 July 1998).

54 See Aleksandr Borodai, "Kavakzskii khaos", *Zavtra* 38: 251 (22 September 1998). See also his "Sud'ba prussov-Rossii?", *Duel* (28 January 1998).

55 *Krasnaia Zvezda* (22 November 1998).

56 See, for example, Semyon Ulanich and Oleg Medvedev, "A Farewell to the Commonwealth", *Business in Russia* (January 1999).

57 Ulanich and Medvedev, "A Farewell to the Commonwealth", 28.

58 BBC Russia Survey (radio), 11 January 1998.

59 "Zyuganov's Attack on Zionism", *Sovetsaia Rossiia* 24 (December 1998).

60 See interview with Valentin Rasputin, *Sovetskaia Rossiia* (reported in Johnson's List, 5 January 1999).

61 Many of Mussolini's ideologues—Roberto Michles, Paolo Orano, Sergio Panunizo—were Marxists before World War I. Similarly, in the 1930s much of the Japanese communist leadership defected to the "national" cause.

62 *Business in Russia* (January 1999): 23.

63 My definition of middle class is based on the ownership of economic property, not education.

64 Alexander Yanov, "Russian Nationalism: Ideology of Counter-Reform", *RFE/RL Reports* (19 December 1989).

19 *Chinese Bridges to Postsocialist Europe*

JEFFREY N. WASSERSTROM

Ten years ago it was still commonplace to think of the People's Republic of China (PRC) and the countries of Central and Eastern Europe as comparable and even connected places. There was no need then for someone like me, who specializes in Chinese studies, to begin a chapter in a book such as this, which focuses on nations that were once part of the former Soviet empire, with an explanation or defense of my essay's inclusion in the volume. Now, as we begin the second decade of the age of the "new world order" or, as it has much more aptly been dubbed, the age of the "new world disorder", the situation is very different.[1] It is useful and maybe even necessary for me to start by justifying my efforts here to bring together the experiences of the PRC and those of European countries that once either clearly belonged to the Soviet empire (such as East Germany) or stood at its fringes (such as Yugoslavia).

This effort will center on the value of focusing on shared characteristics of the postsocialist social and economic transitions that China, like the other countries analyzed in this volume, is undergoing, as opposed to emphasizing only the fact that the PRC is still a Leninist state. Before making this case, however, it is important to do something else: retrace the steps by which comparing China with countries such as Romania and Poland first came to seem such a natural practice and then rather abruptly became an issue that needed to be defended. We need to do this to understand why attempts to combine analysis of these two parts of the world, though still sometimes undertaken, has become much more rare in the 1990s than before.[2]

A Bridge is Made, 1949–1989

Once upon a time, and actually not so long ago, it was routine for social scientists to pair discussion of the PRC with discussion of part—or all— of the Soviet empire. Sociologists concerned with the nature of labor-management relations in Marxist-Leninist states did it. So did economists working on topics such as the role of state-run industries in planned economies and anthropologists doing research on communist family policies. Most commonly of all, perhaps, political scientists concerned with the workings of one-party bureaucracies or the varied forms taken by Marxist doctrines did it. This seemed normal scientific practice in an academic world where there were journals with names such as *Problems of Communism* and in which the cold war functioned to provide a clear-cut basis by which to divide the world.

China was, of course, often treated as a "special case" within this division of states. Initially this was due to Chairman Mao's break with Moscow as well as to the moves toward normalizing Sino-American relations made by U.S. presidents Richard Nixon and Jimmy Carter and their Chinese counterparts. Later, China's status as an exceptional sort of Leninist country was also linked to Deng Xiaoping's decision to embrace market reforms and privatization. Nonetheless, the fact that the PRC was governed by a communist party that had little tolerance for dissent was seen by many western conservative and liberal academics as reason enough to place it on the red (or dark) side of the "communist/free world" divide. For radical scholars, less tied to or even critical of this kind of cold war polemical language, China still seemed worth putting in the same category as other one-party states that followed five-year plans.

Moreover, it is worth remembering that many people living in China and in Central or Eastern Europe before 1990 saw themselves as enmeshed in comparable cultural worlds. Some even thought of themselves as sharing connected fates. István Rév summed up this sense of relatedness. Up through the 1980s, he noted, many Hungarians thought of themselves as almost sharing a "common border" with not only China but Cuba as well—a nice trick of the imagination, he commented, for citizens of a landlocked country.[3] And this feeling of connection was by no means one-sided, as the memoirs of Chinese intellectuals such as Yue Daiyun clearly show. Her wonderful book, *To the Storm*, makes it clear that events taking place and texts produced in places such as Hungary and Yugoslavia between the 1950s and the 1970s often had an impact on how she and those around her understood and acted in their Chinese political world.[4]

There are many other specific kinds of interconnectedness that could be mentioned. There were, for example, the linked visual commentaries provided by the monuments and political posters suffused with Soviet realism and other styles that from the 1950s to the 1980s were produced in China and in various parts of Central and Eastern Europe.[5] In addition, there were decisions made by communist party leaders in one part of the state socialist world that were inspired by actions taken by their counterparts in another section of it. For instance, as Nancy Tucker stresses in a recent essay on the PRC in 1968, Chairman Mao's decision to curtail the most radical phase of the cultural revolution needs to be understood, in part, as a reaction to the Prague Spring.[6]

A Wall Tumbles and a Bridge Falls Down

The unexpected upheavals ten years ago brought forth first a dramatic flourishing and then a shattering of the assumption that the PRC and parts of Central and Eastern Europe were closely tied. They also triggered a turn away from Sino-European comparisons by many—though by no means all—academics. For a time during that epochal year, it seemed that the PRC and parts of the Soviet empire might change in perfect synch. At almost the same moment that round table talks were transforming Polish politics, for example, Chinese demonstrators at Tiananmen Square and in the central plazas of other cities were making demands for direct "dialogue" with officials. The first half of 1989 also saw protesters in both Czechoslovakia and the PRC testing the limits of the regimes' openness by holding, or trying to hold, mourning ceremonies for martyrs. In each instance, dissidents claimed that all they wanted to do was celebrate the memory of a hero who had died too young. The hero in question was the Prague Spring martyr Jan Palach in the one case and the reformist communist party leader Hu Yaobang, who had been demoted in 1987 for being too lenient toward student protesters and then suffered an unexpected heart attack in April 1989, in the other. In each case, dissidents tried to combine these commemorative activities with calls for those in power to live up to the ideals represented by the fallen heroes.[7] Finally, in the second half of the year, after the 4 June massacre and related acts of brutality put an end to the protest movement in the PRC, it seemed to many people that countries in the Soviet bloc were picking up where the Chinese insurgents had left off.

It is still hard to assess just how strong the links really were between the struggles for change in 1989 that occurred in places as far apart from one another as Wuhan from Warsaw, Beijing from Bucharest. Though there were broadly cosmopolitan and internationalist dimensions to what many protesters did and said that year, a wild eclecticism of the symbols and strategies and slogans they turned to, there was also often a self-contained sense to what was going on. It is likely that, at least in many instances, national—or at most regional—influences remained most important, and that attention to what was happening or had happened recently on other continents was of secondary significance in shaping the choices protesters made. Certainly, there is no evidence that Chinese protesters calling for dialogue viewed the Polish round table as a direct influence. Nor did all those who gathered to honor Jan Palach know much about Hu Yaobang, or vice versa. Still, it did seem for a time that all the various yet specific protests were part of the same macroevent, and this alone makes it worth taking seriously the interconnections of various 1989s.

To put this another way, though the influence of European developments on China can be overstated, it certainly meant something when students in Beijing lamented that "Heaven gave Russia a Gorbachev but only gave us a Deng Xiaoping". It also meant something when they wondered if a Chinese "Wałęsa" might emerge from the ranks of the angry workers who joined students on the streets in ever increasing numbers. Meanwhile, though there are people in East European countries who in 1989 were ready to insist that interest in the Chinese protests was much less acute for them than interest in struggles in neighboring lands, there are also those who swear that the Chinese example was very inspirational. Each statement is doubtless true to varying degrees for varying individuals; I have heard both and seen no reason to doubt the speaker's sincerity in either case.

Perhaps all that can be said definitively is that it certainly meant something to many European protesters that autumn that Chinese demonstrators had done what they did that spring—and had done it on television. The sense of shared borders alluded to above, moreover, made at least one kind of connection very direct. A distaste for what Daniel Chirot has referred to as the pervasive "rot" within and growing popular "disgust" toward so many Leninist regimes provided a common vocabulary that year. Even protesters who spoke different languages than and knew little about the specific histories or ideals of their counterparts in other regions found common ground in their shared distaste for corruption and anger at petty forms of official tyranny.[8]

Most significant of all, perhaps, it meant something to the leaders in each part of the state socialist world that, as their authority was being challenged by popular movements, so too was that of their counterparts in other countries. Deng and those close to him were intensely concerned with the Polish dilemma and the example set by Solidarity. This helps explain the strategies of repression they turned to in 1989, from the move to impose martial law in May to the decision to use state violence in June to break the back of the protest movement in both Beijing and Chengdu, where a massacre also occurred. Knowing that martial law in Poland failed to check the rising social movement led by Solidarity in the early 1980s helped convince China's leaders to use armed soldiers to dispel the crowds. It is no accident that the majority of the victims of the massacre were workers, nor that the heads of newly formed autonomous labor unions as well as student protest leaders figured prominently on the regime's most wanted lists. It is also no coincidence that, while some educated youth were punished severely, the harshest sentences tended to be given to workers.

The influence of the Chinese regime's behavior on European leaders is harder to summarize and describe in straightforward terms. Some specific individuals may have eschewed violent solutions in part to escape the international censure that was directed at people such as Li Peng after 4 June, though this seems unlikely in light of the relative mildness of the real impact of this criticism on the PRC. No Chinese leader, after all, fell from power due to being held accountable for the massacres, and the diplomatic and economic consequences of the international condemnation of the crackdown were minimal. At least one East European leader, Nicolae Ceauşescu, seems to have seen in the Chinese regime's actions a model for survival. Others, such as East Germany's leadership, seem to have toyed with, but then finally decided against, imitating Beijing. The one point that is clear is that many leaders, including Gorbachev, had China on their minds late in 1989 and that what happened in China on 4 June was seen as relevant in some way to the dilemmas that faced the countries of Central and Eastern Europe several months later.[9]

Unconnected Shores: 1990–1999

The fracturing of a sense of connection and a turn away from comparison already could be sensed by the very end of 1989, and the pulling apart of the two regions in scholarly and other imaginations became even more dramatic a year and a half later. A kind of bleak last hurrah for the notion of relatedness and comparability came in December 1989, when some of Romania's leaders treated protesters in a brutal fashion similar to that of their Chinese counterparts. But then, before the year ended, Ceauşescu was executed—an event that some Chinese dissidents celebrated as a kind of displaced wish-fulfillment fantasy, the closest thing they could hope to see happen to Deng or his ally Li Peng as punishment for the bloodshed of 4 June. When the new decade began with Deng and Li still in power, even this imagined connection between Romania and China—two countries that had often shared a particularly close bond from the 1960s to the 1980s—became very tenuous at best. There remained the possibility, at that point, of continuing to draw analogies between a reduced Soviet empire and a still intact Chinese one, but even that disappeared in 1991 when the Soviet Union fell apart.

It was not just the reshaping of the geopolitical order that separated the PRC from some of the countries to which it used to be thought similar and linked but also nearly simultaneous—and related—shifts in intellectual fashion. Most notably, the 1990s saw the rise of two different ways of conceptualizing the "post-cold war" world, each of which was tied in some way to the events of 1989 and each of which militated against thinking of the PRC as comparable to any part of Europe. The first of these continued to stress the sharp contrast, beloved by cold war propagandists of the left and the right, between "capitalist" or "liberal democratic" states and "state socialist" or "totalitarian" ones. The difference now was that each set was a different size: nearly all parts of the former Soviet empire were seen as rooted in or at least drifting toward the former, while China was portrayed as among the few proud or benighted hold-out countries of the latter.

One influential version of this was the "end of history" paradigm of Francis Fukuyama, in which China was presented as a land that had been left behind, yet again, by the tide of progress.[10] The only hope for it, in this and other liberal triumphalist readings of 1989, was to try to catch up with the former state socialist countries of Europe and join them in their effort to shed communism and transform themselves into western-style democracies. There were other versions of this worldview as well, however, including a Chinese one that saw the countries of the former Soviet empire as the ones that had stepped out of the Hegelian stream of historical progress. The year 1989—in this reading, equally triumphalist in its own way—was a year in which China resisted an evil tide that had engulfed and destroyed some of its former allies and ruptured the ties between the PRC and various European lands.[11]

The second new way of thinking about the world that militated against viewing the PRC and any part of Central or Eastern Europe as linked and comparable stressed cultural difference. One influential version of this was the "clash of civilizations" paradigm associated with Samuel Huntington, in which China was bracketed off from the former

Soviet empire by virtue of its attachment to Confucian ideals and practices that posed a danger to Western ways.[12] Here again there was a Chinese counterpart in the form of the "Asian values" argument, which put a distinctively positive spin on the same conflict of worldviews.[13] In either case, the end result was essentially the same: to contribute to the push away from comparing the PRC to European countries. In each case, there was a compensatory pull, a move toward linking China to its western and southern neighbors (Japan, Korea, Singapore) as opposed to its northern ones (Russia, other parts of the former Soviet Union, and Mongolia). Similarly, where Central and Eastern Europe is concerned, a focus on "historical" and "cultural" factors of the Huntingtonian sort both pushed Chinese analogies away and made comparisons with neighboring countries seem more appropriate.

In Search of New Bridges

Is all of this merely of historical interest? Should we just note that it used to make sense to think of the PRC as linked to some parts of Europe, but it no longer does, and then move on to matters of contemporary interest? Is there any real reason to continue to think that a giant, still-Leninist country with high growth rates should be compared to much smaller post-Leninist ones that have, in most cases, undergone tough economic times in the 1990s?

These questions are reasonable to ask whether or not one accepts the tenets of either of the new paradigms for thinking about how parts of the world are interrelated as sketched out above. Moreover, if one takes seriously the way people living in particular countries think about their condition and possible futures, there is certainly good reason to ask them. Returning to Rév's comment about "common borders", he brought up the old one between Hungary and the PRC precisely because he thought it was now primarily of historical interest. Being a historian, among other things, he certainly did not mean that this made the idea unimportant, just that now it was the shared history of communism more than the commonality of current experience that could be invoked most easily as a bond tying Hungary to China. To the extent that Central Europeans and East Europeans now think about how their lands fit into larger wholes, it is usually Central Europe, Eastern Europe, or Europe as a whole that is the main point of reference. Likewise, while some citizens of the PRC may think that their country has a special link to other state socialist countries, many are more concerned with how it is situated within an Asian—or, rather specifically, East Asian—cultural sphere.

In spite of these and other reasons to support the idea that the time has come to relegate to the past the idea of placing the PRC and formerly state socialist parts of Europe side by side in our minds, I am convinced we should resist this temptation. There are good reasons for China specialists and scholars working on Central or Eastern Europe to establish a more robust dialogue on the decade stretching from 1989 to the present. Now that the borders connecting these two parts of the world are harder to see (aside, of course, from the always tense physical one dividing China from Russia that runs through Central Asia), forays into comparison may need to be made in more creative and thoughtful ways. They are, nevertheless, still well worth making. I say this in part simply because when trying to find our bearing in confusing transition periods—and both the PRC and the former Soviet empire are in the midst of these—we need all the help we can get. One kind of assistance can come, in this case, from paying attention to how those who are thinking about another, in some way comparable, part of the world are formulating questions, developing models, and pondering the dilemmas of postsocialism.

Most of the rest of this chapter is devoted to describing four approaches to comparison that seem particularly worth pursuing just now. The first is a macrovariety, which involves sweeping assessments of the whole decade and all parts of both regions. The second is a geographically limited variety, which looks for parallels between developments in specific cities or provinces of the PRC and specific countries within Central and Eastern Europe. The third is a temporally limited comparison, which zeroes in on specific moments in time. The fourth is one that moves freely through time, comparing different periods in each region's past.

A final prefatory note about the issue of comparison is in order, however, before each of these four approaches is described in more detail. Despite all the comments above about Sino-European divergence since 1989, a good case can be made that some parts of the former Soviet bloc have become more, not less, like the PRC in the 1990s than they were in the preceding decade. I was convinced that this counterintuitive statement was true before I went to the Budapest conference, and I came away from that gathering even more certain of its validity. This is because, as I listened to the papers that now have been collected as the chapters of this book, I continually heard comments being made about one or another part of Europe that similarly described the Chinese phenomenon. I heard descriptions of an increase in official corruption here and experiments with local elections there. I listened to accounts of a resurgence of virulent forms of nationalism in one part of the region, of the popularity of synchretic apocalyptic cults in another, of the incredible influence of Mafia-like organizations in certain cities, and of the serious environmental crises that threatened to affect the whole region. I took in arguments about nostalgia for more stable totalitarian times among some residents of one area and about the crises triggered by increasing discrepancies between richer and poorer segments of the population in another.

And all the time I found myself thinking the same thing. Namely, if a group of well-informed Chinese intellectuals had suddenly made a wrong turn during a tour of Budapest and been brought into this gathering not knowing what it was, they might easily have drawn a strange conclusion about many of the papers. They might have imagined that a presentation about one or another part of the former Soviet empire was actually a discussion of China in the 1990s.[14]

Broad-brush Comparisons

The main danger of treating the PRC of 1989–99 as essentially the same sort of place as Central and Eastern Europe during this period has already been spelled out; to do so is to efface the importance of the contrast between Leninist and post-Leninist states. If, however, we define each of these parts of the world as undergoing a transition away from socialist economic structures and temporarily bracket off political issues, then a basis for broad comparison remains. China, no less than the former Soviet empire, is experiencing a variety of social traumas right now that are linked to such issues as the privatization of many industries and a scaling back of welfare activities by the state. The high growth rates of the PRC make it a special case in one sense. We need to remember, however, that these growth rates have not equally benefited all citizens of China. The disparity between the experience of haves and have-nots within the PRC has been increasing dramatically in recent years, with laid-off former employees of state-run industries and residents of the hinterland as opposed to coastal regions tending to be the ones left behind by "progress".

This, in itself, suggests one basis for sweeping comparison. Not only can parallels be drawn between the specific hardships that some people in each place are undergoing, but also a similar move from homogeneity to heterogeneity has taken place in each region. Circa 1970, for example, the kind of material lifestyle that typical residents of coastal cities such as Guangzhou and those of the hinterland such as Xian could expect to enjoy were pretty much the same, but this is not true today. The same thing could be said of people living in more and less economically successful parts of the former Soviet empire.

What good does it do, in pragmatic terms, to accept this notion? Here, as in the sections to come, I will try to illustrate the value of thinking along a particular comparative line by referring to some recent publications on a relevant theme. Not surprisingly, given my background, these will typically be works on China that either refer to European parallels or develop approaches to a topic that could be applied to the former Soviet empire. Without going into their arguments in any detail, they should bring to mind some ways that looking at Central and Eastern Europe through the lens of a China specialist might be useful. In some cases, they will also show how the reverse can be true.

Let me begin this search for bases for broad comparison with some discussion of the book *In the Red: On Contemporary Chinese Culture*, a collection of essays by Australian China specialist Geremie Barmé, one of the most perceptive analysts of recent developments in the PRC. Of particular relevance here is Barmé's chapter on "Totalitarian Nostalgia", which leans heavily on the work of Russian specialist Svetlana Boym.[15] Barmé claims that there are both distinctive and generic characteristics to the way that, in the PRC of the 1990s, nostalgia for the security of more totalitarian times has been expressed. In the Chinese case, like the Russian one, according to Barmé, we find this nostalgia articulated through a temper that "harks back to and feeds off lingering totalistic and totalizing tendencies". He stresses differences between European and Chinese varieties of this nostalgia, noting such things as the special role of totalizing ideas in various periods of China's precommunist past. He also emphasizes that the interplay between what Boym calls "utopian nostalgia" on the one hand and "ironic nostalgia" on the other is different in the PRC of today than in the former Soviet empire.[16] Overall, however, it is the similarities rather than the differences that stand out for him. Despite the fact that the communist party is still in control in China and not in the former Soviet Union, Barmé sees many parallel manifestations, sometimes taking similarly perverse forms, of the desire for a simpler, if less free, past that Boym analyses.

Barmé also describes several ways that in China, as in Russia, attempts have been made to manipulate this hunger for stability and use it to further political ends. The revamping of Stalin and Mao as symbols is one area where the parallels are particularly strong, he shows, and Russia and China end up seeming the two 1990s settings where the workings of totalitarian nostalgia are most comparable.[17] But at least implicit in

Barmé's reworking of Boym's arguments is the notion that cultural developments throughout the postsocialist world are likely to have some important points in common. His study is thus likely to be of relevance not just to Russianists but also to those interested in other parts of the former Soviet empire.

A second, very different sort of work that also draws attention, in this case mainly implicitly, to the potential for macrocomparisons is an important new book by political scientist Dorothy Solinger on China's "floating population" and the social problems associated with it. Entitled *Contesting Citizenship in Urban China: Peasant Migrants, the State, and the Logic of the Market*, her study deals with the flood into many cities of rural dwellers, often young men in search of work, that began in the 1980s when bans on internal migration were lifted.[18] There are some parts of her study that do not travel well or at least cannot be transported easily to the Central and East European context. For example, as Solinger notes, there were unique features to the way villagers were tied to the land under Maoism that prevented movement even from one part of the countryside to another. There are also culturally distinctive—though by no means unique—aspects to the disdain for peasants felt by many Chinese urbanites. This prejudice, which remains acute in spite of decades of official propaganda extolling the virtues of peasants as key makers of the revolution, is justly treated by Solinger as analogous to an extreme form of dislike of ethnic "others" assumed to be inferior in every way.

This said, increased internal migration as well as tension between long-time residents of certain places and new groups perceived of as inferior (perhaps temporarily but perhaps eternally so) is an important part of the social landscape in many parts of the world, including much of Central and Eastern Europe. Solinger's study, which uses a varied documentary base and draws on her own ethnographic explorations of the subculture of the "floating population" within Chinese cities, thus has much to offer to those working on related phenomena in the former Soviet empire. Her framing of the problem as one directly tied to renegotiating categories of "citizenship" at a time of economic transition is likely to make it particularly valuable for these scholars. Her actual comments on Central and Eastern Europe are very limited, taking form mainly of passing reference to the lessons on limiting mobility that Chinese communists took from Stalin. Even if she does not, like Barmé, draw directly from the work of a Central or East European theorist, however, she does provide a solid analytical basis on which those with comparative interests can easily build.

The same is true of another recent work, Michael Dutton's *Streetlife China*, which also deals at length with the problems faced by members of the "floating population" as well as those of other marginal or subaltern groups disadvantaged by postsocialist trends.[19] Dutton, a political scientist by training like Solinger (though a much more unconventional one than she), explores in detail the myriad ways that subaltern groups have become scapegoats for social evils and targets of state repression. His book is stylistically and theoretically very different from Solinger's, taking the form of a collage of documents and analysis and looking to postcolonial and neo-Marxist theories for inspiration. Nevertheless, the two books can be read in tandem and successfully played off against one another by anyone interested in the ways that uprooted people survive and struggle amidst the uncertainties of a postsocialist transformation.

Connecting Pieces of Two Worlds

The second type of strategy for bringing together discussion of the PRC and discussion of Central and Eastern Europe in the era of the "new world disorder" involves limiting one's purview to specific sections of each large region. Here, to illustrate this general point, I will confine myself to a single case. This will involve drawing on my own current work on Shanghai. I am specifically concerned with the process by which this metropolis, once dubbed "The Paris of the East", as was Budapest, became a more provincial place under socialism, but now has reasserted itself as a cultural and economic center in the postsocialist period. I see potential value in pairing this Chinese city with several Central and East European ones that were very cosmopolitan urban centers before experiencing socialist interregnums.

My comments below are drawn from an ongoing study of Shanghai's past and present. My study will place this metropolis within the models articulated in some major contributions to urban theory that deal with the global city as a social form and also challenge some of the underlying assumptions of these works.[20]

Of particular interest to me, as already noted, is how Shanghai's degree of integration into or detachment from large-scale economic and cultural systems has varied over time. The pattern of Shanghai's movement into and out of international structures makes it very different from many other major urban centers of today. Unlike Tokyo, for example, which has steadily become an increasingly significant global hub, Shanghai went through a period when it stopped serving these sorts of functions. And unlike some of its competitors within the PRC, such as Shenzhen, which were never thought of as major cities before the 1980s, Shanghai's recent rise to global prominence needs to be seen as both a novel development and a resumption of old patterns. Shanghai thus poses a problem of sorts for much of the theoretical writing on the "global city", including the justly influential and important work by Saskia Sassen. In such studies, one is given a sense that urban centers with certain characteristics move steadily and naturally from being local to national to transnational centers of exchange.[21] The assumption is that cities begin firmly rooted in a national context, but over time, some take on characteristics that detach them from this setting, linking them cultural and financially to other major urban centers in distant parts of the world. Discussions of "postmodern" cities also often frame their arguments within this kind of general evolutionary vision.[22] The fact is, however, that Shanghai was more "global" or at least "cosmopolitan" during its old incarnation as an international treaty-port—or, to use the Chinese phrase, a subdivided "semicolonial" city—than as a socialist metropolis.

In fact, as I have argued elsewhere, in the treaty-port era (1843–1943), Shanghai acquired many of the features that are now described as typical of postmodern or global cities, from its links to distant urban centers to its fragmented internal character. This suggests either that these terms need to be rethought or perhaps that room needs to be made for the idea that some cities were precociously postmodern or global. More to the point, since Shanghai became more closed in on itself and less open to the world after 1949, yet in the 1990s has dramatically begun to be reintegrated into transnational cultural and economic systems, its history suggests that these phenomena can proceed in many ways. It is possible to see stop-and-go movement, even sometimes a circling back and restarting of old patterns, where some urban theorists suggest only the possibility for unidirectional progress.

A final point worth making about the Shanghai case is that its past has played a symbolic and practical role in its resurrection as an international center of cultural and economic activity. It is hard to say just how much weight should be assigned to specific historical factors in this case, since belief in each of them has sometimes been as significant as their actual existence when it comes to convincing the regime and foreign investors to foster the transformation of Shanghai. To one degree or another, however, each of the following factors has played a role, as has the rise to prominence in post–1989 China of national leaders with Shanghai roots: (1) the idea that Shanghai people have personality traits and cultural traditions that make them especially good at doing business and especially open to foreign influences; (2) the idea that the city of Shanghai, despite turning inward during the Maoist era, retained an infrastructure that will aid its reglobalization; and, (3) the idea that its past status as a major center for world trade will facilitate its resurgence as an international center, simply because people around the globe are used to thinking of it as a natural transnational hub.

This very brief description of Shanghai's resurrection as an international hub, with real and imagined ties to various parts of the world through investment and the flow of everything from people to ideas to styles, should be enough to suggest the value of looking for comparisons with some European cities. In its heyday, the Soviet empire led to the turning inward of certain formerly cosmopolitan urban centers, which became more firmly nested for a time within national or, at the most, imperial boundaries. The postsocialist period has seen some of these cities become more internationalized once again, if not necessarily move toward the status of full-fledged global cities. It has also seen some of them—East Berlin being perhaps the most obvious example—return to old, interrupted trajectories. Shanghai is not, moreover, by any means the only city of this sort where assumptions about its past have played a key role in how its future potential has been marketed to the national authorities and the world at large. Budapest, like Shanghai, is a place that tourists and investors think about in special ways in the 1990s, in part because they know that it was called, with good reason, a "Paris of the East" in the presocialist era.[23]

Comparing Moments

Another way to restrict the search for parallels that makes sense in certain cases is to elevate time rather than space to the status of a key variable. Perhaps the most important illustration of this point involves circling back to comments made at the beginning of this chapter about 1989. Here, we see an ironic outcome of the move away from the comparisons between the PRC with Central and Eastern Europe that gained steam at the beginning of the 1990s. Namely, this has led academics to pay much less attention to the similarities between the protests that took place in China and in various parts of the Soviet empire ten years ago than might have been expected. While the events of 1989 were unfolding, it was common for journalists and scholars to note such parallels; some works published in the 1990s have certainly continued to do this, but the tendency has been to focus on divergent results rather than common processes. Hence, it has been more typical for commentators to stress the difference between the success of the protests in the former Soviet empire and the failure of those in China and wonder why the outcomes varied than to explore features the events may have shared.

When it comes to counterexamples that show the desirability of re-linking discussion of the Chinese and the non-Chinese 1989s, a variety of recent works on the PRC bring up issues or develop methodologies that might be of value to those working on Central and East European cases. One worthy of particular attention, in part because it addresses comparative issues quite directly, is a recent essay by sociologist Andrew Walder that focuses on the key question of how protesters were able to carve out the political space to demonstrate in 1989.[24] He stresses the central role played by divisions within the Chinese leadership in opening up the room necessary for a movement to grow. He also, in a related vein, highlights the importance of supportive coverage of some early events by the official media as a factor that helped convince people to take to the streets.

Another recent significant study with clear comparative implications is *Neither Gods nor Emperors* by Craig Calhoun. This is, as the author himself makes clear, not the work of a China specialist per se, but rather that of a social theorist interested in popular protest who happened to be in Beijing during the dramatic events of 1989. Calhoun's interpretations of the struggle—based on his own observations, work done in collaboration with Chinese-speaking research assistants, and analysis of secondary sources and materials in translation—is impressive and innovative. Of particular interest to specialists working on the former Soviet empire may be the attention he pays to the role of friendship in political movements that break out in authoritarian states as well as his comments on issues associated with civil society and the public sphere.[25]

The links between Chinese and European developments in 1989 are also treated in some publications and works in progress that take a collaborative form. Several collections of essays were published in the early 1990s that focused on either the 1989 protests in the PRC or those that took place in parts of the former Soviet empire that year, yet included at least one chapter that paid close attention to the other region.[26] Encouraging signs of developments to come in this line include even more directly collaborative efforts, such as conference papers cowritten by people knowledgeable about different parts of the world. China specialist Yang Guobin and Europeanist Steve Pfaff, for example, are working on a joint presentation on "Anniversaries as Symbolic Mobilization Opportunities" in the former Soviet empire and the PRC.[27]

China's Present and Europe's Past

The final sort of bridge-building that seems particularly worth attempting involves moving through time. What I mean, more specifically, is the effort to compare events that have taken place in China recently with those that occurred at an earlier point in the former Soviet empire. This can be done appropriately or inappropriately, however, and some proponents of the "end of history" teleology have fallen into the trap of doing it in the latter fashion. They have accomplished this by suggesting—misleadingly—that the PRC is destined to follow directly in the footsteps of the nations of the former Soviet empire.

There are many problems with the assumption, implicit in the work of Fukuyama himself and some who have taken their cues from him, that China missed the democratization boat ten years ago but would soon follow along the same post-Leninist course set by countries that had "successful" 1989s. Here, it will be enough just to mention two. The first is that, as other chapters in this volume show, there has not been one path away from Leninism and toward something new in Central and Eastern Europe; there have been many. So if one assumes China will someday "follow" in the footsteps of the formerly Leninist lands of Europe, then this begs a major question: Which footsteps leading in which direction? Another problem is that many residents of formerly Leninist countries have felt that, during the years following 1989, their plight has gotten worse, not better; the "nostalgia" that Boym describes is not always, by any means, an irrational desire to return to a more oppressive way of life.

This latter point is particularly important no matter how big this "many" is thought to be and how valid the feelings of members of this group are considered. This is because China's leaders and the official media in the PRC have made strategic use of the traumas that various parts of the former Soviet empire have experienced in the 1990s. When Central or Eastern Europe is mentioned in the speeches of Chinese leaders or in the pages of mainstream PRC newspapers, they are typically presented in a negative light, and usually countries where things are going particularly badly are singled out for attention. Sometimes this is done in a critical fashion, but more often in a way that is designed to inspire pity and make the citizens of China feel lucky that they have avoided suffering from particular post-1989 social or political crises.

The Chinese handling of the recent events in Kosovo fits this pattern, but perhaps the most significant case in point has been—and remains—that of Russia, which is, with justification, portrayed as having become much weaker internationally and much more troubled domestically in recent years. In 1989, some demonstrators, as noted above, lamented

China's lack of a Gorbachev. In recent years, however, in subtle and not so subtle ways, the Chinese regime has tried to convince the people of the PRC that they were very lucky indeed that, in the late 1980s and early 1990s, heaven gave them a Deng Xiaoping instead. In 1989, one of the strongest rhetorical cards the regime had to play was fear of the potential of the protests to usher in a period of *luan* (chaos) reminiscent of the decade of the cultural revolution (1966–1976). Even this was not, however, a powerful enough image to keep demonstrators from gaining widespread support. Now, when the regime defends the idea that all those who want to see China become a richer and stronger nation must make stability their watchword, the image of the danger of *luan* is linked to a different referent. The cultural revolution era is still sometimes conjured up as a bogeyman, but the fear of the kind of chaos that direct challenges to the regime's authority could bring in their wake is now associated more often with the post-Leninist fate of Russia.

If the "end of history" version of comparing China's present to Europe's past is thus doubly problematic (since it simplifies possible routes beyond Leninism and fails to take into account the influence of post–1989 troubles in the former Soviet empire as a negative example), which version works better? The alternative is one that avoids any sense of inevitability or restricted outcomes, but rather focuses on multiple possibilities and merely looks at how similarities between China now and parts of Central or Eastern Europe then can be used to help us think through complex issues. It is also one that accepts and makes the most of the variability found within the recent and not so recent histories of Central and East European states.

An important case in point among works in progress that take the approach I have in mind is by a Europeanist, not a Sinologist. It is Budapest-based political economist Mária Csanádi's attempt to explore the relevance for China of the model for understanding post-Leninist transformations that she has developed with reference to Hungary and other parts of the former Soviet empire. Three key points about her investigation, which is too complex methodologically and theoretically to do justice to in a short summary, are worth pointing out here. First, the main work it draws on, her own earlier book, *Party-States and their Legacies in Post-Communist Transformation*, is one that takes seriously the considerable variability of experiences of transition that have occurred in Central and Eastern Europe. Second, she leaves open the possibility that the PRC will follow a post-Leninist path that is not quite like that taken by any part of the Soviet empire. Third, she acknowledges the extent to which China has already entered, at least in some senses of the term, a postsocialist phase.[28]

Another important line of analysis that brings together parts of Central or East European history and contemporary developments within the PRC can be found in a book that has already been discussed, Geremie Barmé's *In the Red*. Here, I am thinking particularly of his ongoing efforts to adapt and apply to Chinese phenomena the "velvet prison" idea developed by Miklós Haraszti.

Haraszti's justly acclaimed and controversial analysis of artists under socialism focuses primarily on the situation in the Soviet empire in the early to mid–1980s and the decades leading up to that point. It also includes passing comments on the PRC of the same era, however, and in part because of this, in addition to the elegance of the argument it contains, it has generated a good deal of discussion and some debate among specialists in Chinese cultural studies from 1989 on. Barmé's first major engagement with Haraszti's work took the form of an essay that appeared in the Taiwan-based journal *Issues and Studies* a decade ago, which argued essentially that what the Hungarian analyst had said about European artists under socialism could be used to make sense of the situation in the PRC. This article by Barmé subsequently inspired a rejoinder by Paul Pickowicz, a specialist in Chinese film studies. Pickowicz, writing after the events of 1989 had taken place, saw problems with using Haraszti's model to understand the work of Zhang Yimou and other "fifth generation" Chinese directors. He also criticized Haraszti for being too pessimistic about the potential for change in state socialist countries.[29]

Now, in his new book, far from giving ground in his championing of Haraszti's approach, Barmé extends his application of the "velvet prison" model by showing how it can be used to explicate Chinese cultural trends of the 1980s and of the 1990s. One chapter of *In the Red*, which reworks some of the material first presented in the aforementioned 1989 essay, is called simply "The Chinese Velvet Prison", and Haraszti is invoked in the introduction and in other sections as well. In a chapter on "The Graying of Chinese Culture", for example, Barmé cites approvingly the Hungarian critic's comment that: "The more talented and flexible the state, the more pleasurably it can suck the dissidents' vital fluids into the organism of state culture".[30]

Throughout *In the Red*, Haraszti plays a key role in a general effort by Barmé to link contemporary Chinese trends to those that are taking place—or once took place—in a larger international world of culture. Two other figures, Václav Havel and Milan Kundera, are invoked or quoted in a similar way at different points in the book, but it is Haraszti's influence that is most pronounced.[31] One interesting point to note about Barmé's efforts to make use of the insights of Haraszti and other analysts of European state socialist phenomena is that he skillfully manages to suggest that there is a basic common dynamic at work, yet also makes plenty of room for cultural variation. Neither Europe nor China seems the "exception" to the rule in Barmé's account. Rather, he encourages us to think of each case as one in which we can see change over time and across space taking place within a shared set of politically circumscribed boundaries.

The other key point to mention about Barmé's work here is that this vision of change within parameters allows him to compare pre–1989 Europe and post–1989 China without falling into the "end of history" teleology. There is even a possibility left open—and here it is worth remembering the discussion above of his adaptation of Boym's ideas relating to posttotalitarian nostalgia—that Leninist cultural patterns can remain in force or even return after Leninist political structures have been dismantled. He shows, in short, a tendency to see contemporary China as still very like pretransition parts of the Soviet empire, but neither just like those places nor clearly located behind them on some unidirectional cultural timeline.

In Search of Conclusions

It is hard to know how to wrap up this discussion of comparisons, which has doubtless brought up more questions than it has answered and pointed to roads that might be worth taking more often than it has actually followed any path. Perhaps the best way to proceed is to look briefly at how keeping all of the strategies sketched out above in mind can help shed light on a single specific issue. The most fitting example I can think of is one that has been a recurring theme throughout this essay: the relationships, real and imagined, between the Chinese protests of 1989 and various Central and East European events. Thinking about 1989 as an epochal year illustrates the need to resist the temptation to focus on only one sort of comparative strategy. None of the four methods outlined above is satisfactory on its own, but each has something to offer.

Macrocomparisons across time and space certainly have something to offer in the case of the 1989 movements. This is because there are important common threads connecting not just what Chinese protesters and their counterparts in what was then the Soviet empire were trying to do ten years ago, but also the repercussions of their actions. It is common to think of the PRC demonstrations as having a dramatically different outcome than those in other parts of the state socialist world, but the contrast can be overdrawn. If we want to understand post–1989 Chinese political trends, it is important to see the protests of that year as having brought about some positive changes, even though in the short-run they were crushed.

The fact that the regime came so close to being toppled in 1989 helps explain some of the main directions it has pursued in the 1990s. More specifically, while continuing to suppress—often through brutal measures—direct challenges to communist party rule, China's leaders have made efforts to try to show that they are committed to solving the problems that helped convince people to take to the streets in 1989. Anticorruption campaigns, though bearing only mixed results, have become a routine part of political life in 1990s China. In addition, the state has become a much less intrusive force in the daily life of many Chinese citizens, and more channels have opened through which people can express their grievances, again with the key proviso that these not include demands for an end to one-party rule. The increased experimentation with local level elections, especially in the countryside, has been another post–1989 development that should be seen, in part, as a positive response to the failed protests of that year.

In general, we can say that not only were the Chinese and European protest movements of 1989 comparable in various ways as events—a point already discussed above—but also that the defeated Chinese struggle had some results that paralleled those of much more successful European ones. If, as other China specialists such as Merle Goldman have claimed, China's trajectory since 1989 has at times been more similar to that of many parts of the former Soviet empire than is usually assumed, these parallel results help explain why this has been the case.[32]

This said, neither macrocomparisons nor temporally limited ones nor even some combination of the two exhaust the possibilities for bringing China's 1989 into dialogue with Central and East European events. This is because, when taken as a whole, neither the events that took place in the two parts of the world in 1989 themselves, nor the impact of the various movements on the developments of the 1990s, are completely analogous. There are contrasts as well as parallels to be reckoned with at these levels of generalization. Moreover, regionally limited and temporally staggered approaches also have something to offer.

When it comes to breaking up China and the former Soviet empire into smaller constituent parts, what stands out most is that certain moments in the Chinese movement in particular cities were very similar to certain moments in one or another European country in 1989. The parallel between the Polish round table episode of March and the demand for dialogue by Beijing protesters in May has already been noted, as has the similarity between the abortive Romanian official crackdown of mid-December and the more effective and even bloodier June ones in both Beijing and Chengdu. One can also say that, during the heyday of the occupation of Tiananmen Square, China experienced something very closely akin to a velvet revolution moment, and in the central plazas of some other cities, similar events took place. Even if it lasted just a week or two, and even if it proved to be based as much on hope as on anything else, there was a sense among some Chinese urbanites that the state might dissolve and an alternative order might be created without violence.

Last but not least, if one takes an approach to China's 1989 that tries to link the PRC events to those that occurred earlier in Europe, the failure of the protests of that year can be placed in a new and interesting light. I say this because, while listening carefully to the papers presented in Budapest, I was struck by the extent to which events that took place in Central Europe well before the 1980s were being described as having an impact similar to that of the Chinese protests of 1989.

Comments were made about the Hungarian struggles of 1956 illustrating the difficulty of trying to defeat the state by revolutionary means, while Prague Spring showed in 1968 the impossibility of a reformist leader being able to comprehensively reshape a Leninist regime from within. Post–1968 efforts to transform these two countries and Poland, meanwhile, were presented largely as being carried out by people who simply decided that the best course of action was one predicated on taking for granted the imminent demise or obsolescence of Leninist structures. These led me to ponder the possibility that China's 1989 could be seen as a kind of counterpart to Central Europe's 1956 and 1968 rolled into one—and not just because in all these cases acts of state violence crushed a movement for change. Some thoughtful former participants in the Chinese protests of 1989 have argued that many demonstrators and their supporters fell into the trap of imagining that salvation could come through the actions of one heroic figure within the regime. Some have also criticized the tendency of participants in the movement to frame it as a "revolutionary struggle" to save the "revolution"—and hence fail to see that a completely new approach to changing China was needed. One tendency since 1989, among at least some critical intellectuals and dissidents, has been to move away from looking for a communist party leader who will save the regime from itself. Another has been to look for alternatives to the paradigm of attachment to a sacred revolutionary cause that has, over the course of so many decades, tended to lead mass movements in troubling directions.

Where all this will lead is hard to tell, and here again there is a need to steer clear of teleological fallacies that would have China inevitably following the course set by one or another Central European country. Still, it is tempting to see hope for the citizens of the PRC in the way some have been recently redirecting their energies in a fashion similar to that seen in Central Europe after 1968. Some have worked toward creating new organizations that stand apart from the communist party; others have simply behaved as though the eventual obsolescence of the regime can be taken for granted. Ten years after 1989, the Chinese regime shows no sign of simply withering away and rather gives the appearance of having bounced back quite effectively from the challenge it faced in the months preceding the 4 June massacre. Nevertheless, there remain many sources of discontent within the PRC, and it is still too soon to tell just what toll the legitimacy crisis of a decade ago really took in terms of destroying long-term public faith in the communist party as a moral force. Taking all this into account, and remembering how few people saw serious cracks in the façade of the Soviet empire when only a decade had passed since Prague Spring, it is at least worth wondering what the historians of the twenty-first century will say about China's 1989. One possibility is that they will come to see it as the same kind of beginning of an end as we now see in Central Europe's 1968.

Ironically, and it seems fitting to end this circuitous chapter on such a note, one point that will help determine whether or not this comes to pass is the course that history takes from here in the countries of the former Soviet empire. Even if the borders between these lands and the PRC have become more tenuous and harder to see, they do remain important in this sense: Troubles in Central and Eastern Europe continue to play a key role in the struggle by China's leaders to restore their regime's sense of legitimacy. Every member of the international community has good reason to hope that the second decade of the post–1989 period sees more countries in the former Soviet empire stand out as "successes" when it comes to economic development and democratization than was true in the first. People such as myself, who have a special interest in and concern for China, have an additional one—namely, because moves in that direction in Europe will also, indirectly, increase the likelihood that positive steps will be taken in the PRC as well.

Notes

1 Kenneth Jowitt, *New World Disorder: The Leninist Extinction* (Berkeley: University of California Press, 1992).
2 Some books published in the 1990s that either pay equal attention to each of these parts of the world (or focus on one, but include at least one chapter devoted to the other) are Yanqi Tong, *Transitions from State Socialism: Economic and Political Change in Hungary and China* (Lanham, Md.: Rowman and Littlefield, 1997); Andrew G. Walder, ed., *The Waning of the Communist State: Economic Origins of Political Decline in China and Hungary* (Berkeley: University of California Press, 1995); Paul Bowles et al., eds., *China After Socialism: In the Footsteps of Eastern Europe or East Asia?* (Armonk, N.Y.: M.E. Sharpe, 1996).
3 Personal communication, István Rév to Jeffrey N. Wasserstrom, 28 April 1999.
4 Yue Daiyun and Carolyn Wakeman, *To the Storm: The Odyssey of a Revolutionary Chinese Woman* (Berkeley: University of California Press, 1987). See also Richard Kraus, "Eastern Europe as an Alternate West for China's Middle Class", *Studies in Comparative Communism* 22:4 (Winter 1989): 323–36.
5 For the role of this visual grammar in China, see Harriet Evans and Stephanie Donald, eds., *Picturing Power: Posters of China's Cultural Revolution* (Lanham, Md.: Rowman and Littlefield, 1999); for the Soviet case, see Victoria E. Bonnell, *Iconography of Power: Soviet Political Posters under Lenin and Stalin* (Berkeley: University of California Press, 1997); for comparative perspectives, see Evgeny Dobrenko and Thomas Lahusen, eds., *Socialist Realism without Shores* (Durham: Duke University Press, 1997).
6 Nancy Bernkopf Tucker, "China Under Siege: Escaping the Dangers of 1968", in *1968: The World Transformed*, eds. Carole Fink, Philipp Gassert, and Detlef Junker (New York: Cambridge University Press, 1998), 193–216.
7 For details on the Chinese case, see various contributors to Jeffrey N. Wasserstrom and Elizabeth J. Perry, eds., *Popular Protest and Political Culture in Modern China*, 2d ed. (Boulder, Colo.: Westview Press, 1994); Han Minzhu, ed., *Cries for Democracy: Writings and Speeches from the 1989 Chinese Democracy Movement* (Princeton: Princeton University Press, 1990); and various materials included in the website created for the Long Bow Film Group's controversial prize-winning documentary on Tiananmen, "The Gate of Heavenly Peace", http://www.nmis.org/Gate/. On the European side, two excellent, very different starting points are Vladmir Tismaneanu, ed., *The Revolutions of 1989* (London: Routledge, 1999); and Bernard Gwertzman and Michael T. Kaufman, eds., *Collapse of Communism* rev. ed. (New York: Random House, 1991). The former brings together seminal essays on the events; the latter, dispatches by correspondents for the *New York Times*. Despite having a European focus, *Collapse of Communism* includes some important newspaper reports on China.
8 Daniel Chirot, "What Happened in Eastern Europe in 1989?", in Wasserstrom and Perry, *Popular Protest and Political Culture*, 218–45; also in Tismaneanu, *Revolutions*, 19–50.

9 See the comments on Sino-European connections sprinkled through James A. R. Miles, *The Legacy of Tiananmen: China in Disarray* (Ann Arbor: University of Michigan Press, 1996); on East German plans (later abandoned) to employ a "Chinese solution" to the problems there in Gwertzman and Kaufman, *Collapse of Communism*, 216–22; and on the ironic deterrent influence on European leaders of the PRC's actions in Tucker, "China under Siege", 214.

10 Francis Fukuyama, *The End of History and the Last Man* (New York: Avon Books, 1993).

11 See, for example, the approach taken in Song Qiong et al., *Zhongguo keyi shuo bu* (China Can Say No) (Beijing: Zhonghua gongshang lianhe chubanshe, 1996).

12 Samuel P. Huntington, *The Clash of Civilizations and the Remaking of World Order* (New York: Simon and Schuster, 1996).

13 The mutually reinforcing workings of some forms of western China-bashing and various types of resurgent Chinese nationalism, and the way that "Asian values" ideas work in both, is discussed well in Geremie R. Barmé, *In the Red: On Contemporary Chinese Culture* (New York: Columbia University Press, 1999), 365–77.

14 A useful book to turn to for a quick sense of just how many of the phenomena we typically associate with the former Soviet empire have been affecting post–1989 China is Orville Schell and David Shambaugh, eds., *The China Reader: The Reform Era* (New York: Vintage, 1999). On virulent nationalism, see 291–96 and 519–21; on rising crime rates and mafia-like organizations, see 394–405; on increasing disparities between rich and poor regions, see 357–61; on official corruption, see 131–32; and so on.

15 Barmé, *In the Red*, 316–44; Svetlana Boym, *Common Places: Mythologies of Everyday Life in Russia* (Cambridge: Harvard University Press, 1994).

16 Barmé, *In the Red*, 316, 344.

17 On the Mao revival, see also Geremie R. Barmé, *Shades of Mao: The Posthumous Cult of the Great Leader* (Armonk, N.Y.: M.E. Sharpe, 1996); and Michael Dutton, *Streetlife China* (New York: Cambridge University Press, 1998), 238–71.

18 Dorothy Solinger, *Contesting Citizenship in Urban China: Peasant Migrants, the State, and the Logic of the Market* (Berkeley: University of California Press, 1999); and on the "floating population", see also Schell and Shambaugh, *China Reader*, 362–75.

19 Dutton, *Streetlife China*, 8–13, 62–69, and 86–93.

20 Full elaboration of the arguments presented will be contained in a book, the working title of which is *Global Shanghai*, but some preliminary discussion of the themes introduced can be found in Jeffrey N. Wasserstrom, "Comparing 'Incomparable' Cities: Postmodern L.A. and Old Shanghai", *Contention: Debates in Society, Culture, and Science* 15:3 (1996): 69–90; and Jeffrey N. Wasserstrom, "Locating Old Shanghai: Having Fits about Where it Fits", in *Remaking the Chinese City: Modernity and National Identity, 1900–1950* ed. Joseph W. Esherick (Honolulu: University of Hawaii Press, 1999), 192–210. My discussion of Shanghai builds on recent work by a variety of specialists in the history and present state of that city, and many of them are acknowledged in some fashion in my "Locating Shanghai" chapter. My current work also draws heavily from studies in progress by and ongoing discussions about Shang-

hai's past and present with several people, most notably Robert Bickers, Elizabeth Perry, Steve Smith, and Barbara Mittler.

21 Saskia Sassen, *The Global City: New York, London and Tokyo* (Princeton: Princeton University Press, 1991).

22 On visions of the postmodern city, see Michael Dear, "Beyond the Post-Fordist City", *Contention: Debates in Society, Culture, and Science* 5:1 (1995): 67–76; also Edward Soja, *Postmodern Geographies* (London: Verso, 1989).

23 The preceding section is, admittedly, a somewhat impressionistic one, so it is only fair to note that it was inspired in part by my own impressions of Budapest. Arriving there for the first time in March 1999 to attend the conference at the Central European University, I expected to find a city that reminded me of Vienna, the urban center closest to Budapest, which I had visited in the past. Instead, I was struck by a variety of impressions, including the juxtaposition in some districts of stores and hotels that suggested European architectural styles of the 1930s and generically state socialist concrete apartment buildings from the 1950s that reminded me more of Shanghai. I did not see the same kind of evidence of massively ambitious new building projects that are such a definitive part of 1990s Shanghai, of course. There were, however, many signs in Budapest, as there are in Shanghai, of a city attempting to return to an interrupted path of urban development and resurrect itself as an international hub.

24 Andrew Walder, "Collective Protest and the Waning of the Communist State in China", in *Challenging Authority: The Historical Study of Contentious Politics* eds. Michael P. Hanagan, Leslie Page Moch, and Wayne te Brake (Minneapolis: University of Minnesota Press, 1998), 54–72.

25 Craig Calhoun, *Neither Gods Nor Emperors: Students and the Struggle for Democracy in China* (Berkeley: University of California Press, 1994), 170–73 on friendship and 188–212 on public sphere and civil society. A variety of other analysts have, in part because of the influence of work on the former Soviet empire that deals with similar themes, focused on issues of civil society in looking at China's 1989. See, for example, various contributions to Arthur Rosenbaum, ed., *State and Society in China: The Consequences of Reform* (Boulder, Colo.: Westview Press, 1992); various chapters in Roger Des Forges et al., eds., *Chinese Democracy and the Crisis of 1989: Chinese and American Reflection* (Albany: SUNY Press, 1993); Elizabeth J. Perry and Ellen Fuller, "China's Long March to Democracy", *World Policy Journal* (Fall 1991): 663–95; Jeffrey N. Wasserstrom and Liu Xinyong, "Student Associations and Mass Movements", in *Urban Space in Contemporary China*, ed. Deborah Davis et al., (New York: Cambridge University Press, 1995), 362–93; and Philip Huang, ed., "Symposium: 'Public Sphere'/'Civil Society' in China?", a special issue of *Modern China* 19:2 (1993).

26 Daniel Chirot, ed., *The Crisis of Leninism and the Decline of the Left: The Revolutions of 1989* (Seattle: University of Washington, 1991); Robert P. Miller, ed., *The Development of Civil Society in Communist Systems* (London: Allen and Unwin, 1992); and Wasserstrom and Perry, *Popular Protest and Political Culture.*

27 This paper will be presented in November 1999 at the Social Science History Association annual meeting. It will be part of a panel on "The Democracy Movements and the Upheavals of 1989: Research on Social Movements and Political Change Ten

Years Later" that is to be chaired by Jeff Goodwin, a theorist of revolutionary change. It will also include papers by Jack Goldstone and Daniel Chirot.

28 Maria Csanadi, *Party-states and their Legacies in Post-communist Transformation* (Cheltenham, U.K.: Edward Elgar, 1997).

29 Miklós Haraszti, *The Velvet Prison: Artists Under State Socialism* trans. Katalin and Stephen Landesmann (New York: Basic Books, 1987); Geremie R. Barmé, "The Chinese Velvet Prison in the 'New Age,' 1976–89", *Issues and Studies* 25:8 (August 1989): 54–79; and Paul Pickowicz, "Velvet Prisons and the Political Economy of Chinese Filmmaking", in Davis, *Urban Spaces*, 193–220. Barmé's approach to Haraszti's work—as providing "one the most insightful, albeit irreverent and often tongue-in-cheek, guides to mainland China's post–1976 'new age' of culture"—Barmé *In the Red*, 7—is returned to later. Pickowicz, "Velvet Prisons", begins with a reference to Haraszti as a "brilliant" analyst (194), but ends by saying that "for all the light [his] work sheds on the situation in China, he was, in the end, wrong" (216). Pickowicz claims that Haraszti—and Barmé as well, at least in his earliest use of the "velvet prison" idea—is too hard on artists working under state socialism and ends up painting too bleak a picture of the possibilities for effective and genuinely subversive dissent in such settings.

30 Barmé, *In the Red*, 129; see also Barmé, *In the Red*, xviii, 1–19, 304, and 345; the quote comes from Haraszti, *Velvet Prison*, 159.

31 It is worth noting that some producers as well as analysts of Chinese popular culture are interested in links between Eastern Europe and China. It is surely no mere coincidence, for example, that the title of the controversial rock singer (and more recently rapper) Cui Jian's latest compact disc is "Power of the Powerless", an allusion to a famous piece of writing by Havel.

32 Merle Goldman, "Restarting Chinese History: A Review Essay", *American Historical Review* (forthcoming 2000).

20 Mickiewicz and the Question of Sacred Territory

IRENA GRUDZIŃSKA GROSS

The tenth anniversary of the 1989 velvet revolutions also marks the tenth year of the Yugoslav war. It was ten years ago—on 28 June 1989—that Slobodan Milosević delivered his fateful speech in Kosovo, which celebrated the six-hundredth anniversary of the Kosovo battle, an event central to Serbian national mythology. The gradual disintegration of the Yugoslav federation and the creation of small nation-states according to uncertain and terribly complex ethnic lines followed this event.

The present conflict over Kosovo is the latest chapter in this bloody, destructive war. At this point in time, Serbian ethnic cleansing has reduced the Albanian Kosovar population from approximately 1.8 million to 1 million people. It has been estimated that at least eight hundred thousand Kosovars have been forced abroad, six hundred thousand are believed to be internally displaced in Kosovo, and two hundred thousand are missing. North Atlantic Treaty Organization (NATO) planes are bombing targets in Serbia and Kosovo, and there is no sign that civilian Serbs disapprove of ethnic cleansing; on the contrary, they seem united in facing NATO bombing.

No easy resolution at this stage of the war is at hand. Kosovo, observers believe, is essential to the very essence of Serbian nationalism. "Serbian culture itself is built around elaborate sagas of failure and betrayal, all beginning with the 1389 defeat of Prince Lazar by the Ottoman Turks on the battlefields of Kosovo—a heroic last stand that sanctified Kosovo for all Serbs *for all time*", runs one typical comment (emphasis added). "For centuries", writes the same observer, "Serbs have been taught not only that they sacrificed more than any other Christian European people to resist pagan aggression, but also that their sacrifices have never been appreciated or recognized. Rather, outside powers ungratefully denied them their independence."[1]

It is in fact this "for all time" that I address here. The basis of the fa-
talistic approach to the Balkan wars lies in the conviction that national
symbolic geography is unchangeable. Yet such history is not unique to
the Serbs and has been changed in other countries; thus, although it does
have "staying power", certainly it is not eternal. Moreover, the process of
constructing national myths comes under scrutiny even in today's Serbia.
One of the few certainties about the battle of Kosovo is the significance
of its date—the day of Saint Vitus, 15 June 1389 (28 June according to
the new calendar), on which both the Serbian Prince Lazar and the
Turkish Sultan Murat were killed. The Serbs were defeated, and their
state, which continued to exist for another eighty years, was subjugated
by the Ottoman Turks.

The origin of the legend of Kosovo was religious rather than political or
national. The Orthodox Church quickly placed Prince Lazar among its
saints. The Kosovo battle legend evolved then around two New Testament
motifs: of unconditional sacrifice and of betrayal. In the eighteenth century
it was finally encapsulated in a coherent epic work, enriched a century later
in numerous variations and modernizations. The definitive literary version
of the Kosovo battle was written in 1847 by Petr Petrović Niebosh, a
Montenegrin romantic poet. The battle became a living part of national
tradition, modified and invoked at every historic moment, constituting an
interpretation of history and the model for present behavior.[2]

Other East and South European nations have similar symbolic national histories. Past glories and defeats, betrayals by stronger powers,
civilizing missions toward those who were of other religious persuasions,
and deep feelings of victimization are characteristic of the region. Yet
within this framework, spectacular changes and accommodations have
taken place.

A radical change in the Polish attitude to its sacred territory is one
such case. Forced to relinquish its eastern lands, Poland first adjusted to
its new borders, and then, its seems, almost forgot what was left behind.
It is possible to observe by this example a change in national geography
and a national identity in motion.[3] "For all time" turned out to be finite.

Modern Polish national identity was forged in the first part of the
nineteenth century, at approximately the same time as Serbian identity.
Poland had a long history of statehood, but its state disintegrated in the
seventeenth century, when the historic nation-states of Western Europe
were coming to maturity. "Belated" nations like Italy and Germany, and
even more "belated" East-Central European states, were formed after the
long preparation of "an anticipatory national consciousness disseminated
by propaganda". The main actors in these preparatory efforts were
"writers and historians, and scholars and intellectuals in general, who

laid the groundwork for...subsequent unification of the state by propagating the more or less imaginary unity of the 'cultural nation'".[4] "The exclusive legitimacy of culture-based states" needed a kind of "ethnogenesis" in which "schoolteachers, ethnographers, folklorists and national Awakeners...[went]...to the villages and construct[ed] a national culture from the chaos of regional dialectical variety", thereby transforming peasant culture into high culture so as to permit the building of a political entity that would be coterminous with the state. Only in that way could the nationalist principle of "one culture-one state" have been implemented in Eastern Europe.[5]

The father and codifier of the Polish "cultural nation" was the romantic poet Adam Mickiewicz (along with many of his contemporaries). The year 1998 was the bicentennial of his birthday, and it was the first celebration of a national icon in post-1989 Poland. The country was awash with conferences, speeches, concerts, readings, and performances. Television programs were produced, movies were made. The bicentennial became an occasion to debate issues that are now being addressed in all postcommunist countries: the question of the relationship between newly regained national sovereignty and accession to the larger world community; of the growth of individualism coterminous with the protection of local communal values; of justice and forgiveness, or, to quote Adam Michnik, amnesia and amnesty; of going forward while carrying the burden of recent history.

The terms of the discussions surrounding that anniversary made clear the romantic origin of Polish national consciousness and the continuity of its basic suppositions. Polish public life was described and analyzed through concepts such as political treason, individual betrayal, sacrifice, and redemption. Because of the tradition of statelessness, these terms were—and still are—used in a moral rather than a political sense. The identification of Polishness with Catholicism seems to remain the basis of national identity. Such Polishness is counterposed to western legalism and liberalism (although Poles are undoubtedly the most prowestern nation among the Slavs). The "primordial" people's wisdom is contrasted with the embracing of false knowledge and nonpatriotic values by the elite. Family constitutes a unit of resistance and is the real repository of national tradition, with the woman as the guardian of family ("the nation's hearth"). Men are not politicians but continue to be warriors (or traitors). The "West" continues to misunderstand Polish specificity, although its acceptance into NATO makes one believe that this chronic mistrust is weakening.

It is not accidental that these issues were debated on the occasion of the bicentennial of the birth of a poet. This vision of national life can—

and should—be traced back to the messianic nationalism of Adam Mickiewicz. A few words about him are therefore needed here. Born in 1798, Mickiewicz belonged to the first generation that never knew a sovereign Polish state. (Mickiewicz, one should note, was just slightly older than the codifier of the Serbian Kosovo saga, Petr Petrović-Niegosh). At the time of his birth, Poland was partitioned among Austria, Prussia and Russia, and was not to regain its independence for another one hundred and twenty years. He was a citizen of the Russian empire, living as a child in Nowogródek (now in Belarus), and later studied in Vilnius (now the capital of Lithuania). In the past, these territories were a part of the powerful Polish-Lithuanian Commonwealth. Exiled to Russia as a young man, Mickiewicz did not once set foot in Warsaw or Kraków, or what is now the central part of Poland. He passed his life in exile, mostly in France, nostalgic for the country of his childhood and youth, which he called, in Polish, "Lithuania". He died in 1855 in Constantinople, trying to organize Polish and Jewish military units to fight for Poland's independence.

Mickiewicz was the descendant of poor, minor nobility, most probably of Lithuanian ethnicity (if such a description makes any sense). An ardent Catholic who spoke and wrote in Polish, he had a limited, or nonexistent, knowledge of Lithuanian and a boundless devotion to Poland. Throughout the nineteenth century he functioned in Polish culture as an exemplary patriot and was the embodiment of the very idea of what it is to be Polish. Over the years there were endless rumors and controversies attached to his name: the often-suspected Jewish origin of his mother, the Orthodox Christianity of his father, his own heretical Christian mysticism and life in a Christian sect, and his womanizing. The reasons why he did not join the 1831 anti-Russian insurrection and why he organized Jewish battalions in Turkey are very difficult to ascertain. He was the bearer of Polishness, the common ancestor of all Poles. His poetry inspired awe and love and was absorbed into everyday language, providing it with proverb-like sayings, quotations, and expressions. If we define a classic as a source of quotation, Mickiewicz is such a classic for Poles. By repeating, paraphrasing, or alluding to his words, Poles signal to each other their common national heritage. Several of his characters and literary situations are recognizable to any Pole—even illiterates. Repeating his words is the way in which the nation proves its uniqueness, its authenticity. The mechanism of repetition serves then to maintain a unique identity.

The role Mickiewicz played in the creation of Polish national consciousness was similar to that of other national poets of East-Central Europe. His geographic origin—coming from the borderlands—seems to have been a common pedigree of the founding fathers of early nineteenth-century East European nationalism (Niebosh was a Montenegrin, and Petőfi was of Slovak origin, to name just two of them).[6] These poets, writers, and intellectuals bridged the eighteenth-century vision of the territorial state based on dynastic legitimacy with the nineteenth-century concept of state sovereignty based on nationhood.[7] One could say that they "democratized" state sovereignty, brought it down to *demos* in its original meaning: the people. In Mickiewicz's case the "people" were not so much a single ethnicity as the body of all inhabitants of the historical Polish-Lithuanian Commonwealth and especially as a class—the local peasantry. The Polish nation was not an ethnic concept, but it had a larger sense—it was "a cultural nation", to use the words of Jürgen Habermas. It could not be otherwise, since Mickiewicz's Poland was not even located on what could be called ethnically Polish territories. The plays and poems Mickiewicz wrote were set in what today is Belarus or Lithuania, a part of Europe that used to—but does not anymore—belong to Poland. As Tadeusz Boy-Żeleński said, because of Mickiewicz, Vilnius, rather than Warsaw or Cracow, became the poetic capital of Poland. When, one hundred and fifty years after Mickiewicz's death, the *location* of Poland changed, that *seat* of Poland was as good as forgotten.

The Poland that romantics celebrated and proposed as the common historical homeland for all Poles was located on the Niemen River rather than on the Vistula. These Belarusian or Lithuanian territories of Mickiewicz's works were populated by "medieval" pagans and Orthodox Christians. The settings, both historical and geographical, were far removed from his contemporaneity. Yet the exotic territory and pagans were never an obstacle to the patriotic—and later even ethnic—interpretation of his work. Many particulars were brushed aside or ignored. It was always understood that the Poland of Mickiewicz was true in a nonliteral sense, that independently or in spite of particulars, what he captured was its essence. The fatherland (or rather, suffering motherland) of Polish citizens did not have to be ethnically Polish, did not have to be Catholic; that ideal fatherland was a re-creation of an idealized Commonwealth of Poland and Lithuania, perched towards the East, "civilizing" and christianizing Lithuanian pagans and Ukrainian nobility, submerging barbarian Muscovites, repelling Tartar attacks and invasions. Its greatness disappeared, but the idea of a Catholic and civilizing *antemurale* did persist.

Mickiewicz was a man of the Polish borderlands who celebrated a Poland that already then belonged to the distant past: to put it crudely, a nonethnic Pole who captured in supreme verse an idealized image of an ethnically non-Polish Poland. The Polish *Divine Comedy*—Mickiewicz's

Pan Tadeusz—is the best example of that "misplacement" or dislocation. The imaginary manor of Soplicowo, where the Polish-speaking nobility awaited the arrival of Napoleon's army, is located somewhere to the west of Moscow, but also far to the east of Warsaw (in, it seems, Lithuania).[8] Mickiewicz's Poland—its geographic shape imprecise—was there, in that between-Warsaw-and-Moscow territory.

That vision, shape, and location of Poland gradually changed. Throughout the nineteenth century the concept of Polishness became more and more ethnic. That ethnicization was not due to the forgetting of the patriotic "matrix of Poland"—the Polish Commonwealth.[9] The Polish nobility and intelligentsia kept this matrix alive. Important literature has been written about it, and the books by such writers as Orzeszkowa and Sienkiewicz maintained, so to speak, the "location" of Poland in these ethnically composite territories. The ethnicization of the concept of Poland—the linking of Polishness to blood and the transformation of a cultural nation (of nobility) into an ethnic nation (of all classes)—came with the spirit of the times. Poland was just one of many European nations that gradually redefined itself in ethnic terms. The ethnically complex Mickiewicz and his ethnically complex Poland became purified and cleansed, as did all other East European nations. His work was first poetic and symbolic, but gradually it became even less literal. The nostalgic Soplicowo took on an ethereal, idealized quality, and its quarrelsome inhabitants became family to every Pole.

I mentioned already that during the bicentennial anniversary of Mickiewicz's birth, many problems were discussed that were common to the postcommunist countries. There were also specifically Polish questions: about the persistence of romanticism in Polish patriotism, the place of religion in Mickiewicz's vision of Poland, and some Mickiewicz family secrets, like the mental illness of his wife. There was almost no discussion, however, of the location of Poland, even though the poetic and intellectual, if not moral, authority of another Polish "Lithuanian"—the poet Czesław Miłosz—revived the vision of the Commonwealth of Poland. Throughout his long creative life, Miłosz writes continuously about the Polish-Lithuanian Commonwealth and returns repeatedly to Mickiewicz. (Miłosz believes Mickiewicz made Poles replace all questions, including theology and metaphysics, with national issues. Goodness was on the side of Poles and, Miłosz said, Mickiewicz made God become Polish.) But today the Lithuanian Commonwealth is basically a land of poetry, and Miłosz himself sees it as a place of exoticism.[10] Besides, Poles have more and more trouble understanding the very idea of the Republic of Lithuania and Poland. The link between language, blood, and territory, reinforced by the idea of one religion, delineates the borders of what Poland can be, of how Poles are able to think about their country. In the Commonwealth, nobility was Polish or Polonized; the pan-language was Polish; the peasantry was just that—peasantry. With the collapse of the old class system, the Commonwealth became exotic and obscure. Today we can hardly understand what it was all about.[11]

I wrote above that there was *almost* no discussion of the former location of Poland, but some nostalgic voices were raised and should be noted here. One was that of Jacek Trznadel, who wrote: "*Pan Tadeusz* is a testimony of the strength and reach of Polish culture, the way Roman aqueducts, roads, temples, and amphitheaters outside of Italy are witnesses to the power and greatness of Rome".[12] The Ukrainian city of Lviv, present in Polish consciousness as Lwów, is still celebrated by the poets and writers who were born there: Zbigniew Herbert, Adam Zagajewski, and Stanisław Lem. But the tone of these remembrances is simply nostalgic. It is one issue to leave behind monuments of past greatness (however Trznadel understood these words) and another to claim a territory as one's own. That difference is clearly visible in Kosovo.

The mental and ideological abandonment of territories that used to be (politically) Polish was helped, of course, by several historical calamities, wars, uprisings, and population movements. New states appeared in place of former Polish territories, and no one doubted their legitimacy, especially not the people who believed in the ethnic principle of nation-state. Stalin's creation of these countries "pushed" Poland towards the West, causing her "migration". Although this campaign was primarily the enlargement of Stalin's domain, Poles actively embraced their new location and its tilt toward the center of Europe. That embrace was well-expressed in the short but very meaningful episode that took place in the 1980s: the creation (or return) of the myth of Central Europe—the mostly Czech-inspired idea of Eastern Europe being in reality an integral part of the European West. A series of articles written by Milan Kundera, Czesław Miłosz, and Timothy Garton Ash, among others, and enthusiastically accepted in Czechoslovakia, Hungary, and Poland mark the latest case of East European intellectuals rewriting the concept of national and state loyalties. This very successful rewriting of the mental map of Europe now has been sanctified by the enlargement of NATO.

But it is unclear how the NATO story will end. Today, the national question is back with us in full force. Ethnic cleansing, the redrawing of borders, the appearance of new nations, each claiming a state of its own, seem to continue the process that started in the first half of the nineteenth century. The gradual dissolution of multinational empires led then to the creation of new nation-states, and the European mosaic of ethnicities started to sort itself out. World War II was in itself a gigantic wave of ethnic cleansing and was immediately followed by another. East European Jewry was wiped out; a large proportion of Roma population was annihilated; the Sudeten Germans were expelled from Czechoslovakia. Poland moved west into new territories and had part of its eastern population settled in formerly German towns and villages. These resettled people never returned to their former lands. One could say that this phenomenon was due to the cold war and its freezing of borders. But in all of twentieth-century European history, there are no examples of the return of populations once they have been expelled from their homelands. The unlikely return of Kosovars to their lands would be the first such case.

The former Soviet empire is disintegrating on ethnic fault lines. Undoubtedly, it has been defeated to a large degree by the internal and external resistance of oppressed ethnicities. No matter how small the group, the dream of its own state seems to be the order of the day.[13] Communism transformed itself into nationalism; to use another apt formulation by Adam Michnik, nationalism became the supreme stage of communism. The best, or rather the worst, example of that evolution is Slobodan Milosević, former communist apparatchik and now a virulent Serbian nationalist. The postcommunists in Russia are another illustrative case.

It is unclear where and how this process may end. But one could say that in the case of Poland, the horrendous task of ethnic "sorting" has been completed. Nobody in Poland casts a longing eye on formerly Polish eastern territories. It also seems that present day Germany accepted the fact that its eastern territories are now firmly possessed by Poles, including such "sacred" German places as Danzig and Marlbork. "After 1989 it was generally accepted that borders should stay where they were. This was what had been agreed at Helsinki in 1975, and it remained an article of faith even when this meant accepting the injustices of the post-1945 settlement. Germany finally recognized Poland's western border and gave up all claims to the old eastern territories. The Baltic states too accepted independence within the postwar boundaries and did not seek a return to the pre-1939 *status quo ante*. Stability was too precious to be jeopardized".[14]

The Poles have the look of a nation satisfied with its geographic and political positioning, with the ethnic and religious unity of its population placed "neatly" within state borders. It is a truly unusual situation in Poland's thousand-year history and in European history as well. One often can hear in Poland that religious and national unity assists the development of democracy. This is a truly paradoxical situation: among its neighbors, Poland is the only religiously and ethnically homogenous country; it is therefore tautological that it would have less ethnic and religious conflict. One could question the long-term relationship between democracy (which implies plurality and diversity of subjects) and ethnic and religious monoentity. Even without minorities, Poland has a serious Jewish question, as though a democratic state needs to produce diversity in order to function properly. But if we were to conclude that the mono-ethnic state is more conducive to peace and prosperity, Poland (and Europe) paid an extremely heavy price for this unusual correspondence between borders and ethnicity. That price is being exacted today in the Balkans.

Mickiewicz had a deep respect for the Serbian nation. In his courses in Slavic literature, delivered in the years 1840–44 at the College de France, he discussed the Kosovo battle. "The entire national poetry of Serbs circles around this defeat or painfully reminiscences about it... [T]he old story of this battle is for them a reality to a degree that is difficult to comprehend; their thoughts are not taken by active life, new history, richness of current events. The Serbs, passing through the Kosovo Polje, even now cry as if the battle took place yesterday; they speak about it almost as if about a present event. In the Serb poetry it plays the same role as the battle of Xeres de la Frontera in Spanish poetry: it reigns over every thought. Unfortunately, the Serbs did not have their battle of Tolosa, which for the Spaniards started a new epoch, while for the Serbs the Battle on Kosovo Field opened and closed their political history".[15] The war against Kosovar Albanians does not seem to bring the Serbs out of the Kosovo circle. Their political history still remains closed.

Notes

1 Stacy Sullivan, "Milosević's Willing Executioners", *The New Republic* (10 May 1999): 26–35; both quotes from 30.

2 Olga Zirojević, "The Kingdom of Serbs is Not of This World", *Gazeta Świąteczna* (15–16 May 1999): 14–16. It is important to say that Slobodan Milosević starts his Kosovo speech by acknowledging that the historical facts may not correspond to the current Serbian vision of the Kosovo battle. But it is the emotional truth that is of importance, he says.

3 See Ilya Prizel, *National Identity and Foreign Policy: Nationalism and Leadership in Poland, Ukraine and Russia* (Cambridge: Cambridge University Press, 1998), 12–37.

4 Jürgen Habermas, *The Inclusion of the Other: Studies in Political Theory*, eds. Ciaran Cronin and Pablo De Greiff (Cambridge: MIT Press, 1998), 105.

5 Ernest Gellner, *Conditions of Liberty: Civil Society and Its Rivals* (London: Hamish Hamilton, 1994), 109–24.

6 See also the article by Daniel Chirot, "Herder's Multicultural Theory of Nationalism and Its Consequences", *East European Politics and Society* (Winter 1996): 1–15.

7 See Rodney Bruce Hall, *National Collective Identity: Social Constructs and International Systems* (New York: Columbia University Press, 1999).

8 The poem starts with the famous opening "Oh, Lithuania, my country", and therefore Soplicowo is to be placed in Lithuania. But of course this is not the Lithuania of today, but the "Lithuania" of Mickiewicz's childhood—most probably present day Belarus. Such supposition seems, however, to be profoundly unpatriotic, judging by the remarks of Jacek Trznadel in his "Tajemnicza przyroda w Panu Tadeuszu", in *Tajemnice Mickiewicza*, ed. Marta Zielińska (Warsaw: IBL, 1998), 167–177; see 176. Trznadel considers these territories Lithuanian—that is, Polish—although now "geographically" located "in partibus infidelium" (sic) (175).

9 Ilya Prizel writes that the "aristocratic commonwealth" became "the matrix of a national ideal", in Prizel, *National Identity and Foreign Policy*, 41.

10 See Miłosz's "The Land of Urlo", "Prywatne obowiązki", and "Poszukiwanie ojczyzny", among others.

11 This is well demonstrated by the new cinematic version of "By Fire and Sword", an adaptation to screen of the most popular Polish patriotic book. While Sienkiewicz writes about an arduous fight to keep the lands of the Polish Commonwealth, the movie speaks in an exotic and strange mixture of languages, nationalities, and costumes that illustrate bloody battle scenes succeeding one another without pause and mercy. The movie tried to redress the historical injustices of Sienkiewicz's depiction of seventeenth-century Polish wars, turning the entire enterprise into a barely comprehensible mess.

12 Trznadel, *Tajemnice Mickiewicza*, 176.

13 Faced by the war, Montenegrins and Kosovars started to define themselves as nations. See also "Hail Ruthenia!" in which Timothy Garton Ash describes the national aspirations of Ruthenians. In *The New York Review of Books* (22 April 1999): 54–55.

14 Mark Mazower, *Dark Continent: Europe's Twentieth Century* (New York: Knopf, 1999), 393–94.

15 "Lecture IV of the First Cycle", in Adam Mickiewicz, "Literatura słowiańska", *Collected Works* Vol. IV (Warsaw: 1955), 45.

V Past, Present, Future

21 *Conclusions*

TIMOTHY GARTON ASH

The last time I did this job—concluding a conference—was, curiously enough, in Budapest in 1996. The subject then was the revolution of 1956, forty years on. That was clearly a revolution, and everyone recognized it as such: there was a strong element of popular and violent uprising. It was probably the last revolution in that classical sense in European history. And it had to be forty years on because for thirty years the history of the revolution was systematically traduced in Hungary itself and turned into a "counterrevolution". Only after forty years could we find out what had really happened; we had the documents, and we also could see the consequences of what had happened. Now, ten years on from 1989, our case is quite different. For a start, we spent much of the last two days discussing in what sense this was a revolution. I remember this was often discussed during the events themselves. I remember discussing them in the Magic Lantern Theater in Prague when, five minutes before a press conference to announce to the world what the Civic Forum was going to do, someone said: "But should we call this a revolution? After all, a revolution involves violence". So instead of discussing the soundbite, we spent the last five minutes with Martin Palouš and others wondering if we should call it a revolution. In fact we always have to qualify it; we call it "velvet", we call it "peaceful", we call it "evolutionary", someone in our conference calls it "rebirth" not revolution, I call it "refolution"—a mixture of revolution and reform. Curiously enough the moment when people in the West finally thought there was a revolution was when they saw television pictures of Romania: crowds, tanks, shooting, blood in the streets. They said: "That— we know *that* is a revolution", and of course the joke is that it was the only one that wasn't.

Ten years on, what do we know? First of all, we know more about the consequences. We know that this "revolution" of 1989 not only changed systems throughout Eastern and Central Europe. It changed the whole political map of Europe, and it led directly to the end of the Soviet Union, of the cold war, of the short twentieth century, and to a total redefinition of the Left. There is not a corner of the world that has not in some sense been touched by the consequences of 1989—Central America, China, South Africa, Southeast Asia—so in its consequences it was certainly one of the great revolutions of modern history. Secondly, we know an awful lot about the causes, unlike the Hungarian revolution of 1956, for which we had to wait forty years to know what the Politburo discussed, thanks to the work of our friends in the Cold War International History Project, the admirable 1956 Institute in Budapest, and other contemporary historians, and thanks to the opening of the archives. Just ten years after 1989 we have a very good idea of what actually happened and the causes.

I don't myself think that there are many historiographical revelations and many great secrets waiting to be discovered about the causes of 1989. The trouble is that we have too many causes; the outcome of 1989 has come to be seen as almost overdetermined, as somehow an inevitable result. Thus, for example, we have figures about the hard currency indebtedness of East Germany, and then people say, "You see, East Germany was bankrupt, so it was bound to collapse", but of course this is a fallacy. Countries don't collapse like companies simply because they are bankrupt. Certainly countries don't when they are part of an empire that is armed with nuclear weapons. What we have is what Henri Bergsan called "the illusions of retrospective determinism". It seems to us that everything that happened *had* to happen. We gather neatly in our academic papers all the causes, and what we have lost and forgotten is what people *did not know* at the time. I remember sitting with Adam Michnik on the morning of the historic Polish elections on 4 June 1989. Adam was exhausted and profoundly depressed, not only because he had a hangover, but also because he was not sure; he did not think that Solidarity had won. We did not know. And again, even when Solidarity had won, we did not know it would be possible to form a government led by a noncommunist prime minister. Then I went to East Germany in July 1989. All the dissidents in East Berlin told me that what was happening in Poland and Hungary could *never* happen there, that it was impossible, and they gave very convincing reasons. We did not know.

So throughout that year of wonders, 1989, we were like children at a birthday party sitting at the feet of a conjurer. We gasped at every new trick. I think that sense of wonder and that cloud of unknowing in which we moved was in some sense nearer to the historical truth than we may be today with our illusions of retrospective determinism. For, based on all the evidence we have, the outcome was by no means inevitable; it was perhaps not even highly probable, and there were many turning points at which history might have taken a different path—as it did in China on 4 June 1989. What made the crucial difference was something that perhaps we have talked too little about in the last two days: the role of individuals in history. The outcome, the almost miraculous outcome, was crucially determined by three groups of individuals. The first group is Gorbachev and his colleagues with their strange combination of realism about the depth of the crisis and illusions about the possibility of reforming socialism— illusions without which 1989 would not have been possible.

The second group is the Central European opposition elite with their learning process through the events of 1953, 1956, 1968 and from 1980– 81 to 1989, but also with a longer learning process, a learning process from the whole history of revolution and of radical philosophy, of utopias, summed up by Adam Michnik in the wonderful sentence: "We have learned that those who start by storming Bastille will end up building Bastille". That fundamental lesson from the history of revolution was crucial to the way these revolutions were conducted.

Finally, last but not least, I think we should mention those people inside the regimes, in Poland and Hungary—not so much elsewhere—who were what Hans Magnus Ensenberger has wonderfully called "the heroes of retreat"—the heroes of retreat who recognized the need and had the wisdom to sit down at round tables with the opposition elite and negotiate a transition. They were the F.W. de Klerks of Central Europe.

One of the questions that was raised in this discussion by Martin Palouš was a question to me about the assertion that the revolutions of 1989 produced no big new ideas. I always have difficulty in discussions with Martin Palouš: one of the many things that I have failed to do in my life is to master phenomenology, and so the conversation between an Anglo-Saxon empiricist and a Central European phenomenologist is not always the easiest one. But nonetheless, I have yet to hear what big new ideas emerged from the revolution of 1989 to compare with *"liberté, egalité, fraternité"* of 1789 or to compare with "all power to the Soviets" and the idea of a heaven built upon earth, the communist utopia. There was no distinctively new project for the remaking of society in 1989. The project was in essence one that already existed elsewhere in Europe. It is, I think, an irony that a revolution that was in many ways, as Vladimir Tismaneanu mentioned, a revolution of intellectuals—and in that sense comparable with 1848—produced no new ideas. The one thing the revolution of intellectuals did not produce was any new ideas. It just produced a reality, and in that sense it was the opposite of 1848. All that 1848 left was ideas.

The year 1989 left realities. Yet there was something new; there was a big new idea, and that was the revolution itself—the idea of the non-revolutionary revolution, the evolutionary revolution. The motto of 1989 could come from Lenin's great critic Eduard Bernstein: "The goal is nothing, the movement is everything". It was not just a lesson that Agnes Heller taught us—that no goal is so sublime that it justifies the sacrifice of political freedom—but also the lesson that the means you use them-selves pervert the end. So this was a revolution that was not about the *what* but about the *how*. That particular model of peaceful, sustained, marvelously inventive, massive civil disobedience channeled into an oppositional elite that was itself prepared to negotiate and to compromise with the existing powers, the powers that were (in short, the round ta-ble)—that was the historical novelty of 1989. Where the guillotine is a symbol of 1789, the round table is a symbol of 1989. This is a model that has continuing significance. If you talk to people in South Africa about their transition, they tell you that what happened in Central Europe was vitally important to them, not just because it was the end of the cold war. Aung San Suu Kyi, the opposition leader in Burma, has read all the works of Václav Havel and Adam Michnik and others; she is studying the model of the velvet revolution. And let us not forget there were Kosovar Albanians who spent seven years organizing a massive move-ment of peaceful civil disobedience trying to implement that model with no Jaruzelski on the other side, but also with no help from the West.

Of course this model of velvet revolution, of the round table, has to stand the test of time. There is one particular test that a self-limiting, nonrevolutionary revolution faces, and that is the sense of a missing revolutionary catharsis. The resentment is caused by the fact that people from the old elites are still in power, the cry that we should finish the revolution—in short, the cry for what in Central Europe has been called "decommunization". This, it seems to me, is a test that is intrinsic to the nature of the nonrevolutionary, of the evolutionary, revolution. My own view on this is that to tackle this by means of trials in court, as István Rév has suggested to us, has been deeply unsatisfactory. The purges may be a necessary evil, but they are still an evil and should be highly lim-ited, and certainly such vetting should be individual and strictly appeal-able. However, what is essential to this process is what I call "history lessons"—not just history lessons that are conducted by scholars and journalists but also the kind of public, ceremonial reckoning with the past that we identify with the truth commission. I wish we had had more time to talk here about that subject and why, in effect, we had no truth commissions in Central Europe. In my view, if we are taking the model of 1989 to a wider world, then that model has two vital components. One is the round table and everything that lies behind it, and the other is the truth commission. They are, in my view, twin brothers.

We spent much of our time talking about the other part of our title: what has happened since the struggle for democracy in Central and Eastern Europe. Here we had a problem that characterized a lot of the debate, which is: What are we talking about when we say 1989? Are we talking about the specific phenomenon that I've been discussing—the velvet revolutions in Czechoslovakia, East Germany, Hungary, and Poland; are we talking just about what happened in 1989 in Central Europe; or are we talking about the whole phenomenon of the consequences of 1989 in Southeastern Europe, in the former Yugoslavia, in the former Soviet Union? Of course what we've seen in the 1990s—and this was another theme of this conference—is an extraordinary divergence in postcommunist Europe. What has happened in Central Europe is better than anything we dreamt of even at the end of 1989. What has happened in the former Yugoslavia is worse than our worst nightmare in late 1989. Then we have countries like Bulgaria and Romania that are somewhere in between. It seems to me that the thing we have to accept in this spectrum, and the thing we have to explain, is not the many places where things went wrong, because after forty or seventy years of communism, you would expect that things would go wrong. What we have to explain—the great exception—is that it went so extraordinarily well in Central Europe. This is a mystery, and here again, as several speakers reminded us, we did not know it was not inevitable; that it turned out so well was to a degree the product of individual leadership. Slovakia is a good illustration of this.

One of the curious ideas that came up from this discussion was the idea that the thing that I've been talking about, "Central Europe", was actually a western imperialist notion that was imposed on reluctant Czechs, Hungarians, and Poles. It was said that after 1990, people in Hungary were only talking about Hungary, they were talking about competition; and it was the West that insisted on Central Europe. Well I'm sorry, but we got it from you; we didn't invent it. Admittedly Milan Kundera was living in Paris, Czesław Miłosz was in California, and György Konrád was not seldom in Berlin or Vienna, but nonetheless they are not Americans, Austrians, Frenchmen, or Germans, and there were many intellectuals in the Czech Republic, in Hungary, and in Poland who gave us this idea. It is indeed true that the West then, as it were, played the idea back to Central Europe at the beginning of 1990, encouraging people to live up to their promises of regional cooperation and respect for human and minority rights and all the other good things identified with being Central European. Indeed this institution in which we sit, the Central European University, is itself a rather vivid example of that "playing back" from the West to the region itself. But I would submit that that in itself was a good thing.

It was also said that in fact in private you all say "Eastern Europe". Well, in London, Paris, and Washington, people in private *also* say Eastern Europe. So we have this strange phenomenon of a notion of Central Europe that seems to exist only, as it were, at the public interface between East and West, while in private people on one side and the other still say Eastern Europe. Of course it is not entirely true. There are many people who even say it in private, and I am one of them, but nonetheless there is this very Central European, phantom mirror existence of the concept of Central Europe, in which Richard Holbrooke uses the term because he thinks Václav Havel would like him to, and then perhaps Gábor Demszky uses the term because he thinks Richard Holbrooke would like him to. Despite or perhaps because of this fact, it has become a geopolitical reality, perhaps for the first time in the twentieth century— a geopolitical reality and a very positive one, too. The Czech Republic, Hungary, and Poland are in Central Europe, and they are part of the West to which Central Europe now belongs, you may say in some senses since the eleventh century, but in a very specific sense since 12 March 1999.

Let me say just a word about this complicated relationship between the old West and Central Europe. Several speakers have reminded us critically of the way in which, starting in January 1990, missionaries of democracy, of the free market, of normality descended upon the unconverted of Central Europe and preached—doubtless also from this platform—the true gospel. And like many true gospel preachers it was a very simplified gospel: the true gospel of a sort of two-dimensional democracy. I think myself that we may be talking too much about democracy on its own in isolation.

The idea was that all you had to do was have a free election, and all will be well—and all manner of things will be well. As we have been reminded, they were not, and you can have what has been called "electocracy" or "demokratura"—that is to say, countries that have formally free elections but are in fact semi-authoritarian or even authoritarian regimes, like Slovakia under Mečiar or Serbia under Milosević. We preached the true gospel of the free market, a market much more free and pure than anything we had in our own countries. We preached civil society, the great slogan of post-89, without really quite knowing about what we were talking. Often what it came down to, as many speakers reminded us, was nongovernmental organizations, but the question is whether nongovernmental organizations are like seeds to the beautiful turf of civil society or like that thing called astroturf—artificial grass that covers the ground so the real grass cannot grow. We talk a lot less about a quality that belongs fundamentally to civil society: the quality of civility. Then we weren't clear in our own minds whether we were talking about the citizen or the bourgeois, a distinction that is perfectly framed in German, which uses two different words: *Zivilgesellschaft* and *Bürgergesellschaft*.

I think the irony is that most intellectuals in Eastern and Central Europe and most missionaries from the West were rarely talking about the citizen but about what we have in Central Europe: the bourgeoisie. You have a new growing middle class that is building civil society to defend its own interests. So perhaps after all Karl Marx was right, and what we are looking for is "bourgeois democracy". The irony of all this is that the missionaries of the West came ten years ago to preach lessons from the West to the unconverted, to the barbarians of Central Europe. What we've found at the end of ten years is lessons *for* the West. We came to preach the constitution of liberty, to tell you the ingredients of western normality, and what we found is that we don't know ourselves. We don't know ourselves what is that extraordinarily complex and subtle mixture of ingredients—political, social, economic, cultural, moral, legal—that do make up this elusive thing we call liberal democracy or normality. We don't know ourselves, and that I think has been one of the great experiences of post-89.

Of course, as I have suggested, the Central European story is an extraordinary success story, and if we lose that sense of wonder, we are losing something very vital. Nonetheless, the fact is that throughout Central Europe there is a huge amount of disillusionment. Partly this is still the hangover after the party, and partly it is because the achievement, the greatest achievement, is that Central Europe has become boring. No longer may you live in interesting times, a fantastic achievement that Central Europe has never achieved before, but nonetheless, let's admit it—it is a little boring compared to Kosovo.

Then, of course, there were the unreal expectations. In the French Third Republic there was a saying: *"Comme elle était belle, la république, sous l'empire"* („How beautiful the Republic was—under the empire"). And so: "How beautiful freedom was—under communism". Of course the reality cannot live up to the dream. Then there are the real losers, and there are many real losers; we have discussed them at length. I haven't the time to itemize them, but I will just say one thing. We say "the losers from the transition", or "the losers in the transition;" of course in some sense that is true, but the question that we cannot yet answer at this ten-year point, for which we need another ten years or twenty, is whether these are really just losers in or from the transition, or if they are losers in the normality. That is, whether the new Central European normality is not what everyone dreamed of before 1989, namely Western Europe before 1989—the post-45 West European model of the social market economy—but perhaps something more like what we have in Britain and in the United States, where you have, as a permanent feature of a capitalist bourgeois democracy, an underclass of somewhere between fifteen and thirty percent of the population living in permanent misery. I think we should raise this question.

And finally I think there is a sense of disillusionment because there is nothing new. And this is the one part of the disappointment that I might myself share, because Central Europe has been so extraordinary and so distinctive in the ideas it generated, the political models it developed, up to and including and culminating in 1989, that some of us at least hoped for something distinctive from the 1990s, something slightly different from what we had in the West. I am afraid my answer after ten years is: It isn't there. Of course what you have in the Czech Republic, Hungary, or Poland is a unique mixture of elements; every country has that. But if you look at the political system, the constitution, sport, lifestyle, the press, breakfast television, game shows, wherever you look, you will find copies, and often rather bad copies, of something in the West. I don't say it could have been otherwise, and there are many worse things than that. But what you have is a consumer society as we know it in the West; it is a consumer society characterized among other things by the artificial creation of needs. This is quite unlike the unfreedom of pre-89; but it is a subtle form of human bondage. So there is disappointment. Adam Michnik said that the story of Central Europe has been like a bad American film, because it has a happy ending. I like the happy ending, but I am not very keen on the bad American film.

To conclude, there is one thing mentioned that I would like to raise as a question, although I don't have an answer. Someone said in passing, "...and of course there is the generation of 89". Well, maybe the sociologists have found them and can tell us something about them, but for me one of the great puzzles about the present in Central Europe is: Where exactly is the class of 89? There have been two great distinctive political generations in postwar Europe: the class of 45 and the class of 68. We know who they are, we know for what they stood. They stood for a certain set of ideals and a certain vision of society. They have distinguished representatives. I can't yet find the class of 89—maybe they are sitting at the back of this room? I would say provocatively that while I have met many bright and lively young people eager to seize the chances of freedom, I find them remarkable above all in their appetite for normality—for the normality of travel, of money, of status and yes, of power, often power without principle. But I leave you with that question: Where and what is the class of 89?

Contributors

Sorin Antohi is associate professor of history at the University of Bucharest, and at Central European University, and is currently a fellow at the Center for Advanced Study in the Behavioral Sciences, Stanford.

Valerie Bunce is professor of government at Cornell University.

Karen Dawisha is professor of government and politics at the University of Maryland, College Park and associate director of its Center for the Study of Post-Communist Societies.

Susan Gal is professor of anthropology at the University of Chicago.

Timothy Garton Ash is a fellow of St. Antony's College, Oxford University.

Irena Grudzińska Gross is affiliated with the Ford Foundation and with the Remarque Institute at New York University.

Miklós Haraszti is a Budapest-based writer, editor, human rights activist, and university professor.

Agnes Heller is Hannah Arendt Professor of Philosophy at the New School University, New York. She also teaches at Eötvös Loránd Universtiy, Budapest and József Attila University, Szeged.

Jeffrey C. Isaac is professor of political science at Indiana University, Bloomington and a fellow of the Open Society Institute.

Bartlomiej Kaminski is associate professor of government and politics at the University of Maryland and is affiliated with its Center for the Study of Post-Communist Societies. He also serves as a consultant for DECRG-Foreign Trade, World Bank.

Gail Kligman is professor of sociology at the University of California, Los Angeles.

Adam Michnik is editor-in-chief of *Gazeta Wyborcza,* Warsaw.

Martin Palouš is deputy minister of foreign affairs of the Czech Republic and teaches at the Faculty of Social Science of Charles University (foreign relations division), where he currently serves as vice-dean.

Kazimierz Z. Poznanski is a professor at the Henry M. Jackson School of International Studies, University of Washington, Seattle.

Ilya Prizel is associate professor of Russian area and East European studies at The Paul H. Nitze School of Advanced International Studies (SAIS) of Johns Hopkins University, Baltimore.

István Rév is professor of history and political science at the Central European University and academic director of the Open Society Archives at CEU.

Jacques Rupnik is research director at the French National Foundation of Political Science and is a professor at the Institute of Political Studies, Paris.

Karol Soltan teaches political science at the University of Maryland.

Vladimir Tismaneanu is professor of government and politics and the director of the Center for the Study of Post-Communist Societies at the University of Maryland, College Park. He is also the editor of the journal *East European Politics and Societies.*

Ivan Vejvoda has taught political science and European studies at numerous universities, most recently at Smith College. He is a member of the Institute for European Studies in Belgrade and is currently executive director of the Fund for an Open Society in Yugoslavia.

Katherine Verdery is Eric. R Wolf Professor of Anthropology at the University of Michigan, Ann Arbor.

Jeffrey N. Wasserstrom is associate professor of history at Indiana University, Bloomington; he also serves as associate editor of the *American Historical Review.*

Name Index